COUNSELING WOMEN
OVER THE LIFE SPAN

Judith A. Lewis
Governors State University, Illinois

Bree A. Hayes
The Hayes Group, Georgia

Loretta J. Bradley
Texas Tech University

LOVE PUBLISHING COMPANY ®
Denver, Colorado 80222

Library of Congress Catalog Card Number 91-077048

Copyright ©1992 Love Publishing Company
Printed in the U.S.A.
ISBN 0-89108-222-0

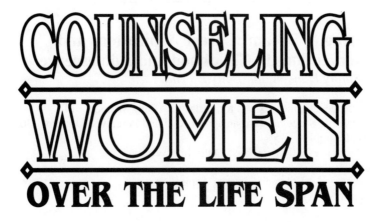

Contents

Part Two

PREPARING FOR WOMANHOOD

Part Three

ADULT WOMANHOOD 97

Part Four

MATURE WOMANHOOD

Part Five
CONCLUSION   **269**

TABLES AND FIGURES

To Our Mothers

Part One

INTRODUCTION

1

Counseling Women About Women's Issues

Bree A. Hayes
The Hayes Group, Athens, GA

There was heaviness in the air as the young woman left my office. She reported that the session was helpful to her, but I was feeling rather frustrated and angry. Why, as we approach the 21st century, are young mothers still experiencing so much guilt around the issue of motherhood? How can bright, competent women spend so much time second guessing every decision they make? Why does it appear that women today are in a no-win situation when it comes to having both a career and a family?

Heather is a 26-year-old married mother of a 2-year-old. She entered into counseling because she had overwhelming feelings of anxiety about working and raising a child. Heather stayed at home with her new baby for the first 6 weeks of his life and then returned to her job as a human resources manager for a large corporation. Everything appeared to be going smoothly for the first 18 months, but then the baby became ill with the flu. The illness was brief and uncomplicated; but from that point, Heather reported a growing uneasiness about leaving Steven at the day-care center while she worked.

Like many other young mothers, Heather is feeling conflicted. She reports that her job is very important to her, both in terms of her career aspirations and its financial rewards. She also readily admits that she could stay at home with the baby and the family would probably survive on one paycheck. But she fears that if she chooses this alternative, she will grow to resent the baby for causing her to make such a sacrifice. She loves her work and she loves her baby. Herein lies the bind, the conflict with which so many women find themselves struggling. "How can I have a professional self without sacrificing a personal self? How can I be independent and still be connected to loved ones?"

It appears that, in our culture, independence and autonomy have traditionally been regarded as necessary traits for healthy personalities. In fact, an important objective of the therapeutic intervention is frequently to free clients of the burden of assuming responsibility for other people's lives, thereby freeing them to find paths that are most gratifying or least conflicting for themselves. With this line of logic, Heather might be counseled to understand that, since her work is very important to her, she must attend to that need and find some ways to cope with her self-imposed guilt about the baby.

More recently, however, we have come to know, through the feminist therapy literature (Butler, 1985), that autonomy and independence are not necessarily the most important characteristics of healthy personalities for all people. In fact, for some people, significantly more women than men, interdependence and relationships may be more profoundly prized than independence and autonomy. A counselor response that persuades Heather to attend to her career and overcome her feelings of guilt misses the point that, for this client, her relationship with her child is as important as her feelings about her career. A traditional counseling approach, based on the premise that autonomy and independence must be achieved, could exacerbate an already painful situation. Clearly, effective counselors must overcome traditional expectations and recognize the individual needs of all clients.

This is a book about counseling women over the life span. It examines three critical issues as they apply to women—careers, society, and health—through a developmental window of three distinct life stages. It is intended to offer a broad perspective on the kinds of problems facing today's women and to address some ways in which counselors can help clients resolve conflict and live effectively and in harmony with their internal values systems.

CAREERS

The world of work is changing rapidly for all of us. High technology has brought computers, robotics, hydraulics, satellites, laser beams, and fax machines to business and industry. The most tedious and time-consuming jobs of the past are now relatively simple and easily accomplished. People who were once required to lift heavy objects can now use hydraulic lifts to do the same job. The assembly line is a thing of the past; robots do the work without the liability of injury or fatigue. And information is transmitted from one country to the next with the mere press of a button.

We have also seen a change in the general composition of the work force. For the past 30 years, the numbers of women entering the work force have steadily increased. It is estimated that by the year 2000 there will be more women than men employed by American organizations (Johnston, Packer, & U.S. Department of Labor, 1987).

This trend can be attributed to many factors. First, since the publication of Betty Friedan's monumental work *The Feminine Mystique* (1963), many women have begun to admit to themselves that cooking, cleaning, and child care were probably not the ultimate career experiences of which they had dreamed. It should be noted that some of these homemakers were college graduates. But if a woman married right after graduation, her college degree was more an insurance policy than a rite of passage into the world of work. And many of these women were told by their own mothers that the point of a college degree was merely "to have something to fall back on in the event that marriage does not work out."

As a result of Friedan's work and the subsequent women's movement, in the 1960s some of these women turned in their aprons for typewriters and joined the ranks of the employed. Other women delayed their entry into the work force until they believed that their children were old enough to be relatively self-sufficient. But whether they left home early in their children's lives or later, women began to experience the challenge of work outside of the home and a paycheck (albeit significantly smaller than a man's) that offered a sense of self-efficacy that they might not have experienced before that point.

At the same time, the United States, embroiled in the Vietnam conflict, began a steady downhill economic trend. Housing, food, and gasoline prices spiraled to the point that even mothers who would have preferred to stay at home entered the work force. It became evident in many cases that if a family wanted to maintain its standard of living, both parents would have to go to work.

The 1970s brought an end to the war and the beginning of a new era for women and work. Many more women began to view college degrees as a means for attaining career aspirations. More women than ever before entered traditionally male graduate schools of law, medicine, engineering, business, and dentistry. Women joined the work force fully expecting to fill many of the positions that had historically been occupied by men. And women began to expect equal pay for equal work.

The influx of women into the work force has brought with it the need for changes that could have an important impact on the quality of work life for all employees. First, people are beginning to be aware of the need to change the benefits available to employees. The needs of a single male employee are typically quite different from the needs of a working mother. Flexible benefits and cafeteria plans offer a wide range of choices to employees. These new plans, which ideally should be offered by all businesses, allow employees to choose those benefits that best fit their lifestyles.

The presence of large numbers of women in the work force has also made it clear that the current shortage of quality day-care is a national emergency. Some companies—but all too few—have made arrangements with day-care centers close to their offices or even offer day-care on the premises. Some hospitals now offer day-care for sick children. Flexible hours are becoming more popular as companies—again, all too few—recognize that there are viable alternatives to a 9-to-5 operation.

Some companies have begun to respond to the wishes of employees (both men and women) who are saying that they are unwilling to move home and family regularly. While it was once mandatory that employees move at the whim of the company, some companies now offer choices. In responsive organizations, employees may choose to turn down transfers without jeopardizing their job standing.

Finally, corporations of the past spoke only of productivity and the bottom line. Employees were viewed as a means for attaining the company's goals and were seldom considered holistically. They were not seen as husbands, wives, parents, or people with dreams. They were treated almost like automatons. Although some corporations remain caught in the past, other successful and more forward-looking organizations still speak of productivity and the bottom line, but they are also acutely aware of the importance of their human resources. They realize that, without a satisfied work force, they cannot reach their highest potential. This changed attitude is frequently referred to as "humanizing" the work place.

There have been many changes in the work place since large numbers of women appeared on the scene. Some might argue that not all of these changes can be attributed to women entering the work force but instead to overall changes in society. We could surely argue, however, that these changes are a direct result of women speaking with a louder voice. The values of interdependence and relationships appear to have grown in importance in the work place.

SOCIETY

Despite the continuing efforts of the women's movement, we still live in a patriarchal society, where there is a fundamental assumption that women have less political and economic power than men. We see this in all aspects of daily living, including family life, business, organized religion, education, literature, finances, and protocol.

For a while it appeared that substantial progress had been made in eliminating sexism in the early stages of the women's movement (1965–1970). However, since that time, and for many reasons, the fervor with which equality was once sought has relaxed. Perhaps young women, who did not have to fight the original fight, took their freedom for granted. Perhaps oppositional forces gained momentum, particularly during the debate and voting over the Equal Rights Amendment. Whatever the cause, it is now apparent that women have lost some significant ground in the quest for equality.

Consider the case of Heather and her guilt about working and raising her child. Heather is not a single mother. She has a husband and her child has a father, who might even be called a "modern father" in that he is willing to spend time caring for his son and regularly assists Heather with the household chores. So why does Heather have a problem?

Perhaps it is not so much Heather's problem as a problem with society. In our culture, as in most cultures, the mother is still seen as the primary caretaker of the children. When a child becomes sick at school or at day-care, it is almost always the mother who is called to come for the child. There appears to be an unwritten code that suggests that the father is not to be disturbed because he is doing very important work. But a mother's work can be interrupted. This code is further reinforced at the work place, in that employers seem much more accepting of women than men leaving the office for family emergencies.

A look at a pediatrician's office offers another example of women as primary caretakers of children. Almost all sick children are accompanied by mothers to the doctor's office. By and large, these are working mothers who must use vacation time for the appointment.

Mothers, not fathers, typically escort children to the dentist, orthodontist, drug store, and clothing store. There are mothers more than fathers at school conferences, open houses, recitals and school plays. Mothers drive children to school and are there to pick them up at the end of the day. Schools have "room mothers." It is mother, not father, who is asked to send in treats for special days. So pervasive is this norm of mother as

Table 1.1
Guidelines for Feminist Therapy

1. Help clients to recognize the harmful effects of sexism in our culture.

2. Assist clients in exploring the inherent harm in sex-role stereotyping.

3. Support clients in their need for nurturance and self-healing through their own inner resources.

4. Continue to use a non-sexist frame of reference.

5. Avoid any hierarchical relationship between you and the client. It should be a collaborative relationship.

6. Attempt to match women clients with women therapists. Group counseling should have only women members and leaders.

7. All therapists should (1) conduct on-going evaluations of their practices; (2) make provisions for low-income clients; (3) continue to examine personal beliefs and lifestyles as they relate to counseling approaches; (4) identify with feminist philosophies and goals; and (5) examine blindspots in approach as they relate to race, class, and sexual orientation.

Source: Adapted from "Guidelines for Feminist Therapy" by M. Butler, 1985, in L.B. Rosewater and L.E.A. Walker (Eds.), *Handbook for Feminist Therapy: Women's Issues in Psychotherapy* (pp. 32–38), New York: Springer Publishing Company.

primary caretaker that those few men who choose to be homemakers often find themselves fairly isolated.

Heather's bind stems from the fact that her career and her relationship with her son are both very important to her. But even if Heather achieved a comfortable balance between work and family, she would continue to feel the external pressure of a society that believes that the only good mother is a full-time mother.

Another critical variable in all of this is society's view of the working woman. One of the downsides of the movement of women into the work force is the sense that women must be superachievers. In their efforts to prove their worth as effective employees, women have been willing to overextend themselves in all directions. Hence, the work ethic for women has become "Keep climbing to the top, even at the expense of your family and even if it kills you."

Clearly counselors must address client problems within the context of the society in which they live. Table 1.1 gives guidelines for counselors working with women clients, proposed by members of the Feminist Therapy Collective, Inc., of Philadelphia.

HEALTH

Most little girls grow up believing that their bodies are bad. It's not that anybody specifically tells them to be ashamed of their bodies, but they often reach this conclusion from a collection of childhood events. Drawing from client stories, I will share some experiences that lead women to believe that their bodies are shameful.

It is quite natural for young children to feel somewhat encumbered or inhibited by their clothes. Hence, they frequently strip down to a more comfortable and natural state. Chloe and her older brother enjoyed taking off their clothes, especially in the summer when it was quite warm. She recalls that she was apparently able to "get away with this" because no one had noticed. But one day, when her father actually did notice, he became outraged and sent Chloe to her room for the next several hours. What most impressed her was that her father did not appear disturbed about her brother's nudity. In fact, to the best of her recollection, her brother was not even punished. It is easy to speculate about Chloe's father's anxieties about his daughter's nudity, but what is more important is the message Chloe was given. There must be something wrong with her body.

As little girls grow up, they are bombarded with warnings about potential abuse, molestation, or rape. It is sad that women must live in an era of paranoia. Conscientious parents begin to tell their girls at a very young age of the dangers outside of the safety of their own homes.

As girls become adolescents and begin to date, they are warned at home and at school about date rape, which is the leading form of rape in our country. They are also warned about safe sex and instructed about the dangers of herpes and AIDS. They are told of the burden of an unwanted pregnancy and reminded that it is their responsibility to ensure that they do not become pregnant.

Still young, they begin to read or hear about women who were raped and subsequently dragged through a long and painful inquisition. In many cases, the perpetrator is not even punished.

It is not hard to see how young girls begin to form an image of themselves and their bodies that is not entirely positive. And if the messages that they receive from their parents and schools were not enough, television commercials tend to finish the job. The most insidious of these commercials are those that advertise douches, which are allegedly designed to make a woman feel fresh and clean. In truth, informed women have come to know that douches are actually bad for their natural chemical balance.

So young women begin to believe that their bodies should be hidden, protected, and disinfected. They have learned that they must be careful on dates; they must irrigate and clean themselves regularly; they must remember to walk in well lit places, preferably with a group of people. If they are raped or impregnated, it is their fault. Who would want the burden of a female body? Fortunately, though these are grim messages, some significant progress has been made in this area over the years.

In the spring of 1969, a group of women in Boston, who later became the Boston Women's Health Book Collective, had grown weary of these messages and the fact that women seemed to know very little about their own bodies. Doing some early research, they found that women consumed the largest proportion of health services in the country. They average 25% more visits to doctors each year than do men; they are admitted to hospitals significantly more frequently than men; they take 50% more prescription drugs than men. Women are prescribed tranquilizers significantly more frequently than are men.

Because most patients are women and most physicians are men, a woman's illness may be compounded by the fact that she must be open to a male examination and analysis of her problem. It would be heartening to be able to say that both men and women physicians treat all patients equally, but this is simply not the case. It is a fact that women's complaints are often dismissed as emotional or hysterical. Consider the fact that the origin of the word *hysterectomy* is from *hysteria*. It was once believed that, if a woman's reproductive system were removed, she would not be so emotional, which was seen as a negative attribute.

The Boston women's group made significant headway in the area of women and health. They met regularly to gather pertinent data about health issues. They shared information from medical journals and books and interviews with doctors. They taught a course for women about understanding their bodies and ultimately organized the first comprehensive book about women's health issues written by nonphysicians, *Our Bodies, Ourselves* (1971).

Today some progress has been made for a select group of women, but there are still many women for whom information or resources are not available. It is typically uneducated, disadvantaged women who suffer the consequences of limited information.

Not long ago, I met with Elana, a 28-year-old woman who described herself as "paralyzed with depression." When we began our exploration, she spoke about a painful childhood filled with sadness and rejection. She could never please her father, despite her efforts to be an exemplary student, a helpful daughter, and a solid member of her community. Her brother Carlos was her father's pride and joy while Elana's best efforts were met only with rejection.

On high-school graduation day, Elana left home in a rage. She spent the next 2 years traveling around with a gang of men and women on motorcycles. Then one morning, after awakening with a drug hangover and a man she did not recognize, Elana decided to return to her old lifestyle. She seemed to escape her situation relatively unscathed, with the exception of a mild case of herpes.

Soon after her return to what she described as her "saner life," she found a respectable job and began to see Enrico. She lived with him for the next 5 years and felt safe and loved. He asked her to marry him several times, but she could not say yes because she had not told him about the herpes. Part of her depression was clearly linked to her belief that, if she told Enrico, he would either leave her or, worse, he would stay out of pity or out of resignation to the fact that he too was infected.

Elana was in a no-win situation on many levels. She felt unclean, immoral, and dishonest. She did not have easy access to information about herpes and was afraid to confide in her family.

The picture is a little brighter for most other women. Women are still concerned about rape, pregnancy, and sexually transmitted diseases, but there is much more information available and fewer taboos about women's bodies. Women are learning to be assertive in talking with physicians, even asking for second opinions about medical procedures. Health centers that specialize in women's unique needs and problems are appearing throughout this country.

Women are learning to take care of themselves through proper diet, exercise, and play. They are learning about the changes they can expect as they get older and acting proactively to extend and enrich their lives.

STAGES OF DEVELOPMENT

We have chosen to discuss women over three basic life stages (young women, adult women, and mature women), because we contend that counselors must have a general understanding of the unique issues and problems women experience in various stages of development. We do not intend to offer an analysis of adult development, but instead to reflect on the issues present for women at different stages of development. We hope that you will find the book helpful in understanding some of the important questions, problems, and concerns of women over the life span.

REFERENCES

Boston Women's Health Book Collective (1971). *Our bodies, ourselves.* New York: Simon and Schuster.

Butler, M. (1985). Guidelines for Feminist Therapy. In L. B. Rosewater & L. E. A. Walker (Eds.), *Handbook of feminist therapy: Women's issues in psychotherapy* (pp. 32–38). New York: Springer Publishing.

Friedan, B. (1963). *The feminist mystique.* New York: W. W. Norton.

Johnston, W. B., Packer, A. E., & U.S. Department of Labor (1987). *Workforce 2000: Work and workers for the twenty-first century.* Indianapolis: Hudson Institute.

Part Two

PREPARING FOR WOMANHOOD

2

Daring to Dream: Career Aspirations and Interventions in Childhood and Adolescence

L. Sunny Hansen and Betty Biernat
University of Minnesota

The career dreams of children and adolescents is a topic of vast scope—one difficult to fit into one chapter of discussion. The topic is particularly complex because we take a broad view of the word "career," reviewing the full range of life planning, including both occupational and family roles. We use this conceptualization of career because family and work roles interact in our culture so frequently.

We also assume that the career development paths of men and women are interactive regardless of lifestyle and that any discussion of change for women requires an examination of information and possible change for men as well. Although there are many different family patterns today, dual earner families now represent more than 50% of families (Bernard, 1981). With both partners working, the mingling of family and work roles for both women and men has become more common. While the primary focus here will be on girls and female adolescents in keeping with the focus of the book, the relationships between the gender roles will also be brought in where it is relevant.

We had hoped to ensure that this chapter would be multicultural, addressing the data on and needs of a racially diverse population. While this has been attempted, a very restricted database and space limitations have kept us from fully describing cultural variations in career aspirations of girls and women of color. Although these populations often have been ignored or underrepresented in research, it is our hope that cultural and ethnic diversity issues will play a stronger role in future research.

A clarification of usage of the words "sex" and "gender" is appropriate here, as these two terms have been used inconsistently in the counseling literature (including by the authors). Our usage here will be consistent with that of Doyle and Paludi (1991): "sex" will refer to physical characteristics of being male and female, while "gender" will be used for the social psychological features ascribed to or associated with assigned female or male status. The components of gender will be described as "gender role stereotypes," "gender roles," and so on, for consistency, though we recognize that many authors continue to use terms such as "sex roles." Our decision reflects our concern about the many definitions for and connotations of the word "sex." We might also note that the concepts related to gender vary along a continuum of femininity and masculinity.

Finally, any discussion of career aspirations in young girls needs to consider the pervasive gender role system that is at the core of our cultural norms. This gender role system has been defined as "the network of attitudes, feelings, and behaviors that results from the persuasiveness of gender role stereotyping in the culture" (Chetwynd & Hartnett, 1978). Gender role stereotyping can be defined as beliefs about the general appropriateness of various roles and activities for females and males. This gender role system directly affects every aspect of career planning for both males and females. It is also indirectly influential because it affects other life choices that interact with occupational choice (such as marriage or child rearing).

Chetwynd and Hartnett (1978) have pointed out three major components of this gender role system:

1. The assignment of stereotypical personality traits on the basis of gender. Females are assigned the stereotype of being dependent, passive, subjective, and subordinate. Males are assigned the stereotype of dominance, aggression, independence, and problem solving.
2. The assignment, by sex, to different categories of labor activities such as "men's work" or "women's work," resulting in occupational sex segregation.
3. The investing of male characteristics, traits, and activities with higher status than those of the female.

The effects of this gender role system in a number of areas of young women's career development will be examined. Later in this chapter, materials, strategies, and programs involved in changing the effects of the gender role system will be provided.

CAREER DEVELOPMENT ISSUES FOR GIRLS AND YOUNG WOMEN

Effects of Gender Role Stereotyping on Initial Career Goals

The gender role system is pervasive in its effects on female and male development. Gender differences in career knowledge and aspirations have been the focus of a number of studies since the 1960s. Before these are reviewed, it seems appropriate to note that in career choice, as in any complex behavior, many other variables interact with gender, including socioeconomic status, geographical region, physical health, sexual orientation, and race/ethnicity. This discussion will focus primarily on exploring gender differences and the apparent effects of the gender role system, with other variables specifically discussed only when they are directly pertinent.

Elementary and Preschool Children

Studies of elementary and preschool children have focused on two types of occupational behaviors: knowledge of gender occupational stereotypes and their application in responding to questions about types of work, and responses about personal career preferences. The relationship between the two factors seems apparent: Knowledge about stereotypes and applying those stereotypes in a general way or to other persons undoubtedly would precede applying them to oneself. Studies on both types of behaviors will be reviewed here.

Early Occupational Stereotypes

Studies of children generally have shown that they demonstrate knowledge of gender role stereotypes about occupations at very early ages. Gettys and Cann (1981) worked with 2- and 3-year old children, asking them whether a male or female doll held a particular job such as a construction worker. They found that most children responded according to traditional gender role stereoypes even in toddlerhood, though this finding has not always been replicated (Tremaine, Schau, & Busch, 1982).

Studies with older grade-school children have yielded fairly consistent results. As Matlin (1987) concluded in her review, children's gender typing of occupations tends to increase from kindergarten to about fourth grade and is more flexible in fifth to sixth grade (Franken, 1983; McKay & Miller, 1982; Tremaine & Schau, 1979). This conclusion is supported by cognitive-developmental theories of intellectual development (Kohlberg, 1966; Piaget & Inhelder, 1969), which postulate that gender role stereotyping is more rigid at younger ages. When children move into the stages of concrete and formal operational thinking, they develop cognitive styles that are conducive to more flexibility.

In regard to gender typing in older students, Shepherd and Hess (1975) compared groups of kindergartners, eighth graders, college students, and adults. They found lessened gender typing with age, with an especially large decrease in adulthood confirming the trend toward more flexibility about occupations with age.

Early Occupational Preferences

Studies of actual occupational preference have not been as consistent. Most research has confirmed a tendency for grade-school children to choose occupations in accordance with gender role stereotypes (McKay & Miller, 1982; Tremaine & Schau, 1979). Some studies also have indicated that girls as a group generally tend to state a smaller number of occupations than boys and tend to choose more gender stereotyped jobs (Looft, 1971a, 1971b; Zuckerman & Sayre, 1982). Nurse and teacher often composed a large percentage of the girls' choices, whereas boys' choices tend to be distributed over a wider variety of occupations. However, some recent studies of elementary children have contradicted this last set of findings, at least for older girls. Tremaine et al. (1982) found that, while each gender did prefer culturally stereotyped jobs and girls' choices showed less range, second-grade girls' preferences were less culturally gender stereotyped than boys'.

Kriedberg, Butcher, and White (1978) looked at second- and sixth-grade students in replication of an earlier study by Looft (1971a, 1971b). These authors found that male and female second graders nominated almost the same number of occupations, though they were mostly traditional choices. In the sixth-grade sample, both sexes again nominated equal numbers of choices, but the girls made more flexible choices. All the males, but only half of the females, chose traditional occupations.

In another study, Franken (1983) compared preschool, second-grade, and fifth-grade boys and girls on vocational aspirations and reported that boys did name a greater number of occupations overall than girls, though the differences were not great. Preschool boys and girls named 8 and 9 occupations respectively, while fifth-grade boys and girls listed 15 and 12 occupations respectively. She also noted that 53 of 60 boys in her sample chose male stereotyped occupations while 23 of 60 girls chose male or neutral occupations.

Lavine (1982) investigated the relationship between 7- to 11-year-olds' career choices and the proportion of males working in those jobs. She found that boys' choices averaged 89% male participation, whereas girls' choices averaged 41% male participation. The authors interpret this finding as suggesting that girls are less restricted in career choice, a finding also supported in a recent study of adolescent girls and boys (Hedin, Erickson, Simon, & Walker, 1985).

Reviewing these and other studies suggests several conclusions about career preferences in grade school:

1. Many, if not most, expressed personal career choices in elementary school that conform to cultural stereotypes.
2. Girls appear to be more flexible than boys with regard to personal choices and cultural stereotypes.
3. There is contradictory evidence in recent studies about differences in range of occupations for females and males in elementary school.

More research is needed to clarify data on the expressed range of occupational choices for this age group as well as to determine whether societal changes are leading elementary students to choose from a wider range of occupations than they have been socialized to expect.

Adolescent Career Attitudes and Stereotypes

Studies of adolescent career choices appear to show some effects from changes in cultural views about gender stereotypes. In 1978, Marini reviewed research from the previous two decades on gender differences in adolescent career aspirations. She concluded that there were gender differences in two particular areas of career choice. Adolescent girls indicated lower educational aspirations than boys, and girls chose different occupations than boys in accordance with gender role stereotypes. These findings, of course, are consistent with the results of studies on children's career aspirations and indicate the continuing influence of gender role socialization on early career choices. However, more recent studies have suggested some changes in adolescent aspirations.

Occupation Choice and Aspiration

In her study of all 9th and 12th graders (N = 1,234) in nine Illinois high schools, balanced on rural, urban, and inner-city locations, Farmer (1983) found that boys and girls had similar educational aspirations. She also found that females scored significantly higher than males on socioeconomic level of occupational choice and that 35% of females expressed nontraditional choices. The higher socioeconomic level of girls' occupational choice is likely to be due to the fact that many stereotypical female occupational choices (such as teacher or nurse) tend to fall in the middle and upper middle range of occupational distribution.

Using an instrument adapted from Super and Culha's (1976) *Work Salience Inventory*, Farmer (1983) also unexpectedly found that females scored higher on a measure of career commitment. Higher scores on this scale were seen as reflecting a higher interest in long-term career prospects and advancement. Surprisingly, she also reported that males more than females endorsed plans to share parenting and career roles with their spouses. However, the items varied by gender. Boys were agreeing that it was very important to them to share parenting, whereas girls were responding that it was very important to them to share equally in the financial support of their family. Because each gender did not respond to each question, gender comparisons cannot be made on the sharing of both responsibilities.

Farmer's data are surprising, given Marini's conclusions about earlier studies. Yet two other studies conducted in the early 1980's found similar educational aspirations and similar level of occupational aspirations for females and males (Card, Steel, & Abeles, 1980; Tittle, 1981). These studies suggest that efforts to reduce the influence of the gender role system may be affecting adolescent girls in areas of educational aspirations, career commitment, and a number of nontraditional choices, while boys may view parenting as more their responsibility than previously.

This conclusion is further supported by the results of the Minnesota Youth Poll study (Hedin et al., 1985). This 1984 project involved a survey of 725 Minnesota high-school students in 115 focus discussion groups from urban, suburban, and rural schools and one adolescent treatment center. These subjects were a geographically selected representative sample of Minnesota students who were polled on a variety of questions, including their expected career at age 30. The Minnesota Youth Poll found that females tended to have both higher and lower aspirations than males. Fourteen percent of females chose clerical or service work, while 63% chose professional work, in contrast to 3% and 38% of males, respectively. Males overwhelmingly (93%) selected occupations stereotyped as male, whereas females were more flexible. Forty-two percent of girls chose stereotypical female work, 46% chose stereotypical male work, and 11% percent chose gender-neutral work. Males also were notably more rigid about gender and career, with 75% listing jobs that females could not do, including fire fighter, police officer, and politician. In contrast, 50% of young women felt there were jobs females could not do, and they primarily involved some type of physical limitations such as priest, professional football player, and ditch digging.

Hedin et al. (1985) found considerable inconsistency and ambivalence in the attitudes of the female adolescents in particular. Girls were more likely to see barriers to achieving their goals than were boys. Main reasons were the job market, lack of money, not having the necessary career skills, not knowing "the right people," and a lack of knowledge of career options.

These results clearly point to the need for further work with boys and girls about career stereotypes. The importance of directly addressing the effects of socialization for males is emphasized by their more rigid career–gender attitudes. These attitudes not only affect their own choices but could likely cause strains in relations with colleagues at work as well as spousal conflict by clearly different attitudes regarding females' career abilities and role expectations. Further, the impact of male attitudes on females' aspirations needs to be considered. Clearly, with the constant interrelations between the sexes, the attitudes of one sex will affect the behavior of the other.

Work and Family Roles

In keeping with the expanded definition of career (Hansen, 1984; Miller, 1984; Richardson, 1981; Super 1980), a review of adolescent expectations about the interaction of employment and family responsibilities is appropriate. As discussed above, Farmer (1983) reported that high school boys more than girls endorsed a plan to share parenting and career roles with their spouses, though the sexes responded to different questions and the difference was small in absolute terms.

In the Minnesota Youth Poll (Hedin et al., 1985), high-school youth indicated a range of attitudes about items on life roles. Two-thirds of both females and males accepted the Cinderella myth that most young women want to marry successful handsome men who will take care of them for the rest of their lives so they will not have to work outside the home. Girls' responses indicated a belief that work might be important to them but they ought to seek permission to do so. For both sexes, the woman's income often was viewed as supplemental. Both males and females considered ideal the Superwoman Model, one who is successful in homemaking, career, child rearing, community affairs, and keeping her husband happy.

The Minnesota Youth Poll also found rather traditional attitudes about care of young children. While only 2% of their female sample expected to be homemakers at age 30 (consistent with Farmer, 1983), 63% of females said they would not work outside the home when they were pregnant or had small children. Again note the discrepancy between these adolescent perceptions and the reality of women's participation in the workforce (60% of married women with children under 18). Forty-five percent of males versus 33% of females felt "somewhat or extremely unprepared" to raise children adequately. Thirty-three percent of males and 16% of females rated themselves in these unprepared categories for running a household, while 26% of males and 16% of females felt unprepared to balance home and work responsibilities. These findings suggest that future couples would be likely to juggle home and family responsibilities in relatively traditional ways, with the female partner being responsible for housework and staying at home to raise small children.

While not a study of career choice but of gender role attitudes, a national study of 3,000 high-school seniors by Herzog and Bachman (1982) found a great deal of traditional response in both males and females. Although both sexes favored equal opportunity for women, young women favored it more strongly. It is significant that in attitudes toward work and family, neither the females nor males thought a woman should work outside the home if she had small children (this in spite of the reality that more than 50% of women with preschool children are in the workforce). While both sexes felt restricted in their role choices, males felt they have less flexibility than females.

Adolescent Ambivalence

A similar study of expectations and attitudes of female and male students in a private Midwestern high school found unexpectedly stereotyped attitudes about the roles of women and men (Gilligan, 1986). In another study, McBean (1986) observed that high school students responded stereotypically to a dilemma involving brothers and sisters sharing household tasks and sibling care with their single parent working mother. A pattern in many of these studies seems to be that both sexes recognize new options are possible but have contradictory feelings about choosing them.

In summary, these studies indicate the ambivalence both girls and boys experience about career/family roles. As Hedin and her colleagues noted:

> It appears that both sexes, but especially girls, have mastered the importance of work to women's identity, the need for women to have high aspirations and the like. Yet, at the same time, they also believe in all the old myths about being taken care of, about work as a way to fill the time and get some extra pin money. Young women, indeed have heard the conflicting messages about what women should be and do and seem to have incorporated all of them! (1985, p.3)

Further, these studies indicate that, despite some ambivalence, adolescent females are benefitting to some extent from changing and more flexible societal attitudes about women's careers and from direct school efforts to reduce adolescents's gender role stereotyping. These changes result in apparent increased educational aspirations for adolescent females, an increase in nontraditional career choices for females, and perhaps increased career commitment for females. Males, however, do not appear to reflect society's and school changes in either their own choices or in their general views about gender and career. They may be changing in their perception of their responsibility for sharing parenting responsibilities, but many still hold to traditional cultural stereotypes about men's and women's roles in work and family.

Differential Treatment of Female and Male Students

The influence of the gender role system can be seen clearly in the differential treatment males and females receive in the schools. This differential treatment is thought to be connected to women's career choices and to later behavior in the workplace (Epperson, 1988). The abundant literature on this topic emphasizes the need for efforts to publicize the fact, increase parent and teacher awareness, and change gender discrimination in the schools. While concern has been expressed about all levels of education, this discussion will focus on elementary and secondary education in keeping with its emphasis on children and adolescents.

Teacher–Pupil Interactions

A number of studies on gender role stereotyping in the schools have examined teacher actions. Teachers have been found to give more positive and negative attention to boys than to girls (Brophy & Good, 1978). In a study of teacher–pupil interactions in fourth-, sixth-, and eighth-grade classes, Sadker and Sadker (1982) found that boys receive significantly more praise, criticism, and remedial help. In their study of teacher–pupil interactions in more that 100 classrooms (English, social studies, science, and mathematics) with diversity in race and backgrounds, they found that (1) male students receive more teacher attention and are given more time to talk, (2) teachers generally are unaware of the presence or impact of the bias, (3) brief but focused training (of educators) can reduce or eliminate gender bias from classroom interaction, and (4) increasing equity in classroom interaction increases teacher effectiveness as well. They point out that equity and effectiveness are not competing but complementary concerns (Sadker & Sadker, 1982).

Epperson (1988), in a brief review of the literature, noted, that compared with girls, boys:

—are five times as likely to receive the most attention from teachers.
—are eight times as likely to call out in class.
—outtalk girls by a 3 to 1 ratio.
—are twice as likely to demand help or attention from the teacher, to be seen as model students, or to be called on in class.

In a review of literature on stereotyping in schools in Western Europe and North America, Sundal-Hansen (1984) found this differential treatment to exist across cultures.

These findings suggest that teacher behavior reinforces the gender role system that gives more status to males. Boys then learn to expect more attention and status while girls learn lower self-esteem. Teachers may thus, often unconsciously, help shape girls into a dependent style and teach girls to accept the greater status and attention given to males.

Other studies have noted the impact of teachers on children's play. Serbin, Connor, and Iler (1979) found that teachers were more likely to call on a boy to demonstrate how to play with a stereotypically masculine toy and that when a new toy is introduced with stereotyped comments, children respond in a stereotyped manner, playing only with toys seen as appropriate for their sex. Teachers also have been found to often encourage other gender stereotyped activities as well (Fagot, 1981).

Another interesting line of research has addressed teacher impact on attributions for success and failure in girls and boys. Teacher behaviors such as levels of criticism and praise may encourage girls to attribute success to external factors (such as luck) and failure to internal factors (such as ability) while encouraging the reverse for boys. The effects of boys and girls adopting these attributional styles may be to encourage a "can do" attitude in boys, while girls may be left with low self-efficacy or feelings of mastery. Girls may feel that effort contributes little to their success and correspondingly lower their goals and efforts. They may be discouraged from participating (and hence from achieving), have lowered self-esteem, and prematurely limit their choice of course and career options. These effects may be continued as young women go onto college. Epperson's (1988) article also reported that valedictorians developed less self-esteem and self-confidence with age. This confirms earlier studies that found that females develop more negative self-concepts with age. Whether this is changing as women's lives are changing is subject for future research (American Association of University Women, 1991).

A somewhat different perspective on bias in teacher–student relations was seen in the 1985 Minnesota Youth Poll (Hedin et al., 1985). This population (described earlier) was asked, "Do you think girls are treated differently than boys in school?" "In what ways?" Half of the girls and two-thirds of the boys thought the sexes were treated differently. The majority of boys responded that girls were "disciplined less stringently, given better grades for less work, and were more trusted and favored by teachers" (p. 15). Female agreement responses were more varied; some agreed with the boys, though they tended to feel that the differential treatment was often warranted by the boys' behavior. Another theme in female responses was that teachers have higher expectations of girls and expect better behavior and grades of girls.

These responses about girls' preferential treatment do appear to fit with the research data about more negative attention for boys. It is probably an accurate perception that males receive more severe punishment, given research data on that topic. It is interesting to note that the students' perceptions do not match with findings about more positive attention for males. Gender role stereotypes may be reflected here in that the students may perceive a more favored, visible status for males as a "normal" state of affairs and not even construe it as differential treatment. Further work to clarify student (and teacher) perceptions about differential treatment for girls and boys is called for and would confirm if these views are common. Nonetheless, it appears that the effects of socialization and unconscious attitudes and behaviors continue to exist and still appear to have negative impact on the career development of girls and perhaps boys as well.

Race and Gender Effects

There is little information on the combined effects of gender and race on teacher interactions. Even sources that present excellent overviews on education and career, such as the book *Black Adolescents* (Jones, 1989), have virtually no information on the combined effects of gender and race. This is unfortunate, as the effects of a double membership in minority groups for black females appear to not be simply additive. For example, black adolescent females tend to rate themselves more positively than white females on some characteristics (e.g. warmth, steadiness) in spite of the presumed negative effects of racial and gender discrimination for this group. One recent study has found that black girls report high self-esteem from elementary school through high school, while many white girls experience a drop in self-esteem from elementary school to high school (American Association of University Women 1991). Yet we cannot ignore that African-American girls and women, as well as other minority women, experience the double whammy of race and gender bias and discrimination in this society. While some women of color may have moved out of the domestic service occupations, 1989 figures indicate that more than half of all African-American and Hispanic women workers are employed in clerical and service occupations. African-American women also experience unemployment at more than twice the rate of white women. In 1989, 12 million women of color were in the labor force (62% of African-American, 48% of Hispanic, and 70% of white female heads of families). More than half of the black and

Hispanic women had incomes below the poverty level. Even more telling, only 29% of Hispanic and 34% of African-American women workers attained educational levels beyond high school compared with 43% of white women workers (National Commission on Working Women, 1988).

These statistics have important implications for the career guidance of girls and women of color. While it is recognized that many studies are of Caucasians, it is essential that more studies be conducted on the career development of girls and women of color, and, even more important, more interventions be created to reduce the barriers and expand the options available to them. Even less information appears to exist on other racial minorities, though the added stress of adolescence on minorities has been noted (Rode & Bellfield, 1990). Given the increase in cultural and ethnic diversity predicted for future American society and current concerns about a multicultural approach to education, a more extensive research base is called for in the areas of teacher interactions in education as well as in other career development areas (Betz & Fitzgerald, 1987; Matlin, 1987).

It is imperative to mention here that counselors have a responsibility to adjust their counseling in order to be helpful to clients of varying ethnic and racial backgrounds. While an openness to creative techniques along with knowledge of cultural norms is helpful, some specific information about particular ethnic groups is detailed below. (Counselors are referred to Pedersen, Draguns, Lonner, and Trimble, 1989; and McGoldrick, Pearce, and Giordano, 1982, for additional background and techniques.) These descriptions are intended as general information about the cultures; obviously the information is not applicable to all individuals of any ethnic group, and counselors need to remember that, as with gender, within-group differences may be greater than between-group differences.

African-American Girls and Women

Counseling with members of the African-American or black community requires the counselor to be aware of African-American culture and the common extended kinship network that includes blood relatives and nonrelated persons. This network is likely to be a crucial influence on a young person's general development and career development. African-American girls are less likely to have as traditional an image of the mother role as white girls, because for most black women, working outside of the home is the norm. African-American girls and women often prefer and expect to combine marriage, children, and employment without significant role conflict. Counselors need also to consider the social, socioeconomic, religious, and broader ecology of the African-American family and its community in working with a member of this group and to be prepared to assist the client in dealing with socioeconomic concerns, racism and sexism, and other constraints in career planning. Creating a sense of empowerment and competence for black female clients is critical and can be aided by a therapeutic focus on strengths rather than problems.

Latino and Hispanic Girls and Women

Latino cultures vary considerably by specific ethnic background, including Mexican, Cuban, Puerto Rican, South American, and Central American. Cultural commonalities tend to include a close extended family network, traditional gender roles, and encouragement of nurturance over autonomy. A polite formal style with strangers and a flexible attitude about time are also characteristic. The emphasis on connection with family should not be viewed necessarily as pathological. As Falicov noted:

> The process of individuation, for example, is universal, but its characteristics, which include quantity and quality of differentiation, behavioral markers, timing and implementation, vary from culture to culture. Thus, a therapist perceiving a need for greater individuation in a 9-year-old Mexican American boy, may encourage him—in the Anglo pattern—to seek friendships outside the home by joining a neighborhood club or to take more responsibility by getting a newspaper route. On the other hand, his parents may feel that giving him a few household chores and allowing him to run an occasional errand—duties that do not warrant payment of an allowance—are sufficient acknowledgement of more maturity. (1989, p. 159)

Asian-American Girls and Women

Asian-American cultures are also extremely varied according to geographic region and include Japanese, Chinese, Korean, and Filipino, as well as more recent refugees and immigrants from Southeast Asia (Laotians, Hmong, Vietnamese, Malaysians, Cambodians, and Indonesians). Some common traditions include highly developed feelings of obligation to family and culture, unquestioned male authority over family, and emphasis on fitting in socially, with shaming the mechanism for reinforcing appropriate social behavior. Direct discussion of topics may be avoided and great care taken not to impose on another person. Counselors are likely to be viewed as authority figures and will be likelier to work successfully with Asian-American clients by being directive and by showing respect for family roles such as a mother's close relationship with her son. Knowing that problems are likely to be minimized and referred to indirectly may be helpful in understanding the client's situation. In addition, realizing that a client may attempt to tolerate great stress rather than impose on a counselor may be important.

Other cultural backgrounds may present different challenges for counselors helping girls and women to develop their potential in a democratic society. Helpers will need to be sensitive to ways in which cultural tradition may perpetuate the gender role system and keep women from obtaining the education, the opportunity for expanded life options, and other human rights that a pluralistic society assures to all.

These brief sketches are provided to emphasize the varied backgrounds female clients bring to counseling and to stress counselors' need to ascertain a female client's cultural identity and to be familiar with her culture. As noted above, however, each client is first and foremost a unique individual, and careful exploration of the culture's relevance for the client and her values, goals, and aspirations is needed rather than an assumption of its influence. Counselors also need to be aware of the ways in which cultures—and the roles of women and men in them—are changing.

Erosion of Female Career Aspirations from Childhood to Adolescence

One specific concern in the career psychology of women has been the issue of girls abandoning occupational dreams due in part or perhaps primarily to the effects of the gender role system. Gottfredson (1981) described a process of occupational circumscription whereby, as a child grows older, the number of occupational alternatives that he or she considers is lessened. This process was thought to begin as early as age 6 when children eliminate occupations perceived as inappropriate for their gender. Thus, the gender role system directly causes a girl who may want to be a construction worker to eliminate this aspiration as she perceives that males greatly dominate this field. In the second phase, occupations are eliminated due to concern about fit with social class self-concept and with general ability level. Finally, in the third phase, careers are eliminated in light of perceived personal interests, abilities, and values.

Changes in Career Choice and Aspirations

Theories such as Gottfredson's have resulted from and have led to research on the nature of changes in occupational choices from childhood to adolescence. The studies generally have compared occupational choices among preschool and elementary children of various ages. Unfortunately, as Harmon (1989) has noted, longitudinal studies following subjects' choices are very rare, which is especially true about tracking childhood choices through adolescence. Studies of this type are needed to specify the effects of aging on career choices. The few studies addressing issues related to gender differences in change of choice will be reviewed here.

Kriedberg, Butcher, and White (1978), as mentioned earlier, studied sixth-grade students' career choices. Both sexes nominated equal numbers of careers, with girls indicating more flexible choices. These authors noted, however, that when asked what they probably would really be when they grew up, three-fifths of the girls with nontraditional choices changed to traditional ones, suggesting that these girls did not expect to achieve their initial aspirations.

The study by Farmer (1983), also discussed earlier, found 9th- and 12th-grade students to score similarly on aspirations, with its author suggesting little change in goals with age.

An intriguing study by Homs and Esses (1988) compared 8th-, 10th-, and 12th-grade females in Canada on four criterion variables and several predictor variables. The four criterion variables were career commitment, occupational aspirations, educational aspirations, and vocational certainty. Two sets of significant relationships were found. Higher career commitment and more prestigious occupational aspirations were seen in girls who had higher grades, either masculine or androgynous trait dispositions, more liberal attitudes toward women, and higher socioeconomic status. Older girls from a lower socioeconomic background with high commitment to marriage and family were found to have high career commitment and certainty, but lower educational and occupational aspirations. The authors concluded that, as these young women aged, they perhaps became more aware of difficulties in combining work and family roles, suggesting but not actually demonstrating a lessening of educational and occupational aspirations with age. The authors also stressed the importance of looking at career and family goals separately for females and the need for counseling to address both of these life areas. While also desirable for young men, such work and family counseling seems imperative for young women if in fact they are struggling with decisions about future life. Clinical experience with young adult women indicates they often think of their future in relation to both life roles, whereas men often will be thinking about career success with little thought to marriage and family.

One of the few studies to take a longitudinal approach to this topic was conducted by Grant and Sleeter (1988). These authors followed 24 lower middle-class racially diverse students over 7 years and recorded their vocational goals and dreams. What these authors found was a lowering of aspirations from 8th-grade to 12th-grade along with narrowing options, for both males and females. The girls in the 8th-grade reported more ambitious career goals than the boys, though their choices were gender stereotyped and became more so toward graduation. The authors noted the critical importance of the school environment for students, particularly in the practice of tracking students in 10th-grade in either college preparatory classes or vocational courses. Students who were unsure about their future course were generally put into an academically undemanding vocational track, a practice which these authors believed negatively affected the students' academic self-concept and goals. They report that only 3 of the 13 students who planned in the 8th-grade to attend a 4-year college actually did so, for various reasons. The sample in this study was small (24 students), with no described differences between boys and girls. Through quotations and case studies, these authors conveyed their students' sense of frustration and lack of future planning. Carmen drops plans to study to be a legal secretary because "she is sick of school-boy problems and boring classwork. She simply wanted to be away from the hassles of school" (p. 24). Larry regrets having taken the easy course "cause I feel like I coulda learned more if I went, if I took some harder classes. There's a lot of kids that just, they're smart, but they just take easy classes and not, you know, they're not learning nothing. Once you get into senior high, you don't even have to take math, you know, not at all" (p. 25). The trend toward abandoned dreams that these authors reported is alarming.

Earlier studies (e.g., Astin & Myint, 1971) documented the shift for many women after high school for their high-school vocational choices, particularly if they had reported nontraditional career plans. While a few authors have indicated some trend in this direction for sixth graders (Kreidberg et al., 1978), the extent to which adolescents abandon occupational goals is unclear. Questions on this topic include whether there is significant change in goals at this age—especially for those students interested in nontraditional careers, whether the apparent change takes place during high school, and how plans for college or vocational school affect career choices. These data are needed in order to know where best to focus efforts at change.

Environmental Influences

Research efforts have attempted to pinpoint both environmental and psychological factors related to vocational persistence or change. Those environmental factors influential in females' career planning will be briefly mentioned here, while strategies to alter or counteract these factors will be discussed later. See Betz and Fitzgerald (1987) for a detailed discussion of these influences.

Parental Influence

The importance of parental behaviors and attitudes on career choice is well known. As Whiston (1989) noted, relatively little attention has been paid to integrating a family systems perspective into career-counseling theory. Yet parents, of course, are a strong, if not primary, influence on children's development. Parents shape gender roles by differential play, speech patterns, and other behaviors with infants and children. Because Chapter 3 will address general gender role socialization, we will discuss only parental influences directly related to career aspirations and choice at this point.

A number of students have demonstrated the influence of various parental factors on career aspirations. Sorenson and Winters (1975) reviewed the literature in this area and noted that girls whose mothers are employees are generally more approving of working mothers. They emphasized that, "The relationship is not direct, it is complex and influenced by education and socioeconomic level, the degree of mother's role conflict, the attitude of the father toward the mother's employment and many other variables" (p. 40). Family socioeconomic status appears to be a very influential factor in girls' career aspirations and is, of course, tied to the types of occupations parents expose their children to, to economic realities about higher education, as well as to mothers' employment. Betz (1989) emphasized an important point when she noted that:

> A non-directive parental stance and a null educational environment add up to apparent neutrality and, thus, apparent freedom of choice, but the external environment has NOT been neutral—it has been "marking her ballot" [Bem & Bem (1976)] with messages pushing traditional directions for 18 or 20 or 22 years. If this is the equation, can it add up to free choice? I argue that it does not. Note that unless this young woman receives some support, possibly from a counselor, for the other side of the equation, that is, for a broader range of life options, the societal pressures are likely to overdetermine her decisions. (p. 138)

Father's education and mother's occupational status also have been found to be related to occupational aspirations (Burlin, 1976). These are thought to reflect, to some extent, socioeconomic influences. Childhood play activities are found to be correlated with later career choices, with non–gender stereotyped play correlating with nonstereotyped career choice (Cooper & Robinson, 1989; Metzler-Brennan, Lewis & Gerrard, 1985).

Sexual Violence

Various forms of violence against women may have profound effects on their life choices. Early sexual abuse, sexual harassment, and sexist attitudes can deeply affect a female child or adolescent's self-concept, self-esteem, and expectations. Although there is abundant literature on sexual violence and the incidence of violence against women, it has necessarily focused primarily on negative psychological effects more than on career choices and decisions. Nonetheless, in spite of societal progress in reducing sexist and harassing behavior, the media constantly report incidents of violence, which can have lasting effects on the victims, especially in feelings of shame and self-worth. Some of these relate to sexual harassment and assault by athletes in cases in which parents and school officials assume a "boys will be boys" stance. The most tragic of these have resulted in the female adolescent committing suicide. These socialized attitudes of domination and subordination are basic in the effects they have on the self-esteem and life options of girls and women at all ages.

Influence of Peers and Professors

Attitudes still exist in high school that young women should not be too bright; if they are, they should not show it. One of the authors experienced a vivid example of this when her adolescent daughter, an honor student, did not want her high school friends (particularly her boyfriend) to know that she was receiving the outstanding physics student award. Peer influence also prevented her from applying for membership in the National Honor Society as a junior despite being urged to do so by her teachers and advisor. She went on to major in mathematics in college, but discouraging messages from a college physics professor, in a class in which there were 42 men and only 3 women, influenced her decision to drop college physics in spite of having achieved an A minus the first semester.

Changing Family Patterns

One of the realities mentioned earlier in this chapter is that today and in the future, there are and will be varied family patterns. The traditional family today comprises only about 10% of families (Levitan, Belous, & Gallo, 1988), with single-parent families (mostly women with children and many of them in poverty) comprising 28%. Other family types include blended or restructured families, extended families, and the two-earner family that today is the dominant family pattern (more than 50%). The gay-lesbian lifestyle, estimated to be about 10% of the population, and role-reversal families are other family patterns. It is possible that people may move in and out of more than one of these patterns at different life stages. It is our assumption, however, based on demographic projections, that 90% of women and men will continue to marry and 80% to have children in heterosexual marriages (Hansen & Minor, 1989).

Social Supports

One critical factor that emerges in research as influential in career/life planning for women and men is perceived social support for career aspirations from parents, teachers, and peers (Farmer, 1980, 1985; Saltiel, 1986). Unfortunately, research indicates that girls and boys with career aspirations that do not fit gender stereotypes tend to be ignored, disparaged, or left to their own devices (Hackett & Betz, 1981). Availability of role models is another factor. Role models can be scarce for children and adolescents with nontraditional career plans (Miller, 1986). Another significant factor to be considered is the young woman's plans for marriage and family and the support she receives around whether to marry or not and whether career, marriage, and family can be combined (Fitzgerald & Crites, 1980). Because theorists have proposed that women's identity may be grounded in their relations with others, it is imperative to better understand how family plans interact with career plans and changes. Given current trends, many, if not most, future couples are likely to be dual-earner couples, and both women and men will likely need assistance in planning to meet the challenges of their multiple roles.

Black adolescent females traditionally have been found to have greater expectations about combining employment and family roles (Matlin, 1987), perhaps because black women have for generations worked outside the home. They also have higher educational and vocational aspirations than black adolescent males, though their achievement as a group sadly fails to match their aspirations. Racism and sexism have provided barriers to both black females and males, and the negative effect on black males is addressed in other literature (Moore & Leafgren, 1990).

Additional Psychological Factors

In addition to the environmental factors, it should be noted that researchers have identified a number of psychological factors related to career aspirations and achievement, some of them already mentioned. Others include development of an expressive or instrumental identity, self-concept, self-efficacy, and perceived ability level.

Expressive or Instrumental Identity

One psychological factor that has been studied in relation to career choice is the formation of a predominantly instrumental or expressive identity. An instrumental identity would primarily consist of a sense of personal agency expressed in behavior that is rational, analytical, independent, decisive, competitive, and self-directed. Someone with an expressive identity would, by contrast, more often exhibit communal traits such as being expressive, nurturant, integrative, cooperative, subordinate, and gentle. As the originator of these concepts—David Bakan (1966)—noted, the agentic traits have been assigned to males and the communal traits to females in Western culture. However, Bakan and others have proposed that a balance of agentic and communal traits is optimal for an individual (Block, 1973).

Gottfredson's (1981) model of career choice linked these concepts to career circumspection by postulating that adolescents eliminate occupations that are perceived to be inconsistent with their expressive or instrumental identity. Hollinger (1988) tested this proposition with gifted and talented female adolescents and concluded that these young women did vary in occupational interests, competencies, and preferences in relation to perceived instrumental and expressive identity. She has advised that adolescent career counseling needs to facilitate self-exploration and to help adolescents see the relationship between personal traits and the many appropriate career options available. The counselor might note that she does not see early career eliminations as irreversible but rather feels that counselors can aid clients in reexamining such decisions to decide if the early decisions were appropriate.

Risk-Taking

While risk-taking as a factor in women's life planning has not received a lot of attention, this is an important area for future research, especially in relation to girls and women making nontraditional choices that do not conform to the stereotype of "women's occupations" and roles. A qualitative study of 46 selected women leaders in a range of occupations found that 90% of them saw themselves as risk-takers (Sundal-Hansen, 1987).

Self-Concept

Self-concept has long been viewed as a factor in career development, and sex is seen as one important determinant of self-concept (Gottfredson, 1981). A recent study on adolescent self-concept researched self-esteem in 3000 children between grades 4 and 10 and found differences by sex and race (American Association of University Women, 1991). Elementary boys and girls were similar in that 67% of boys and 60% of girls replied that it was always true that "I am happy the way I am." But by middle school, only 37% of girls gave that response, compared to 56% of boys; by high school, the girls' positive responses were down to 29% and the boys' to 46%. A broader self-esteem index echoed this more dramatic self-esteem drop in girls.

Different patterns in self-esteem were found for girls of different races in the AAUW study. The percentages of white girls who chose "always true" in reply to the statement "I am happy the way I am" dropped from 55% in elementary school to 29% in middle school and 22% in high school. Black girls' responses went from 65% on that item to 59% to 58%, respectively, suggesting that they are much less likely to view themselves negatively. Hispanic girls' replies went from 68% "always true" in elementary school to 54% in middle school and 30% in high school, showing the largest drop in self-esteem. These findings suggest that gender and race play an important part in self-esteem that is then likely to affect future career plans and choices. The value of intervention to aid self-esteem in girls is clearly supported by this study.

Self-Efficacy and Aspirations

Self-efficacy refers to the expectation or belief that one can successfully perform a given behavior. Hackett and Betz (1981) have pointed out the implications of self-efficacy theory, first proposed by Bandura (1977), for gender differences in career aspirations and achievement. They postulated that low or weak expectations of self-efficacy constitute one set of internal barriers to women's pursuit of and achievement in careers.

Gender differences in self-efficacy are thought to derive from differential experiences in growing up. Four areas of experiences are thought to be related to this concept. *Performance accomplishments* refer to differences in the variety of tasks accomplished due to gender roles and differences in attributions about task performances, with women relying more on luck as an explanation for success. *Vicarious learning* refers to the lack of role models in books, media, and society, especially for nontraditional pursuits. *Emotional arousal* involves the higher levels of anxiety seen in females, which are felt to be detrimental to both task performance and efficacy expectations. *Verbal persuasion* describes the encouragement and persuasion one receives from others. Females are presumed to receive less support for achievements and career than males, giving them lower self-efficacy (see Table 2.1).

What then can be summarized about erosion of female children's or adolescents' occupational/career dreams? It is clear that further research is needed to clarify the amount of change for both girls and boys from childhood through adolescence. Further data are needed to confirm whether changes, if they occur at this level, are related to lack of support, to failure of the school to counsel and track students appropriately, to interfering factors such as plans to marry or pregnancy, or to increased concerns coming from dating and peer relationships (such as harassment and sexist attitudes and behavior). When these factors are clarified, interventions can be more appropriately planned to specifically thwart erosion of occupational goals and dreams of expanded life options in childhood and adolescence.

Besides examining attitudes toward occupations and life options, we have presented evidence of persistent socialization for segregated work and family roles. While some changes have occurred, there is a remarkable consistency across studies on traditional attitudes toward appropriate gender roles.   There is also evidence of ambivalence as

Table 2.1
Postulated Effects of Traditional Female Socialization on Career-Related
Self-Efficacy Expectations

Sources of Efficacy Information	Examples of Socialization Experiences Typical Among Females	Effects on Career-Related Self-Efficacy
Performance accomplishments	Greater involvement in domestic and nurturance activities, but less involvement in sports, mechanical activities, and other traditionally "masculine" domains	Higher self-efficacy with regard to domestic activities; lower self-efficacy in most other behavioral domains
Vicarious learning	Lack of exposure to female role models representing the full range of career options. Female models largely represent traditional roles and occupations	Higher self-efficacy with regard to traditionally female roles and occupations; lower self-efficacy in nontraditional occupations
Emotional arousal	Higher levels of anxiety reported	Further decreases in both generalized and specific self-efficacy
Verbal persuasion	Lack of encouragement toward or active discouragement from nontraditional pursuits and activities e.g. math, science	Lowered self-efficacy expectations in relationship to a variety of career options

Source: From "A Self-Efficacy Approach to the Career Development of Women" by G. Hackett and N. Betz, 1981, *Journal of Vocational Behavior, 18*, p. 333.

adolescents think about themselves and their future. It appears there is still a great deal of work to be done in helping young girls and women fulfill their potential by reducing the psychological and environmental barriers that limit them.

COUNSELING STRATEGIES: EXPANSION OF REAL AND PERCEIVED OPTIONS

Environmental and psychological factors related to career development of girls and young women have been described. Counselors have moved toward asking specifically how girls and boys can be encouraged to expand their life career options rather than to circumscribe them. Issues of prevention and intervention will be dealt with in the last section. This section will respond to the issue of how counselors can work with young clients to ensure their consideration of the widest range of possible career and life role options.

Providing Gender-Fair Counseling

Unfortunately, previous research has found that gender-biased counseling is fairly common among counselors. Although progress has been made in reducing the most blatant forms of bias, high-school counselors have been found to choose lower-paying occupations and occupations with less education for female case studies than for male case studies (Donahue & Costar, 1977), to indicate agreement with misinformation about gender and career (Bingham & House, 1973), and to demonstrate negative reactions to males aspiring to a nontraditional occupation (Fitzgerald & Cherpas, 1985). While many programs were created in the 1970s to increase awareness of counselors, teachers, and other educators about sexism and gender bias, and Title IX led to the elimination of the most blatant bias and discrimination, there is evidence that subtle bias still exists. After sex equity programs almost disappeared in the 1980s, new efforts in the 1990s indicate the problems did not go away, and new initiatives in multicultural and gender fair education (and counseling) are underway in several states (Hansen & Harless, 1988).

Gender fair career-counseling strategies clearly need to begin with the careful examination of the counselor's (and other educators') attitudes about gender. While some still trivialize it, use of nonsexist and gender-neutral terminology is crucial, as is keeping abreast of current information about gender and careers, demographics of work and family, and life roles. Counselors need to be knowledgeable about common misinformation in the culture also, such as the common misperception that full-time employment for women causes behavior problems in their children. Counselors need to be aware of these ideas in order to help make explicit some of the misgivings students may have about certain occupations or life plans and to prepare them for likely reactions to their choices. They also need to help change the traditional socialization that inadequately prepares youth for the realities of women's and men's roles in the 21st century.

Evaluating Assessment Instruments

As Diamond (1975) pointed out in the first wave of gender equity awareness, evaluating career assessment instruments for bias is an important facet of increasing options for both sexes. More recently, Deason and Bolyard (1988) listed criteria for evaluating assessment materials and emphasized its importance, as it has been demonstrated that some instruments tend to channel clients into traditional occupations by gender. Guidelines for constructing, administering, and interpreting tests still need to be heeded to assure both racial and gender equity.

Developing Gender-Fair Career Programs

One critical component in expanding career options is to implement career development experiences at all grade levels. As noted earlier, research has demonstrated that gender typing of occupations and gender-stereotyped vocational choices can begin even prior to the school years. Early intervention is most likely in encouraging students to keep their career options open. Needless to say, the career development curriculum, if one exists, needs to be reviewed for elimination of any gender discriminatory materials or information, as well as for discerning what gender-related areas may have been excluded. Appropriate preservice and inservice training of counselors, teachers, and other people who will deliver the program is needed, so that both traditional and nontraditional careers are positively explored for each sex, and educators continue to be sensitized to their own unconscious biases and stereotyping about male and female roles. Specific materials and programs will be referenced in another section of this chapter. However, delaying specific occupational choices until later in high school or college might allow students to consider a wider range of options and to avoid early circumscription, though it is recognized that career decisions often are made early in some fields, such as mathematics, science, and music. More about these systematic programs appears later in this chapter.

Assuring Accurate Information

Of equal importance in both individual counseling and career development programs is the need for the student to investigate and attain information on other aspects of career planning besides occupational information *per se*. While students need to know facts about emerging and disappearing jobs, they also need to know facts about the composition and distribution of the work force, gender data, and societal trends. As noted earlier, females' career planning seems to be very closely related to their plans for marriage and family, and both sexes need information and assistance in making realistic plans about multiple roles, whatever type of family lifestyle they prefer. Addressing issues of both individual work goals and family relationship goals is important. Direct confrontation in classes and in counseling about common erroneous stereotypes or beliefs such as the idea that women do not work after they have children or that men cannot work part-time or that Prince Charming will take care of Cinderella could aid students in clarifying their values and beliefs as well as improving their information. Students may not have sought or been exposed to up-to-date, accurate information about what girls and women do, can do, and are likely to do. They may not realize that their information is biased or can be confirmed or disproved objectively. Some, of course, may refuse to acknowledge their own stereotypes.

Encouraging Risk-Taking

As previously noted, the encouragement of risk-taking behaviors in girls may also be helpful in encouraging them to expand their life/career options, as risk taking correlates with their willingness to try new experiences and ideas. Girls can be encouraged to attempt new tasks and activities in academic and nonacademic areas such as courses, sports, hobbies, part-time work, and volunteering. (Of course, they should not be encouraged to take foolish risks that have a high probability of negative outcomes.)

Encouraging Nontraditional Choices

The importance of providing social support and role models for students considering nontraditional careers is emphasized by research that demonstrates how students are influenced by these factors. Apart from personally being supportive, counselors can arrange job visitations, interviews with role models, and mentorships for students aspiring to nontraditional occupational goals. They can help girls and women understand

Table 2.2
Employment of Working Women in Traditional and Nontraditional Jobs

Traditional Occupations	% Female	Nontraditional Occupations	% Female
Secretary	99.0	Engineer	7.6
Child care worker	97.0	Mechanic	3.1
Registered nurse	94.0	Dentist	8.6
Telephone operator	90.0	Data processing equipment repairer	8.6

Source: From the National Commission on Working Women or Wider Opportunities for Women, 1988, p. 1.

their own socialization and encourage them to keep options open through persistence in critical filter subjects such as mathematics and science. Clubs or support groups for students in nontraditional careers or course work are another source of social support.

In relation to nontraditional careers for women, it is instructive to note that in 1989, only 9% of all working women were employed in nontraditional jobs (i.e., jobs in which 75% or more of those employees are men). Table 2.2 from the National Commission on Working Women of Wider Opportunities for Women (1988) is self-explanatory.

During 1989, 60% of professional women worked in the two traditional female occupations of teaching and nursing. While the proportion of women in such professional fields as medicine, law, business, and dentistry has increased, the current employment statistics still suggest a pattern of extremely slow change in opening up nontraditional occupations for women and men.

Advocating School Policy Changes

Specific structural and school policy changes that counselors might work toward include flexible course selection and scheduling that does not track students into courses that foreclose later consideration of college attendance or discourage them from vocational fields that offer nontraditional and often high-paying options in the trades and crafts. Suggesting or supporting nontraditional courses and nonpunitive opportunities to take course electives would allow for expansion of students' interests and help to eliminate the imbalance in traditionally perceived men's and women's occupations.

Providing Activities to Enhance Self-Efficacy

Given concern about the effects of self-efficacy experiences on females' career development, counselors are faced with the question of how to intervene to counteract the development of low expectations of self-efficacy. One essential step in career counseling that would help females become aware of differences with self-efficacy expectations is gender role analysis. This technique involves focusing on the costs and benefits of fulfilling the traditional female role versus a more nontraditional one. Fitzgerald (1984) and Sundal-Hansen (1984) have noted the importance of helping girls and women to recognize the benefits of the choices made so far, and ways for them to transcend their socialization. Active discussion of these topics, especially in a group setting, can help young women develop a sense of mastery over their environment.

Promoting Self-Efficacy in Mathematics

Another issue that has received considerable research attention is women's sense of self-efficacy in mathematics. Because math functions as a gate to further study in the sciences and related fields, taking fewer courses in high-school math can effectively shut the door to further work or a major in those areas. In spite of extensive research and program development on girls and women in math and science in the 1970s and 1980s, the underrepresentation of women in these fields is still dramatic, and the underrepresentation of women of color even more so.

Betz and Hackett (1983) described the specific components of math self-efficacy and studied gender differences in these areas. Betz and Fitzgerald (1987) suggested that girl's math self-efficacy could be raised by requiring 4 years of math for all students, by providing overt support for girls in math, by making math-anxiety programs available, and by special programs designed to encourage girls' interest, confidence, and participation. (See Humphreys, 1982, for additional programs.)

Finally, directly addressing the four causes of low self-efficacy expectations can be an appropriate preventative measure (see Table 2.1). Working with parents, teachers, and the educational system to increase exposure to a variety of role models for women and men, increasing support and encouragement for nontraditional career and life choices, and encouraging a variety of tasks for both genders would be examples of ways to change the areas of vicarious learning, verbal persuasion, and performance accomplishments (Betz and Hackett, 1983).

Developing a Sense of Agency

A career development issue related to self-efficacy is what has been called a "sense of agency." This concept pertains to feelings of control over what happens in one's life, also called "destiny control." There is considerable evidence that a sense of agency is related to good mental health, and it is a central concern of career development, especially in Western culture. Girls and women, and particularly women of color, may not identify with the concept, especially if they are outside the opportunity structure and feel victimized by a system they cannot change. Providing encouragement and support, success experiences, and programs in which they can effect even small changes in their lives or in schools or other institutions may help to increase their sense of agency. Many recent programs try to achieve this goal, using the notion of "empowerment."

Addressing Gender Discrimination

A related issue is the need to address the topic of gender discrimination directly, especially concerning employment. Research suggests that young women are aware of the added barriers they may face in meeting their goals. The Minnesota Youth Poll by Hedin et al. (1985) found that 90% of the high-school respondents thought that the differential treatment males and females receive at home and school affected their future plans and aspirations. About half—mostly females—focused on the psychological impact and stated that females could have less confidence and competence due to being overprotected. The other half noted that the differential treatment caused young people to choose stereotypical careers. In addition, these authors analyzed responses from a *Minneapolis Star Tribune* Junior Journals column printed in 1983. The question asked about preference for being male or female, and 2,000 essays from 10- to 18-year-olds were received. While not a random sample, 12% of this population specifically noted gender discrimination as a factor in their choice. Seventeen percent of the girls mentioned this factor. Clearly, adolescent females are not unaware of this barrier to their goals and dreams, and, as Epperson (1988) has pointed out, these barriers may be the precursors of further barriers in their adult employment.

Self-efficacy may, therefore, be enhanced by ensuring that both genders are informed of progress against gender discrimination as well as alternative methods of confronting discrimination in their own lives. These adolescents need to be aware that discrimination is illegal and of the channels of official action as well as techniques that can be applied in interpersonal encounters. Feelings of mastery and competence will be aided by having a repertoire of responses to deal with gender discrimination, rather than accepting it as a discouraging but uncontrollable part of our society. Many of the policy statements and brochures for students on gender discrimination and sexual harassment developed by schools and colleges still need to be widely disseminated and implemented.

This review of counseling strategies has been brief. Further information on other counseling-related materials and activities will be given in the next sections. Counselors have many opportunities to act as change agents for gender (and racial) equity in the schools. The role of counselors facilitating positive change recently has been affirmed in the Common Values statement of the American Association for Counseling and Development (AACD, 1989). By committing themselves, counselors will help to reduce barriers of race, gender, and disability for their students and assure that all students have the opportunities to fulfill their potentials, a goal to which the counseling profession, the schools, and society profess commitment.

CASE EXAMPLES

Helping young girls and women dare to dream can be a challenging yet rewarding experience. As previously pointed out, despite progress made in the past 10 to 15 years in reducing barriers to life career options for women, myths and stereotypes persist. One of the major tasks of counselors is to provide direct support, encouragement, and information as well as to be leaders in creating and implementing programs that will enhance the life career options of girls and women. The counselor must also be culturally sensitive to differences in attitudes and values that clients from diverse cultures may bring. In this section, we provide a few case examples from elementary, middle-school, and secondary-school levels that can be used to help teachers, counselors, and other educators (including counselor educators) better understand and develop skills to empower girls and adolescents in specific situations in which they find themselves.

While these examples are based on actual cases, names and certain data have been changed to protect the identity of the students. Appreciation is expressed to the graduate students in counseling who provided some of them.

The Case of Susan

Susan is a 14-year-old white female ninth-grade student who lives with her parents in a metropolitan area of the Midwest. Her father did not complete high school, is a construction worker, and spends a lot of time watching television. Her mother completed high school, married immediately, never worked outside the home, and feels that her daughter needs to learn secretarial skills, or nursing, or something "to fall back on just in case."

Susan is well-developed sexually, attractive, and well-groomed. She appears somewhat sullen, shy, but is smiling hesitantly as she comes to the school counselor with an unspecified problem. She appears to become more comfortable in the interview only when speaking about her academic accomplishments but appears uncomfortable talking about other aspects of her life.

This student has excellent academic achievement but says, "I don't know who I am; therefore I don't know what direction to follow in school. I don't know what I want to be but I know I have to plan my high-school program."

"I like to study. I really like history and math. Dad says that's ridiculous. He says with a shape like mine, I'll get married and don't need college. But he's really strict where boys are concerned—almost like he doesn't trust me."

"My friends think I'm crazy to want to study. Maybe they're right. My teachers listen to me and think I'm OK. I don't know what mom thinks. She's sort of wishy-washy."

Hesitantly, the client verbalizes her discomfort with her advanced physical development—that boys look at her and giggle or tease, so she tries to wear loose clothes. She also slouches significantly.

A number of questions can be considered in examining this situation, including the following:

1. What do you think Susan's problem is?
2. How would you try to help her?
3. With which issue would you try to help her deal first?
4. How might you involve Susan's parent or teachers in counseling?
5. How could you help her with her sexuality concerns, particularly relationships with her peers?
6. What might be the long-term consequences of Susan's problem?
7. What kinds of things can you do to help empower her at this critical stage of her life?

The Case of Elizabeth

Elizabeth was born and raised in a rural area in the central part of a southwestern state. The oldest of six children, including four boys, she spent the majority of her time growing up in the family home cooking, baking, and cleaning to assist her mother in raising the family.

She was a good student in grade school, sometimes accused of being a "teachers' pet," but happy receiving good grades, high marks on achievement tests, and being very involved in school plays and other student presentations. Her participation in school activities changed drastically when she transferred to a large junior high school for her ninth grade—suddenly the number of classmates rose from 11 to 437; in addition, the school was some distance away from her home, which brought the limitations of being a "bus kid."

Being very practically motivated, she decided to make the best of the situation and become more highly achievement motivated—grades became even more important. She participated in activities offered during the school day, becoming involved in choral activities and taking a lot of pride in being accepted into each progressively more sophisticated choral group throughout her high school days.

In her youth, she and her brothers and sister had not been encouraged to associate with the "town kids" because there was always too much work to be done. Her parents also made an effort to control adolescent peer group influence. With her participation and interests increasing through her junior- and senior-high school days, she looked more and more for reinforcement and recognition from her school classmates, so the division from her childhood peer group became wider and wider. This was further widened by acceptance after tryouts, elections, or other competition into Senior Choir, Girls' State, and National Honor Society. She developed in those years a strong feeling of independence and sought only a few close friends with many "friendly" associations—she was alone, but never lonely.

In her coursework she attempted to select those courses that would benefit her most in her future career. Being highly achievement- and academics-motivated, she chose some of the typical collegiate track courses; on the other hand, her dreams of going to college after graduation had to be tempered with realism that this was a financial impossibility for her family. Therefore, she also chose classes in the clerical/secretarial track and home economics. She accepted her parents' conclusion that college was out of the question for her due to limited finances and the fact that no one in her family had ever gone to college.

The realism of impending graduation and getting that all-important "first job" was frightening and scary for her. However, with some gentle prodding and encouragement from her parents, she applied for a number of clerical positions. The most intriguing was the possibility of working for the U.S. government in Washington, D.C. Looking back, she feels that she was much braver and daring then and went off to an exciting new experience as a secretary in the capital! Her strong set of values plus a few cautionary statements from her father carried her through the first year of financial worries, homesickness, and challenges experienced by every other 18-year-old the first time away from home.

After an interesting year, she returned to her home state to accept a position as an assistant manager in a retail store. While she enjoyed working with the customers and the merchandise (jewelry) in the store, she was not quite satisfied with her life. After 6 months, she went to her community counseling center.

While other questions might evolve from a group of counselors or teachers, the following are provided as a guide:

1. What are Elizabeth's salient personality characteristics?
2. What do you observe about her development from her early years in a rural family home to her late teens?

3. How was Elizabeth's experience in the rural area different from her experience in the larger junior high school?
4. What was her relationship with her peers? With her parents?
5. If you were to counsel Elizabeth in high school, how might you have helped her to pursue some wider options?
6. What kind of help would you provide as she comes to you as an 18-year-old with a year of secretarial experience and 6 months in retail?
7. What would be your role in facilitating Elizabeth's career development at this stage of her life?

The Case of Maria

Maria's family were migrant workers in a small rural town in the Midwest. The town is heavily blue collar with most workers employed by the local textile plant, the town's largest employer. Some, like her family, lived in a trailer and worked on the local onion farms. Maria is the third of six children, three boys and three girls. Her mother has been home taking care of the family.

Maria is now an 18-year-old Hispanic woman who dropped out of school at 16. She hated school and wanted to go to work. After 2 years, she finds that she cannot qualify for more than low-paying menial jobs, mostly cleaning.

Maria has been involved in drug use but saw a mental health counselor to help her kick the habit. She has abstained from drug use for the past several months. Her counselor suggests that she return to her high school counselor for career guidance. She currently is living with a friend, is unemployed and on welfare, and has a 6-month-old baby. She wants more out of life but realizes she has to find some way to support herself and her baby. She didn't realize life would be so difficult and that it would be so hard to get a good-paying job. She has lost touch with her parents.

Maria's high-school grades through her sophomore year were mostly C's with an occasional D and B. Her test records suggest that she has an IQ of 120 and that she has high mechanical and spatial ability. She thinks she should become a secretary since "that's what most women do."

As the career counselor in Maria's high school, how would you try to help her?

1. What are Maria's priority issues?
2. With which issue would you try to help her first?
3. What would be your relationship with the mental health counselor?
4. What are the barriers Maria faces in trying to work out a better life for herself and her baby?
5. What specific strategies would you suggest to help her?
6. What other agencies might be of help to Maria?
7. In this most difficult but common situation, what changes are needed for you to be of help to Maria?

The Case of Janette

Janette is an 18-year-old white female who has just graduated from a large suburban high school with a graduating class of 600. She did well in school (graduated in the top fourth of her class) with a B+ average in a fairly academic program. She followed the college track and thought it would be nice to go to college but knew her parents, who were divorced when she was 11, couldn't afford to help her. They also didn't see much value in it "for a girl," as she'd probably get married anyway. She was an excellent volleyball player and a member of the women's team.

Janette's father, who is a recovered alcoholic, works as the foreman for the city maintenance crews, and her mother works part-time at a local nursing home. They are a Polish Catholic family with strong religious attitudes and traditions. Her two brothers went to work as laborers after high school. One of them was a running back on the football team and was a C+ student in school.

Janette has a boyfriend she has been dating since her junior year. He has worked part-time and summers for an uncle who is a contractor. He plans to get a job as a carpenter and does not plan on further schooling. He would like to get married and does not see any reason for her to go to college. She would eventually like to get married and have children and feels she should stay home with children if she is going to have them. She has heard that it's possible to have a career and family, but she doesn't really think it's true.

Janette comes to you as her school counselor during her senior year.

1. What is the key issue for Janette?
2. How would you characterize her?
3. How do you think various people might be influencing Janette in her decisions? Her parents? Her boyfriend? Her teachers? Her coach?
4. What strategies would you use in counseling Janette?
5. What else would you need to know to empower her to make her own decisions?
6. Who else might you involve in counseling?

The Case of Julie

Julie is a 17-year-old white female junior at Milburn High School in a western town of 30,000. There are 250 in her high school class. She comes from a working-class Norwegian immigrant family and is the oldest of three children. She has two brothers, 13 and 10. Her mother is a homemaker and earns some money as a part-time seamstress. The family lives in the lower half of a duplex not far from the meat-packing plant where her father works. Neither parent went to college, both have only a high school education; though Julie is a good student in school, they do not pressure her or particularly encourage her about planning for the future. They think she should get enough education to get a good job, probably as a secretary. They know a lot of women are working these days, but they come out of a religious background that says "a woman's place is in the home."

Julie has pretty much accepted her parents' values but she does like going to school and thinks she will probably apply to the local Vo-Tech Institute, where many of her friends have gone and study office work or cosmetology. She has an A average and has taken a strong academic program through her junior year. She received some encouragement from her mathematics teacher to think about going on to college. Her boyfriend is a senior, and they have quite a serious relationship. He works part-time at a gas station and plans to go to Vo-Tech to study auto mechanics.

Julie comes to see her counselor for a "career planning interview" scheduled with all students. She recently has gained some new friends in a journalism class, as she is one of the newspaper editors, and some of them have suggested she think about going to college. She thinks it might be fun but she has no money and doesn't think it would be possible. It's just not expected in her circles.

Julie expects to get married some day but has no immediate plans. She comes for her junior interview with the counselor.

You might ask several female students to role play a "career planning group" in which it is Julie's turn to present her problem. Or you might use the simulated interview, asking two participants to role play two different segments. The questions would need to be modified if a support group approach is used.

1. How would you start the interview with Julie?
2. What more would you need to know about her?
3. How well does Julie know herself?
4. How well does Julie know what options might be available to her?
5. What kind of financial aid might be available if she were to decide to go to college?
6. What kinds of other influences is Julie experiencing in making her decisions regarding post–high-school plans?
7. What strategies would you use in helping Julie make informed career decisions?
8. What do you do when a student's values and expectations are different from those of her parents?

The Case of Whei Lee

Whei Lee is a senior at a metropolitan high school in the Midwest. She has just received notice of acceptance with financial aid at two fine liberal arts colleges in her home state (her family moved there as refugees from Cambodia). Unlike most of her female peers, she will attend college and prepare for a law career.

Whei Lee came to the United States at age 6. She has been very active in school activities, including tennis, declamation, Southeast Asian culture, and National Honor Society. She was a President's Scholar, and ranks 10th in her class of 320 students, following a demanding academic schedule. She has also worked at a local Arby's restaurant and is currently a manager there.

Whei Lee's family is very much a part of the Southeast Asian culture in her community, where her father is a respected leader of the clan. She has many half-brothers and -sisters from her father's other marriages. She has a brother who teaches in a vocational-technical school and another who is in medical school. Her parents speak no English and have no formal education either in their home country or in the United States. Her father is a retired farmer, and the family is on welfare.

Whei Lee intends to become a lawyer and wants to help those who are poor and oppressed, especially her people. The college she will go to is predominantly white middle class, and she has some fears about finding her place there. Whei Lee is not thinking about marriage. In her culture, marriages are arranged, and it is common for young women to be married by 13 or 14. Whei Lee is very involved in the youth group of the church that sponsored her family.

Whei Lee feels she has a lot of control over her life decisions. Although she is very different from her parents, she respects their wisdom and support. Whei Lee is straddling two cultures: American and Cambodian. The greatest pressure she feels is her ethnic culture's beliefs about the place of women, who are primarily wives and childbearers with no rights of their own. Few women have broken out of those prescribed roles. She feels the most important thing she wants to do is help other Cambodian women out of what she perceives as their cultural barriers that keep them subservient and ignorant.

Whei Lee has had a very good relationship with you as her counselor and comes to you now to discuss her conflict about being in two cultures and wanting to bring about change, especially for women. She also wants to discuss her choice of law as a career and potential conflict in going to a predominantly white college away from her family.

1. What are the major issues with which Whei Lee is dealing at the present time?
2. What forces may have been operating to help her break from the tradition of her family culture and pursue a nontraditional path for her gender and culture?
3. What barriers do you think Whei Lee will face as she goes to a predominantly white college?
4. What conflicts might emerge as she further distances herself from her own culture and yet attempts to change it?
5. How likely is it that Whei Lee will achieve her goals?
6. What next steps will she need to take in the next 4 years as she shapes her own career development and life decisions?
7. How can she be empowered to achieve her goals?

The Case of Jessie

Jessie is a 15-year-old African-American student who is finishing her sophomore year in an inner-city high school. She lives with her single parent mother in a public housing project. Her mother works as a part-time cook at a local restaurant.

Jessie has an excellent voice and is a soloist with a Gospel Choir in her Baptist church. She also is in the All-School Choir in her school. Jessie has a B average in her last two years and has taken a general curriculum. SRA achievement tests have shown that she is in the 85th percentile in comparison with national norms and that she is especially strong in science and mathematics. She is debating whether to take more math as she is not sure she needs it. A striking and tall girl, 5 feet 10 inches tall, Jessie plays on the girls' basketball team, a sport which she loves. She expects to get a job when she finishes high school but has not done any future planning beyond that. She doesn't think of career planning because she doesn't see herself having a career. Recently she has been identified for a community mentoring project for minority students but is somewhat skeptical of what it would provide.

Jessie has two brothers and two sisters who are older and out on their own. Only her closest sister finished high school. One of her brothers got kicked out of school, and she doesn't know what he is doing. Her other brother works as a janitor at an elementary school. Her mother is a very warm and loving person who cares a great deal about her children. She also is very involved with the church.

Jessie comes to you to plan her last 2 years of high school as all sophomores are expected to do.

1. What kind of person is Jessie? What else do you need to know about her?
2. What are the issues she faces as she plans her high school programs?
3. What barriers does she face as she thinks about her own life and career decisions?
4. What does Jessie think she wants to do? What expanded career options might she need to know about?
5. What are the possibilities for further education?
6. What would you advise Jessie about the rest of her senior high program?
7. How could you help to empower Jessie to use her potential?

The young women you have met in this section have a variety of dreams. Some are competent and decisive, with a real "sense of agency," while others live a life filled with barriers that appear to hold little hope. Some are ambivalent and uncertain and are being influenced by past socialization, institutional policies, family pressures, cultural norms, and current peer relationships to make or not to make certain decisions in their lives. The case examples here are based on real young women with real problems, though each case is a composite, with details and identities changed to protect the identities of the young women. In all of the cases, the importance of education is a key factor.

Additional resources and methods to work with students, parents, teachers and to effect change in educational systems in these areas will be described in the next sections of this chapter.

PROBLEM PREVENTION AND SYSTEMATIC INTERVENTIONS

Consultation with Parents and Teachers

Counselors are likely to be called upon to consult with parents and teachers in groups or as individuals around issues of career selection as well as other areas involving gender equity. In his or her role as change agent, a counselor initiates consultation with these influential partners to insure gender-equitable treatment and support for students in fulfilling their potential. While some of the general material listed in the resource section could be useful in consultation (e.g., Sadker & Sadker, 1982; Hansen, 1981), the counselor will find these specific resources for workshops with these groups, including material to recommend for teacher use.

School-Based Career Development Programs

Besides typical counseling and consultation activities to enhance the career development of girls and young women, one of the most promising interventions is a systematic kindergarten through 12th-grade career development program in the schools.

Fortunately, today there is a resurgence of interest in such programs in the schools, driven perhaps by the reality of change and recognition of the priority students and their parents give to career needs. While career guidance conceptualizing flourished in the 1960s and career education was prominent in the 1970s, the 1980s saw diminished career development and career guidance in the schools, due in part to the increased emphasis on "back to the basics" in the educational reform movement. A new initiative toward expanded career development programs is in progress, involving counselors as team leaders working with teachers, parents, community, and students themselves and developing multifaceted career experiences integrated into the regular curriculum. These programs could have positive effects on both girls and boys, especially if attention is given to an expanded concept of career, focusing on life roles and the changing roles of women and men in work and family.

While the scope of this chapter precludes a detailed discussion of such career development programs, it is important to present a brief scenario of program characteristics that could influence the dreams and plans of young girls and women.

Programs developed in the 90s must attend to the global changes challenging our values, such as nuclear weapons, computers, migration, bioengineering, human rights, environmental degradation, and moral and ethical breakdowns. They must also address current changes within American society such as plural family patterns, greater cultural and ethnic diversity, and the dramatic changes in women's involvement in work and public life. The changing workplace is going to have a dramatic impact on the lives of girls and women and their ability to implement their dreams, especially in times of recession and work displacement. Corporate and public policy (e.g., regarding family and medical leave, poverty, child care, and work-family issues) will have to change before new life patterns can become a reality.

It is our position that, with the growing recognition of the interaction of work and family, new career development programs in the schools need to move beyond the traditional trait and factor matching of persons with jobs to helping children and youth understand the relationship between work and other life roles, the pervasive stereotyping that still exists, the different career socialization of girls and boys, and the need to consider nontraditional career options.

Hansen and Minor (1989) have suggested that the career development curriculum should include the following areas: (1) career decision making skills; (2) work and family issues in the United States and across cultures; (3) changing roles of women and men and gender issues; (4) changes in the work place and job market; (5) changes in the family; (6) life role planning; (7) economic independence and survival skills (and, we would add, multicultural and relationship skills, (8) entrepreneurs and job creation; and (9) managing change, negotiation, and transitions. Hansen also suggested that "spirituality," often ignored in career planning, has become more central in people's lives and should be a part of a developmental career planning program. She uses a definition of "spirituality" as "the core of the person—the center from which meaning, self, and life understanding are generated" or "the deep integration, wholeness, a sense of the interrelatedness of all of life." She also compares it to one's mission and sense of purpose, or, as mythologist Joseph Campbell called it, "following your bliss." Spirituality takes on special meaning in women's lives as they seek identity and empowerment and struggle for balance in work and family. Hansen has developed these ideas further in her model of "Integrative Life Planning" (Hansen, 1988; Hansen & Yost, 1989), an extension of her work on BORN FREE (Hansen, 1981).

A few career development programs have begun to implement a more expanded and integrated view of life planning. *The National Guidelines For Comprehensive Career Development* (National Occupational Information Coordinating Committee, 1989) were created with the involvement of several national professional associations, several of these divisions of the American Association for Counseling and Development. The packets consist of training modules for five settings (elementary schools, middle/junior high schools, high schools, post-secondary institutions, and community and business organizations) with competencies for students/clients at each level and a model for implementation of programs. Like many of the earlier federal, nonfederal, state, and national models of the 1970s, the guides contain goals and objectives for each developmental level, now focused on the areas of self-knowledge, educational and occupational exploration, and career planning. While the guidelines have brief sections on work and life roles and occupational and gender stereotyping, they are still heavily focused on work, give minimal attention to work and family linkages, and provide only surface attention to gender and multicultural issues.

One program that attempts to deal with the life role issues is *I'll Take Charge*, a 4-H–based program being disseminated nationally through the national 4-H center (Walker & Coble, 1989). The program uses video and experiential activities to teach career-planning concepts to 4-H members and their parents and can be used in or out of school.

While Gysbers and Henderson (1988) have offered an excellent guide for the process of developing and implementing a school guidance program and gave considerable attention to career guidance, in our view the sample curriculum provided does not deal adequately with career development of girls/women, work-family issues, multicultural issues, or societal changes.

The new momentum for systematic career development programs will need input from counselors who are aware of the need to integrate gender-fair and multicultural content in a central way. Recent state regulations requiring emphasis on these areas in school curricula may help provide support for continuing the task begun in the 1970s of assuring gender and racial equity in the schools. For this to happen, counselors and teachers will need to see themselves as team leaders and change agents for all kinds of equity.

Particularly they will need to:

❑ Examine their attitudes and practices to be sure they have eliminated both blatant and subtle stereotypes.
❑ Integrate new knowledge about women and gender roles, work and family, stereotyping and socialization, and gender/racial equity into career programs.
❑ Advocate for public policy changes that bring policies into greater congruence with realities of global and societal change and women's and men's changing roles.

❑ Insist that career guidance programs include the broader concept of career, with emphasis on integrative life planning and purpose and meaning, as well as educational-occupational choices.

❑ Help students, teachers, and prospective teachers become positive agents for change (Hansen & Harless, 1988).

While the focus of this chapter is girls and young women, career development programs must recognize that as women's lives change, men's lives will change, too. Programs need to help boys *and* girls understand themselves, stereotypes, and gender issues at different stages of their development. They also need to understand female and male socialization and to be helped to transcend it. If they are going to implement the preventive, developmental approach advocated by the counseling and human development professions, they will need to allocate part of their time to tasks that reflect proactive programs for change—not only one-to-one counseling after problems have occurred. Counselors and teachers will need to use their creativity and commitment to equity and human development in developing K–12 career development programs that will make a difference in the lives of both sexes.

BROAD-BASED ATTEMPTS TO ALLEVIATE CAREER STEREOTYPING: BORN FREE AS AN EXAMPLE

An example of a program designed to take a multifaceted approach to reduce career-related gender role stereotyping and to expand career options in educational institutions is presented here. Project BORN FREE, one of the first gender equity projects supported by the Women's Educational Equity Act, was developed in 1976 by a team of university-based faculty and graduate students involved in counseling and career development education. They collaborated with teachers, counselors, and administrators from 14 different educational institutions—elementary schools through vocational institutions. The goals of this comprehensive program are to provide teachers, counselors, and other educators with (1) a conceptual framework for examining limits on career options for women and men, (2) a process for bringing about change in career-related gender role stereotyping, (3) a set of materials useful for accomplishing both. The acronym of the program, BORN FREE, expresses these goals: to **B**uild **O**ptions, **R**eassess **N**orms, and **F**ree **R**oles through **E**ducational **E**quity.

The conceptual basis for BORN FREE is the expanded definition of career development as a continuous life-long process focused on individuals examining and making self-directed decisions about educational, vocational, and lifestyle options. Girls and boys, men and women are encouraged to make career decisions in accordance with individual talents, abilities, and interests rather than societal expectations. Part of the decision-making process needs to involve opening up possibilities for new roles and combinations of roles for individuals. Equally important is the need to learn which roles are most satisfying to individuals in line with their talents, preferences, and needs, as they realize that old patterns of choice do not match the current variety of life career options. Consideration of a variety of emerging life patterns and career alternatives is encouraged, such as dual-earner couples or families; equal partnership relationships in which both partners share financial, household, and parenting responsibilities; and child-free relationships.

BORN FREE operates from the conceptual framework of the Minnesota Career Development Curriculum (CDC) model (Tennyson, Hansen, Klaurens, & Antholz, 1975), which emphasizes the broad concept of career, including the integration of employment roles with other life roles. Students are to master the competencies of developing and clarifying a positive self-concept, acquiring a sense of control over one's life, acquiring knowledge of the world of work and lifestyles options, acquiring knowledge of the career decision-making process, and applying management skills to life roles. BORN FREE adds to this framework the concept of "career socialization," defined as "the differential experiences, influences, and processes used to prepare females and males for the educational, occupational, and lifestyle roles and choices society has defined as being appropriate for their particular sex" (Hansen, 1977).

The BORN FREE program has a number of components. One element involves a systems analysis for educational institutions committed to addressing the gender role and stereotypical issues related to career development. This self-analysis enabled the BORN FREE staff at each site to identify institutional policies and practices that facilitate or inhibit the availability of career options and the development of career aspirations and competencies in students. The goal of this component is to foster enduring change in institutions by motivating faculty and parents to recognize a problem exists and to want to change. They are also taught principles of change and how to become a change agent in their own institution. The program recognizes that only after problems are identified and acknowledged by staff can solutions be identified and offered.

Another component of the BORN FREE program is a set of training packets for elementary, secondary, and postsecondary/higher education institutions. In the development phase, prototype materials and resources for reducing career-related gender role stereotyping were distributed as examples, though staff at each institution were encouraged to create a unique BORN FREE training packet and action plan of their own for addressing the gender equity problem. BORN FREE training packets contain a set of definitions, guidelines for workshop leaders, a summary of the review of literature for the appropriate level, and cognitive and affective learning strategies based on appropriate goals and objectives, along with selected resources and a "fact pack" consisting of compilations of statistics on the status of women and men in education and work. The final training materials also incorporate principles and guidelines for faculty and parent teams to be change agents for gender equity in their own institutions.

The more-than-200 original and adapted learning strategies in the packets have both experiential and cognitive elements. Readings, discussions, simulations, role plays, videotape films, self-evaluations, and quizzes and introspective exercises are included. A total of 50 to 60 hours of training is possible using the packets, to be tailored for each institution's needs and arranged in needed combinations for inservice training from 2 hours to 2 weeks.

Nine half-hour color videotapes are also part of the BORN FREE program. The stimulus tapes consist primarily of short personal interview statements from children, youth, parents, and staff in the original schools and colleges about career choices and changes for women and men. In the interviews, subjects talk about lifestyles, societal expectations, educational-vocational opportunities, and career decisions. The tape's titles reflect their focus, such as "Women: Choices and Changes," "Parents as Influencers," and "Why Change?" Each tape has a viewer's guide with discussion questions, general instructions for use, and background information about the BORN FREE program. Although some of the hairstyles and clothes may seem a little dated and the fact sheets need updating, the content and themes are as valid today as when originally developed. That fact emphasizes that change comes slowly in the area of gender equity.

Finally, the BORN FREE staff developed a number of training designs of varying length. Two training institutes (one local and one national) were held to test the designs. Extensive content and process evaluations of the training institutes were conducted with very positive results.

Since BORN FREE was introduced in 1976, hundreds of local, national, and international institutions have used its materials and ideas. The program's success was validated in field testing and the materials have enjoyed wide dissemination. Nonetheless, the BORN FREE program is only one example of a broad-based preventive program. A variety of solutions are needed to reduce gender bias and gender role stereotyping and to expand career/life options for all people.

SUMMARY

In a society of rapid changes in both cultural norms and technology, counselors need information and specific skills to help prepare young clients/students for their future lives and to enable them to reach their potential. While this chapter has focused primarily on girls or young women, we recognize the need for a systems approach to gender-related career development issues. The influences on young people's life/career attitudes and choices are many; interventions for change need to be extensive and multifaceted. We have attempted to summarize what has been found in research about gender-related influences on children's and adolescents' life/career development and to expand thinking about career to include the interaction of work and family. We also have addressed techniques, programs, and resources for counselors and other educators to use in implementing change.

The shape of our future society is, of course, the primary factor in revising counseling practices and career development curricula and programs. Some changes have been widely predicted–the continuing presence and influence of women in the workplace in large numbers; the likely increase in two-earner families; the increase in single-parent families, most headed by women; fathers' increased involvement in child care; the increase in service jobs; and the increased numbers of people of color in the population and in the workplace. These predicted changes challenge counselors to design and implement counseling and career development programs that reduce barriers of race and gender and better prepare female and male clients/students for the demands and changing characteristics of work and family in the 21st century. Young people's ability (and especially women's ability) to "dare to dream" depends on the support they receive from counselors, parents, teachers, and the workplace. We hope that this chapter contributes to efforts to create a supportive climate for the career development of young people, especially girls and women.

RESOURCES FOR ENHANCING CAREER ASPIRATIONS

While enormous progress was made in gender equity in the 1970s with the passage of the Education Amendments of 1972 and the Women's Educational Equity Act, activity was sharply reduced in the 1980s as schools embarked on educational reform but ignored gender equity issues. The 1990s appear to be witnessing a renewed call for attention to issues of multicultural and gender fair education and counseling. Most of the resources listed in this section represent the many programs and initiatives begun in the 1970s, many of which still continue as established programs today.

Counselors seeking to implement programs or changes to encourage all students to achieve their potential will find many materials to aid their efforts. A sampling of books, programs, and audiovisual materials as listed here can be used as resources in changing counselor strategies, in assisting student choices, and as general references. Sources of additional information are also included.

Resources on Counseling-Based Strategies

Anderson, T., & Barta, S. (1983). *Multicultural nonsexist education in Iowa schools; Guidance and counseling.* Des Moines: Iowa State Department of Education.

Beymer, L. (1989). *Improving equity career guidance in Indiana junior high and middle schools: Results and recommendations for a three-year project.* Terre Haute: Indiana State University Department of Counseling.

Deason, M., & Bolyard, K. (1988). *Gender-fair career counseling strategies.* Indianapolis: Indiana Commission on Vocational and Technical Education.

Fitzgerald, L. (1984). Career counseling women: Principles, procedures, and problems. In D. Lea & Z. Liebowitz (Eds.) *Adult career development* (pp. 116–131). Alexandria, VA: National Career Development Association.

Hansen, L. S., & Harless, D. (1988). *Sex equity in guidance and counseling.* Ann Arbor, MI: Counseling and Personnel Services Clearinghouse.

Hansen, L. S., & Yost, M. (1989). Preparing youth for changing roles and tasks in society, work, and family. In Comprehensive Career Development Project for Secondary Schools, *Career development: Preparing for the 21st century* (pp. 119–137). Knoxville: University of Tennessee.

O'Malley, K. M., & Richardson, S. (1985). Sex bias in counseling: Have things changed? *Journal of Counseling and Development, 63,* 294–298.

Stiegler, C. (1980). *How-to strategies for sex equity: The role of the counselor.* (Report #LBY 41580). Frankfort: Kentucky State Department of Education, Bureau of Vocational Education. (ERIC Document Reproduction Service No. Ed 281 900)

Wellesley College Center for Research on Women. (1989). Making a difference in the lives of teen-agers: Center for research on adolescence. *Research Report, 7* (2).

Other Program Resources

The following resources are intended to be helpful to counselors participating in a school's implementation of a career development program. Listed are materials that take a comprehensive view; additional component materials found in the previous section may also be relevant.

Gysbers, N., & Henderson, P. (1988). *Developing and managing your school guidance program.* Alexandria, VA: American Association for Counseling and Development.

Hansen, L. S. (1978). Promoting female growth through a career development curriculum. In L. Hansen & R. Rapoza, *Career development and counseling of women.* (pp. 425–442). Springfield, IL: Charles C Thomas.

Jackson County School District. (1982). *Career education program for elementary students: Science.* Jackson, MI: Jackson County School District.

Kouzekanani, K., & Knight, J. (1983, December). *Career education for the recruitment, retention, and placement of students in vocational education program areas not traditional for their sex.* Paper presented at the convention of the American Vocational Association, Anaheim, CA.

Louisiana State Department of Education. (1983). *Adult responsibilities curriculum guide. Secondary vocational home economics programs (eleventh and twelfth grade levels). Bulletin 1710.* Baton Rouge: Louisiana State University, Division of Vocational Education.

National Occupational Information Coordinating Committee (NOICC). (1989). *The national career development guidelines—elementary schools, middle/junior high schools, and high schools.* Washington DC: Author.

Tate, R. (1981). *Traditional vs. nontraditional: Expanding career choices. Middle school unit (or high school unit).* Bloomington, IN: Bloomington Department of Human Resources.

Tennyson, W. W., Hansen L. S., Klaurens, M., & Antholz, M. B. (1980). *Career development education: A program approach for teachers and counselors.* Alexandria, VA: National Career Development Association.

Walker, J., & Coble, T. (1989). *I'll take charge* (Program developed for National 4H Program in coordination with Pillsbury Co.). St. Paul: University of Minnesota, Extension Division.

Women's Educational Equity Act Program. (1987). *Excellence and equity, 1977–1987.* Newton, MA: Educational Development Center.

YMCA of Boston. (1981). *Connections. A program for middle school students about women and work and skills for good jobs. Leader's guide.* Boston: Author. (ERIC Document Reproduction Service No. ED 198 385)

Resources for Direct Assistance to Students

Bingham, M., Edmondson, J., & Stryker, S. (1985). *Choices: A teen woman's journal for self-awareness and personal planning.* El Toro, CA: Mission Publications.

Bingham, M., Edmondson, J., & Stryker, S. (1985). *Challenges: A young man's journal for career self-awareness and personal planning.* El Toro, CA: Mission Publications.

Carvell, F. (1979). *Choices and challenges—A student guidebook about nontraditional career opportunities.* Los Altos, CA: Carvell Education Management Planning, Inc. (ERIC Document Reproduction Service No. ED 212 768)

Cauley, C. D. (1981). *Time for a change: A woman's guide to nontraditional occupations.* Tulsa: Ellis Associates. (ERIC Document Reproductions Service No. ED 212 768)

Lindner, A., & Mellen-Sullivan, D. (1987). *Career planning workbook: From astronaut to zoologist, career survival kit for teen education and employment.* Madison, WI: Vocational Studies Center. (ERIC Document Reproductions Service No. ED 312 404)

For Parents and General Audiences

Boyer, M., & Horne, A. (1989). Schools and parents: Partners in career equity guidance for young adolescents. *Equity Career Guidance Project Monograph No. 2.* Terre Haute: Indiana State University Department of Counseling.

Canora, V. (1981). *Parent awareness: Sex equity training package. Unlocking nontraditional careers.* (Research and Development Series No. 215c). Columbus: The Ohio State University. (ERIC Document Reproduction Service No. ED 277 371)

Fagan, L. J. (1980). *Expanding opportunities through sex equity in vocational education* (Inservice Instructional Unit XA). Jackson: Mississippi State University.

Feminist Northwest of Seattle, WA. (1976). *Project awareness: A multistate leadership project addressing sex discrimination issues in education.* Olympia, WA: Office for Equal Education.

Hansen, L. S., Johnson, D., Teeson, T., & Hatfield, T. (1977). *Project BORN FREE. Selected review of the literature on career development and sex-role stereotyping at the secondary level.* Minneapolis: University of Minnesota, Project BORN FREE.

Sechler, J. (1981). *Communication skills. Sex equity training package. Unlocking nontraditional careers.* Columbus: The Ohio State University.

Van Buren, J. (1988). *Working for change: Planning a gender equity workshop.* West Lafayette, IN: Purdue University, Vocational Education Section.

For Teachers

Calabrese, A. (1984). *Rainbow shave ice, crackseed, and other ono stuff. Sex equity goodies for the classroom.* Honolulu: Hawaii State Department of Education. (ERIC Document Reproduction Service No. ED 244 133)

Idaho State Department of Education. (1982). *Sex equity resources for Idaho schools.* Boise: Idaho State Department of Education.

Jolly, S., & Forrester, J. (1981). *Sex equity in the classroom: Teacher strategies.* Jackson: Mississippi State Department of Education. (ERIC Document Reproduction Service No. ED 219 551)

McCune, S. D., & Matthews, M. (1978). *Implementing Title IX and attaining sex equity: A workshop package for elementary–secondary and post-secondary educators.* Washington, DC: Council of Chief State School Officers; U.S. Department of Health, Education, and Welfare, Office of Education.

Pfiffner, K. J. (1983). *Choosing occupations and life roles. Teacher's handbook.* Charleston, WV: Appalachia Educational Laboratory. (ERIC Document Reproduction Service No. ED 233 224)

Wright, J. (1981). *Creative options for children of the eighties. Reducing stereotyping in career education K–6. A manual to assist the classroom teacher.* Gray: Maine School Administrative District 15.

General Resources

American Institutes for Research. (1980). *Programs to combat stereotyping in career choice.* Palo Alto, CA: American Institutes for Research.

Giallourakis, M., & Lorenz, M. (1984). *Wo-mentoring: Can it work?* Hammon, LA: American Business Communication Association. (ERIC Document Reproduction Service No. ED 259 356)

Hansen, L. S. (1984). *Eliminating sex stereotyping in schools: A regional guide for educators in North America and Western Europe.* Paris, France: United Nations Educational, Scientific, and Cultural Organization (UNESCO).

Hollenbeck, E. (1983). *Together we can. Annual Texas vocational guidance summer workshop proceedings.* Denton: North Texas State University. (ERIC Document Reproduction Service No. ED 227 234)

Illinois State Board of Education. (1982). *Bibliography of available sex equity resources.* Springfield: Illinois State Board of Education. (ERIC Document Reproduction Service No. ED 240 021)

Martino, S., & Watson, J. (1988). *Educational equity options. A resource bibliography.* Washington, DC: Wider Opportunities for Women, Inc. (ERIC Document Reproduction Service No. ED 306 388)

Pelcak, D. (1977). *Selected review of the literature on career development and sex-role stereotyping at the elementary level.* Minneapolis: University of Minnesota, Project BORN FREE.

Sadker, M. P., & Sadker, D. M. (1982). *Sex equity handbook for schools.* New York: Longman, Inc.

St. Paul Public Schools. (1982). *America's women of color: Integrating cultural diversity into non-sex-biased curricula. Minority women: An annotated bibliography.* Newton, MA: Education Development Center. (ERIC Document Reproduction Service No. ED 221 503)

Sprung, D. (1975). *Non-sexist education for young children: A practical guide.* New York: Citation Press.

Sullivan, K. A. (1976). Changes in girls' perceptions of the appropriateness of occupations for females through films with counter sex-stereotyping. *Dissertation Abstracts International, 36,* 51–64.

Tibbetts, S. L. (1975). Sex roles stereotyping in the lower grades: Part of the solution. *Journal of Vocational Behavior, 6,* 255–261.

Vicenzi, H. (1977). Minimizing occupational stereotypes. *Vocational Guidance Quarterly, 25,* 265–268.

Virginia State Department of Education. (1989). *Vocational gender equity project abstract 1988–89.* Richmond: Virginia State Department of Education. (ERIC Document Reproduction Service No. ED 311 254) (These also exist for years 1987–88.)

Women in nontraditional careers (WINC): Journal and curriculum guide. (1982). Washington, DC: Superintendent of Documents, U.S. Government Printing Office.

Women's Educational Equity Act Program. (1983). *216 resources for educational equity.* Beverly Hills, CA: Sage.

Women's Educational Equity Act Program. (1987). *Celebrating a decade of equity 1977-87.* Newton, MA: WEEA Publishing Center, Educational Development Center.

REFERENCES

American Association for Counseling and Development. (1989). *A strategic plan for the Association.* Alexandria, VA: Author. (mimeo)

American Association of University Women. (1991). *Shortchanging girls, shortchanging America.* Washington, DC: Author.

Astin, H., & Myint, T. (1971). Career development of young women during the post-high school years. *Journal of Counseling Psychology, 18,* 386–393.

Bakan, D. (1966). *The duality of human existence.* Chicago: Rand-McNally.

Bandura, A. (1977). *Social learning theory.* Englewood Cliffs, NJ: Prentice-Hall.

Bernard, J. (1981). The good provider role: Its rise and fall. *American Psychologist, 28,* 512–526.

Betz, N. (1989). Implications of the null environment hypothesis for women's career development and counseling psychology. *The Counseling Psychologist, 17,* 136–144.

Betz, N., & Fitzgerald, L. (1987). *The career psychology of women.* Orlando, FL: Academic Press.

Betz, N. E., & Hackett, G. (1983). The relationship of mathematics self-efficacy expectations to the selection of science-based college majors. *Journal of Vocational Behavior, 23,* 329–345.

Bingham, W. C., & House, E. W. (1973). Counselors' attitudes toward woman and work. *Vocational Guidance Quarterly, 28,* 512–526.

Block, J. (1973). Conceptions of sex roles: Some cross-cultural and longitudinal perspectives. *American Psychologist, 22,* 16–32.

Brophy, J. E., & Good, T. (1978). *Teacher-student relations: Causes and consequences.* New York: Holt, Rinehart and Winston.

Burlin, F. (1976). The relationship of parental education and maternal work and occupational status to occupational aspiration in adolescent females. *Journal of Vocational Behavior, 9,* 99–104.

Card, J., Steel, L., & Abeles, R. (1980). Sex differences in realization of individual potential for achievement. *Journal of Vocational Behavior, 17,* 1–21.

Chetwynd, J., & Hartnett, D. (Eds.). (1978). *The sex-role system.* London, England: Routledge and Kegan Paul.

Cooper, S., & Robinson, D. (1989). Childhood play activities of women and men entering engineering and science careers. *The School Counselor, 35,* 338–342.

Deason, M., & Bolyard, K. (1988). *Gender-fair career counseling strategies.* West Lafayette, IN: Purdue University.

Diamond, E. E. (1975). Guidelines for the assessment of sex bias and sex fairness in career interest inventories. *Measurement and Evaluation in Guidance, 8,* 7–111.

Donahue, T., & Costar, J. (1977). Counselor discrimination against young women in career selection. *Journal of Counseling Psychology, 24,* 481–486.

Doyle, J., & Paludi, M. (1991). *Sex and gender.* Dubuque, IA: W. C. Brown.

Epperson, S. (1988). Studies link subtle sex bias in schools with women's behavior in the workplace. *Wall Street Journal,* Sept. 26.

Fagot, B. (1981). Male and female teachers: Do they treat boys and girls differently? *Sex Roles, 7,* 263–272.

Falicov, C. (1989). Mexican families. In M. McGoldrick, J. Pearce, & J. Giordano. (1982), *Ethnicity and family therapy* (pp. 134–163). New York: Guilford Press.

Farmer, H. (1980). Environmental, background, and psychological variables related to optimizing achievement and career motivation for high school girls. *Journal of Vocational Behavior, 17,* 58–70.

Farmer, H. (1983). Career and homemaking plans for high school youth. *Journal of Counseling Psychology, 30,* 40-45.

Farmer, H. (1985). Model of career and achievement motivation for women and men. *Journal of Counseling Psychology, 32*, 363–390.

Fitzgerald, L. (1984). Career counseling women: principles, procedures, and problems. In D. Lea, & Z. Liebowitz (Eds.), *Adult career development* (pp. 116–131). Alexandria, VA: National Career Development Association.

Fitzgerald, L., & Cherpas, C. (1985). On the reciprocal relation between gender and occupation: Rethinking the assumptions concerning masculine career development. *Journal of Vocational Behavior, 27*, 44–62.

Fitzgerald, L., & Crites, J. (1980). Toward a career psychology of women: What do we know? What do we need to know? *Journal of Counseling Psychology, 27*, 44–62.

Franken, M. (1983). Sex role expectations in children's vocational aspirations and perceptions of occupations. *Psychology of Women Quarterly, 8*, 59–68.

Gettys, L., & Cann, A. (1981). Children's perceptions of occupational sex stereotypes. *Sex Roles, 7*, 301–308.

Gilligan, C. (1986, October). *Adolescence reconsidered*. Gisela Konopka lecture, St. Paul campus, University of Minnesota. (mimeo)

Gottfredson, L. (1981). Circumscription and compromise: A developmental theory of occupational circumscription. *Journal of Counseling Psychology, 28*, 545–579.

Grant, C., & Sleeter, C. (1988). Race, class and gender and abandoned dreams. *Teachers College Record, 90*, 19–40.

Gysbers, N. C., & Henderson, P. (1988). *Developing and managing your school guidance program*. Alexandria, VA: American Association for Counseling and Development.

Hackett, G., & Betz, N. (1981). A self-efficacy approach to the career development of women. *Journal of Vocational Behavior, 18*, 326–339.

Hansen, L. S. (1977). *An examination of the concepts and definitions of career education*. Washington, DC: National Advisory Council for Career Education.

Hansen, L. S. (1981). BORN FREE: Career development, sex roles, and social change. *IAEVG Bulletin*, Proceedings of 10th World Congress, Sept. 1980, 13–24.

Hansen, L. S. (1984). *Eliminating sex stereotyping in schools: A regional guide for educators in North America and Western Europe*. Paris: France: United Nations Educational, Scientific, and Cultural Organization (UNESCO).

Hansen, L. S. (1988, January). Integrative life planning: Work, family and community. Paper presented at national conference on the Transformation of Work and Workers, Orlando, FL: National Career Development Association.

Hansen, L. S., & Harless, D. (1988). *Sex equity in guidance and counseling*. Ann Arbor, MI: Counseling and Personnel Services Clearinghouse.

Hansen, L. S., & Minor, C. (1989). Work, family and career development: Implications for persons, policies, and practices. In D. Brown, & C. Minor (Eds.), *Working in America: Status report on planning and problems* (pp. 25–42). Alexandria, VA: National Career Development Association.

Hansen, L. S., & Yost, M. (1989). Preparing youth for changing roles and tasks in society, work, and family. *Career development: Preparing for the 21st century* (pp. 119–137). Knoxville: The University of Tennessee.

Harmon, L. (1989). Longitudinal changes in women's career aspirations: Developmental or historical? *Journal of Vocational Behavior, 35*, 46–63.

Hedin, D., Erickson, J., Simon, P. I., & Walker, J. (1985). *Minnesota youth poll: Aspirations, future plans and expectations of Minnesota youth*. St. Paul: Center for Youth Development and Research, University of Minnesota.

Herzog, A., & Bachman, J. (1982). *Sex role attitudes among high school students*. Ann Arbor, MI: University of Michigan; Survey Research Center, Institute for Social Research.

Hollinger, C. (1988). Toward an understanding of career development among gifted/talented female adolescents. *Journal for the Education of the Gifted, 12*, 62–79.

Homs, V., & Esses, L. (1988). Factors influencing high school girls' career motivation. *Psychology of Women Quarterly, 12*, 313–328.

Humphreys, S. M. (1982). *Women and minorities in science: Strategies for increasing participation*. Boulder, CO: Westview Press.

Jones, R. (1989). *Black adolescents*. Berkeley, CA: Cobb and Henry.

Kohlberg, L. (1966). A cognitive-developmental analysis of children's sex role concepts and attitudes. In E. E. Maccoby (Ed.), *The development of sex differences* (pp. 82–173). Stanford, CA: Stanford University Press.

Kriedberg, G., Butcher, A., & White, K. (1978). Vocational roles choice in second and sixth grade children. *Sex roles, 4*, 175–181.

Lavine, L. D. (1982). Parental power as a potential influence on girls' career choice. *Child Development, 53*, 658–663.

Levitan, S. A., Belous R. S., & Gallo, F. (1988). *What's happening to the American family?* Baltimore: The Johns Hopkins University Press.

Looft, W. (1971a). Sex differences in the vocational aspirations of elementary school children. *Developmental Psychology, 5*, 366.

Looft, W. (1971b). Vocational aspirations of second grade girls. *Psychology Reports, 28,* 242–244.

Marini, M. M. (1978). Sex differences in the determination of adolescent aspirations: A review of the research. *Sex Roles, 4*, 723–753.

Matlin, M. (1987). *The psychology of women*. New York: Holt, Rinehart and Winston.

McBean, A. J. (1986). *Adolescents and the male sex role: Preliminary data on late adolescent attitudes and investigation of a methodology*. Unpublished master's thesis, University of Minnesota.

McGoldrick, M., Pearce, J., & Giordano, J. (1982). *Ethnicity and family therapy*. New York: Guilford Press.

McKay, W. R., & Miller, C. A. (1982). Relations of socioeconomic status and sex variables to the complexity of worker functions in the occupational choices of elementary school children. *Journal of Vocational Behavior, 20*, 31–37.

Metzler-Brennan, E., Lewis, R., & Gerrard, M. (1985). Childhood antecedents of adult women's masculinity, femininity and career role choices. *Psychology of Women Quarterly, 9*, 371–382.

Miller, J. V. (1984). *The family-career connection: A new framework for career development*. Columbus: The Ohio State University National Center for Research in Vocational Education.

Miller, R. (1986). Reducing occupational circumspection. *Elementary School Guidance and Counseling, 20*, 250–254.

Moore, D., & Leafgren, F. (1990). *Men in conflict*. Alexandria, VA: American Association for Counseling and Development.

National Commission on Working Women. (1988). *Fact sheets on working women*. Washington, DC: Wider Opportunities for Women, Inc. (ERIC Document Reproduction Service No. ED 299 401)

National Occupational Information Coordinating Committee. (1989). *National guidelines for comprehensive career development programs*. Washington, DC: Author.

Pedersen, P., Draguns, J., Lonner, W., & Trimble, J. (1989). *Counseling across cultures*. Honolulu: University of Hawaii Press.

Piaget, J., & Inhelder, D. (1969). *The psychology of the child*. New York: Basic Books.

Richardson, M. S. (1981). Occupational and family roles: A neglected intersection. *Counseling Psychologist, 9*, 13–23.

Rode, P., & Bellfield, K. (1990). *The next generation: The health and well-being of young people of color in the Twin Cities*. Minneapolis: Urban Coalition of Minneapolis.

Sadker, M. P., & Sadker, D. (1982). *Sex equity handbook for the schools*. New York: Longman.

Saltiel, J. (1986). Segmental influence: The case of educational and occupational significant others. *Adolescence XXI, 83*, 615–622.

Serbin, L. A., Connor, J. M., & Iler, I. (1979). Sex-stereotyped and non-stereotyped introductions of new toys in the preschool classroom: An observational study of teacher behavior and its effects. *Psychology of Women Quarterly, 4*, 261–265.

Shepherd, W., & Hess, D. (1975). Attitudes in four age groups toward sex role divisions in adult occupations and activities. *Journal of Vocational Behavior, 6*, 27–39.

Sorenson, J., & Winters, C. (1975). Parental influence on women's career development. In S. Osipow (Ed.), *Emerging women: Career analysis and outlooks*. Columbus, OH: Charles E. Merrill.

Sundal-Hansen, L. (1984). Interrelationship of gender and career. In N. Gysbers (Ed.), *Designing careers* (pp. 216–247). San Francisco: Jossey-Bass.

Sundal-Hansen, L. (1987). The life career journey for men and women: Traditions, transitions, and transformations. *Canadian Journal of Guidance and Counselling, 3*, 3–54.

Super, D. (1980). A life span, life-space approach to career development. *Journal of Vocational Behavior, 16*, 282–298.

Super, D., & Culha, M. (1976).*Work Salience Inventory*. Unpublished manuscript.

Tennyson, W. W., Hansen, L. S., Klaurens, M. K., & Antholz, M. B. (1975). *Educating for career development*. St. Paul: Minnesota Department of Education [Reprinted by National Career Development Association, A program approach for teachers and counselors.]

Tittle, C. (1981). *Careers and family: Sex roles and adolescent life plans*. Beverly Hills, CA: Sage Publications.

Tremaine, L., & Schau, C. (1979). Sex-role aspects in the development of children's vocational knowledge. *Journal of Vocational Behavior, 14*, 317–328.

Tremaine, L., Schau, C., & Busch, J. (1982). Children's occupational sex typing. *Sex Roles, 8*, 691–710.

Walker, J., & Coble, T. (1989). *I'll take charge*. St. Paul: University of Minnesota, 4H Extension Division.

Whiston, S. (1989). Using family systems theory in career counseling: A group for parents. *The School Counselor, 36*, 343–348.

Zuckerman, D. M., & Sayre, D. H. (1982). Cultural sex-role expectations and children's sex-role concepts. *Sex Roles, 8*, 853–862.

3

The Impact of Gender Role Socialization

Loretta J. Bradley and L.J. Gould
Texas Tech University

Bree A. Hayes
The Hayes Group, Athens, GA

W hy do people act the way they do? This is probably one of the world's most frequently asked questions, and the answer is at once very simple and exceedingly complex. Basically, people act the way that they do because they have been methodically socialized to do so. *Socialization* is the process by which an individual learns and internalizes society's expectations concerning what is appropriate behavior for his or her sex, age, and current place in society. "What we term masculine and feminine is not linked in any biological sense to being a male or a female but rather is established by society" (Basow, 1986, p. 4). In our society today, females are socialized to play the role of subordinate.

Miller (1986) has pointed out that, when a society labels one group as dominant and another as subordinate, members of the subordinate group are limited to narrowly defined roles and are closed out of opportunities to perform the functions that are preferred by the dominant group. A cultural mythology develops to "prove" that subordinates have inherent characteristics that make their social limitations appropriate.

Subordinates are described in terms of, and encouraged to develop, personal psychological characteristics that are pleasing to the dominant group. These characteristics form a certain familiar cluster: submissiveness, passivity, docility, dependency, lack of initiative, inability to act, to decide, to think....If subordinates adopt these characteristics they are considered well-adjusted. (Miller, 1986, p. 7)

Unfortunately, "subordinates absorb a large part of the untruths created by the dominants" (Miller, 1986, p. 11), especially if no alternative concepts are available, and society's expectations become self-fulfilling prophesies.

In order to play the role society has chosen for her, the female child must learn to follow several unwritten rules.

> The first psychological demand that flows from a woman's social role is that she must *defer* to others—follow their lead, articulate her needs only in relation to theirs. In essence, she is not to be the main actor in her own life. (Eichenbaum & Orbach, 1983, p. 7)

Because the woman sees herself as secondary and unimportant, she is prepared to follow other rules: avoiding self-containment and separateness, allowing her identity to be defined by her relationship to a male, anticipating others' needs, and taking responsibility for ensuring that these needs are met.

Some aspects of this social role are passed from mother to daughter.

> Mothers and daughters share a gender identity, a social role, and social expectations. They are both second-class citizens within a patriarchal culture and the family. In mothering a baby girl a woman is bringing her daughter up to be like her, to be a girl and then a woman. In mothering her son she is bringing him up to be like others. (Eichenbaum & Orbach, 1983, p. 37)

If the family is traditional, the young girl also observes that her father's role is very different than her mother's and that other family members, including her mother, defer to him.

The family, in socializing its young members, is simply carrying out its part in ensuring that current cultural norms are maintained. Although Eisler (1987) described times in prehistory when women and men lived in communities based on a model of partnership rather than domination, recorded history tells a story of gender-based stereotypes.

SOCIALIZATION: A CULTURAL PERSPECTIVE

Women's recorded role in history has been at the mercy of male historians; as a result, women have not been granted much of a role in history. In modern times, much of the woman's role has been based on obligations.

Primitive cultures provide a key for understanding roles in modern industrialized societies. Cultures pass through stages of development just as people do. Even though all societies may not have originated as hunting and gathering groups, each modern society is probably rooted in some type of agrarian economy. In all cultures, food production is the most important economic occupation within the group. Involvement in food production does not necessarily mean that all members of the group are in the fields or working with the herds. They may be in the marketplace selling manufactured goods or even going to the office and bringing home a paycheck. They are, in one way or another, tending to the needs of the family or group unit (E. I. Montgomery, personal communication, July 2, 1990). Another important role within the group is child care. Hammond and Jablow (1976) have determined that the primary role of women in cultures around the world is family-oriented. The young girl's education is directed toward being a good wife and mother, and that education entails not only the skills that she will need but also the values and attitudes of her feminine role.

Hunters and gatherers tend to be more egalitarian in sex roles than more complex groups. Nevertheless, all groups have sexual division of labor. Within primitive cultures women, not men, gather up to 80% of the food that feeds the tribe. The man is the hunter because it is the more dangerous occupation and requires following the movement of prey. It would be difficult to conduct the hunt in the presence of small children. Gathering, however, poses no problem in the practice of child rearing; it is slower, less dangerous, and leaves time for the mother to not only protect her children but also begin training them in the culture. Thus, the economic occupation and the family occupation merge without loss of status for the woman. However, with the development of farming, the status of women within the culture begins to devalue. Men still continue to hunt while women are tied to the farm with the children. As farming progresses, the ownership of land becomes individualized within families rather than the group ownership of early farming cultures. When ownership becomes an issue, it is usually the man who acquires the status of owning land, with the result that the woman's status is lowered.

In considering the evolution of culture, it is apparent that the woman remains family-oriented and responsible for the care of children while the man becomes more involved in subsistence or economy. Thus, increasing division of labor by gender roles occurs within the culture as the complexity of the culture increases (D'Andrade, 1966; MacCormack, 1980; Whyte, 1978). Whyte (1978) has stated that in more complex cultures, women tend to have less authority in domestic matters, have fewer property rights, are less independent, and suffer from more sexual restrictions. Further, women are likely to be restricted from participation in political and leadership positions. Rubin (1975) has stated that, with the increase in cultural complexity, a woman is more likely to be seen as a man's economic asset, or even his property.

> Women are given in marriage, taken in battle, exchanged for favors, sent as tribute, traded, bought, and sold. Far from being confined to the "primitive" world, these practices seem only to become more pronounced and commercialized in more "civilized" societies (p. 175).

According to Lyon (1986), in today's culture, women are still fighting the stereotype of the Victorian-era cult of womanhood, which established a pattern of distinct social and occupational spheres for women and men for an agrarian society that no longer exists. O'Kelly (1986) has said that first women were stereotyped as weak, passive, frivolous creatures; then the psychologists, anthropologists, and sociologists attempted to find proof that these stereotypes were in fact correct. She further stated that probably the most important reason why women receive negative and stereotypical treatment is that males control the institutions that generate and disseminate the cultural image. O'Kelly concluded:

> In general, things associated with the powerful, the privileged, and the prestigious are considered important. Power in other spheres of our society translates into power and influence in the cultural sphere. Since females are the subordinate sex, that which is concerned with women or associated with women is not deemed significant. (1986, p. 57)

Whether the study is of a primitive or a modern society, evidence demonstrates that the influence of women (and men) on the socialization process of girls begins early. Very small girls observe firsthand the dictates of a social code that defines women's and men's roles. Much of what a young girl initially observes about the socialization process occurs in the family; it is here that she learns what is expected of her. From the family she learns what is good or bad; what she can or cannot do; what she must do or dare not do; what she should do because she is young, not old; and what she should do because she is female, not male.

CHILDHOOD SOCIALIZATION

Sexism in Child Rearing

Gender role socialization begins in infancy with the parents' reaction to the child (Biller, 1971; Block, 1983; Fleishman, 1983; Hoffman, 1977; Honig, 1983) and involves more than wrapping baby boys in blue blankets and baby girls in pink blankets. At birth one of the first questions asked is "Is it a boy or a girl?" Based on the answer, specific behaviors follow. Babies are quickly surrounded by appropriate sex-type clothes (e.g., pink, lace on frilly dresses for baby girls) and sex-type toys (e.g., cuddly white, soft toy kittens for baby girls). Mothers are more likely to breastfeed a daughter than a son. In their interactions with infants, mothers encourage more vigorous activity from infant boys and less active play from infant girls (Hoffman, Paris, Hall, & Schell, 1988). Mothers respond more verbally to girls and more physically to boys when their infants babble (Kagan, 1971).

After leaving the hospital, the baby's gender role socialization continues (Fagot & Leinbach, 1987; Maccoby & Jacklin, 1974). Belotti (1976) has stated that the process occurs when the infant first enters the home with the way that the room is decorated, the toys the baby is given, and the way he or she is treated by both parents. "Sex role stereotypes are definitely not inborn or biologically determined. Children learn from the people [parents] around them what it means to be masculine or feminine" (Weinraub & Brown, 1983, p. 47). Other research on parental reactions to infants has demonstrated that the parents of male children show a higher frequency of response and provide more stimulation and feedback to their sons than to their daughters (Belotti, 1976; Korner, 1978; Lamb, 1977; Maccoby & Jacklin, 1974; Stern & Karraker, 1989; Weitzman, Birns, & Friend, 1985).

Another area in which parents begin to socialize the child to gender roles is that of the choice of toys. Parents are more likely to choose a toy that they consider consistent with the sex of the child (Belotti, 1976; Eisenberg, Wolchik, Hernandez, & Pasternack, 1985; Peretti & Sydney, 1984). For example, boys are encouraged to ride tricycles and play with toy cars, whereas girls are encouraged to play with dolls. Although girls may be encouraged to ride a tricycle, boys are seldom, if ever, encouraged to play with a doll. By 3 years of age, children tend to avoid toys that are associated with the other sex (Matlin, 1987; Roopnarine, 1987). Further, at 3 years, children begin to show differences in the type of play in which they engage. Boys tend to prefer more active play, while girls tend to imitate adults. Girls also tend to be less sex-typed in their choice of toys. In a study of children's ability to discriminate objects according to gender stereotypes,

Thompson (1975) found that by 2 ½ years of age, most children were capable of making sex-typed decisions.

As children mature, parents continue to behave differently with boys than with girls (Fleishman, 1983; Hoffman, 1977; Honig, 1983). With sons, parents stress achievement, aggressiveness, and competition. The boy is given independence earlier. He is taught to control effect and be responsible. Parents, especially fathers, tend to be less tolerant of behaviors in sons that deviate from the traditional stereotypes and tend to more often employ physical punishment. With daughters, parents tend to show more physical closeness and greater warmth. Further, parents usually demonstrate more confidence in the truthfulness and trustworthiness of daughters and show greater reluctance to punish girls. Mothers tend to be more restrictive and engage in closer supervision of activities with girls than boys. Although parents are less distressed by deviation from traditional stereotypes with daughters, they still expect them to behave like "ladies."

School Influence

After the family, the most important area of socialization is the school. Researchers (Serbin, O'Leary, Kent, & Tonick, 1973; Weinraub & Brown, 1983) have demonstrated a gender bias in the manner in which teachers respond to students that shows more involvement with males. School tends to be an expanding experience for boys and a restricting one for girls (Block, 1983). One area of concern in schools is the under-achievement of girls (Mickelson, 1989; Reis, 1987; Ullian, 1984). The difference in achievement motivation between boys and girls appears in the sixth grade, when girls appear to be caught between socialization and intelligence. They have been taught to be quiet and nonaggressive and do the work that they are given, thus causing differential treatment in the classroom. Boys are more likely to talk out and demand the teacher's attention, which leaves the girls somewhat ignored. In addition, girls' achievement is motivated toward winning social approval and friendship with others. Although girls do well in school, they are not prepared to compete in areas where aggressive behavior is an asset. The perceived conflict between femininity and success is a dilemma for the female adolescent and is often carried into adulthood and the work place (Gilligan, 1982).

Peer Influence

Another area that is important in the socialization process of children is peer socialization. The choice of playmates depends on the sex, not the masculinity or femininity, of the child. Maccoby (1988) has called gender segregation a group process not dependent on the individuals involved. Boys show a greater preference for same-sex playmates (Lockheed, 1986). Carter (1987) stated that gender segregation is important in the acquisition of and adherence to gender-typed behavior because it is an endorsement and enforcement of the stereotypical norms. Gender segregation is demonstrated early in the school experience and seems to be a product of both sex and age (Roopnarine, 1984; Silbern & Katz, 1986).

By adolescence, both boys and girls are concerned with self-image. Girls are concerned with attractiveness and their self-concept depends on their looks; boys are more concerned with effectiveness (Matlin, 1987). Same-sex friendships tend to be particularly intense between 14 and 16 years of age.

Media Influence

Other influences on socialization of girls during childhood and adolescence are books and television. Both sexes tend to prefer books that portray sex-stereotypical characters and activities over nontraditional characters, though girls appear to be slightly less rigid (Ashton, 1983; Kroop & Halverson, 1983). Both Durkin (1984) and Jeffries-Fox and Jeffries-Fox (1981) have stated that television is responsible for some of children's stereotypes about sex roles and occupations. Papilia and Olds (1989) reported that:

> By the time the child has graduated from high school, he or she will have watched more than 25,000 hours of television including 356,000 commercials. Children will have seen about twice as many males as females on the screen, and they will have observed that the sexes act quite differently. Traditionally males on television have been more aggressive, more active and more competent than females, who have been portrayed as submissive, inactive and interested mainly in either keeping house or becoming more beautiful. (p. 237)

In a study of textbooks' role in the socialization process, Weitzman, Eifler, Hokada, and Ross (1972) reported that, as with television, women are portrayed differently from men. In their textbook study, girls were depicted in a less active role than boys. Further, girls were represented more often in the traditional roles of homemaker, nurse, and teacher. In contrast, boys were seen in more active roles and higher level positions. In one example, the authors found a textbook that implied girls were inept in math. Boys were more often presented with the more exciting roles, whether in solving mathematics, deriving words, or selecting careers.

In investigating the impact of newspapers on gender role socialization, Macklin and Kolbe (1984) reviewed 64 ads directed toward children and found that although most of the ads were neutral in direction they contained more males than females. They further discovered that male-oriented ads were bolder and showed more aggression, but showed no more activity than neutral ads.

Is there a way to combat gender role stereotyping in young girls and adolescents? Weinraub and Brown (1983) have suggested several things that parents can do. First, parents should call attention to role reversals when they occur and model that type of behavior to children. Second, parents should distinguish between the existing stereotypes and personal conformity to them. Third, parents should place stereotypes in their sociohistorical framework. Fourth, parents should help children deal directly with undesirable stereotyping when it occurs and develop skills to aid them in transcending stereotyping, but children should also be prepared for the possible discrimination that they will face. In the school setting, Lee (1976) has suggested that teachers become aware of their stereotyped behavior and make sure that all children are given equal access to attention and materials. Katz (1986) has suggested that modeling nonstereotypical behavior can be most effective in changing student's stereotypes.

PROBLEMS RESULTING FROM SOCIALIZATION

A major part of socialization is the formation of individuals' expectations about their role in society. When that role is unsatisfactory, unfulfilling, or contradictory or when the role is in transition, the individual experiences problems that may seem irreconcilable. The primary problems resulting from the socialization process are powerlessness, lack of options, anger, and low self-concept. These problems seldom occur in isolation because of the close relationships between them.

Power is defined as the right and ability to do, act, and effect. Because society places limits on their rights and abilities and often gives control of their life to another, girls and women are more vulnerable to both perceived and real powerlessness. Thus when girls grow up to become women it is no surprise that women have less financial and political power than men and are, therefore, less likely to be able to effect the making of the laws that govern their lives. Girls are not taught to seek out and use power as boys are. In fact, girls are taught to surrender power to boys and to be subordinate in appearance if not in fact. It is the woman who surrenders her family name and takes the man's name when she marries. Because girls and women are conditioned to the role of second-class citizen, it is often difficult for them to acknowledge power issues in their lives. Horwitz (1982), in a study of gender roles and power, has stated that the lack of power is responsible for most psychological problems, regardless of gender.

Another area in which girls and women face problems is the belief that both their behavioral and emotional options are limited. Girls, unlike boys, are not taught to consider options, weigh possibilities, and make decisions based on personal wants and needs. A girl is likely to undervalue her skills and abilities. She may have inadequate communication skills that limit her ability to communicate clearly and directly because she has been socialized to be a mediator and conciliator. Girls stifle their true emotions. Later, when they are women, they often feel that their emotions are invalid and not worthy of expression. Throughout life, girls and women are socialized to care for others more than themselves. They often believe that they are to be nurturing, sensitive, affectionate, understanding, kind, helpful, and cooperative at all times. These ideas are so ingrained during childhood that, when the girl attains womanhood, she often feels that she has no right to consider her own emotional wants and needs above those of others because that would be selfish.

A girl or adolescent feeling that she lacks options in her life and overwhelmed by feelings of powerlessness and unmet emotional expectations is likely to experience a great deal of anger. Although she may direct her anger outward at others who may or may not deserve it, a girl will more often direct anger inward, where it manifests as enervation or depression. Society does not sanction the expression of anger by girls (and women); not only is it unmannerly and unladylike, but it is also an implied takeover of a role reserved for men and boys.

Self-concept is determined by the value placed on the individual's existence by society, by significant people, and by oneself. Because society does not place the same value on the feminine experience as it does on the masculine, girls are often troubled by low self-concept. Instead of being taught to be independent and autonomous, girls and women are socialized to be dependent on others, traditionally a father, husband, or brother, often to the point that they do not believe that they have the right to their own direction. Socialized from birth to be dependent on others, it is no wonder that some girls, and later adult women, live life through another to the point that they are incapacitated by the thought of having to live independently. This way of thinking is not innate—it results from socialization.

STRATEGIES

As noted in this chapter and throughout this book, young girls and women often appear to experience low self-esteem. This is most evident in comments such as, "This is too hard; I cannot do this; find someone else to do the job." In identifying the characteristics of positive self-esteem, Frey and Carlock (1984) and Vernon (1990) have identified people with high self-esteem as accepting of self and others, integrated, optimistic, confident, realistically oriented, and realizing they can determine a lot of their own fate. These are traits typically stressed in the socialization of men. In contrast, women have not been socialized to think of themselves in these terms.

It is with this realization that many teachers, counselors, and well-intended parents suggest that we must increase the self-esteem of our young women through assertiveness training, gender-fair career counseling, and other related structured activities designed to promote increased levels of self-efficacy. On the face of it, these strategies might appear to be effective, and they are certainly better than no intervention at all. However, they may also reinforce the notion that the problem lies within the girl and not within the system. The overwhelming message is that these poor girls have a problem and we will have to fix them by increasing their levels of self-esteem. Once again, we blame the victim for having a problem.

In fact, it is not these young women who have the problem, but rather the society in which they live, which continues to promote the idea that only men can be successful. High school girls have only to look around in their schools to see which gender occupies the leadership roles. In their houses of worship, they can look to the platform to see who fills the chairs. They can read newspapers to see which gender provides national and local leadership. These young women do not have a problem with self-esteem; the only problem they have is seeing the world as it is and trying to find the context in which they fit.

Perhaps a strategy that does not necessarily involve training, counseling, or structured activities might prove much more effective in increasing levels of self-efficacy and self-worth. Perhaps to rethink this problem as one that does not exist within our young women but within our society might provide an answer that could have a powerful impact on generations of women to come. Specifically, the school could be the microlaboratory for a gender-fair, egalitarian existence for men and women. Leadership would be equally divided, with as many women as men in the roles of superintendent, principal, vice-principal, and department chairs. Faculty would also be better balanced, with as many females as males in the fields of math and science. Men could also be better represented in the field of home economics. Elementary-level teachers would count as many men as women within their ranks.

Other strategies, using the school as a microcosm for society, might include asking women who have been successful in any capacity to be available to students as role models and mentors. Schools might also invite men who support equality for women to visit with the boys and girls to share their points of view. Schools should certainly use gender-fair textbooks and be sensitive to sexist language in any form, from student writing to school correspondences to parents.

Schools might also offer courses concerning women's issues to both boys and girls, including women's history and cultural diversity. Schools might provide a forum for discussion about ways to achieve equality for all students throughout the school.

In summary, schools have a tremendous opportunity to take a proactive leadership role in promoting higher levels of self-esteem for female students, not only by "doing" something to them, but by "being" the best example of what they are trying to promote. It is our contention that if schools expect male and female students to be equally successful and they reinforce this expectation through their own staffing and organizational behavior, self-esteem among female students will increase in the future.

CASE EXAMPLES

The Case of Melissa

Melissa is a 12-year-old girl who is in seventh grade. Throughout her elementary years in school, Melissa has been a model student. While her favorite classes have been math and science, she has performed equally well in English and social studies. In extracurricular activities, Melissa has been very involved with sports (soccer, volleyball), cheerleading, piano, and dance. Her mother has often exclaimed, "I have a taxi service for Melissa. It seems as if all I ever do is take her from one activity to another."

This year, Melissa's parents and teachers have noticed a change in her academic work. While her first report card contained lower grades, they were still good grades. Her parents attributed this to the adjustment to junior high. Melissa's grades have continued to get lower each 6 weeks. It is now second semester, and Melissa is making average grades. The junior high counselor has talked with Melissa in an attempt to ascertain why her grades have changed so dramatically from sixth grade. Although Melissa was kind and polite to the counselor, it was obvious that she was not concerned about her grades. The counselor decided to call her parents and suggested a conference between the parents, Melissa, and the counselor.

During the conference, it became apparent that Melissa was uncomfortable. When asked about her change in grades, Melissa simply shrugged her shoulders. When her parents said that perhaps some of her extracurricular activities should be reduced, Melissa reacted. She said that her major goal was to be popular; in order to be popular, she must participate in a lot of activities. Further, she said that if she were a "brain" she didn't have a chance of being popular. During this session, it was evident that peer pressure was operating and was a likely source of Melissa's change in attitude. At the end of the session, Melissa said she would see a counselor. The parents agreed to give counseling a chance before insisting that her social activities be curtailed.

During counseling, Melissa said that some of her peers had teased her because she made good grades. Further, she said that one of the boys that she likes had told a friend that he wasn't going to go with a girl who was smarter than he. Melissa said she realized that she couldn't be both a good student and popular. In view of this, she decided she would choose to be popular.

In the course of counseling, it was evident that Melissa was struggling with her identity. Her peers had certain gender role expectations for girls, and Melissa responded by conforming. Her gender role socialization had left her with internal barriers to achievement. For example, Melissa was afraid of academic success because she believed that if she were brighter than the boys they would not like her. Thus, her success at school depended on her support from her peers.

In counseling, it was clear that Melissa preferred to make good grades; she realized she had lowered her math and science grades because she had been told those classes were for boys. At first, the counselor employed a cognitive approach in therapy. She helped Melissa realize that she should not feel guilty about her intelligence. Further, she helped Melissa consider alternative plans. With time, the counselor moved to gender-aware therapy (Good, Gilbert, & Scher, 1990), which is a synthesis of feminist therapy and knowledge about gender, to help Melissa examine gender stereotypes. In gender-aware therapy, Melissa was helped to understand that the counselor valued Melissa's rights to select views and behaviors that were congruent for her regardless of gender roles.

Through gentle questioning in counseling, Melissa realized that her peer group could stifle future career endeavors. While she stated that it was very important to her to be popular, she could see reasons to try to improve her grades. During individual counseling, Melissa decided that, while she would not be assertive with her answers, she was going to make a greater effort to complete her homework and study for exams. At the time of this writing, Melissa, along with other students her age, attends a support group. It has been helpful for Melissa to share her problems with other teen-agers and to realize they have very similar problems.

The Case of Brandi

Brandi is a 16-year-old high school junior attending a private girl's school in the South. She is an open, gregarious person who is well liked by almost everyone she meets. Brandi is an only child who admits to being sheltered by her parents. They were sad when she decided to go away to attend a private high school, but they came to accept her decision because they knew the high school in their small town was not strong academically. Brandi makes excellent grades and is involved in many extracurricular activities at her school. She lives with two other girls in a dormitory on the high school campus.

Soon after the beginning of the fall semester, Brandi went to a party with a college sophomore who was the cousin of a friend at school. The party was at his fraternity house. Brandi, who normally does not drink, was persuaded to have several drinks. Her date then took her upstairs to his room and forced her to have sexual intercourse with him. Afterward, he fell asleep, and Brandi quickly dressed and went to her dormitory. She barely made it to the dormitory before she was sick. She showered and locked herself in her room, where she cried all night.

For the next few days, she refused to leave her room. Her roommates were worried about her, but they could not get her to tell them what was wrong. Finally, one of her roommates, Lindsey, got the story of what had happened from Brandi and insisted on taking her to the counselor at the high school.

At first, Brandi did not want to talk to the counselor. She was too ashamed to admit what had taken place. The counselor was a gentle and understanding woman, who let Brandi know that nothing she could say would make the counselor think less of her. She told Brandi that rape often makes the victim feel that she did something wrong and that the rape was not her fault. She listened when Brandi began to talk about the assault and validated her feelings of pain and anger.

As counseling progressed, the counselor explained to Brandi that rape violates the victim's basic operating assumptions. Janoff-Bulman (1985) has listed three assumptions that are destroyed by victimization. The first is personal invulnerability, which is the sense of protection from stress and anxiety associated with the threat of misfortune. When one is victimized, the assumption of invulnerability is destroyed. Second is the perception of the world as a meaningful and comprehensible place in which, if one is good, nothing bad will happen. With victimization, one is forced to face the fact that bad things happen to good people. Last is the assumption that individuals see themselves positively and have relatively high self-esteem. Victimization causes one to have serious concerns about self-perception. The counselor helped Brandi to identify the assumptions that had been destroyed and helped her begin to rebuild them.

The counselor also used cognitive therapy interventions such as self-monitoring of activities, graded task assignments (e.g., going out alone), and identification and modification of maladaptive cognitions, as described by Frank and Stewart (1983). Brandi was terrified about her parents' reaction. She said, "I know they'll be disappointed in me. I couldn't stand that." It took some time for the counselor to convince Brandi that she was reacting in a stereotypical manner, expecting to be blamed and taking the responsibility for the rape.

It took several months for Brandi to begin to regain her self-confidence and self-esteem. She and her parents decided to file charges against her attacker even though she was afraid that the fact that she had been drinking would be used to make her look like she was a willing participant. "I can't let him do to someone else what he did to me. I couldn't live with myself," she said one day. Brandi continued in counseling for several months, including the time of the trial, which was very hard on her. She was pleased when the rapist was convicted and sent to prison.

RESOURCES FOR YOUNG GIRLS AND ADOLESCENTS

Young girls and adolescents have been affected by socialization patterns that for centuries have been instilled in and perpetuated by cultures. Young girls, teachers, parents, and counselors need to be aware of resource materials (books, pamphlets, audiovisuals, and so on) that are available to give young girls and adolescents contemporary, accurate, and nonstereotyped information about individuals and their society. Some of the resources listed in this chapter are resources that the young girl can read; others are resources for educators. The listing of resources is intended to be exemplary, not comprehensive.

Since 1977, the Women's Educational Equity Act (WEEA) has existed to promote the concept of sex equity in education. Core to this concept is the belief that to help all students reach their fullest potential, sex equity must be an integral part of planning and instruction. The Women's Educational Equity Act Publishing Center was established to help meet this purpose. The following are examples of some of their publications:

❏ *A Mindset for Math*—This is a resource to reduce math anxiety in girls at the upper elementary/junior high levels. The program focuses on the math-anxious female student and provides techniques for reducing the fear of math.

❏ *Circle of Women*—This resource guide and manual addresses the major problems facing the Native American woman as she attempts to balance and synthesize traditional and contemporary roles.

❏ *Hand in Hand: Mentoring Young Women*—Materials for training minority career women to be effective mentors for minority high school girls are provided.

❏ *Maximizing Young Children's Potential*—A nonsexist manual for early childhood trainers, whose purpose is to foster mutual respect between the sexes, to free girls and boys from stereotypical training, and to provide a variety of nonsexist teaching techniques and offer suggestions for classroom implementation.

❏ *Sources of Strength*—This resource focuses on women and culture. Its purpose is to help high school students understand their own and others' cultural roots. A cultural comparison section expands awareness of the lives of African, Chinese, American, and African-American women.

❏ *Teen Parenting*—Ways to meet the special needs of the pregnant or parenting teen are stressed.

❏ *The Woman Within*—Eight workshop sessions to build positive behaviors are described. Focus is on overcoming fears, taking risks, and identifying and eradicating negative patterns.

❏ *Women in American History*—Set against a background of social change and historical events between 1907 and 1920, this resource focuses on the stories of Native American, Black, and Anglo women whose lives and work influenced the development of the United States.

In addition to books, pamphlets, and guides, WEEA also publishes audiovisual materials. Examples of audiovisuals include:

❏ *American Women of Color*—Cultural diversity is integrated into non-gender-biased curricula with engaging filmstrips featuring historic and contemporary topics.

❏ *Born Free*—*Born Free* is a training packet designed for K–12 and post-secondary teacher-training programs, whose purpose is to reduce gender role stereotyping in career development. Each training packet includes activities, a trainer's guide, and journal reprints on sex roles and careers for multiethnic groups. Videotape cassettes are provided, and each cassette contains a viewer's guide.

❏ *Competence is for Everyone*—A curriculum for teaching critical thinking skills, this resource contains videocassettes for K–12 that include such topics as different people, in the minority, male and female, and competence in our society.

❏ *Sex Stereotyping in Education*—This K–12 program includes an audiotape cassette, bibliography, instruction sheet, and handouts. Its purpose is to help eliminate sex stereotyping in the classroom. Examples of cassette topics include: "Girl, Boy, or Person: Beyond Sex Differences"; "Sex Stereotyping in Math Doesn't Add Up"; "Exercising Your Rights: Eliminating Sex Bias in Physical Education"; and "Diagnosing the Problem: Sex Stereotyping in Special Education."

❏ *Venture Beyond Stereotypes*—A workbook and videocassette are provided in this resource designed to assist teachers in combatting children's sex stereotyping. The videotape series "Jill and Jack: Fact and Fiction" explores how cultural patterns and values affect us all.

Many additional resources are available. Information about other materials may be obtained from WEEA Publishing Center, Education Development Center, 55 Chapel St. Suite 200, Newton, MA 02160. Their telephone number is 800-225-3088.

Advocacy Press, a division of the Girls Club of Greater Santa Barbara, an affiliate of Girls Clubs of America, has published a series of books on life planning for young girls. These include *Changes: A Woman's Journal for Self-Awareness and Personal Planning*; *Choices: A Teen Woman's Journal of Self-Awareness and Personal Planning*; *Career Choices: A Guide for Teens and Young Adults*; and *More Choices: A Strategic Planning Guide for Mixing Career and Family*. Career Choices has been described as the book that does for teens what *What Color Is Your Parachute* does for adults. Some of the Advocacy Press books have been national best sellers. These include *Minou* and *Father Gander Nursery Rhymes*. In *Minou*, Minou lives a Cinderella life until tragedy strikes, and she is unprepared to care for herself. In *Father Gander Nursery Rhymes*, attention is directed to sexist, racist, and violent attitudes that have roots in the nursery. In this book, Father Gander revises some of the traditional verses and adds some new ones to create positive images of sex roles and relationships. Information on these books may be obtained from Advocacy Press, P.O. Box 236, Suite 222, Santa Barbara, CA 93102.

The National Women's History Project, 7738 Bull Rd., Windsor, CA 95492, publishes a variety of K–12 curriculum materials. Their materials include posters, games, bulletin board display kits, books, magazines, and videos. Examples of their materials include a bulletin board on women and the Constitution, posters on women depicting their roles in history, and curriculum units on women's history, and American women in science. Curriculum units are available for elementary-, middle-, and high school-levels. The project also conducts workshops to promote national recognition of multicultural women's history.

The Organization for Equal Education of the Sexes, 808 Union St., Brooklyn, NY 11215, publishes posters that present positive images of women representing different races and ethnic groups achieving in many different fields. Examples of women on their posters include Eleanor Roosevelt, Helen Keller, Florence Nightingale, Lucy Stone, Marie Curie, and Susan B. Anthony; examples of less familiar women include Elizabeth Blackwell (first U.S. woman to receive a degree in medicine), Barbara McClintock (winner of the Nobel Prize for her work in genetics), Ida B. Wells-Barnett (investigative reporter), Kate Chapin (writer), Kyung-Wha Chung (concert violinist), Fannie Lou Hamer (civil rights leader), and Elizabeth Cady Stanton (women's rights leader).

Lifelines, a four-page newsletter is included with each poster and contains information about the woman on the poster.

Other sources of resources for young girls include the Council on Interracial Books for Children, Racism and Sexism Resource Center for Education, 1841 Broadway, New York, NY 10023. This center publishes a variety of multicultural and nonsexist materials for elementary and secondary schools. The Feminist Press at City University of New York, 311 E 94th St., New York, NY 10128, is a nonprofit, educational organization that publishes nonsexist books, including children's books, curriculum materials, bibliographies, and biographies. Garrett Park Press, Inc., Garrett Park, MD 20896, publishes books, pamphlets, bibliographies, and charts on such topics as sex equity and career guidance. Information Systems Development, 1100 E 8th St., Austin, TX 78702, maintains a computer database of historical biographies of Hispanic women. This company publishes materials on women, major ethnic groups, and maintains files on women's studies programs. Wider Opportunities for Women, 1325 16th St., NW, Washington, DC 20005, publishes a newsletter, *Women at Work*, as well as other materials to help women and girls consider nontraditional career options. The Women's Action Alliance, The Sex Equity in Education Program, 370 Lexington Ave., Room 603, New York, NY 10017, has published materials on sex-fair education for elementary and secondary children. The Alliance has published *The Neuter Computer: Computers for Girls and Boys* in an attempt to encourage greater use of computers by girls.

Some universities have established centers to conduct research and publish materials on gender and education and gender and career development. The Project on the Study of Gender and Education at Kent State University, The Mary Ingraham Bunting Institute at Radcliffe College, The Wellesley College Higher Education Resource Services, The Center on Education and Training for Employment at The Ohio State University, The Curriculum Publications Clearinghouse at Western Illinois University, and Vocational Studies Center at the University of Wisconsin at Madison are examples. A listing of organizations and centers conducting research on women is available from the National Council on Women, 47-49 E 65th St., New York, NY 10021. Companies have published materials to encourage women to consider nontraditional careers. Examples include a videotape, "Anything You Want to Be" sponsored by Bell Telephone, and a career booklet, "Take It from Us...You Can Be an Engineer" sponsored by General Electric.

Journals have provided good resources on such topics as women and achievement, gender issues, and mathematics and the gender gap. Good articles by Becker (1989), Friedman (1989), Kahle (1984), Linn, Benedictis, Delucchi, Harris, and Stage (1978), Linn and Petersen (1986), and Linn and Pulos (1983) have appeared in recent journals.

In addition to these resources, we encourage young girls to read current literature on gender role socialization, building assertiveness skills, self-esteem building, women in society, women in leadership roles, preparing for womanhood, and career decision making. Teachers, counselors, and librarians are viable resources for suggesting good books in these areas. The school library, local public library, and bookstores should also have books for loan or purchase. For older girls, university conferences, university libraries, and bookstores provide opportunities for obtaining additional resources.

PROBLEM PREVENTION AND SOCIAL INTERVENTIONS

Milestones to Help Young Girls

Young girls and women have come a long way since the turn of the century. Although there is still much progress to be made, the changes resulting from social, economic, and political forces have helped pave the way for young girls. A chronology of milestones that have affected women in the 20th Century is presented in Table 3.1.

As Table 3.1 illustrates, in American society women have not been considered equals of men. Yet milestones have been made in this century as legislation has been passed to reduce socialization patterns that have plagued women for centuries. While most of the events have directly affected adult women, they have provided opportunities for young girls to begin to break the vicious cycle of gender stereotyping that would have otherwise imprisoned them for the rest of their lives.

Title IX of the 1972 Education Amendments is the law that perhaps most directly influences young girls during their early years of training. Title IX was passed by Congress because of the discriminatory and differential treatment of students by sex. Title IX states: "No person shall, on the basis of sex, be excluded from participation in, be denied the benefits of, or be subjected to discrimination under any education program or activity receiving federal financial assistance." After the law was passed, it was sent to the Department of Health, Education and Welfare's Office for Civil Rights to establish specific guidelines for its implementation in schools. The Title IX implementation regulation was signed into law in 1975. A complete copy of the Title IX Regulation may be obtained from the Office for Civil Rights, Department of Education, 330 Independence Ave., SW, Room 1656, Washington, DC 20201.

In discussing why Title IX is necessary, Sadker and Sadker (1982) concluded:

> Girls were often denied the opportunity to enroll in traditionally male courses such as industrial arts and boys were often denied the opportunity to enroll in home economics. Girls' physical education programs were generally inferior to boys' programs. Top female athletes frequently were denied access to coaching and other athletic opportunities. In 1970–1971, while women were 67% of all school teachers, they were only 15% of all principals and 0.6% of all superintendents. (p. 42)

All education institutions that receive federal funds are covered by Title IX. This includes virtually all of the public schools and post-secondary institutions in the United States.

The language of Title IX makes it very clear that it is a violation of the law to treat students differently or separately on the basis of sex. All activities offered by schools must be equally available to all students. The regulation covers in detail the following areas that relate to elementary and secondary students: course offerings, physical education, athletics, counseling, employment assistance, financial assistance, health and insurance benefits, marital and parental status, extracurricular activities, and facilities (Sadker & Sadker, 1982). Although many unresolved issues remain for Title IX, it is a viable means to reduce sexism in education.

The Vocational Educational Amendments and the Carl D. Perkins Vocational Education Act directly assisted young girls. The Vocational Education Amendments of 1976 mandated that gender role stereotyping and gender bias must be eliminated from all vocational education programs. The Carl D. Perkins Vocational Education Act, passed

Table 3.1
Milestones for Women in the 20th Century
_____

1903 National Women's Trade Union (WTUL) is established at the American Federation of Labor convention.

1905 WTUL–Illinois branch seeks federal investigation of working women's conditions. WTUL lobbies with other women's organizations.

1907 Bill is passed to fund reports on women's working conditions. From 1907–1910, 19 volumes of reports unveiling the poor working conditions (health, wages) of women workers are published. Lobbyists continue to press for the establishment of a women's office in the Department of Labor.

1913 A Woman's Division as a subdivision in the Bureau of Labor Statistics is established.

1917 The Committee on Women in Industry is established by the Council of Defense. Women's branches are established by the Board of Labor Standards, the U.S. Railway Administration, and the Ordinance Department. As World War I causes a shortage of labor, the U.S. Employment Service campaigns to replace men with women in every place that women are capable of filling.

1918 The War Labor Administration establishes Women in Industry Service (WIS). WIS seeks to formulate standards for employment of women, including a 48-hour work week, equal pay, sanitary, and safe work conditions. Two years later the WIS was transformed into the Women's Bureau.

1919 The First International Congress of Working Women meets in Washington, DC. The Congress later becomes the International Federation of Working Women.

1920 The Women's Bureau in the Department of Labor is established by Congress with Mary Anderson as director.

The 19th Amendment is passed, giving women the right to vote.

1923 The National Women's Party, through Alice Paul, introduces the first amendment to the Constitution on the equality of women.

The Federal Government Classification Act passes establishing that government salaries will be based on job duties not sex of employee.

1932 The Federal Economy Act, Section 213, requires that one spouse resign if both husband and wife work for the federal government. A study revealed 75% of those resigning were women.

1933 Frances Perkins becomes the first woman cabinet member as Secretary of Labor.

1938 The Fair Labor Standards Act establishes a minimum wage and other standards to protect workers in lower paying jobs.

1941 The Fair Employment Practices Commission is established to help alleviate discrimination against blacks. Black women try to get employed in the better-paying factories.

1942 The War Manpower Commission actively recruits women workers to fill labor shortages created by World War II. The National War Labor Board issues an order allowing employees to equalize wages for men and women. The government lowers the legal working age for women from 18 to 16 years.

1948 The Economic and Social Council of the UN advocates that women should receive the same pay as men for equal work.

1955 The White House Conference on Effective Use of Womanpower looks at gender stereotypes and the limitations they place on women's employment.

1961 The President's Commission on the Status of Women is established.

1962 Presidential memorandum bars discrimination against women in government hiring.

1963 Equal Pay Act passed by Congress.

1964 The Civil Rights Act is passed, including Title VII, which prohibits firms with 15 or more employees from gender discrimination.

The Equal Employment Opportunity Commission is established.

1967 The Age Discrimination in Employment Act is passed to prevent discrimination of workers 45–65 years.

1968 Executive Order 11246 as amended by 11375 prohibits gender discrimination in employment by employers with federal contracts of over $10,000 and requires filing an affirmative action program.

1971 The National Women's Political Caucus is formed. The Department of Labor requires that employers take positive action on discrimination of women.

1972 Equal Employment Opportunity Act is passed.

Title IX of the 1972 Education Amendment is passed.

1979 Sexual Harassment Guidelines establish that sexual harassment is an unlawful employment practice.

1981 The Economic Recovery Tax Act is passed. This act increases tax credits for child care.

1984 The Retirement Equity Act of 1984 provides an easier means for women to collect retirement.

Source: Adapted from "A U.S. Progression: Milestones toward Equality," 1986, *International Altrusan, 64,* pp. 10–12.

by Congress in 1984, provided special funding to schools to establish activities that would eliminate gender role stereotyping and gender bias. Some of the projects funded were activities to encourage young girls to consider nontraditional careers, to recognize women in history, and to participate in projects designed to eliminate gender role stereotyping in the schools.

The Carl D. Perkins Vocational and Applied Technology Education Act of 1990 also provides help for young girls and women. In allocating funds, the Act mandates that no less than 3% be spent on sex equity and no less than 7% be allocated to displaced homemakers, with 0.5% being considered a float between the two categories. The Act is very specific in providing guidelines for state programs. For example, Part B of the Act states that programs must be established to provide single parents, displaced homemakers, and single pregnant women with marketable skills and to promote the elimination of gender bias. Section 222 of the Act outlines the gender equity programs. This section explicitly states that activities (programs, services, comprehensive course guidelines, and counseling) must be provided to eliminate gender bias and stereotyping in secondary and post-secondary education. Further, this section states that preparatory services must be available for girls and women aged 14 through 25 to assist them in supporting themselves and their families. Dependent-care services and transportation are also funded for individuals participating in the program.

Congress passed the Displaced Homemakers Self-Sufficiency Assistance Act in 1990 and it was signed into law by President Bush. The Act (PL 101-554) will provide money for displaced homemakers.

Although much remains to be accomplished, these acts have helped to reduce gender bias and in turn have provided more opportunity for young girls and women to become more participant members of society.

Laws against child abuse have also directly benefitted young girls. There are historical and cultural variations in child abuse, and what qualifies as abuse in one culture may not qualify in another. In some cultures, children have been and still are subjected to brutal discipline, foot-binding, skull-shaping, and ritual scarring. Traditionally, children in the United States have been viewed as the property of their parents; as such they have had few basic rights.

In recent years, the number of reported incidents of child abuse has increased dramatically. Each year child abuse alters, shatters, and shortens the lives of more than a million children. According to the Children's Division of American Humane, the number of reported cases of child abuse has more than doubled since the mid-1970s (Craig, 1989). Social prevention measures have been taken, and states have established laws against child abuse that cover physical abuse, neglect, sexual abuse, and emotional maltreatment. Abuse prevention groups have been established in all states to protect children. Laws require that any person having cause to believe a child is being abused must report the case to any local or state law enforcement agency and to the nearest Child Protection Service, Division of the Department of Human Services. Failure to report suspected child abuse within 48 hours is a misdemeanor. Sexual abuse, while affecting both boys and girls, has more commonly been a problem for young girls. Although laws on child abuse have helped to protect young children, estimates are that 1 girl in 4 and 1 boy in 10 will be sexually abused.

In addition to the passage of laws, organizations have been established to support and encourage opportunities for young girls. Most of these organizations have been established by women who realized that young girls grow up in a society that will render them powerless and dependent unless social interventions are provided. Again our listing of organizations is exemplary, not comprehensive.

Some organizations have been established or have had subdivisions established to be sure sex equity is provided in educational settings. These include the American Association of University Women, American Association for the Advancement of Science Office for Opportunities in Science, American Business and Professional Women's Association, Girls Clubs of America, Inc., National Association for Girls and Women in Sports, National Association for the Education of Young Children, National Coalition for Women and Girls in Education, National Organization for Women, Organization for Equal Education of the Sexes, Wider Opportunities for Women, and Women's Action Alliance.

Some professional organizations have established networks, committees, and professional publications to enhance opportunities for young girls and women. Examples include American Association for Counseling and Development, American Home Economics Association, American Library Association, American Psychological Association, American Society of Allied Health Professions, National Education Association, National Science Teachers Association, Social Science Education Consortium, Society for Women Engineers, and the Association for Women in Science.

Other organizations have been established to provide activities, training, and special programs for young girls and women. These include Campfire Girls, Girls Clubs of America, Girl Scouts of America, Tri-Hi-Y, and the Young Women's Christian Association.

There are organizations at the state and federal level to provide direct assistance to young girls and women as well as indirect services to state departments of education and local school districts. The United States Department of Education Office of Elementary and Secondary Education, the United States Department of Labor, Employment and Training Administration, and the United States Department of Labor, Women's Bureau are examples. Other government organizations include the United States Commission on Civil Rights and the United States Equal Employment Opportunity Commission.

Young girls and women should be aware of the activities of the League of Women Voters in the United States. The League is a nonpartisan, nonprofit political action group that lobbies on national issues and educates the public in citizen education. The League disseminates its publications to schools, conducts public forums, and distributes nonpartisan election information.

The National Women's Hall of Fame, 76 Fall St., Seneca Falls, NY 13148, may be unfamiliar to many young girls and women. It celebrates the contribution of American women to American culture. The Hall has a permanent exhibit to illustrate the achievements of American women who have overcome barriers and enhanced possibilities for young girls and women. It provides exhibits, publications, and audiovisuals. Each March, the Hall sponsors a poster and essay contest for students in grades 4–12.

When young girls and women are made aware of the organizations that exist to help them solve problems and provide resources, then organizations for young girls and women can make a difference. Unfortunately, there are no quick and easy ways to break down gender role socialization barriers that have existed for centuries, but organizations like those listed here have made a significant difference. Although change has been slow, change has nevertheless been realized. These organizations offer some of our most viable hope that tomorrow's generation of young girls will not have to suffer from sex role socialization like those of today. Addresses for organizations listed in this chapter may be obtained at local libraries and from state and local agencies. In addition, many of the organizations listed in this chapter have been described by Sadker and Sadker (1982).

SUMMARY

This chapter has described the impact of gender role socialization. A cultural perspective was discussed to give the reader a brief background in the history of gender role socialization. Parental, school, peer, and media influences were discussed in conjunction with the problems resulting from socialization. Strategies for helping to minimize the effects of stereotyping socialization were offered. Resources for both young girls and educators have been included. The laws affecting sex role socialization were discussed, and a list of organizations to support and encourage opportunities for young girls was presented.

Lorber (1986) has referred to gender as the linchpin of social order. In our culture and all others, an individual's role in society is determined first by gender and the accompanying stereotypes, and then one is judged by personal accomplishments. Stereotypes and gender roles have always been a part of culture because they were created to maintain the status quo, which is the cultural inertia that maintains the equilibrium of the culture. Typically, therefore, culture change takes generations, unless forced by a catastrophe of monumental proportions. For example, consider the time involved in the women's rights movement. Women gained the right to vote on August 19, 1920, and more than 70 years (two generations) later, women are still underrepresented in all aspects of government from the city council level to Congress. Enough support could not be obtained to pass the Equal Rights Amendment. Yet social interventions have had an impact on the lives of young girls and women. Without doubt, recent laws and cooperating organizations have helped and are continuing to help young girls and women to recognize that new roles and expectations should be available to them.

REFERENCES

Ashton, E. (1983). Measures of play behavior: The influence of sex-role stereotyped childrens' books. *Sex Roles, 9,* 43–47.

Basow, S. A. (1986). Gender stereotypes: Traditions and alternatives (2nd ed.). Pacific Grove, CA: Brooks/Cole.

Becker, B. J. (1989). Gender and science achievement. A reanalysis of studies from two meta-analyses. *Journal of Research in Science Training, 26,* 141–169.

Belotti, E. G. (1976). *What are little girls made of? The roots of feminine stereotypes.* New York: Schocken Books.

Biller, H. B. (1971). *Father, child, and sex role.* Lexington, MA: Heath Lexington Books.

Block, J. H. (1983). Differential premises arising from differential socialization of the sexes: Some conjectures. *Child Development, 54,* 1335–1354.

Carter, D. B. (1987). The roles of peers in sex role socialization. In D. B. Carter (Ed.), *Current conceptions of sex roles and sex typing: Theory and research* (pp. 101–121). New York: Praeger.

Craig, G. (1989). *Human development* (5th ed.). Englewood Cliffs, NJ: Prentice-Hall.

D'Andrade, R. G. (1966). Sex differences and cultural institutions. In E. E. Maccoby (Ed.), *The development of sex differences* (pp. 174–204). Stanford, CA: Stanford University Press.

Durkin, K. (1984). Children's accounts of sex-role stereotypes in television. *Communication Research, 11,* 341–362.

Eichenbaum, L., & Orbach, S. (1983), *Understanding women.* New York: Basic Books.

Eisenberg, N., Wolchik, S. A., Hernandez, R., & Pasternack, J. F. (1985). Parental socialization of young children's play: A short-term longitudinal study. *Child Development, 56,* 1506–1513.

Eisler, R. (1987). *The chalice and the blade.* San Francisco: Harper & Row.

Fagot, B. I., & Leinbach, M. D. (1987). Socialization of sex roles within the family. In D. B. Carter (Ed.), *Current conceptions of sex roles and sex typing: Theory and research* (pp. 89–100). New York: Praeger.

Fleishman, E. G. (1983). Sex role acquisition, parental behavior, and sexual orientation: Some tentative hypotheses. *Sex Roles, 9,* 1051–1059.

Frank, E., & Stewart, B. D. (1983). Treating depression in victims of rape. *Clinical Psychologist, 36,* 95–98.

Frey, D., & Carlock, J. (1984). *Enhancing self-esteem.* Muncie, IN: Accelerated Development, Inc.

Friedman, L. (1989). Mathematics and the gender gap: A meta-analysis of recent studies on sex differences in mathematical tasks. *Review of Educational Research, 59,* 185–213.

Gilligan, C. (1982). *In a different voice: Psychological theory and women's development.* Cambridge: Harvard University Press.

Good, G. E., Gilbert, L. A., & Scher, M. (1990). Gender aware therapy: A synthesis of feminist therapy and knowledge about gender. *Journal of Counseling and Development, 68,* 376–380.

Hammond, D., & Jablow, A. (1976). *Women in cultures of the world.* Menlo Park, CA: Cummings Publishing.

Hoffman, L. W. (1977). Changes in family role, socialization, and sex differences. *American Psychologist, 32,* 644–657.

Hoffman, L., Paris, S., Hall, E., & Schell, R. (1988). *Developmental psychology today* (5th ed.). New York: Random House.

Honig, A. S. (1983). Sex role socialization in early childhood. *Young Children, 38,* 57–70.

Horwitz, A. V. (1982). Sex role expectations, power, and psychological stress. *Sex Roles, 8,* 607–623.

Janoff-Bulman, R. (1985). The aftermath of victimization: Rebuilding shattered assumptions. In C. R. Figley (Ed.), *Trauma and its wake: The study and treatment of post-traumatic stress disorder* (pp. 15–35). New York: Bruner/Mazel.

Jeffries-Fox, S., & Jeffries-Fox, B. (1981). Gender differences in socialization through television to occupational roles: An exploratory approach. *Journal of Early Adolescence, 1,* 293–302.

Kagan, J. (1971). *Changes and continuity in infancy.* New York: Wiley.

Kahle, J. B. (1984). *Girls in school/women in science: A synopsis. Paper presented at the meeting of the Women's Studies Conference,* Greeley, CO. (ERIC Reproduction Service No. ED 243 785)

Katz, P. A. (1986). Modification of children's gender-stereotyped behaviors: General issues and research considerations. *Sex Roles, 14,* 591–601.

Korner, A. F. (1978). The effect of the infant's sex on the caregiver. In H. Bee (Ed.), *Social issues in developmental psychology* (2nd ed.) (pp. 78–84). New York: Harper & Row.

Kroop, J. J., & Halverson, C. F. (1983). Preschool children's preferences and recall for stereotyped versus nonstereotyped stories. *Sex Roles, 9,* 261–272.

Lamb, M. E. (1977). The development of mother-infant and father-infant attachments in the second year of life. *Developmental Psychology, 13,* 637–648.

Lee, P. C. (1976). Reinventing sex roles in the early childhood setting. In M. D. Cohen & L. P. Martin (Eds.), *Growing free: Ways to help children overcome sex-role stereotypes* (pp. 187–191). Washington, DC: Association for Childhood Education International.

Linn, M. C., Benedictis, T., Delucchi, K., Harris, A., & Stage, E. (1978). Gender differences in national assessment of educational progress science items: What does "I don't know" really mean? *Journal of Research on Science Teaching, 24,* 267–278.

Linn, M. C., & Petersen, A. C. (1986). A meta-analysis of gender differences in spatial ability: Implications for mathematics and science achievement. In J. S. Hyde & M. C. Linn (Eds.), *The psychology of gender* (pp. 67–101). Baltimore: John Hopkins University Press.

Linn, M. C., & Pulos, S. (1983). Male-female differences in predicting displaced volume: Strategy usage, aptitude relationships, and experience influences. *Journal of Educational Psychology, 75,* 86–96.

Lockheed, M. E. (1986). Reshaping the social order: The case of gender segregation. *Sex Roles, 14,* 617–628.

Lorber, J. (1986). Dismantling Noah's ark. *Sex Roles, 14,* 567–580.

Lyon, E. (1986). The economics of gender. In F. A. Boudreau, R. S. Sennott, & M. Wilson (Eds.), *Sex roles and social patterns* (pp. 149–189). New York: Praeger.

Maccoby, E. E. (1988). Gender as a social category. *Developmental Psychology, 24,* 755-765.

Maccoby, E. E., & Jacklin, C. N. (1974). *The psychology of sex differences.* Stanford, CA: Stanford University Press.

MacCormack, C. P. (1980). Nature, culture and gender: A critique. In C. P. MacCormack & M. Strathern (Eds.), *Nature, culture and gender* (pp. 1–24). Cambridge, England: Cambridge University Press.

Macklin, M. C., & Kolbe, R. H. (1984). Sex role stereotyping in children's advertising: Current and past trends. *Journal of Advertising, 13,* 34–42.

Matlin, M. W. (1987). *The psychology of women.* New York: Holt, Rinehart & Winston.

Mickelson, R. A. (1989). Why does Jane read and write so well? The anomaly of women's achievement. *Sociology of Education, 62,* 47–63.

Miller, J. B. (1986). *Toward a new psychology of women*, (2nd ed.). Boston: Beacon Press.

O'Kelly, C. (1986). The nature versus nurture debate. In F. A. Boudreau, R. S. Sennott, & M. Wilson (Eds.), *Sex roles and social patterns* (pp. 23–62). New York: Praeger.

Papilia, D., & Olds, S. W. (1989). *Human development* (4th ed.). New York: McGraw-Hill.

Peretti, P. O., & Sydney, T. M. (1984). Parental toy choice stereotyping and its effects on child toy preferences and sex-role typing. *Social Behavior and Personality, 12*, 213–216.

Reis, S. M. (1987). We can't change what we don't recognize: Understanding the special needs of gifted females. *Gifted Child Quarterly, 31*, 83–89.

Roopnarine, J. L. (1984). Sex-typed socialization in mixed-age preschool classrooms. *Child Development, 55*, 1078–1084.

Roopnarine, J. L. (1987). Mothers' and fathers' behaviors toward the toy play of their infant sons and daughters. *Sex Roles, 14*, 59–68.

Rubin, G. (1975). The traffic in women: Notes on the "political economy" of sex. In R. R. Reiter (Ed.), *Toward an anthropology of women* (pp. 157–210). New York: Monthly Review Press.

Sadker, M., & Sadker, D. (1982). *Sex equity handbook for schools* (2nd ed.). New York: Longman.

Serbin, L. A., O'Leary, K. D., Kent, R. N., & Tonick, I. J. (1973). A comparison of teacher response to the preacademic and problem behavior of boys and girls. *Child Development, 44*, 796–804.

Silbern, L. E., & Katz, P. A. (1986). Gender roles and adjustment in elementary-school children: A multidimensional approach. *Sex Roles, 14*, 181–202.

Staff. (1986). A U.S. progression: Milestones toward equality. *International Altrusan, 64*, 10–12.

Stern, M., & Karraker, K. H. (1989). Sex stereotyping of infants: A review of gender labeling studies. *Sex Roles, 20*, 501–522.

Thompson, S. (1975). Gender labels and early sex role development. *Child Development, 46*, 339–347.

Ullian, D. (1984). Why girls are good: A constructivist view. *American Journal of Orthopsychiatry, 54*, 71–82.

Vernon, A. (1990). Self-development across the life span. *Counseling and Human Development, 23*, 1–11.

Weinraub, M., & Brown, L. M. (1983). The development of sex-role stereotypes in children: Crushing realities. In V. Franks & E. D. Rothblum (Eds.), *The stereotyping of women: Its effects on mental health* (pp. 30–58). New York: Springer Publishing.

Weitzman, L., Eifler, D., Hokada, E., & Ross, C. (1972). Sex-role socialization in picture books for preschool children. *Journal of Sociology, 77*, 1125–1150.

Weitzman, N., Birns, B., & Friend, R. (1985). Traditional and nontraditional mothers' communication with their daughters and sons. *Child Development, 56*, 894–898.

Whyte, M. K. (1978). *The status of women in preindustrial societies*. Princeton, NJ: Princeton University Press.

4

Health Risks in Children and Adolescents

Cheryl L. Mejta
Governors State University

O ver the course of the 1980s, the health and wellness movement became entrenched in American culture. With increased awareness of the connection between lifestyle behavior patterns and health status as well as the continuing rise in health care costs, our society began to focus on the prevention of disease, disability, and death. Although morbidity and mortality rates for children and adolescents are lower than those for adults (National Center for Health Statistics, 1990a), disease prevention and health promotion programs focused on developmental periods is important for several reasons. First, the origins of many unhealthy lifestyle behavior patterns in adults can be traced to childhood and adolescence. Second, to perhaps an even greater extent than with adults, disability and death during childhood and adolescence are often directly attributable to controllable factors. Finally, health risks for some children and adolescents are imposed by their adult caretakers rather than freely chosen.

Within the past several years, female health issues have received increased attention. Although research on the health issues, practices, and behaviors of female children and adolescents is limited (Vinal et al., 1986), what we do know suggests that there are important gender-related differences in mortality rates and health risks that make it imperative that we target our clinical and research efforts separately on the health status of female children and adolescents.

HEALTH ISSUES FOR FEMALES IN CHILDHOOD AND ADOLESCENCE

During childhood and adolescence, the leading cause of death for female and male children and adolescents are similar. As seen in Table 4.1, the primary causes of death for females and males are motor vehicle accidents, homicide/legal interventions, malignant neoplasms, diseases of the heart, suicide, and cerebrovascular disease. Gender-related differences, however, are seen in overall mortality rates. In comparison to their male counterparts, female children and adolescents have lower mortality rates. According to the National Center for Health Statistics *Monthly Vital Statistics Report* (1990b), the mortality rate per 100,000 is 20.3 for female children 5 to 14 years old and 51.1 for female adolescents 15 to 24 years old. The comparable mortality rates for male children and adolescents are 29.9 and 150.8, respectively. This discrepancy in mortality rates is primarily the result of higher rates of fatal motor vehicle accidents, homicides/legal interventions, and suicide within the male adolescent population.

Although the health risks experienced by female children and adolescents are not as likely to be immediately fatal, they are likely to have immediate and delayed psychological consequences, long-term physical consequences, and decreases in the quality of life. The major health risks affecting female children and adolescents fall into the following categories: violent and abusive behaviors, sexual behaviors, health risks, substance abuse, and body image.

Health Risks Associated with Violent and Abusive Behaviors

Health risks within this category involve violent and abusive behaviors inflicted upon female children by those in a caretaking role (e.g., child abuse) or self-inflicted (suicide). The National Center on Child Abuse and Neglect (1988) reported a 74% increase in the incidence of child abuse between 1980 and 1986; physical abuse increased by 58%, and sexual abuse increased by 300%. Across the past three decades, adolescent suicide rates have nearly tripled (Institute of Medicine, 1990).

Child Abuse

In 1984 Congress offered the following definition of child abuse and neglect:

> The physical and mental injury, sexual abuse or exploitation, negligent treatment, or maltreatment of a child under the age of eighteen, or the age specified by the child protection law of the State in question, by a person (including any employee of a residential facility or any staff person providing out-of-home care), who is responsible for the child's welfare. (Child Abuse Prevention and Treatment Act, 1984)

In 1986, the National Center on Child Abuse and Neglect (1988) commissioned a study of the national incidence and prevalence of child abuse and neglect. The results indicated that more than 1½ million children in the United States experience abuse or neglect. The study also found that females were more likely than males to experience abuse; the rate of abuse per 1,000 children was 13.1 for females and 8.4 for males. Females were also more likely than males to be injured or impaired as a result of the abuse; the rate of physical injury/impairment per 1,000 children was 3.5 for females and 2.0 for males. Because child abuse generally is under-reported, these rates probably should be higher. Hampton and Newberger (1985) found that only 60% of abuse cases

Table 4.1
Primary Causes of Death for Children and Adolescents (Rates per 100,000)

Primary Cause of Death	Male	Female
Motor vehicle accidents	29.05	10.08
Homicide/legal interventions	23.95	5.90
Malignant neoplasms	5.20	3.75
Diseases of the heart	5.15	2.10
Suicide	15.58	1.89
Cerebrovascular disease	0.55	0.53

Source: From *Health United States,* National Center for Health Statistics, 1989, Washington DC: U.S. Government Printing Office, DHHS Pub. No. (PHS) 89-1232.

for children below 5 years of age were reported, and only about 25% of abuse cases for adolescents 12 to 17 years old. Repeat offenses were noted by these authors to be common among child abusers.

Child abuse generally is divided into three major categories: physical, sexual, and emotional. Table 4.2 compares the rates of the three categories of abuse for females and males. Across all forms of abuse, rates of abuse are higher for females than males. The discrepancy in abuse rates is particularly apparent for sexual abuse. Females children and adolescents may be more likely to experience abuse because they are more vulnerable than their male counterparts. Females may be less likely to protect themselves because they are socialized to be less assertive and to internalize blame for bad outcomes. In addition, females are physically less powerful.

Physical Abuse Physical abuse has been defined as the intentional, nonaccidental use of physical force or act of omission aimed at hurting, injuring, or destroying a child (Gil, 1971). It is the most frequently occurring form of abuse for females (6.4 per 1,000) and males (5.0 per 1,000) (National Center on Child Abuse and Neglect, 1988). It also is the most likely form of abuse to be reported, probably because it is the most easily identified and recognized (National Center on Child Abuse and Neglect, 1988).

Most researchers and clinicians suggest that this figure underestimates the true incidence of child physical abuse. White, Snyder, Bourne, and Newberger (1989) reviewed the results of a national survey on family violence within two-parent families with children between the ages of 3 and 17. They reported that 82% of the 3- to 9-year-olds, 66% of the 10- to 14-year-olds, and 34% of the 15- to 17-year-olds had been victims of some form of violence during the year. Severe parental violence (threatened or assaulted with a lethal weapon) directed toward 3- to 17-year-olds was estimated at 3.8% (38 out of 1,000 children).

Reported cases of physical abuse used to determine the incidence of abuse typically involve the most obvious cases. More subtle cases of physical abuse, however, can be equally as damaging to a child's psychological well-being. Mellody, Miller, and Miller (1989) used a broader criterion to define physical abuse that focuses upon the question,

Table 4.2
Sex Differences in Rate of Specific Forms of Abuse (Rates per 1,000)

Sex	Type of Abuse		
	Physical	Sexual	Emotional
Female	6.4	3.9	3.8
Male	5.0	1.1	2.9

Source: From *Study Findings: Study of National Incidence and Prevalence of Child Abuse and Neglect—1988*, National Center on Child Abuse and Neglect, 1988, Washington DC: U.S. Government Printing Office.

"Was the child's physical person treated with respect, or was it attacked or ignored?" They suggest that the following messages are given to a child when he or she is physically abused: The body is not worth being respected, one has no right to be free from painful touches, and one has no right to control what happens to his or her own body. In a survey of family violence within two-caretaker families, it was found that 1% reported very severe violence toward their children (kicked, bit, punched, beat up, threatened with or used deadly weapons), 7% reported hitting the child with an object such as a stick or belt, and 39% reported slapping or spanking their children (Gelles, 1987).

In families where child physical abuse occurs, violence appears to be a common interactional pattern; families who engage in one form of familial violence are likely to engage in other forms of familial violence (Strauss, 1988). In a survey of the literature on family violence, White et al. (1989) derived the following conclusions: (a) women who experienced spouse abuse were more likely to physically abuse their children, (b) sibling violence was more likely in families where parents were violent toward children, and (c) children who experienced parental violence were more likely to use violence against their parents.

Bittner and Newberger (1981) developed and White et al. (1989) further discussed an etiological model of family violence that involves an interaction among child vulnerabilities and stresses, parental vulnerabilities and stresses, and family stresses. Child factors associated with abuse include parental perceptions of the child as physically, mentally, temperamentally, or behaviorally different or as difficult. Parental factors related to behaving abusively toward a child include the parent's ability to understand and empathize with the child and the parent's own childhood exposure to violence or deprivation. Family factors associated with child abuse include an impaired attachment relationship between parent and abused child, absence of a parent, social isolation of the family, and structural factors such as poverty, unemployment, poor housing, family size, and lack of access to child care. These authors also noted that child abuse occurs more frequently in families who accept violence as a normative means of socializing children.

There are direct and indirect health risks associated with physical abuse. Physical injury or death is the most obvious result of abuse. Among children between the ages of 5 and 14 years, homicide is the third leading cause of death (National Center for Health Statistics, 1989). Accidents and nonfatal injuries (e.g., falls, burns, drownings, shootings) also occur as a result of child neglect and abuse (Wissow, 1990).

Immediate and delayed psychological health risks associated with physical abuse perhaps are the most likely consequences. The effects of physical abuse are influenced by the following factors: (a) child's age and developmental level at the time of the abuse, (b) frequency and nature of the abuse, and (c) the total emotional milieu in the home (White et al., 1989). Common adverse consequences of physical abuse include (a) developmental delays in cognitive, language, and motor skills/abilities, (b) emotional impairment, especially in the development of a positive self-concept, (c) difficulties managing aggression, and (d) impaired social relationships. Hibbard, Ingersall, and Orr (1990) found that, in response to physical abuse, females had greater emotional reactions (e.g., trouble sleeping, difficulty with anger, thoughts of suicide, and difficulty making friends). Males, on the other hand, had greater behavioral reactions (e.g., use of alcohol and drugs, running away, attempting suicide).

Sexual Abuse   Child sexual abuse has been defined by Browne and Finkelhor (1986) as forced or coerced sexual behavior imposed on a child or sexual activity between a child and a person who is 5 or more years older, irrespective of whether coercion was involved. Sexual abuse may involve contact acts, which are intrusive or involve fondling of the genitalia, or noncontact acts, which include deliberate exposure to sexually abusive acts (Wissow, 1990).

Many sexual abuse cases remain hidden because (a) there are no visible physical signs of abuse, (b) victims tend to internalize responsibility, and (c) adults tend not to believe the children's disclosures (Daro, 1988). Therefore, it is difficult to estimate the true prevalence of child and adolescent sexual abuse. The National Incidence Study, sponsored by the National Center on Child Abuse and Neglect (1988), reported that females were nearly four times as likely to be sexually abused as males. The rate of sexual abuse for females was 3.9 cases per 1,000 children, whereas the rate of sexual abuse for males was 1.1 cases per 1,000 children. Sexual abuse cases composed 30% of all female abuse cases and 13% of all male cases.

In examining the literature on sexual abuse, we found the following patterns: (a) the victim of sexual abuse is most likely to be a female (Burgess, 1985; Wissow, 1990); (b) the perpetrator of sexual abuse is most likely to be a male (DePanfilis, 1987); (c) most cases of child sexual abuse (76%) involve a person that the child knows (Finkelhor, 1979); and (d) the most common form of sexual abuse is between a father or father figure and his daughter (DePanfilis, 1987). A girl's risk for sexual abuse increases if the principal father figure is a stepfather. In one survey, it was found that 17% of the women were sexually abused by a stepfather and 2% of the women were sexually abused by a biological father (Russell, 1984). Furthermore, 47% of the cases involving stepfathers compared to 26% of the cases involving biological fathers were defined as very serious. Finkelhor and Baron (1986) found two peak periods of the onset of sexual abuse: 6 to 7 years old and 10 to 12 years old. They further found that children experienced the abuse in silence for an average of 3 to 4 years before the abuse was disclosed to someone.

Five family conditions where father-daughter incest is most likely to occur have been identified: emergence of the daughter as the central figure of the household; relative sexual incompatibility of the parents; willingness of the father to seek a partner outside the nuclear family; pervasive fears of abandonment and family disintegration; and unconscious sanction of the incest of the mother, who condones or promotes the daughter's sexual role with her father (Lustig, Dresser, Spellman & Murray, 1966).

Browne and Finkelhor (1986) reviewed the empirical literature on the effects of female child sexual abuse. Their overall conclusions were that "sexual abuse is a serious mental health problem, consistently associated with very disturbing subsequent problems in some important portions of its victims" (p. 72). Initial effects of the child sexual abuse (reactions occurring within 2 years of the termination of abuse) substantiated within the research were fear, anxiety, depression, anger, hostility, and inappropriate sexual behavior. The long-term effects of female child sexual abuse substantiated by the literature were depression, self-destructive behavior, anxiety, feelings of isolation and stigma, poor self-esteem, tendency toward victimization, and substance abuse.

The impact of sexual abuse is influenced by several factors, including the relationship of the perpetrator to the victim, the type of sexual activity, degree of coercion, and parental response to disclosure. The research literature suggests that greater trauma is experienced when the perpetrator is a father or father figure, the abuse involves intimate sexual contact (e.g., genital contact), the perpetrator uses force, and the parental responses to the disclosure are negative (Browne & Finkelhor, 1986).

Emotional Abuse Of all forms of child abuse, emotional abuse is probably the most frequent kind of abuse but also the most difficult to define. Mellody et al. (1989) have suggested that emotional abuse occurs through verbal abuse, social abuse, and neglect or abandonment of dependency needs. Verbal abuse involves screaming, name calling, ridiculing, and listening to verbal abuse directed toward someone else. Social abuse occurs when parents directly or indirectly interfere with child's access to peers. Neglect of dependency needs occurs when the child's needs for emotional nurturing are not met well enough and the child is shamed. Abandonment of dependency needs occurs when emotional nurturing needs simply are not met—either one or both parents are unavailable. The rate of emotional abuse is 3.8 cases per 1,000 female children and 2.9 cases per 1,000 male children. Emotional abuse cases compose 29% of all female abuse cases and 34% of all male abuse cases (National Center on Child Abuse and Neglect, 1988).

Summary Although the major categories of child abuse have been discussed separately, the literature suggests that there is a high correlation among the different forms of abuse within families. For example, Daro (1988), looking at cases in which physical abuse had been reported, found emotional abuse in 76% of the families and neglect in 39% of the families. While there are specific reactions to certain forms of abuse, Wissow (1990) summarized some of the major reactions of children in response to child abuse. These include delays in cognitive and social development, separation difficulties, poor self-esteem and self-hatred, attachment difficulties, and internalization of blame for the abuse and family problems.

Suicide

According to the National Center for Health Statistics (1989), suicide is among the top five leading causes of death for female children and adolescents between the ages of 5 and 24 years of age. The suicide rate for female children between the ages of 5 and

14 is estimated to be 0.25 per 100,000 female children. Because of the controversy over whether children are emotionally and cognitively capable of committing suicide, non–illness-related childhood deaths often are attributed to "accidents" rather than to suicide (Orbach, 1988). Childhood suicide rates, therefore, may be underestimated. As female children move into adolescence, their suicide rates increase. The suicide rate for females between the ages of 15 and 24 is 3.5 per 100,000 female adolescents (National Center for Health Statistics, 1989). Although the psychological challenges posed by adolescence may account for some of the increase in number of suicides, Orbach (1988) has postulated that the self-destructive process resulting in suicide frequently has its roots in early childhood experiences.

Both sex and race differences are found in the rates of suicide. Across age groups, the suicide rate is higher for white females than for black females (age group 5 to 14 years: 0.3 versus 0.2, respectively; age group 15 to 24 years: 4.7 and 2.3, respectively) (National Center for Health Statistics, 1989). Across ages and races, the suicide rate for males is higher than for females (age group 5 to 14 years: 1.0 versus 0.25, respectively; age group 15 to 24 years: 17.6 versus 3.5, respectively) (National Center for Health Statistics, 1989). While more males than females actually commit suicide, more females than males may attempt suicide. Hawton (1986) reported that the female to male ratio for attempted suicide is between 3:1 and 9:1. Males may be more likely than females to succeed in committing suicide if attempted because of differences in the methods used. Males are more likely to attempt suicide using violent means such as firearms, whereas females are more likely to attempt suicide with poisons (Hawton, 1986). According to the Institute of Medicine (1990), the adolescent suicide rate has been increasing across the past three decades.

In attempting to explain child and adolescent suicide, Orbach (1988) proposed the Unresolvable Problem Hypothesis. Briefly, the hypothesis suggests that the suicidal child is pressured to solve a problem that he or she cannot avoid but that is unresolvable for one of the following reasons: (a) the problem is beyond the child's capabilities, (b) the child's attempts to solve the problem are blocked, and (c) the child is not allowed to use new problem solving approaches. He further proposes that suicidal behaviors develop through the following sequence of experiences: the child feels intolerable pressure and develops a depressed attitude; the child makes initial unsuccessful attempts at adjusting and coping; frustrations accumulate and wear down emotional strength; the idea of suicide appears; the child attempts to adjust through self-destructive means; environment's response to self-destructiveness escalates pressures on the child; the child's pessimistic view of life is confirmed, as is the idea that suicide is the only solution; and new frustrations continue to accumulate leading to the ultimate act of self-destruction.

Orbach (1988) reviewed the literature on factors contributing to and causing childhood suicide. Personality factors increasing the risk of suicide in children were depression, especially if accompanied with despair and hopelessness; cognitive rigidity and inflexibility limiting problem solving abilities; and an obsessive preoccupation with death. Life circumstances associated with childhood suicide were parental self-destructive tendencies such as depression or suicidal tendencies; negative childhood experiences affecting levels of self-esteem, depression, and hopelessness such as child abuse, loss, and family crises; and familial atmosphere of stress and tension. Family patterns contributing to childhood suicide were families with multiple problems; families who dealt with internal conflict and problems by scapegoating a child; and families with closed systems and unhealthy symbiosis.

Health Risks Associated with Sexual Behaviors

According to the Year 2000 Objectives for the Nation (Public Health Service, 1989) 19.2% of adolescents first had sexual intercourse at age 15 or younger and 47% of adolescents 15 to 19 report some current sexual activity. Yet only 57% of adolescents 19 or younger report effectively using contraceptives at first sexual intercourse. These sexual practices result in increased rates of teen-age pregnancy, sexually transmitted diseases, and HIV infection.

Teen-Age Pregnancy

In comparison to most other developed nations, in the United States adolescent pregnancy, abortion, and childbearing rates are considerably higher even though sexual activity begins at the same age (Institute of Medicine, 1990). The pregnancy rate per 1,000 females is 1.3 for girls between the ages of 10 and 14, 30.6 for females between the ages of 15 and 17, and 81.0 for females between the ages of 18 and 19 (National Center for Health Statistics, 1989). This translates to about one million teen-age pregnancies each year. Many of these teen-age girls obtain abortions. The abortion rate (number of abortions per 100 live births) is 141.2 for girls under 15 years old and 71.7 for females between the ages of 15 and 19 years old (National Center for Health Statistics, 1989).

There are health and social consequences for teen mothers and their children. The risk of maternal death is 3 times higher for adolescent mothers than for mothers aged 20 to 24 (Institute of Medicine, 1985). Finally, life options for teen-age mothers are restricted. For example, females who were teen-age mothers show lower achieved income and educational levels than other females (Institute of Medicine, 1990).

Young maternal age, coupled with low socioeconomic status, are factors associated with poor pregnancy outcomes. Women under the age of 17 are at particular risk of delivering low-birth-weight infants. Adolescent women with less than a high school education are 70% more likely to give birth to low-birth-weight infants than are high school graduates. Low-birth-weight infants, who weigh 1 ½ pounds or less at birth, are born with poorly developed muscle tissue, very little body fat, low stores of iron, and an inadequately mineralized skeleton (Institute of Medicine, 1985). According to the National Center for Health Statistics (1990c), low birth weight is the greatest single hazard to infant health.

Malnutrition, as well as the lack of prenatal care, directly affects the health of the mother and infant. The nutritional needs of pregnant adolescents must support their own development as well as that of their fetus. Adolescent pregnancy adds fetal nutritional needs to those of the mother. Consequently, adolescent pregnancy presents a very high risk for low infant birth weights.

Studies of high risk groups, such as pregnant adolescents and poor women, have demonstrated that early and consistent prenatal medical care can greatly increase the chances of producing healthy babies. An expectant mother with no prenatal care is three times as likely to have a low-birth-weight baby as one who has prenatal care. Unfortunately, pregnant adolescents are among those groups least likely to procure prenatal care (Institute of Medicine, 1985).

In Healthy People Year 2000, the Institute of Medicine (1990) reported that adolescents have been sexually active for an average of at least one year before they seek contraceptives. They attribute the causes of the unintended pregnancies to the unavailability of family-planning services and teen-agers' reluctance to obtain and use contraceptives.

Sexually Transmitted Diseases

Two and one half million teen-agers become infected with a sexually transmitted disease each year; a teen's risk of contracting a sexually transmitted disease is estimated to be 2 to 3 times higher than that of someone aged 20 or older (Institute of Medicine, 1990). Hein (1984) reported that the highest rates of cytomegalovirus (CMV), chlamydial cervicitis, and pelvic inflammatory diseases are found among 15- to 19-year-olds. Because of anatomic and physiological differences, adolescent girls may be at higher risk for contracting STDs than adult women (Hein, 1984). Although the risk of contracting an STD is high, only one third of adolescents consider themselves to be very well informed about STDs (Institute of Medicine, 1990).

Acquired Immunodeficiency Syndrome

In 1990, Human Immunodeficiency Virus (HIV) infection was listed among the 10 leading causes of death for children aged 1 to 4 and young people aged 15 to 24 (National Center for Health Statistics, 1990b). Using data supplied by the Centers for Disease Control, the National Center for Health Statistics (1989) estimated that about 2% of the diagnosed AIDS cases involve children and adolescents under 20 years old. Children under 5, who contract the virus from their mothers while *in utero*, represent the majority (70%) of these cases. Adolescent females, aged 13 to 19 years, represent 18% of all adolescents with AIDS and 0.8% of all females with AIDS.

Although the percentage of female children and adolescents with AIDS is small, there are several indicators suggesting that female adolescents in particular are engaging in behaviors placing them at risk for HIV infection. Females between the ages of 20 and 29 years old make up 8% of all AIDS cases and 28% of females with AIDS (National Center for Health Statistics, 1989). Because the latency between HIV infection and the development of AIDS averages 5 to 7 years, many of these young adults with AIDS probably were infected with HIV between the ages of 13 and 24 years.

Several studies examining adolescents' knowledge of, attitudes toward, and belief about AIDS support the contention that adolescents are engaging in behaviors placing them at risk for AIDS. DiClemente, Zorn, and Temoshok (1986) surveyed 1,326 high school students in San Francisco. The majority of students knew that AIDS could be transmitted through sexual intercourse (92%), sharing intravenous drug needles (81%), or receiving infected blood through a transfusion (84%). However, only 60% of the students knew that using a condom during sexual intercourse lowered the risk of becoming HIV-infected.

In further analyses of this data, DiClemente, Zorn, and Temoshok (1987) examined attitudes and beliefs about AIDS. They found that the majority of students perceived AIDS as being a serious disease; about 51% stated that they would rather contract any other disease than AIDS. The majority of students (74%) also reported fears about getting AIDS. Female adolescents were more likely than male adolescents to report a high level of susceptibility to AIDS (57% of the females versus 47% of the males).

Kegeles, Adler, and Irwin (1988) examined sexually active adolescents' knowledge about, attitudes toward, and actual use of condoms. Of those adolescents who were sexually active, about 25% of the females reported that their partners used condoms and about 45% of the males reported that they used condoms. Only 2.1% of the females and 8.2% of the males reported using condoms every time they had intercourse. Females tended to report little intention of having their partners use condoms, whereas males tended to report that they were likely to use condoms. Females were uncertain about whether or not their partners wanted to use them, whereas males believed that their partners wished them to use condoms.

Health Risks Associated with Alcohol and Drug Use

Testimony for the Year 2000 Health Promotion/Disease Prevention Objectives (Public Health Service, 1989) has indicated that drug abuse is the most serious threat to the health and well-being of our children and adolescents. Adolescents who are substance abusers are at high risk for physical, social, and psychological problems. For instance, adolescent substance abuse plays a causal or contributing role in juvenile delinquency, adolescent suicide, and intentional and unintentional injury, including motor vehicle accidents.

Two recently conducted national surveys provide information about the prevalence of substance use among female children and adolescents. In 1985 the National Institute on Drug Abuse (NIDA) conducted a national household survey to measure the prevalence and correlates of drug use in the United States. A total of 3,095 12- to 17-year-olds (1,557 males and 1,538 females) and 1,505 18- to 25-year-olds (642 males and 863 females) participated in the study. Females' drug use patterns are remarkably similar to males' drug use patterns. For most drug classifications, about an equal percentage of females and males reported having ever used the drug, having used the drug in the past year, and having used the drug in the past month. Two exceptions are smokeless tobacco, which more males than females use, and psychotherapeutic drugs, which more females than males use.

In examining females' drug use patterns specifically, the NIDA-sponsored survey found that about 26% of the females reported trying an illicit drug, with 16% reporting use within the past year and 9% reporting use within the past month. The most common drugs used by adolescent females were alcohol, cigarettes, and marijuana. Regarding alcohol, 47% tried alcohol, 41% used alcohol within the past year, and 24% used alcohol in the past month. Alcohol was used once a week or more by 4% of the adolescent females. With regard to cigarettes, 39% tried cigarettes, 22% smoked cigarettes within the past year, and 11% smoked cigarettes in the past month. Regarding marijuana use, 18% tried marijuana, 14% reported use within the past year, and 7% used within the past month. Marijuana was smoked once a week or more by 4% of the female adolescents.

For all other drug categories, reported use was less than 10% of the female adolescents surveyed.

Johnston, O'Malley, and Bachman (1988) also conducted a national survey of high school seniors. These authors also noted diminishing differences between the sexes in their substance use patterns. The following differences in substance use, however, were noted. Males were more likely to use most illicit drugs. High school females, however were slightly more likely than males to use stimulants and tranquilizers. Females were slightly more likely to smoke cigarettes than their male counterparts in high school.

Health Risks Associated with Body Image

Leon and Dinklage (1989) have defined body image as "the perception and evaluation of one's own body" (p. 250). Female adolescents experience tremendous physiological and physical changes. This is also a period when female adolescents begin defining their sexuality. Often these physical changes are accompanied by acute self-awareness, at times resulting in self-consciousness. In looking for female role models to help define oneself, female adolescents are confronted with society's ideal image of the female as thin and beautiful. In attempting to comply with society's ideal female, many female adolescents become preoccupied with their weight and physical appearance. For some female adolescents, this preoccupation with weight and appearance can lead to the development of eating disorders. Adolescence is a major risk period for anorexia nervosa and bulimia. Even if the female adolescent avoids developing an eating disorder, she is often dieting. Nutritional deficiencies frequently result from following diets designed to produce weight loss with minimal or no concern about nutrition.

ETIOLOGY OF HEALTH-RISK BEHAVIORS

The empirical and clinical literature increasingly recognizes that health-risk behaviors are strongly associated with one another. That is, people who engage in one type of health-risk behavior are likely to engage in other types of health-risk behaviors. Generally, it is thought that health-risk behaviors are multidetermined. As related to child and adolescent health-risk behaviors, however, there are at least three etiological considerations: characteristics and tasks associated with this developmental period, health risks comprising constellation of problem behaviors as proposed by the Problem Behavior Theory, and health-risk behaviors as expressions and symptoms of child neglect or abuse.

Certain characteristics of later childhood and adolescence make it likely that females will experiment with health compromising behaviors (Jessor, 1984); (a) peers, who may encourage experimentation with health-risk behaviors, become more influential in the female's life, (b) the female has greater access to health compromising substances and more opportunity to use them, and (c) health-risk behaviors may be an attempt to cope with the pressure and stress attached to this developmental period.

The Problem Behavior Theory was formulated by Jessor and Jessor (1977) in an attempt to explain adolescent health-risk behaviors. The theory posits that factors in the personality system, the perceived environment system, and the behavior system interact to affect the individual's propensity toward health-risk behaviors. Jessor (1984) summarized the research results on the Problem Behavior Theory. Within the perceived environment system, propensity toward health risks was associated with low parental support and control, high peer controls, low compatibility between parental and peer expectations, low parental influence relative to peer influence, low parental disapproval of high risk behaviors, and strong peer models and approval of health-risk behaviors. Within the personality system, propensity toward health risks was associated with lower value placed on academic achievement, higher value placed on independence, greater value placed on independence relative to achievement, lower expectations for academic achievement, greater social criticism and alienation, lower self-esteem, external locus of control, greater tolerance of deviance, weaker religious beliefs, and greater importance attached to positive functions relative to negative functions of health-risk behaviors. Within the behavior system, propensity toward health-risk behavior was associated with lesser involvement in conventional behaviors and institutions and greater involvement in other problem behaviors.

Some of the clinical literature on addictions and abuse, especially as articulated by Bradshaw (1988, 1990) and Miller (1981, 1990), postulated a common underlying etiology for health-risk behavior. Briefly, it is suggested that addictions, compulsive behaviors, and other health-risk behaviors surface from experiencing dysfunctional and nonnurturing parenting as a child. More specifically, a person who was raised in a family where parental need satisfaction was emphasized while the child's needs were neglected, ignored, or punished is relatively more likely to engage in health-risk behaviors until he or she can identify and resolve these early experiences.

COUNSELING INTERVENTIONS

Interventions Focused on the Child or Adolescent

There are more than 230 alternate forms of counseling for children and adolescents identified within the literature (Kazdin, 1990). As with counseling for adults, many questions have been raised about the effectiveness of counseling with children and adolescents. In a review of 75 outcome studies on counseling with children and adolescents, Casey and Berman (1985) concluded that counseling with children and adolescents is as effective as counseling with adults. Compared to untreated children, treated children's outcomes were better. There was no evidence to suggest that one form of counseling was superior to another. Kazdin's review of the child and adolescent psychotherapy literature provided further evidence for the effectiveness of treatment compared to no treatment in resolving children's and adolescents' problems.

To be effective, counseling strategies and interventions for children and adolescents need to be developmentally specific (Shirk, 1988). Most counseling approaches for children and adolescents emphasize one or more of the following goals:

1. Validation of the child's/adolescent's experiences and feelings as they relate to less-than-nuturing or traumatic experiences.
2. Developmentally appropriate "working through" of feelings and reactions.
3. Correction of developmental deficits resulting from less-than-nurturing caretaking.
4. Promotion of behaviors that are psychologically and physically health-enhancing.

Tuma (1989) listed four general factors, similar to those operational in counseling with adults, that promote change in children and adolescents. These are the opportunity to express and master feelings about traumatic events; the child's or adolescent's expectation of change, which is influenced by parental attitudes and counseling discussions; attention from the counselor as communicated through the counselor's empathy, warmth, and genuineness; and the counselor's reinforcement of the child's or adolescent's attempts to resolve problems in healthy ways.

Shirk (1988), however, has cautioned against relying on insight alone to produce healthy change. He suggested that in addition to the direct harmful effects of dysfunctional and nonnurturing families, additional maladjustment results from disruptions in negotiating developmental tasks and acquiring age-based competencies. Therefore, insight into early experience of abuse is not sufficient for emotional and behavioral change. Shirk (1988) also recommended skills training to correct developmental deficits.

Interventions Focused on the Family

Commonly used parent-focused approaches to modifying dysfunctional and unhealthy parent–child interactions include training in child management skills (e.g., use of positive reinforcement and nonviolent discipline methods), parent education and support groups to further understanding of parental responsibilities and to learn different child rearing approaches, anger and stress management to learn self-control and to develop appropriate coping skills, and treatment of antecedent conditions in the family (e.g., health problems, marital discord, financial and job problems, violence) (Wolfe & St. Pierre, 1989).

Community-Based Interventions

A common characteristic of dysfunctional families is that they are isolated from their extended families and the community (Strauss, 1988). Without social contacts, the family has no support system to help them alleviate stress. In addition, the family has no reference group with which to compare the appropriateness of present behaviors as well as to develop alternate and more successful behaviors. Linking these families to social and community organizations and services can be effective in reducing social isolation and family dysfunction.

Parents Anonymous (P.A.) is one community service that has been effective in reducing family dysfunction. P.A. is a national self-help group for parents who define themselves as abusive (physically, emotionally, or sexually) to their children. Groups meet regularly, usually weekly, to provide support to members. Although participation is voluntary, many group members share their histories as related to their abusive behaviors. In addition to a chairperson who leads the groups, each group has a professional sponsor who serves as a consultant and referral source. An outside evaluation reported by MacFarlane and Lieber (1978) indicated that abusive parents who participate in P.A. show almost immediate reductions in the frequency of verbal and physical abuse; further, abuse continues to decrease over time. In addition, P.A. members showed increases in self-esteem, social contacts, knowledge of child development, and ability to deal with stress. Finally, members rated P.A. as useful in helping them deal with their child abuse problems.

CASE EXAMPLES

The Case of Kim

Kim is a 16-year-old female who was brought to a mental health center for counseling after her mother discovered a suicide letter written by Kim to a friend. In the letter, Kim stated that she felt as though she was a disappointment to her parents and that she was not good enough. She also stated that it would be easier for everyone if she were dead. Her intention to commit suicide was expressed several days after a heated family argument that resulted in her mother holding Kim while her father hit her.

An assessment of the family yielded the following information. Until about 5 years earlier, Kim's father had been an alcoholic who drank. He stopped drinking without assistance from a counselor or self-help group. He shows signs of a classic "dry drunk syndrome." He is a self-focused, angry, and bitter person with intense feelings of inferiority. He demands respect and obedience from his daughter. Kim's mother is a self-described Adult Child of an Alcoholic (ACOA); her father was an alcoholic and she married an alcoholic. She has extremely high aspirations and expectations for her daughter. She expects her to follow the path she has set down for her without deviation or failure.

In this family, Kim has minimal opportunity to develop a clear sense of herself and to separate from the family in healthy ways. Family counseling was initiated with the immediate goal of stopping the verbal raging and physical abuse by helping the family resolve conflict and disagreements through communication, negotiation, and anger management. A later goal was to help the family more successfully negotiate the current developmental transition involving the separation of the daughter from the parents. Each parent also has unresolved family-of-origin issues suggesting additional individual counseling; the parents resisted this intervention. The daughter, however, did enter individual counseling with primary goals related to increasing self-esteem, separating issues belonging to her parents from her issues, continuing the individuation process, developing self-enhancing coping and problem solving skills, and recognizing life-sustaining options.

The Case of Pat

Pat is a 15-year-old female who was placed into an adolescent, residential, substance abuse treatment facility by her mother and stepfather. For the past year, her parents reported that they were unable to manage her behavior. She typically stayed out past her curfew; she often came home drunk. On several occasions, the parents were called by the high school because of their daughter's behavior. She increasingly skipped classes. When she attended classes, she was disruptive and verbally abusive to the teachers. At the time she entered treatment, she had been suspended from school for verbally attacking the assistant principal.

Her substance abuse assessment yielded the following information. Pat began using alcohol at age 13. For the past 6 months, she has been drinking 3 beers daily; on weekends, she drinks 6 to 8 beers each day. She smokes about one pack of cigarettes daily. She also smokes a marijuana joint every few days. Pat indicated that all of her friends use drugs. She also reported unsafe sexual contacts with her boyfriend. She had an abortion about 6 months ago. Pat has two older brothers, ages 18 and 20. The 18-year-old brother also used drugs, but he has been substance-free for one year. Her father died in a car accident about 3 years ago, and her mother remarried about 1½ years ago.

It was recommended that Pat complete the 4-month residential program she now is attending. The program includes participation in adolescent-focused groups, female-specific groups, individual counseling, and peer-facilitated mutual aid groups (self-help groups). Her counseling sessions need to address loss issues related to her father's death and her abortion, developing non-drug-related coping skills, establishing a peer group supportive of healthy behaviors, and developing drug-refusal skills and assertive skills. Pat also needs to receive information about sexual behaviors and important precautions to reduce the risk of AIDS, another pregnancy, and STDs. Barriers to changing her sexual behaviors need to be addressed. Family counseling is also suggested to address issues concerning the addition of the stepfather into the family and establishing clear, consistent, and age-appropriate limits for their daughter.

RESOURCES

Self-Help/Mutual Aid Groups

❏ Alcoholics Anonymous (AA)
  General Service Office
  P.O. Box 459
  Grand Central Station
  New York, NY 10017
  (212) 686-1100
❏ Al-Anon/Alateen
  P.O. Box 862
  Midtown Station
  New York, NY 10018-0862
  (212) 302-7240

❏ Families Anonymous (FA)
  P.O. Box 344
  Torrance, CA 90501
  (213) 775-3211
❏ Parents Anonymous (PA)
  P.O. Box 2943
  Station A
  Champaign, IL 61820
  (217) 359-2350

Information and Referral Resources

AIDS

❏ AIDS Hotline/Public Health Service
  Office of Public Affairs
  200 Independence, SW
  Washington, DC 20201
  (800) 342-AIDS

❏ United States Public Health
  Services/Technical Information
  Services Center
  1600 Clifton Road
  Atlanta, GA 30333
  (800) 447-2437

Child Abuse

❏ Clearinghouse on Child Abuse and
  Neglect Information
  P.O. Box 1182
  Washington, DC 20013
  (301) 251-5157

❏ National Center on Child Abuse
  and Neglect Department of Health,
  Education, and Welfare
  Washington, DC 20201

General Health
❑ National Health Information
   Clearinghouse
   P.O. Box 1133
   Washington, DC 20013
   (800) 366-5683

Substance Abuse
❑ Just Say No Foundation
   1777 N. California
   Suite 200
   Walnut Creek, CA 94596
   (800) 258-2766

Suicide
❑ KIDSRIGHTS
   3700 Progress Blvd.
   Mount Dora, FL 32757
   (800) 892-KIDS
❑ National Adolescent Suicide Hotline
   3080 N. Lincoln Avenue
   Chicago, IL 60657
   (800) 621-4000

Pregnancy
❑ National Pregnancy Hotline
   (800) 852-5683

❑ National Institute on Drug Abuse
   5600 Fishers Lane
   Rockville, MD 20857
   (800) 662-4357

❑ Youth Suicide National Association
   1825 Eye Street, NW
   Suite 400
   Washington, DC 20006
   (202) 429-2016

PROBLEM PREVENTION AND SOCIAL INTERVENTIONS

Female children and adolescents are particularly appropriate targets for health education, health promotion, and risk-reduction efforts. First, childhood and adolescence are critical periods for the formation and consolidation of health-related attitudes, values, and behaviors (Vinal et al., 1986). Health-risk behavior patterns established during adolescence pose immediate and long-term risks. The deaths and disabilities occurring during these ages are to a large extent preventable because they are mostly the result of behavioral health-risk factors. Also, certain characteristics of adolescence (e.g., experimentation, peer influence, risk taking, perceived invulnerability) increase the likelihood that adolescents will experiment and possibly adopt health compromising behavior.

Many health education and promotion programs focus on total abstinence from activities posing health risks (e.g., abstinence from sexual activity, all drug use). There are other possible goals, however, that are more closely aligned with the developmental, behavioral, and social issues and realities of childhood. Based upon the assumption that normal adolescent development involves some experimentation with health-risk behaviors, Jessor (1984) proposed three strategies to reduce the health consequences of risk behaviors: minimization (e.g., controlled, moderate, or responsible involvement in the behavior), insulation (e.g., eliminating the serious, irreversible, or long-term consequences of experimentation), and delay of onset (postponing the initiation of health-risk behavior).

An additional factor to consider in developing health education and promotion programs for female children and adolescents is the focus of the program. Many health education and promotion programs for children and adolescents focus on a specific health behavior or concern (e.g., smoking). The empirical literature, however, points to a high correlation between health compromising behaviors. Therefore, health education programs should be more global in their orientation and focus on the constellation of health compromising behaviors practiced by children and adolescents. On the basis of his research findings that health-risk behaviors result from a pattern of personality, environmental, and behavioral factors, Jessor (1984) has suggested that health education programs address the multicausal nature of health-risk behavior.

The PRECEDE model (Predisposing, Reinforcing, and Enabling Causes in Educational Diagnosis and Evaluation) was developed by Green, Kreuter, Deeds, and Partridge (1980). The model provides a framework for developing health education and promotion programs. The three factors directly related to health behavior are predisposing factors, reinforcing factors, and enabling factors. Predisposing factors function to motivate a person to act; they include knowledge, attitudes, values, and perceptions related to health behaviors. Enabling factors allow a person to perform a health behavior; they include availability of resources, accessibility, referrals, and health-behavior skills. Reinforcing factors influence the maintenance of health behaviors; they include attitudes and behaviors of health professionals, peers, parents, and other people influential in the person's life. Green et al. (1980) suggested that the content of health education and promotion programs be based upon an assessment of these three factors as they relate to health behaviors of a given population.

SUMMARY AND CONCLUSIONS

It is no longer acceptable to discuss children's and adolescents' health-risk issues without reference to gender. The literature clearly demonstrates gender-related differences in mortality rates, health risks, and health issues and concerns. To develop effective health intervention strategies for females, it is critical that research of females' health issues increase in order to establish a knowledge base equivalent to that on males' health issues.

The level and type of health intervention also needs to consider the underlying factors contributing to health compromising behaviors. A female adolescent may be participating in health compromising behaviors as a reflection of psychological issues related to abuse or trauma, as age-appropriate experimentation, or as a part of a multiple problem behavior pattern. Different health-behavior interventions will be effective depending upon the etiology of the health-risk behavior.

Finally, we need to examine the expected goals of our health intervention strategies. Too often, health intervention goals are inconsistent with what we know about normal adolescent development and behavior (e.g., abstinence from sexual activity). To be effective in reducing health risks, our health intervention goals need to reflect an understanding of the group to which the intervention is directed.

REFERENCES

Bittner, S., & Newberger, E. (1981). Pediatric understanding of child abuse and neglect. *Pediatrics in Review*, 2, 197.

Bradshaw, J. (1988). *The family*. Deerfield Beach, FL: Health Communications, Inc.

Bradshaw, J. (1990). *Home coming: Reclaiming and championing your inner child*. New York: Bantam Books.

Browne, A., & Finkelhor, D. (1986). Impact of child sexual abuse: A review of the research. *Psychological Bulletin, 99*, 66–77.

Burgess, A. (1985). *The sexual victimization of adolescents*. Washington, DC: National Center for the Prevention and Control of Rape, (ADM) 85–1382.

Casey, R., & Berman, J. (1985). The outcome of psychotherapy with children. *Psychological Bulletin, 98*, 398–400.

Child Abuse Prevention and Treatment Act of 1974. (1974). Public Law 93-247 88 STAT.4. Laws of 93rd Congress 2nd Session. *U.S. Code Congressional and Administrative News, 1*, January 31, pp. 4–8.

Daro, D. (1988). *Confronting child abuse: Research for effective program design*. New York: Free Press.

DePanfilis, D. (1987). *Literature review of sexual abuse*. Washington, DC: National Center on Child Abuse and Neglect, (OHDS) 87-30530.

DiClemente, R., Zorn, J., & Temoshok, L. (1986). Adolescents and AIDS: A survey of knowledge, attitudes, and beliefs about AIDS in San Francisco. *American Journal of Public Health, 76*, 1443–1444.

DiClemente, R., Zorn, J., & Temoshok, L. (1987). The association of gender, ethnicity, and length of residence in the Bay area to adolescents' knowledge and attitudes about Acquired Immune Deficiency Syndrome. *Journal of Applied Social Psychology, 17*, 216–230.

Finkelhor, D. (1979). *Sexually vicitmized children*. New York: Free Press.

Finkelhor, D., & Baron, L. (1986). Risk factors for child sexual abuse. *Journal of Interpersonal Violence, 1*, 43–71.

Gelles, R. (1987). *Family Violence*. Newbury Park, NJ: Sage Publications.

Gil, D. (1971). Violence against children. *Journal of Marriage and Family, 33*, 637–657.

Green, L., Kreuter, M., Deeds, S., & Partridge, K. (1980). *Health education planning: A diagnostic approach*. Palo Alto, CA: Mayfield.

Hampton, R., & Newberger, E. (1985). Child abuse incidence and reporting by hospitals: Significance of severity, class, and race. *American Journal of Public Health, 75*, 56–60.

Hawton, K. (1986). Suicide in adolescents. In A. Roy (Ed.), *Suicide* (pp. 135–150). Baltimore: Williams and Wilkins.

Hein, K. (1984). The first pelvic examination and common gynecological problems in adolescent girls. *Women and Health, 9*, 47–63.

Hibbard, R., Ingersall, G., & Orr, D. (1990). Violent and abusive behavior: Behavioral risk, emotional risk, and child abuse among adolescents in a nonclinical setting. *Pediatrics, 86*, 896–901.

Institute of Medicine (1985). *Preventing low birth weight*. Washington, DC: National Academy Press.

Institute of Medicine (1990). *Healthy people year 2000: Citizens chart the course*. Washington, DC: National Academy Press.

Jessor, R. (1984). Adolescent development and behavioral health. In J. Matarazzo, S. Weis, J. Herd, N. Miller, & S. Weiss (Eds.), *Behavioral health: A handbook of health enhancement and disease prevention* (pp. 69–90). New York: John Wiley.

Jessor, R., & Jessor, S. (1977). *Problem behavior and psychosocial development: A longitudinal study of youth*. New York: Academic Press.

Johnston, L., O'Malley, P., & Bachman, J. (1988). *Illicit drug use, smoking, and drinking by America's high school students, college students, and young adults: 1975–1987*. Rockville, MD: National Institute on Drug Abuse.

Kazdin, A. (1990). Psychotherapy for children and adolescents. In M. Rosenzweig & L. Porter (Eds.), *Annual review of psychology* (pp. 21–54). Palo Alto, CA: Annual Reviews, Inc.

Kegeles, S., Adler, N., & Irwin, C. (1988). Sexually active adolescents and condoms: Changes over one year in knowledge, attitudes, and use. *American Journal of Public Health, 78*, 460–461.

Leon, G., & Dinklage, D. (1989). Obesity and anorexia nervosa. In T. Ollendick & M. Hersen (Eds.), *Handbook of child psychopathology* (2nd ed.) (pp. 247–264). New York: Plenum Press.

Lustig, N., Dresser, J., Spellman, S., & Murray, T. (1966). Incest: A family group survival pattern. *Archives of General Psychiatry, 14*, 31–40.

MacFarlane, K., & Lieber, L. (1978). *Parents Anonymous: The growth of an idea.* Washington, DC: National Center on Child Abuse and Neglect, (OHDS) 78-30086.

Mellody, P., Miller, A., & Miller, J. (1989). *Facing codependence.* New York: Harper and Row.

Miller, A. (1981). *The drama of the gifted child.* New York: Basic Books.

Miller, A. (1990). *Banished knowledge: Facing childhood injuries.* New York: Doubleday.

National Center for Health Statistics (1989). *Health United States: 1988.* Hyattsville, MD: Public Health Service, (PHS) 89-1232.

National Center for Health Statistics (1990a). *Advance report of final mortality statistics, 1988. Monthly Vital Statistics Report, 39*(7), supplement. Hyattsville, MD: Public Health Service, DHHS Pub. No. (PHS) 91-1120.

National Center for Health Statistics (1990b). *Births, marriages, divorces, and deaths for June 1990. Monthly Vital Statistics Report, 39*(6). Hyattsville, MD: Public Health Service, DHHS Pub. No. (PHS) 90-1120.

National Center for Health Statistics (1990c). *Health United States, 1989 and preventive profile.* Hyattsville, MD: Public Health Service, DHHS Pub. No. (PHS) 90-1232.

National Center on Child Abuse and Neglect (1988). *Study findings: Study of national incidence and prevalence of child abuse and neglect—1988.* Washington DC: U.S. Government Printing Office.

National Institute on Drug Abuse (1985). *National household survey on drug abuse: Main findings 1985.* Rockville, MD: Author, (ADM) 88-1586.

Orbach, I. (1988). *Children who don't want to live.* San Francisco, CA: Jossey-Bass.

Public Health Service (1989). *Promoting health/preventing disease: Year 2000 objectives for the nation.* Washington, DC: U.S. Department of Health and Human Services.

Russell, D. (1984). The prevalence and seriousness of incestuous abuse: Stepfathers vs. biological fathers. *Child Abuse and Neglect, 8*, 15–22.

Shirk, S. (1988). The interpersonal legacy of physical abuse of children. In M. Strauss (Ed.), *Abuse and victimization across the life span* (pp. 57–81). Baltimore: The Johns Hopkins University Press.

Strauss, M. B. (1988). Abused adolescents. In M. B. Strauss (Ed.), *Abuse and victimization across the life span.* Baltimore, MD: The Johns Hopkins University Press, pp. 107–123.

Tuma, J. (1989). Traditional therapies with children. In T. Ollendick & M. Hersen (Eds.), *Handbook of child psychopathology* (2nd ed.) (pp. 419–437). New York: Plenum Press.

Vinal, D., Wellman, C., Tyser, K., Stites, I., Leaf, J., Larson, A., & Graves, J. (1986). A determination of the health-protective behaviors of female adolescents: A pilot study. *Adolescence, 21*, 87–105.

White, K., Snyder, J., Bourne, R., & Newberger, E. (1989). *Treating child abuse and family violence in hospitals.* Lexington, MA: Lexington Books.

Wissow, L. (1990). *Child advocacy for the clinician: An approach to child abuse and neglect.* Baltimore: Williams and Wilkins.

Wolfe, D., & St. Pierre, J. (1989). Child abuse and neglect. In T. Ollendick & M. Hersen (Eds.), *Handbook of child psychopathology* (2nd ed.) (pp. 377–398). New York: Plenum Press.

Part Three

ADULT WOMANHOOD

5

Beyond the Mommy Track: The Adult Woman's Career Development

Loretta J. Bradley
Texas Tech University

Linda B. Rudolph and Susan Kupisch
Austin Peay State University

CAREER DEVELOPMENT ISSUES FACING ADULT WOMEN

Balancing Home and Career

> *Men Produce and Women Reproduce.*
> *This is a man's job—this is a woman's job.*
> *Men go out and make the living.*
> *Women stay home and care for the family.*

These stereotypes about women and work have pervaded American society for decades. It is unfortunate that women have been placed into one track and men into another (higher) track. Basically, women are in a mommy track and men in a work track. Yet a close perusal of work indicates that it does not have to be dichotomized as his or hers.

Prior to the industrialization of America, most Americans lived in an agrarian society where work responsibilities were shared by men and women. Women worked with the men in the fields, and both cared for the animals and gardens. In families where businesses and shops were owned, women and men operated the business together. In the home, women and men shared the responsibility for child care, with women being more responsible for the younger children and girls while men assumed more responsibility for the boys. In the preindustrial era, the woman's active participation in the economic life of the family was not only feasible but necessary; every person was needed to provide food, clothing, and shelter.

With the coming of the industrial revolution, the relationship between work and family changed. The industrial revolution emphasized specialization and mass production in a factory setting. Quickly the factory replaced the home as a work center. Because labor was centralized in factories, the woman's role of mother was separated from her role as economic provider. In most instances the two roles were alienated, thus dichotomizing the work roles of men and women. Consequently, important issues arose about who would care for the children and who would work outside the home. As Gibson and Fast (1986) wrote, "Women had to choose between supervising their children and contributing to the economic support of their families. Society decreed that their primary responsibility was the former" (p. 52).

For many women, there wasn't really a choice. It was expected that the woman's major duty was to stay home and care for the family—at least that was the expectation for those who could afford to stay home. Economic need forced some women to enter the paid work force. Their numbers are reflected in the 1850 Census, which estimated that more than 250,000 women worked in factories, with this number increasing to 330,000 by 1870. By 1900 about 20% of women 14 years and older were in the paid labor force (Gibson & Fast, 1986).

As a distinct middle class emerged, many women no longer had to work for economic gain, yet many wanted to work to increase self-satisfaction, foster independence, and accumulate assets. For some women the need to get beyond their front gate was pressing; they saw a host of problems that were virtually ignored. Because paid work was not viewed as a viable option, many women volunteered their time to local hospitals and charities. Many became involved in the abolition and temperance movements, while others campaigned for women's suffrage. Some women tried to enter the professions; while a few were successful, most met resistance.

Although many women entered the paid work force during World War II, most returned home when the men returned from the war. In the decade following World War II, work-saving devices in the home became widespread. No longer did women have to spend hours laundering, canning foods, and sewing clothes; these items could be purchased "ready made." Women became consumers, not producers. In addition, laws required children's school attendance, and thus children were in school most of the day. These changes wove a new pattern for the American woman, a pattern that relieved her from many home responsibilities. Consequently, since World War II women have entered the paid labor force in unprecedented numbers.

Changes in the Work Force

One of the most striking changes in the character of the current labor force is the increase in the employment of women. As Table 5.1 illustrates, in 1900, 18.8% of women

Table 5.1
Women in the Labor Force

Year	Number of Women (Thousands)	Percent of Women (16 yrs & older)
1900	5,319	18.8
1920	8,637	21.4
1940	12,845	25.4
1960	23,268	37.8
1970	31,580	43.4
1980	45,611	51.6
1988	54,904	56.6

Source: Adapted from *Information Please Almanac: Atlas & Yearbook*, 1990, Boston: Houghton Mifflin.

16 years and older were in the labor force. Forty years later, 25.4% were working for pay. Since 1940 the number has risen steadily; by 1980, more than half (51.6%) of the women were in the labor force. In 1988, 56.6% of women were employed for pay.

The figures are even more striking for mothers working for pay. In 1940, less than 15% of mothers with young children were working outside the home (Kiger, 1984). In 1969, for the first time in history, a majority of American mothers of school age children held paid jobs (Papalia & Olds, 1989). As Table 5.2 illustrates, 56.1% of mothers with children under 6 years were working for pay in 1988, while 73.3% of mothers with children 6 to 17 years were in the paid labor force. This is a dramatic change from 1955, when the percentages were 18.2 and 38.4, respectively.

When the data were analyzed by geographic area, Gibson and Fast (1986) found that the highest percentages of mothers with children under 6 years old working for pay were in the deep South, while the lowest percentages were found in Utah and certain northeastern states (Pennsylvania, New York and Massachusetts). While the South and New England had the highest percentages of working wives, the lowest percentages were found in West Virginia, Kentucky, Pennsylvania, Ohio, Michigan, and Utah.

Despite the rapid increase in the percentage of women in the paid labor force, women continue to work in traditionally female occupations. In the 19th century, women were employed as seamstresses and domestic servants. In the late 19th and early 20th centuries, teaching and clerical work were women's occupations (Gibson & Fast, 1986), although these jobs were usually held by Anglo women. Black women were mainly found in the labor force as servants in private households and retail sales positions. Black women dramatically increased their numbers in the professions between 1960 and 1981.

Current data support the basic trends described earlier. In 1988, 44.6% of employed women were employed in technical, sales, and administrative support with 25.2% in managerial and professional careers. Almost 18% were in service occupations with 8.9% working as operators, fabricators, and laborers. Only 2.3% were in precision production craft and repair while 1.1% were in farming, forestry, and fishing (*Information Please Almanac*, 1990).   In contrast, few men are found in lower paying service and clerical

Table 5.2
Mothers in the Labor Force

Year	With Children 6 to 17 Years	With Children 6 Years or Less
1955	38.4	18.2
1965	45.7	25.3
1975	54.8	38.9
1980	64.4	46.6
1985	69.9	53.5
1988	73.3	56.1

Source: Adapted from *Information Please: Almanac Atlas & Yearbook*, 1990, Boston: Houghton Mifflin.

work. Instead, men are usually found in the higher salaried professional, managerial positions, and skilled blue collar trades (Gibson & Fast, 1986). Although women have made inroads into traditionally all-male occupations, their progress is slow.

Since World War II, the most dramatic change in the work force has been the increase of married women. In the course of two generations, combining work and family has become a viable lifestyle for the American woman. Despite this trend, career and homemaking are still often viewed as competing roles.

In evaluating the impact of work on the lives of women, Dabrowski (1984) reported that "employed mothers have higher self-esteem, better self-images, more readily accept themselves, and display fewer physical symptoms than do homemakers" (p. 63). In studying a group of working class women living with their husbands and having at least one child in first or second grade, Stokes and Peyton (1986) reported "those women employed outside the home were more satisfied with their lives, had higher self-esteem, and fewer psychiatric symptoms than full-time homemakers" (p. 301). Similarly, Barnett and Baruch (1985) concluded that "employment outside the home has positive psychological consequences for women both as a source for enhancing well-being and as a buffer against stress from other roles" (p. 137).

Multiple Roles

Despite the many positive aspects of working, all is not bliss for the American woman working outside the home, especially for the woman trying to balance career and family. In studying the relationship between multiple roles and distress, Barnett and Baruch (1985) reported that the role of mother, not wife or paid worker, accounts for most of the role overload. Mothers experienced more role conflict than childless women. Highly educated women employed outside the home experienced more role conflict than their less well-educated counterparts. In discussing their findings, the researchers concluded, "The role of parent rather than that of paid worker is the major source of stress for women in the middle years" (p. 143).

Piotrkowski and Katz (1982) reported that the quality of work life is linked to the quality of both marital and parent-child relationships. Kandel, Davis, and Raveis (1985) concluded that in married women who were mothers marital stress was less positively correlated with depression among employed than unemployed women. On the other hand, work related stress was more highly correlated with depression among mothers than nonmothers. The researchers concluded that work reduces the effects of marital stress but parenthood exacerbates the effects of work related stress. Similarly, Cleary and Mechanic (1983) found that the correlation between marital dissatisfaction and depression is lower in employed than unemployed women. In contrast, parental dissatisfaction was strongly correlated to depression in employed women. Studying English women, Brown, Bhrolchain, and Harris (1975) found that among women without close confidants and exposed to stressful events, only 14% of employed women experienced psychiatric symptoms as compared to 79% of women who were not employed.

Despite the positive aspects of balancing home and career, women report work overload and role conflict. These conflicts are described in the following case of Janet.

Janet is at her office and has just heard that her faculty meeting has been cancelled. She is glad that she has 2 extra hours. Her calendar is so full each day that she seldom has any time for herself at work. Sadly, this situation repeats itself when she arrives home, for she is pulled in various directions by her husband and children. Janet asks, "What would I really like to do with these 2 hours?" She knows she would enjoy getting together at lunch with a close friend. She gives this some thought and concludes, "but what I really should do is go to the mall and purchase some back-to-school clothes for the children. I haven't had much time to attend to their needs." Janet decides to shop for the children's clothes.

Janet experienced conflict between what she wanted to do and what she told herself she should do. Like many women, Janet had assumed the additional role of provider without a commensurate reduction in her child rearing role (Bird, Bird, & Scruggs, 1984; House, 1986). While her husband helped with the children, he did not devote as much time to their family as Janet did.

Although results of studies comparing the time women spend in household labor and child care versus the time men spend vary, the trend is universal. Stokes and Peyton (1986) reported that women who work full time still perform more than 75% of the housework and more than 50% of the child care. Shelton (1990) found that women with preschool age children spend 15.0 hours per week in household labor and 10.2 hours in child care. Men spend 8.2 hours and 2.8 hours, respectively. Women employed full time with school age children spend 18.9 hours on household labor and 2.7 hours on child care, whereas men spend 11.7 hours and 1.1 hours, respectively. Gaddy, Glass, and Arnkoff (1983) found that husbands spend an average of 7.41 hours a week with their children, while mothers spend 17.85 hours.

Some researchers (Juster, 1985; Robinson, 1988) have reported that men have been spending more time on household tasks in recent years, while other researchers (Coverman, 1985; Coverman & Sheley, 1986; Sanik, 1981) concluded that men's time commitment has not changed appreciably. Despite some controversy regarding the amount of time men spend on household tasks, women, whether employed or unemployed, performed the majority of household tasks (Campbell, 1988; Ragins & Sundstrom, 1989). Furthermore, men and women spend their time differently on these tasks.

> Women prepare dinner and wash dishes; men dry dishes and run errands....Employed women do more housework and child care tasks in the morning than do their husbands and they accomplish the housework and child care while doing other things (e.g., eating breakfast). (Shelton, 1990, p. 119)

Although studies across race are sparse, Miller and Garrison (1982) cited research indicating that black husbands do more household chores than their white counterparts. Preferences for traditional differentiation of household roles are higher for Chicanos than for Anglos and relatively higher for Chicano women than Chicano men. Black males are less traditional than white males in their preferences for allocating household roles. The researchers further reported that a "husband's income is the best prediction of shared housework; controlling for race, wife's education, and wife's employment, high income husbands are less likely to share in the housework than are low income husbands" (p. 241). In families with three or more children, Miller and Garrison (1982) reported that there is more sharing of the housekeeper role. However, in the largest families, those with five or more children, there is less role sharing, and there is no direct effect of children under 12 years old on the household sharing of work when race, husband's income, and employment status are controlled.

In summary, while there appear to be changes in role sharing, women's employment does not produce role equity. Given the inequity in the woman's dual role, an obvious question arises: How can a more equitable balance be achieved? Although initially this may seem like a simple question, its solution represents a very complex process flanked by decades of tradition in which the role of mother has more obligations than privileges.

Equitable Balance of Roles

Child rearing is the arena presenting the greatest problem for the dual career woman. An egalitarian marriage where responsibility for children and household tasks were equally shared would enhance the women's pursuit of the roles of homemaker and paid worker. Researchers (Gaddy et al., 1983; Price-Bonham & Murphy, 1980; Rapoport & Rapoport, 1973; Rice, 1979) have reported that successful women with high career aspirations had husbands who supported their careers.

Family constraints more negatively affect women's careers than men's. In recent years, alternative structures have appeared in the life cycle patterns of women. Many of these patterns have allowed women to more adequately balance their dual roles. One obvious change is the marked decline in the number of children, resulting in a smaller family size and less time required for mothering. This "extra" time has been transferred to other roles. A second change is the later onset of pregnancy, with delayed motherhood associated with higher education and increased labor force participation (Gerson, Alpert, & Richardson, 1984; Richman, 1988; Schwartz, 1989a; Wilkie, 1981). Another change is the number of married women who are electing to remain childless (Bram, 1984; Lott, 1973). While there are various reasons for this decision, many women view career and child rearing as competitive roles. Some women have decided that the balancing of career and child rearing presents too many obstacles to undertake.

To be successful in balancing home and career, employed mothers need good child care, which is often a difficult service to find. One way to combat the child care issue is to employ a housekeeper who either lives in or is available during the hours that the employed mother works. For some women this is an option but for most, a full time housekeeper is out of the question. Gerson et al., (1984) reported that half of the child care for children of working mothers is done by family members; this is much more frequent among black and Hispanic families. Approximately one-fourth of children are cared for by a sister or friend. While there are various reasons for the selection of family or friend as the major caretaker, money is likely an issue; many women cannot afford outside help. The choice of child care for poor mothers, which includes the mothers of more than 25% of white American children and 50% of black American children, is prohibitive. For this group, preferred child care is not an option. It remains an option for only a select few, usually the employed woman working in a professional or managerial position.

Another option for child care is the day-care center. The number of children being cared for in day-care centers is increasing, although not every mother can afford day-care, nor is it available to all mothers. Even among those for whom day-care is an option, many mothers express concerns about the effects of day-care centers on their children. Some of the concerns center on the child's exposure to different values, poor relationships, or communicable diseases. Further, mothers are concerned about the development of bonding between mother and child, although research has not found any significant differences between bonding among employed and unemployed mothers.

Despite the concerns, day-care centers provide a viable service for working mothers. Progressive companies are locating day-care centers at the work site, thus making day-care a part of their fringe benefit package. The convenience of having the child at the site where the parent, usually mother, is employed allows time with the child during the workday as well as during travel to and from work each day. Day-care centers usually offer more than baby-sitting; they assist children in developing interpersonal relationships and stimulate learning activities. In addition, some progressive companies are providing day-care for sick children. As primary caretaker, one of the major concerns of the employed mother is the care of the child when he or she is ill.

Another support that enhances the integration of home and career roles is the concept of the flexible work schedule. In its simplest form, flexibility is the time to take off a few hours a day or week to do work at home or to complete important tasks away from the work site. A creative program called *flextime* allows employees to determine the hours that they work each day as long as the hours total a specific number each week. Other innovative practices include parental leave for mothers and fathers, sabbaticals, shorter work weeks, part-time work sharing, and career relocation counseling for the "tied spouse," the spouse who moves when the other spouse moves. These programs offer assistance to the employed woman and her family as they find ways "to help the worker adapt to the family and not the family to the work" (Hansen, 1987, p. 127).

In addition to company support, other services helpful to the employed woman have been initiated. A woman in Wisconsin established Chicken Soup, Inc., to provide child care for sick children. This company picks up children from school and cares for them until the parent returns. Some orthodontists have a van service that transports school children to their appointments. Likewise, a woman in New York established an after-school transportation service to take children to sports practices and games, ballet lessons, piano lessons, birthday parties, and so on. Another support, perhaps one too often overlooked by employed women, is the relationships with supervisors, peers, and subordinates (Campbell, 1988; Ragins & Sundstrom, 1989). These relationships can provide invaluable encouragement and support as well as enhance the woman's credibility within the organization. Ragins and Sundstrom (1989) cited several studies indicating that successful female managers recognized the importance of mentors for their careers. Although most mentoring research has been conducted in business and industry, Busch (1985) reported on mentoring in graduate schools. Her research, like that in business and industry, found that mentoring can be an important variable in a successful career.

In summary, traditional role expectations create barriers for women trying to balance family and career. While much progress has been made in recent years, family and career roles still remain more competitive than cooperative.

Equity in the Work Place

Since the 1960s business and industry have been under legal and moral pressures to eliminate inequities among workers, especially those affecting minorities and women. Inequity takes many forms, including restriction of opportunities for employment and advancement, disparate treatment within the organization (such as harassment, discrimination, and parental leave policies), and salary differences.

Title VII of the Civil Rights Act of 1964 prohibits discrimination on the basis of sex, including the hiring, firing, training, program entry, transfer, and promotion of employees. The law also bans sexual harassment and the discrimination of employees on the basis of pregnancy, childbirth, or related conditions. The Equal Pay Act of 1963 makes it illegal to pay personnel differentially based on gender. Persons responsible for the same type of work at the same level of employment, based on skill, effort, responsibility, and working conditions, must be paid on the same pay schedule and receive equal benefits. Executive Order 11246 prohibits organizations with federal contracts from discriminating against employees or job applicants. Through this order, organizations must validate personnel policies and staffing, reflecting integration of personnel.

Although these laws were passed over 20 years ago and the courts have upheld the legislation, many cases of discrimination are still reported. A substantial number of complaints filed with the Equal Employment Opportunity Commission under Title VII of the Civil Rights Act are related to pay, promotion, and occupational discrimination related to gender (Fischer, 1987).

Most data indicate that women in today's work place continue to be employed in dead-end jobs, earn lower pay, and receive limited benefits compared with men. Women work in helper and support related careers; men are more likely to work in supervisory or blue collar jobs. Today's skilled trade and craft workers are also men, as they have been historically. Men still hold most management positions, even in traditionally female occupations. In 1986, only 2 of the 500 largest industrial and 500 largest service companies had women CEO's; in one case the family controlled the company stock, and the other shared the job title with her husband. In spite of many pressures for change, job segregation is still the norm.

Women earn about 68 cents for every dollar earned by men. Even in the same occupation, women typically have lower salaries. The disparity in income has not changed significantly for more than 30 years. Sorensen (1987) reported that "in 1983, full-time female workers earned only 64% as much as full-time male workers—the same ratio as 1955" (p. 227). In 1988–1989, this ratio was 68.2% according to statistics published in *The American Woman 1988-89: A Status Report* (Rix, 1988). Larwood and Gattiker (1989) concluded from their review of male and female career patterns that a substantial amount of data verifies the existence of a gender-differentiated job market.

Those jobs considered "women's work" usually have paid salaries considerably lower than male jobs of comparable value. In recent years, there have been efforts to implement "comparable worth" policies to reduce the disparity between men's and women's earnings. According to Smith (1988), those who support comparable worth seek equality of pay for jobs performed by men and women considered to be of "equal worth" to the employer. Sorensen (1987) studied the impact of a comparable worth policy in five locations, and her initial results suggested that comparable worth policies would have significant positive effects on women's earnings. Smith (1988), however, argued that legislation would cover only certain groups of women, such as those employed by governmental or large private employers in female-dominated jobs. Noncovered workers would lose under these policies. The total effect of comparable worth policies continues to be controversial, and legislation mandating equal pay based on this concept is not likely to be enacted at an early date.

Women may encounter their first job discrimination when they apply for a job. According to Ragins and Sundstrom (1989), there is some evidence that, because of the "good old boy" network, men have more information about job openings, especially those at higher levels. Biased attitudes from those in power, ordinarily white males, may favor employees who are similar—other white males. We have all heard stories about the woman who was pushy on the job, difficult in the office, did not have the respect of co-workers, or got pregnant and wanted maternity leave at the wrong time. It is less threatening to hire Charlie, a friend of Fred's and a "regular guy," than to risk coping with gender differences. Hiring Charlie will not disrupt the team.

Even if employment is based on submission of resumes and interviews, resumes from male applicants tend to be rated higher, especially in traditionally male-dominated fields. Because they behave differently and have different work experiences, women may not be perceived as adequate for the position. They are often stereotyped as emotional, less stable, passive, indecisive, and more prone to health problems and absenteeism. Women may be seen as more committed to home and children than to career. Employers fear they are just working until they can marry or until a baby arrives. These stereotypical attitudes are more likely to be found among people who are traditional in attitudes, more authoritarian, less educated, and who have low self-esteem (Powell, 1988). Unfortunately, employers with these characteristics are plentiful, and they continue to interfere with women's attempts to advance in the job marketplace.

Even when a woman is successful in obtaining a position, it is probable that she will enter the ranks at a lower level than a male with similar credentials. Likewise, she will not advance as quickly as her male cohorts, even after several years (Ragins & Sundstrom, 1989). Women encounter additional barriers to their advancement as they seek promotion and higher level jobs. Feuer (1988) suggested several of these barriers;

for example, a more stringent set of behaviors is required for women in higher status and management positions, and they are expected to become more male-like to succeed. They are watched more closely, and it is easier for them to be criticized or "fall from grace." They are not expected to be as competent as their male counterparts; therefore, they must be better in order to justify their holding a "male" position.

For many years power has been in the hands of men; they hold lower expectations of women's ability to lead in organizations (Feuer, 1988). Thus, women are pigeonholed in traditional, gender-stereotyped jobs, offering little power or opportunity for advancement. They are not part of the male mentoring system, not expected to fraternize with the males other than in traditional relationships, and have few appropriate and successful role models.

Management training, mentoring, and back-room advice are not always available to women seeking higher level positions. The view that managerial, supervisory, and power require decision making and problem solving skills not possessed by women impedes women's advancement, although research has found no gender differences to support this contention. Many males continue to resist the idea that men should work for women managers, supervisors, or leaders. Morrison and Glinow (1990) contended that there is strong evidence that white women and people of color encounter a "glass ceiling" as they attempt to enter management positions. Morrison, White, and Velsor (1987) concluded from their data and that of The Center for Creative Leadership that:

> Many women have paid their dues, even a premium, for a chance at a top position, only to find a glass ceiling between them and their goal. The glass ceiling is not simply a barrier for an individual, based on the person's ability to handle a higher level job. Rather the glass ceiling applies to women as a group who are kept from advancing higher because they are women (p. 13).

They further reported that should women break the glass ceiling, they may then hit a "wall of tradition and stereotype that separates them from the top executive level" (p. 14), the area of greatest power.

Women who advance in organizations may be placed in positions with little authority or decision making. Their titles often reflect this status, such as assistant to the president or assistant vice president, or they may head a female-oriented division such as personnel, office management, human resources, or food services rather than finance, production, or engineering (Powell, 1988). Seldom are they found in powerful positions where direction is determined and major financial decisions are made.

Women who forge ahead and strive beyond traditional roles face some degree of discomfort. Their presence may illicit distrust or benign assumptions about their motives. They are watched with a more suspicious eye because they are different. To be successful they must learn rules of behavior that conflict with the socialized roles women learn in youth. They must be comfortable with self as a female, yet overcome gender to succeed. It is a narrow road where errors are noted quickly. If too uncomfortable, women may defend themselves by attacking others or slipping back into the comfortable female role of the status quo.

Powell (1988) summarized factors he believes continue to contribute to problems for women in the work place:

1. Males who have not worked with females in the work place rely on old assumptions.
2. Males protect the status quo in the reward/opportunities structure.
3. Institutional policies have not been changed to reflect equity among workers.
4. Leaders may make decisions that are best for them, not what is equally fair.
5. Men and women do not fully understand or accept gender-related behavioral differences.
6. Women's passivity serves to their detriment in the work place; they are conditioned to give in to males.
7. Women may not be ready for entry into some positions due to limited background experiences.
8. The labor market is competitive in areas of high demand.
9. People resist change unless it is to their obvious benefit.

A discussion of women in the work place would not be complete without some reference to Felice Schwartz's suggestion to business and industry that they create a two-track career path for women: one for women interested in pursuing a career and foregoing child rearing and a new career path for "career-and-family" women, which has been called the "mommy track." Strong protests and accusations of traitor to the women's movement were heard at this suggestion (Hopkins, 1990). In her articles, Schwartz (1989a, 1989b) recognized the many barriers to women's career advancement as well as the fact that men do not always understand successful women. Her arguments were based on the projected need for both types of women to provide for the work force of the future.

Castro (1990) pointed out that having children can definitely affect career mobility and advancement, suggesting that employers may categorize working women into two categories: mothers and achievers. Castro, like Schwartz, suggested that working mothers be placed in gentler career paths where they are not pressured to compete and where they are given the convenience of flexible time schedules to accommodate children's schedules. Only the women who are willing to sacrifice family would be viewed as executive types. Female manager turnover is higher than male, possibly due to the conflicting pressures of job and family. Liberated from the apron string but not the umbilical cord, mothers may accept the helpful benefits of the mommy track while sacrificing career and lifestyle opportunities in the future.

The "mommy track" is an extremely controversial idea. Some believe that the suggestion once again will place women in a second-class position, reinforcing the idea that they were never meant for full-time employment; others find the idea a comforting alternative to balancing home, children, and job, arguing that multiple roles may conflict and create a pressure that can be resolved only by reducing investment in one of them. On the other hand, research has shown that married women are more satisfied with their jobs than single women, suggesting that role accumulation can be positive, if not too overwhelming. The strains of combining marital and work responsibilities can be compensated for by feelings of gratification both at home and work.

Although the mommy track may be one solution for some, it is not an acceptable alternative to all women. However, the problem of assisting women with dual roles must be confronted. Women are increasingly involved in the work place. Currently 43% of the work force are women, and the majority of them are married. By the turn of the century, it is estimated that 75% of all families will be two-career families. Guinn (1989) projected that white males will make up only 15% of the available new workers by the millennium and that the dominant worker will be female, married, and of childbearing age. Companies requiring new workers will be faced with the need to change to attract and keep the new worker, who will have different characteristics from the typical worker of the past.

As long as women are expected to jump off the career track to deal with family responsibilities, they will be at a strong disadvantage in the work place (Rix & Stone, 1984). Working mothers have to make decisions that often limit career advancement, particularly when they compete with males for the same positions. Since the years of child rearing are the most crucial years for job competition and struggles for the fewer upper-level positions, women limit their movement up the ladder. The corporate world and professional arenas do not change policies or expectancies to accommodate the pressure of working mothers (Rix & Stone, 1984). The norm has been based on the male employee in the traditional role, one not considerate of family demands.

Sexual harassment, a form of sexual discrimination, continues to be a very real issue with which women must cope in the organizational climate. In 1980, the U.S. Equal Employment Opportunity Commission (EEOC) defined sexual harassment as:

> Unwelcome sexual advances, requests for sexual favors, and other verbal or physical conduct of a sexual nature constitute sexual harassment when (1) submission to such conduct is made either explicitly or implicitly a term or condition of an individual's employment, (2) submission to or rejection of such conduct by an individual is used as the basis for employment decisions affecting the individual, or (3) such conduct has the purpose or effect of unreasonably interfering with an individual's work performance or creating an intimidating, hostile, or offensive working environment.

Such behavior is a violation of Title VII of the Civil Rights Act of 1964, as amended, and Title IX of the Education Amendments of 1972. Based on this legislation, many employers have established policies prohibiting sexual harassment and established procedures for addressing complaints. Policies and procedures do not necessarily remedy the problem. Survey data indicate that about 70% of women experience sexual harassment on the job, and some authors think that as high as 95% of all complaints are not reported. Complaints range from touching inappropriately and lewd comments to demands for sexual intercourse. Such experiences leave women feeling embarrassed, angry, guilty, and ashamed, as well as intimidated and confused about what to do.

Because many complaints have been successfully resolved in the courts in favor of women, harassment and other forms of discrimination have become more subtle in recent years. Many of the attitudes continue, but remarks are not as overt and efforts to keep women out of certain activities are justified by "logical reasons" other than gender. Policies are in place, but not strongly supported; remarks are passed off as jokes; passive forms of exclusion are used such as retreating to the men's room to continue discussions during a meeting break; and suggestions by women that exclusion is occurring are greeted by accusations of being a "libber" or "too sensitive." Sexual harassment and sexual discrimination are difficult issues confronted by women. Many times there is no clear evidence of the behavior, and perceptions do differ. Only when organizations state policies clearly, provide leadership in modeling appropriate behaviors, educate employees by providing information on discrimination, and assist those who have experienced this trauma will the incidents begin to decrease.

Factors Influencing Women's Career Choices and Aspirations

"What do you want to be when you grow up, Johnny?" "I want to be a fireman or a doctor." "What do you want to be when you grow up, Janie?" "I want to be a mommy or a nurse." As young as 4 and 5 years of age, children are asked about their career goals. Although no assumption is made that children are ready to make career decisions or choose from the multitude of future opportunities, their answers reflect early socialization patterns that begin to shape the selective process of career development. Career issues are tied closely to gender identity and role stereotyping. For boys and girls, career aspirations typically are different. Even when some girls aspire or dream about nontraditional fields, they perceive constraints in reaching those aspirations and goals early in adolescence. They begin to think they cannot do the same things that boys can, and aspirations are lowered (Marini & Brinton, 1984).

Personal factors in decisions concerning work have changed over the past 40 years (Powell, 1988). Age, race, and ethnicity are still correlated, however, with one's likelihood to work and the type of work atmosphere. Education significantly affects job type and status. Family conditions, including presence of a husband, his attitude toward work, age, and number of children also have an impact upon a woman's likelihood to work and level of responsibility.

Larwood and Gattiker (1989) have suggested that women's career development differs due to social factors that affect their lives, such as gender role stereotypes, family expectations, job discrimination, entry level jobs available, the reward structure of organizations, and birth control options. King (1989) believes that one tends to shape a career within existing environmental constraints. While boys are free to explore any career for which they have the ability and interest, girls are more dependent upon mother for direction and are more likely to restrict opportunities in order to assure family cohesion. Their role has been defined as one of supporting men's careers by taking care of the home and family. They have been socialized to assume the nurturing role (Diamond, 1989). Whether working or not, women have the bulk of family responsibility for children, spouses, and dependent older family members. Few women have learned to expect anything different; knowing the expectations, they prepare for them appropriately.

The woman's own family may limit her choice and career aspirations. Women continue to handle the bulk of the home responsibilities, and the difficulty of balancing home, children, and career has been addressed earlier. Mobility may become an issue; men will move their families to achieve upward mobility, but few husbands will follow wives in their career paths. Women may choose to leave their career or avoid advancement because of the difficulties of handling all their responsibilities and the fear that advancement will bring more stress. Past trends have indicated that more women who obtain higher level managerial or executive positions tend to be single or divorced and have fewer children than men in comparable positions. Few men view marriage and family as constraints; in fact, these relationships probably contribute to male success.

Carol Gilligan (1982) addressed female development issues and contends that women follow a path of interpersonal relatedness and caring, whereas men follow a path of separateness and independent achievement. In the work place, women tend to view the work setting in terms of family and value high morale and approval, rather than situating themselves for leadership or promotion (Freeman, 1990).

COUNSELING STRATEGIES

Theories and Strategies for Women

Career development theory has received criticism, frequently for its failure to include women. Brooks (1984) wrote that "Existing theories were formulated primarily to explain the career development of men, and since women's career development is different from men's, the existing theories are inadequate" (p. 355).

Early attempts to include women in career theories were made by Psathas (1968), Super (1953), and Zytowski (1969). Super proposed his theory of career development as a five-stage developmental model. Although Super's original theory was based on his work with white males, he intended his theory to be applicable to both men and women. Super described four career patterns for men and seven for women. The seven for women were: stable homemaking, conventional (working followed by marriage), stable working, double-track (working while homemaking), interrupted (working, homemaking, and working, either while homemaking or having given up homemaking), unstable (recycling), and multiple trial (Super, 1984). Although Super was among the first to acknowledge the complexity of women's career paths, his patterns were criticized because they focused too heavily on the homemaker role. Clearly Super's idea of the implementation of self-concept as a "product of interaction of inherited aptitudes, physical makeup, opportunity to observe and play various roles and evaluations of the extent to which the results of role playing meet with the approval of superiors and fellows" (Super, 1990, p. 207) is applicable to women. It is the impact of the socialization process on the career choices of women that Super's theory does not adequately address. The early attempts of Psathas (1968) and Zytowski (1969) to explain the career development of women were also criticized because they did not adequately address the multiplicity of women's roles. Zytowski's nine postulates were criticized because he viewed the role of homemaker and paid worker as mutually exclusive; further he implied that women with high career commitments were deviant (Brooks, 1990).

There seems to be basic agreement that the career development of men and women differs. Agreement ends and disagreement begins when career patterns are explained. Methods to develop theory to explain the career development of women have resulted from three approaches. Brooks (1990) described the approaches as:

One approach has been to apply a theory from one realm to another. Hackett and Betz's (1981) application of self-efficacy theory to vocational behavior is an example....A second approach is to create a new theory....Astin's (1984) and Gottfredson's (1981) attempts are examples....A third approach is to suggest ways in which additional concepts can be incorporated into existing theory. Forrest and Mikolaitis's (1986) relational identity model is an example of this approach. (pp. 365-366)

Other models to explain the career development of women have been proposed by Farmer (1985) and Betz and Fitzgerald (1987). These models will be discussed later in this chapter.

Self-Efficacy

Hackett and Betz (1981) proposed a self-efficacy approach to understanding the career development of women. Their approach used the social learning theory developed by Bandura (1977) to conceptualize women's career behavior. According to Bandura, a sense of efficacy is the conviction that one can successfully execute a behavior required to produce a specific outcome. Self-efficacy implies that individuals will attempt behaviors which they believe they can perform and avoid those behaviors they believe they are unable to perform.

Bandura (1982) described perceived self-efficacy as influencing behavior in three ways:

> It influences (1) the choice of activities to be engaged in, (2) the quality of an individual's performance, and (3) persistence in difficult tasks. It also helps a person withstand failure. Individuals who do not possess a sense of efficacy typically dwell on personal deficiencies and believe that potential obstacles are formidable. (p. 122)

In describing self-efficacy, Bandura (1982) concluded: "Perceived self-efficacy involves self-appraisal; it is not a fixed act or simply a matter of knowing what to do" (p. 122). In discussing perceived self-efficacy, Bandura stated that men considered themselves efficacious for careers traditionally held by both men and women. In contrast, women considered themselves efficacious for careers traditionally held by women.

Low self-efficacy expectations often prevent an individual from attempting a task while high self-efficacy encourages the individual to attempt a task. Using this concept, Hackett and Betz (1981) hypothesized that self-efficacy is a major determinant in career choice and behavior. According to their model;

> The continuing limited and disadvantaged position of women in the labor force and the limited range of career options from which most women choose may be due, at least in part to differential expectations of self-efficacy among women versus men. In other words, the lack of behaviors that would facilitate women's pursuit of and achievements in careers correspondent with their individual capabilities and talents is postulated to be due to the lack of strong expectations of personal efficacy in relation to career related behaviors....Low or weak expectations of self-efficacy are viewed as a major means by which barriers to women classified as internal are manifested in career related behaviors. External barriers to women, e.g., discrimination, sexual harassment and lack of support systems, represent obstacles which require strong self-efficacy expectations to surmount. (p. 329)

Hackett and Betz (1981) discussed four sources of information pertinent to the development of efficacy expectations: (a) performance accomplishments (men are more likely to have gained accomplishments in a wider variety of areas), (b) vicarious learning (women have limited representation in nontraditional roles as portrayed in the media and educational materials), (c) emotional arousal (women score higher on anxiety measures with high levels of anxiety being debilitating for both performance and efficacy), and (d) verbal persuasion (males have received more encouragement for career pursuits than women). Mainly resulting from the socialization process, information from the four sources is less accessible to women than men. In their model, Hackett and Betz hypothesized that the strength of efficacy may be particularly important in the career development of women.

In a later study, Betz and Hackett (1983) found math self-efficacy to be related to the extent students selected science-based college majors. College males had higher math self-efficacy than college women; in turn, college males more often chose science-based college majors. Math aptitude did not predict the major; however, math self-efficacy combined with gender, number of years of high school math, and math anxiety significantly predicted college major. Taylor and Betz (1983) found self-efficacy to be significantly related to career indecision. Moreover, high self-efficacy was significantly correlated with decisiveness, and self-efficacy was not related to academic ability.

In studying women's efficacy expectations, Campbell and Hackett (1986) found women's self-efficacy to be more strongly affected by success and failure than men's self-efficacy. Women more often than men attributed success to luck, while failure was attributed to lack of ability. O'Hare and Beutell (1987) also found men scored significantly higher on self-efficacy than women; they concluded men approached the career decision making process as though it were a challenge.

With regard to empowerment strategies to enhance self-efficacy, Lent and Hackett (1987) suggested:

> Societal beliefs and expectations transmitted to women via socialization experiences, may pose strong barriers through their effects on self-efficacy cognitions. Percepts of personal efficacy were seen as an important mechanism through which differential sex-role socialization experiences affect the career development of women. To the extent that traditional socialization experiences foster biased exposure to sources of information for acquiring efficacy expectations, many women may develop strong efficacy beliefs regarding their ability to succeed at nontraditional (male-dominated) career pursuits. In effect, self-efficacy beliefs may then serve as potential internal barriers to women's career choices and achievements. (p. 368)

Strategies to increase self-efficacy include training to expand women's perceived career options and enrolling in math and science classes to keep a wider variety of career options open. Moreover, self-efficacy training should involve minorities and individuals with disabilities. These individuals may receive inadequate or biased information about careers. Reentry counseling and preretirement counseling with women should include self-efficacy strategies, for at this stage of career development women often receive discouragement about what they can do.

Self-Concept

In developing a theory of occupational aspirations, Gottfredson (1981) advocated that "the importance of social class, intelligence, and sex are often taken for granted" (p. 545). Gottfredson's theory tried to systematically explain their importance. She believes that self-concept is a useful link for understanding the process and approaches related to career development. Gottfredson described four stages in the development of self-concept: orientation to size and power, to sex roles, to social valuation, and to the internal, unique self. In describing orientation to sex roles, Gottfredson (1981) wrote:

It is only in Stage 2 [6–8 years] that they begin to grasp the concept of sex roles....Sex role stereotypes appear to develop in the same way that occupational images do....Consensus on sex stereotypes among children occurs despite known variability in parental role behavior....Differences in intelligence and developmental level would therefore be expected to be associated with more androgynous interests, and this does seem to be the case because people who aspire to high-level jobs have less sex-typed interests than people who aspire to low-level ones. (p. 560)

Brooks (1990) concluded, "Gottfredson's explanation of why women are in lower-status, lower-level positions is that these occupations are compatible with their self-concepts and views about accessibility" (p. 376). Thus Gottfredson is saying that the gender self-concept develops at an early age. In view of this, Newman (1990) cautioned "Because gender self-concept develops at an early age, compromise on the dimension of sex-type in occupational choice is the least likely. This would seem to have especially important implications for women in view of early socialization processes" (p. 29). If Gottfredson's assumptions are correct, counselors may need to implement strategies to allow women to consider career aspirations at a very early age.

Sociopsychological Model

Astin (1984) proposed a theoretical model to describe women's occupational behavior. Her model is a sociopsychological model that explored how needs drive the individual and how early socialization shapes the differential interests of women and men. Her model is:

A need-based sociopsychological model which incorporates four important constructs: motivation, expectations, sex-role socialization, and the structure of opportunity. It is a developmental model intended to explain changes in career choice and work behavior, changes that can be observed not only in the lives of individuals but also in whole groups (i.e., women) over time....The model defines both the psychological factors (work motivation, expectations) and the cultural-environmental factors (sex-role socialization, the structure of opportunity) that interact to produce career choice, which in turn is implemented into work behavior. (p. 119)

Astin (1984) indicated that there are three basic motivations for work: survival, pleasure, and contribution. All people expend energy to satisfy the three basic drives. While the needs that motivate humans to engage in work are the same for men and women, Astin concluded that men and women differ in their work expectations, that is in their perceptions of what types of work are available or accessible to them. Moreover, she believes that expectations are derived from sex-role socialization and the perceived structure of opportunity; expectations are "shaped by one's unique personal experiences, including the lessons learned in childhood and adolescence as one tries to satisfy basic needs and larger social forces" (p. 121).

Astin (1984) described the socialization process as the key to understanding how expectations develop in the life of the individual. During the early socialization process, the values of a particular society are embedded by play, family, school, and work. In American society, these have been distributed across gender lines. Astin cautioned that the early socialization process is not the only force that shapes work expectations. The other major force is the structure of opportunity, which is influenced by distribution of jobs, gender-typing of jobs, discrimination, job requirements, economy, family structure, and reproduction technology. The structure of opportunity differs for men and women; in American work history, opportunities have been more limited for women, minorities, and persons with a disability.

In applying counseling strategies, Astin's (1984) model suggests that career indecision may occur in a woman because she lacks understanding about which of the three needs (survival, pleasure, contribution) are most important to her or which career would be best in meeting her needs. Further, this theory implies that it is important for the counselor to ascertain how the woman perceives her structure of opportunity. For adult women, the structure of opportunity may change. Changes in the economy, family structure, and job requirements can enhance or decrease career opportunities for women. The counselor needs to be cognizant of and plan for the change in opportunities, especially as they influence the career development of adult women.

Relational Identity

Forrest and Mikolaitis (1986), drawing from works by Gilligan (1982) and Lyons (1983), wrote about relational identity. Women's sense of identity is primarily derived from connections to others. "Self is perceived in the context of connection with and responsiveness to others" (p. 80). On the other hand, men define their identity with phrases that seem to portray separateness. "Their [men] sense of self is created by differentiating themselves from others in terms of abilities and attributes" (p. 80). The researchers suggested that identity is crucial to both men and women, though its emergence is derived from different vectors. Their thesis is that relational identity can be adapted and used with existing career theories, in particular that of Holland (1985). In adapting their model to Holland's theory, the counselor should assess the woman's relational identity. If, for example, the woman described herself in terms of connections and responsiveness to others, then she would most likely prefer a work environment where responsiveness to others is valued and procured.

Multidimensional Models

Farmer (1985) proposed a model of career and achievement motivation for women and men. Her model is a multidimensional model that attempted to extend previous models. Farmer advocated that motivation is influenced by three interacting sets: environment, personal, and background. In turn, motivation influences the three sets. Motivational dimensions are influenced by aspiration, mastery and career. Background variables related to motivation are gender, social status, school location, race, age, math ability, and verbal ability. Personal variables related to motivation include academic self-esteem, expressive and independent perceptions of self, cooperative and competitive achievement styles, effort and ability, intrinsic values, personal unconcern, and homemaking commitment. Environmental variables related to motivation include parental support, teacher support, and support for women working. In research conducted with her model, Farmer (1985) reported:

> It is important to know the long-range career motivation patterns....For young women aspiration and mastery were enhanced when they perceived support from teachers for their

achievements. For young men aspiration, but not mastery, was enhanced when they perceived support from parents for their achievements....Long-range career motivation parent support was more important for young women and teacher support for young men. (p. 387)

According to this model, career motivation is set early in life, with mastery and aspiration occurring later. In counseling adult women, Farmer (1985) stressed the importance of experiencing support at home for "young women who experienced support for their achievements at home would be more likely to have high career commitment" (p. 387). Similarly it is important for the counselor to ascertain present support, for adult women's aspirations are likely to be dependent on the support they receive from significant others.

Betz and Fitzgerald (1987) developed a model of women's career choice that integrated various variables that other researchers reported important in understanding women's career development. Previous work experience, academic success, role model influence, and perceived encouragement were the four independent variables predicted to directly influence the three independent variables of attitudes toward work, attitudes toward self, and gender role attitudes, which in turn influenced the two dependent variables, lifestyle preferences and plans and realism of career choice. Reviewing their model, Newman (1990) stated, "This attempt to integrate the many variables that affect women's career choices is clearly one of the most promising contributions to theory development to date" (p. 30). Among the implications for practice is the need for counselors to recognize the many variables that can influence, either positively or negatively, women's selection of careers. Clearly, counselors can play a viable role by helping women consider the factors that contributed to their past career endeavors as well as factors currently influencing and likely to influence future career patterns.

Finally, in considering the career development of women, it is important to recognize that patterns may differ because of differences in socioeconomic level, race, and ethnic groups. Many of the theories advocate the selection of a career that is congruent with the client's interests, abilities, and values. Certainly the idea is good; however, its implementation is not always feasible. Some women do not have the financial or the social resources to pursue the optimal career. Many do not have the opportunity to explore careers because they must accept the first available job in an effort to provide food, clothing, and shelter. Brooks (1990) identified an important issue when she wrote "Research on special career development problems of ethnic groups must be interpreted cautiously, both because of the confounding of race, class, ethnic and economic variables and because of cultural-disadvantage assumptions" (p. 386).

Factors Affecting Women's Career Advancement

In discussing characteristics for women aspiring for top positions, Bardwick (1979) concluded that the qualities of confidence, competitiveness, ambition, assertiveness, and task orientation are necessary for advancement in organizations as they currently exist. However, in their review of the literature, Ragins and Sundstrom (1989) concluded that women generally have lower self-confidence than men, which may affect their expectations of successful outcomes even when their performance is good, and thus lead to lower career aspirations. Further, they reported that women also appear to have lower expectations than men, especially with regard to salaries.

Traditional female personality characteristics do not appear to correlate well with women's advancement. Ragan (1984), using the Bem Sex Role Inventory with 100 women, found that high achievers had higher mean scores on the masculine scale and lower mean scores on the feminine scale than lower achievers. Boardman, Harrington, and Horowitz (1989) reported that successful career women were higher in the need for achievement than affiliation and tended to have an internal locus of control.

Most women are socialized from birth for the passive, dependent roles traditionally accepted as appropriate for them. Boy and girl babies are talked to by adults in different tones and the messages are different. Girl babies are told how cute and sweet they are; boy babies are told to grow up and be tough like their dads. Boy children play games with guns, footballs, and trucks; girl children play with dolls, doll houses, and nurse's kits. Boys are allowed to venture farther from home and climb trees; girls are encouraged to stay close and help mother around the house. Teachers and school counselors still suggest that boys be doctors, scientists, and lawyers; girls should be secretaries, teachers, and nurses. Higher education for girls is not as highly valued as it is for boys. All of these overt and subtle socializing pressures reinforce the girl's thoughts and feelings about her worth in the work world. She is reinforced for being the helper, supporter, and caretaker, not for being assertive, self-confident, and independent, traits required for success in the work world. Should she try to develop these characteristics or to enter a career field not traditionally female, such as engineering, medicine, or financial management, she may also be told that her husband and family should come first.

Women who attempt to break away from socializing forces in order to have a successful career may have trouble because they lack self-confidence; this problem is often reflected in their behavior. Women often use less decisive language and end their statements on a note of question, asking for reassurance for their statements. Research has shown that women are interrupted in their speaking more often than men and have less opportunity in meetings to make their points. They are more reluctant than men to "market" themselves and more often play down their contributions to a project. Unfortunately, women continue to have few role models of women who have "made it." Therefore, it may be difficult for them to know what is appropriate for their particular job.

Ragins and Sundstrom (1989) believe that the differences in achievement orientation may be related to socialized role expectations and values. Women reared in homes where fathers encourage women's achievement as well as women with achievement-oriented mothers are more likely to succeed in the work world. Women have been socialized as to appropriate behaviors, roles, and attitudes. Women are expected to achieve in the home and family environment, not in the work place.

There continues to be a perception that a career woman is neglecting her home and children, and she may not be thought of as being as truly "feminine" as the woman who stays in her traditional role. The idea that women should be satisfied with home and family life touches the most sensitive of American values. If women wanted to work outside the home, they were considered less than wives and mothers, shirking family responsibilities for personal ambition. If women have to work to support their families, that is accepted as long as they do not want to stay in the job market beyond the time of need and do not seek to better themselves from it (Gutek & Larwood, 1989). It is difficult, in fact, for women to articulate dissatisfaction with their life path because they may never really conceive of an alternative. How could the natural order that has been traditional for centuries—for their mother and their mother's mother—be oppressive? How does one accept that without feelings of anger and dissonance?

Most women enter the work force marginally rather than by way of a directed career. The career track is not planned or probably even considered. Not preparing for a lifetime of work means that women do not tend to seek out educational opportunities to prepare for getting ahead. While men have been sent away to schools to study with the best instructors or to receive advanced degrees, women have stayed home and been educated conveniently. They have gone to 2-year trade schools, taken a few courses at a time, and tried to continue to budget time between family and education. Instead of seeking out the best route for themselves, women tend not to confront or divert money from the family, but passively accept what is available. To do anything else would be viewed as self-centered, nagging, or an invitation for abuse. Willful women have not been viewed by either gender as behaving appropriately.

Ragins and Sundstrom (1989) pointed out that women are more likely than men to make choices that lead them into jobs unsuited to advancement. They are not encouraged to obtain the level of education or training that males receive. Moreover, they are not encouraged to pursue skilled jobs that pay well, such as plumber or contractor. Their skills are not valued highly in the track leading toward leadership roles. There are fewer opportunities financially, but the number of single or divorced women heading households with children increases daily. The single working mother is becoming the fastest growing class of poor Americans. Women often select jobs that require little training and offer little chance of advancement; by selecting traditionally female jobs, they receive lower pay, and lower status, and have less power. Seldom do they consider a professional specialty that is associated with leadership and power roles such as school administrator, counselor director, or human resources manager.

Women seldom plan for their careers. When they do consider nontraditional careers, they may face resistance and pressure from family and friends; they may find it easier to choose a traditional role and avoid inner conflicts about appropriate roles for women (Ragins & Sundstrom, 1989).

Women who do succeed in their career choices often continue to feel uncomfortable and isolated. Some are in positions held by women for the first time, or they are among relatively few women in the organization. Most have no role models for patterning their behaviors. Morrison et al., (1987), in conjunction with The Center for Creative Leadership, have supported the ideas that successful women must take risks but never fail, be tough but not macho, be ambitious but not pushy, take responsibility but follow others' advice. Obviously these constraints make it almost impossible to avoid unfavorable perceptions. Should a woman adopt more masculine characteristics in order to succeed, or should feminine leadership provide a different and complementary view in organizations that will result in positive returns (Loden, 1985)? Until there are role models and additional support systems, women are left to find their way through the obstacles and barriers with little guidance.

Counseling Strategies for Attaining Goals

Because of socialization, societal pressures, limited experiences, and learned self-defeating behaviors, women interested in pursuing a career often need a support network and the opportunity to learn new skills. Perosa and Perosa (1987) suggested that a variety of counseling techniques be employed to help women with career decisions, including behavioral, cognitive, developmental, Adlerian, paradoxical, and Bowenian family systems approaches.

Counselors working with career women will need a variety of techniques to assist them in exploring and understanding their roles and needs, as well as techniques required for coping with expectations on the job and in the home. One of the first concerns encountered by counselors may be the lack of adequate self-confidence. Strategies designed to improve feelings of self-worth and clarify identity are basic to most counseling approaches. Values clarification techniques will encourage women to set a direction for their lives based on values that are not in conflict and are truly important in their lives. Cognitive techniques, especially those that attack irrational ideas, have been effective in counteracting self-defeating thoughts women carry with them from social pressure and early socialization. The behavioral strategies of desensitization and stress reduction ease anxious feelings and fears about confronting new situations. Time management is an essential skill for most women as they attempt to balance all roles. Family systems theories can help counselors deal with career issues related to family responsibilities, including lack of support from husband, parents, and children (Perosa & Perosa, 1987). Perhaps most of all, working women need a support group (friends, colleagues, family, mentors, and so on) to provide them a listening ear during the times of self-doubt and confusion. They need true friends or confidants who will assist them with feedback about their behavior and encourage them to assess the realities of situations encountered in their everyday struggles.

Unfortunately, counseling theories that address career development traditionally have been based on males and therefore give little assistance to counselors seeking to help women in their careers. Only recently has consideration been given to the possibility and the acknowledgement that career patterns and influences may vary by gender. It is still surprising to see new literature on career development continue to take a unidirectional approach. Riverin-Simard (1988) described what she conceived as phases of working life for the typical adult:

Landing on the job market	Age 23–27
Seeking a promising path	Age 28–32
Grappling with an occupational path	Age 33–37
Testing new guidelines	Age 38–42
Searching for guiding thread of life experiences	Age 43–47
Considering last chances	Age 48–52
Seeking a promising exit	Age 53–57
Pulling toward retirement	Age 58–62
Dealing with retirement	Age 63–67

But theories that are designed for the typical male do not fit most women today. Of necessity, women will probably behave more and more like men in the development of careers as more enter the work place and seek career advance (Gutek & Larwood, 1989). But we are in a period of rapid social change in gender-related behavior, and it is difficult to put the older and younger woman worker in a unidimensional plan for stage-related career development. Even with the changes, women's careers will remain different for several reasons (Gutek & Larwood, 1989):

1. There are different expectations for men and women regarding appropriateness of jobs and kinds of jobs for which they prepare.
2. Husbands and wives are differentially willing to accommodate themselves and each other's careers.
3. The parent role is differentially defined.
4. Women are faced with more constraints in the work place, including discrimination and stereotypes detrimental to advancement.

Gutek and Larwood (1989) suggested that an adequate look at women's career development must address the following:

1. *Career preparation:* The education and training necessary for career entry and advancement.
2. *Opportunities available:* The acquisition of appropriate experiences, motivation to buck opposition in nontraditional fields and areas of limited opportunities and ability to deal with stereotypes about role behavior.
3. *Marriage and locality restrictions due to family responsibilities:* Acceptance of the working wife and husband's mobility.
4. *Pregnancy and children:* The interruptions created by child-rearing responsibilities.
5. *Timing and age:* Women have different career patterns depending upon whether career or marriage stability occurred first.

Powell (1988) also looked at the different work behaviors of men and women, particularly in management positions. He contended that individuals have to make several decisions about working that heavily affect their career path. First, each person formulates career aspirations, interests, and preferences, a process which begins quite early in childhood. As ideas accumulate with time, decisions are influenced by the realities of our experiences. Second, decisions to work or not to work are made from time to time. Women have been freer to drop in and out of the work force for periods of time, although advances in career opportunities are often diminished in the process. Third, decisions are made by each individual to explore job opportunities and to choose one job over another. These decisions affect career path, direction, and stability.

Studies on career decision making show that decisiveness tends to increase with age. A study by Kinner, Brigman, and Hoble (1990) showed that people enmeshed with their families of origin are more likely to have difficulty making career decisions. Individuation appeared to contribute to both the career planning and decision-making processes; therefore, autonomy and independence were positively correlated with career development and advancement. The implication for the socialization of women is that the factors facilitating career development are often not the factors emphasized in the upbringing of women in our culture.

Women plan for marriage but not for separation from dependent relationships. They plan for children but not for children growing up and becoming independent from them. They may plan for college but not for a career path. They usually do not consider that most of them will spend one-third of their adult years alone. Richardson (1974) described three career patterns for women:

1. Continued uninterrupted work pattern, usually when she has no children or delays marriage and childbirth.
2. Work-oriented with equal priority given to work and family responsibilities. She works most of her adult life but drops out periodically for limited periods of time.
3. Homemaking, assuming the traditional family role.

What factors determine the pattern women will take? Authors have made many suggestions, but there appears to be no single factor that contributes to the different work expectations of males and females.

Feuer (1988) found that the women in her study did not tend to make conscious career commitments to career advancement until they reach their 30's which was much later than males. They planned to advance through hard work, training, and additional educational study, but they did not address the political aspects of the work place such as whom to impress and whom to associate with for support. They did not build strategies for gaining entry into the "old boy network" and still tried to be the traditional mother who took responsibility for rearing young children. A well-conceived career plan that visualizes strategies for moving up unquestionably will pay off for the average woman. Those who planned consistently enjoyed better career paths and felt successful. Not planning or avoiding goal setting led to being stuck in dead-end jobs.

CASE EXAMPLES

The Case of Mary

Mary is an accountant for a law firm in Indianapolis. After graduating from high school, she attended college. She worked part time to pay for her schooling. Throughout college, Mary was a motivated student, and she graduated with honors. She accepted her first position as accountant to a business executive in Houston. Mary was an excellent employee and was promoted to direct eight other employees.

After working for 2 years Mary met and married Dale; they have two daughters. After the children were born, Mary took off from work to be with her family. While she enjoyed her family, Mary missed her career. When she talked to Dale about returning to work, he was adamant that he wanted her to stay home with the children. Although Dale was a good husband and father, his work history left much to be desired. He seemed to change jobs frequently, usually because he was fired or about to be fired. In fact, it was his job change that brought the family to Indianapolis.

After moving to Indianapolis, Mary returned to the labor force. She has been employed in her current job for 4 years and has received excellent raises and several promotions.

Recently Mary's employer announced she was moving to Dallas to accept a partnership in a large law firm. She asked Mary if she would be willing to move to Dallas and accept a position as supervisor of the accounting division. The new job offered a large pay increase and an excellent benefits package. Mary really wanted to accept the position, but she wondered if Dale and the children would be willing to move. During dinner, Mary discussed her new opportunity with Dale. To her dismay, Dale informed her that he would not consider "following her" to Dallas. Mary was so distressed that, she decided to seek counseling.

In discussing her situation with a counselor, Mary indicated that she wanted to accept the new job, but she felt she was not being fair to Dale. When the counselor pointed out that she had moved from Houston to Indianapolis because of Dale's position and it was now Mary's turn to make a career move, Mary seemed perplexed. It was evident that Mary perceived herself in the context of her connections with others. For her the decision to accept the new job was externally controlled, and she did not seem to be considering her own needs and desires. During the sex-role socialization process, Mary had internalized social norms regarding appropriate sex-role behaviors. The counselor employed many of the concepts from Astin's (1984) model and helped Mary consider her needs and not just the needs of her family. Through counseling, Mary was able to widen her beliefs about her career development. She accepted the position in Dallas.

The Case of June and Joyce

June and Joyce are 38-year-old women who were considering changing careers. Both women described their present careers as depressing and unsatisfactory. Each realized she was experiencing burnout in her present position. Further, June and Joyce realized they needed to change careers soon. June weighed the advantages and disadvantages of changing careers. As she considered her situation, she described herself as a conscientious worker, good learner, and willing and capable of learning new ideas. In contrast, Joyce began her self-inspection by deciding that despite being a hard worker she was not sure she could be successful in a new career. She feared she would not live up to the new employer's expectations. June decided to change careers while Joyce decided to just "put up with her boring job."

In reviewing the cases of June and Joyce, it was evident that June exhibited a higher sense of self-efficacy than Joyce. According to Bandura (1982), self-efficacy influences the choice of behaviors to be engaged in. In this example, June believed in herself ("I can do the new job") and decided to change careers. Individuals who do not possess a sense of self-efficacy dwell on the negatives and fear the obstacles that might be. Joyce believed the potential obstacles in the new job might be more than she could master. Thus, she decided to remain in her present career.

In counseling, the counselor helped Joyce consider how she reacted to change. Issues such as uncertainty about an outcome, possibility of failure, and self-efficacy were discussed. Realizing the effects of gender-role socialization, the counselor helped Joyce counteract its effects. Through counseling, Joyce learned to pursue greater utilization of her abilities and talents. Her counselor helped her find significant role models; here she was exposed to women with strong perceived self-efficacy. At the time of this writing,

Joyce was making good progress in counseling. While not as efficacious as June, Joyce nevertheless was learning to believe in herself.

RESOURCES FOR WOMEN

Women often feel alone and confused in their search for assistance in climbing the career ladder or coping with the barriers that interfered with their advancement. Where do they turn for help?

As stated previously, indications are that women turn to their own professional organizations first in their efforts to find support and advance women's issues. Most professional organizations have formed women's caucus groups or networks to provide encouragement and disseminate information. Programs on women's concerns may be scheduled as a part of conferences; these groups offer women periodic seminars for the development of specific skills. There are women's organizations in some professions; the Society of Women Engineers and Women Law Studies are examples. The Women's Bureau, U.S. Department of Labor, Washington, DC 20210, will provide information on issues concerning working women, women with families, job rights, alternative work patterns and other topics.

Professions also may provide special training or other opportunities to women through institutes, conferences, internships, or mentoring programs. Educational institutions often have women's centers with brochures, books, and counseling. The American Council of Education supports women in education in many ways; the National Identification Program is one successful component of this program that provides networks, direction, and other opportunities to women seeking high offices in education. The Project on the Status and Education of Women, Association of American Colleges, 1818 B Street, NW, Washington, DC 20009, develops and publishes materials addressing issues that affect women's status in educational institutions. Other professions may have similar national organizations designed to facilitate women's advancement into leadership positions.

In addition to professional organizations, national groups such as the National Organization of Women (NOW), 1736 R Street, NW, Washington, DC 20009. and the American Association of University Women (AAUW), 2401 Virginia Avenue, NW, Washington, DC 20037, strongly support the concerns of women. In some instances, they also provide financial assistance with legal issues. Local groups representing NOW will be found in larger towns and cities, and branches of the AAUW are more often located near a college or university. Local groups of other business and professional women can provide both personal and career support to women in their daily activities. More information about various resources may be obtained from the Federation of Organizations for Professional Women, 200 P Street, NW, Room 1122, Washington, DC 20036.

Women are also encouraged to read current literature on women's issues, business, and leadership. Books on leadership and management, self-esteem, dealing with people, assertiveness, office politics, the history of the women's movement, and other women's concerns will give readers information needed for discussing issues as well as suggestions for improving personal skills. Women must also be knowledgeable about local and world events and developments in their professions or work areas in order to converse intelligently and contribute to solving the problems in their work place. Personnel in local bookstores and libraries can suggest best sellers in these areas. A list of publishers that specialize in literature for women should be available at the local library. Books on the contributions of women in all professional areas are available through special presses along with books that relate to the history of women's progress, different lifestyles of women, self-help information, and even books, pamphlets, or newsletters to assist with career advancement. A list of organizations and centers conducting research on women may be obtained from the National Council for Research on Women, 47-49 East 65th Street, New York, NY 10021.

Women who believe that they have experienced discrimination may want to consult with the regional or national offices of the Equal Employment Opportunity Commission. The Equal Employment Opportunity Commission is the federal enforcement agency for discrimination covered by Title VII of the Civil Rights Act of 1964, the Age Discrimination in Employment Act of 1967, and the Equal Pay Act of 1963. The national office is located at 2402 E Street, NW, Washington, DC 20507. The Directory of Organizations Working for Women's Educational Equity may be obtained from the U.S. Department of Health, Education and Welfare, Women's Educational Equity Communications Network, 1855 Folsom Street, San Francisco, CA 94103. The Department of Education, Office for Civil Rights is responsible for enforcing federal requirements in programs that receive funds from the Department of Education. A brochure describing their services is available from the U.S. Department of Education, Office for Civil Rights, Washington, DC 20202.

These are only examples of the many types of resources available to assist women. However, although there are a variety of programs, activities, and materials available, most organizations still ignore or avoid discussion of women's issues. Women must continue to struggle to build a strong foundation, establish networks, and work to achieve equality in all areas of their lives.

PROBLEM PREVENTION AND SOCIAL INTERVENTIONS

Organizational Strategies to Help Women

Institutions and organizations have reacted to equal opportunity pressures in a number of different ways. Some have seen an opportunity to develop a more diversified and talented work force and have actually recruited and trained women employees; some have met only minimum requirements of laws, and a few organizations have ignored issues related to gender discrimination, hoping the whole movement will go away (Powell, 1988). At one time the responsibility for achieving equality was placed totally on women. It was up to them to change attitudes and behaviors. More recently, some organizations have begun to make planned and responsible efforts to assist women. Predictions are that in the next century the majority of the work force will be women and minorities, and these organizations want to be prepared. They cannot afford to ignore the talent present in more than 50% of the population.

Most current literature affirms that support from the chief executive officer and other leaders of the institution or corporation is absolutely essential if women are to succeed.

This support must take the form of sincere moral support as well as financial backing for the programs and activities assisting women. It includes showing respect for women and treating them as people of equal worth in the board room and in all areas of the work place. Until there is this commitment, little effort will be made to recruit, train, promote, and support women.

Loden (1985) has suggested that one of the first steps should be a review and revision if necessary of all policies and procedures governing the institution. The following questions should be asked: Are there women in jobs other than traditionally female jobs? Does the hiring policy subtly discriminate against women through procedures that have applications reviewed by all-male committees? Are the qualifications written so that most women will be screened out? Has modern technology been considered as a method for allowing more flexibility in time on the job? Is there a sexual harassment policy that clearly describes unacceptable behavior? Are complaints of discrimination or harassment treated fairly and objectively? Is there equal pay for equal work among men and women? Does the performance appraisal include items fair for feminine leadership traits? Are policies written to assure that women are promoted at a rate equal to that of their male counterparts? These and other policies and procedures will send a clear message about the role of women in the work place.

Another effective method for ensuring that women's views and talents are considered in the work place is for the leadership to be consciously aware of the number of women appointed to serve on boards and policy-making committees. Organizations truly interested in having women's perspectives recognized and incorporated into their approaches will make sure that at least two or more women serve in these important areas; a "token" woman on boards or committees often finds it difficult to be heard and to have her ideas received seriously. In addition, they can place women in positions that require little client contact. Women are often hidden in personnel, assigned to work on domestic issues, or given a job in the stacks of research data. Clients who cannot work with a woman representative because she is a woman are probably not the type of client preferred by the company anyway. In reality, most clients find that the competence, interest, and attention of women company representatives more than offsets any questions they may have had about dealing with a woman.

Other subtle discriminations may prevent women from advancing as rapidly as men. In some companies one way to advance is to show your abilities by handling "tough assignments." These might include leading a task force on a particularly controversial and sensitive area. It might involve negotiating with employee grievances. It could involve managing a declining division to turn it around toward profitability. It could involve supervising a group of very traditional males or females. But frequently, women are not viewed as capable of these assignments, thus reducing their opportunities to "shine." Consideration must be given to the talents of women employees when these opportunities arise; they should not be excluded without being offered the opportunity to accept the assignment.

Another area in which women are sometimes the target of subtle discrimination is in jobs that require travel, especially if most in the group are men. The thinking may go along these lines: It's too difficult and expensive to make hotel reservations for a mixed group; people will gossip; she would not want to go out of town and leave her husband or children; she will not fit in when we go out to dinner or socialize in the evening; what will we talk to her about during the times we are not in meetings. These are not acceptable reasons for restricting women's career opportunities.

Many organizations have elected to support women's advancement through education and training programs. Workshops and seminars on self-awareness, leadership, skill building, working together, and career planning abound. Group discussions that focus on sexual harassment, risk taking, and the use of power are helpful, allowing women and men to explore their thoughts about themselves and their working relationships.

Men have recognized for many years the benefits of having a powerful mentor to teach them the ropes, provide inside information, and act as an advocate. As few women have reached positions of leadership or power, women have a more difficult time establishing this helpful relationship. Males are often reluctant to mentor women, fearing the gossip that could label the relationship as sexual in nature or not being willing to risk their own credibility by supporting a woman. Organizations interested in supporting women's advancement can find ways to encourage mentoring relationships. Both the mentor and the person being mentored should benefit from the interactions.

Reminding corporations of affirmative action laws and regulations may be considered a negative way to encourage equal opportunity for women, yet companies that have held seminars on affirmative action and set goals for hiring and promotion have been among the more successful ones in improving the status of women in their organizations. Letters, brochures, workshops, and seminars should be constant reminders of the necessity for addressing these issues.

Loden (1985) believes that women can help themselves in a number of ways. They should learn about the issues in order to have the knowledge required for answering questions and raising issues. Women must refuse to be a party to collusive relationships or those that reinforce and accommodate old, negative attitudes. Men have benefited for years through a network of friendships and acquaintances; women must learn to support one another for their mutual benefit. Women do not have to fully accept the masculine world of business, but they can demonstrate their competence through sharing their vision and providing a different but effective style of leadership.

Equal opportunity, attitudes toward women, and child care issues traditionally have been primary concerns of working women. Because women have been and continue to be the primary caregivers for children, the burden and stress of balancing family and work falls on the woman. Because of child care responsibilities, women are seen as being absent from work more often, spending too much office time on the phone running the home, and not interested in their jobs because they want to be at home with their children. Recently, more enlightened companies have recognized the need for women in the work place and have implemented programs to assist. Some have established corporate child care centers; some run referral services for good child care; some offer informational seminars; and others provide financial assistance to parents for child care (Stautberg, 1987). The U.S. Congress has debated a bill providing for parental leave in support of child care. These are not easy issues to resolve, but the family of the 21st century is not the same as the family of the 20th century and neither are the workers. The work place, as well as women, must address the issue of families if the labor force of this century is to meet the needs of an expanding economy.

Powell (1988) has offered the following suggestions for helping women overcome occupational segregation and reduce the differentiation of career choice:

1. Enlighten recruiters about stereotypes and how to adequately assess job potential.
2. Help all youth become aware of career opportunities in all fields.
3. Actively search to hire females and males in nontraditional fields.
4. Provide staff development opportunities in the work place on appropriate professional behavior.
5. Institute and reinforce ways to reduce sexual harassment in the work place.
6. Encourage female mentorships, particularly for those reentering the work force.

There are many management initiatives that organizations can take to encourage advancement in female employment. The following list highlights some, but not all, of those initiatives:

1. Affirmative hiring patterns
2. Salary equity
3. Promotion and transfer representativeness
4. Training opportunities for advancement potential
5. Equity in opportunities for leadership and decision making
6. Reduction in number of dead-end jobs
7. Career planning services, including career laddering
8. Child care support at the work place

To promote equal opportunity, organizations must make sure that current decisions and practices enhance the employment, development, and retention of members of protected groups, not just refrain from discrimination (Powell, 1988). Discrimination is now looked upon as uneven distribution across occupation and job level and differences in earning potential. Patronizing and coddling women are damaging practices whose time is passed.

Recommendations from the Project on the Status of Women (Ehrhart & Sandler, 1990) for improving the climate for women in medical schools and teaching hospitals include suggestions that would be beneficial to all organizations:

1. Develop outreach strategies to encourage young women of all races to consider nontraditional occupations and advanced positions.
2. Ensure that the organization is committed to gender equity through policies and programs implemented institution-wide.
3. Ensure that all recruiting and admissions personnel are committed to women's participation in all occupations and to a gender-fair work place.
4. Ensure that all women have access to advice and mentoring from leaders in the organization.
5. Hold workshops and discussions about the effects of an intimidating climate, the importance of role models and mentors, and the availability of programs for women entering the field.

6. Hold meetings to discuss attitudes toward women as colleagues and superiors.
7. Encourage women to get involved in support groups, both within the organization and in larger professional circles.
8. Provide support services for women to help them cope with the stresses of social, family, and career pressures.
9. Ensure that women are hired and promoted in the organization by developing and monitoring specific recruitment and promotion procedures.

SUMMARY

This chapter has described and summarized the adult woman's career development. Women's increased participation in the labor force has been accompanied by a greater awareness of the need to understand the factors that promote and impede career development of women. A series of issues face adult women, including balancing home and career, self-efficacy, motivation, social and economic support, discrimination, equity, and sexual harassment. These and other issues were addressed throughout the chapter.

Although most career development theories were originally formulated to explore the career development of men, this chapter focused on theories and models designed to explain the career development of adult women. Attention was given to strategies for adapting career counseling theories to meet women's needs. Case examples were provided to integrate theory and practice. The final portion of the chapter was devoted to interventions designed to help women solve work place issues.

The future may bring a blend of masculine and feminine styles into the work place. Androgyny may become the expected pattern of characteristics, the ideal for both genders. Work and family responsibilities may blend and receive equal emphasis in the lives of both genders. It would be an adult lifestyle for both parents to be involved with the rearing of their children and to feel they enjoy the opportunity to develop their career interests and talents; the two will not be viewed as conflicting or competing but enriching life. With adults working more years before and after the rearing of children, they will not feel the pressure to handle so many responsibilities at one time. As society learns that the early years of childhood are critical and that we all share in the responsibility for our collective "next generation," developmental child care will be available for all mothers, with acceptable connotations. The home and work place arenas will not be so far apart psychologically and will have a healthier balance. Personal, social, and achievement aspects of self will not be viewed separately but holistically. Perhaps this vision will be realized sometime in the next century.

REFERENCES

Astin, H. S. (1984). The meaning of work in women's lives: A sociopsychological model of career choice and work behavior. *Counseling Psychologist, 12*, 117–133.

Bandura, A. (1977). Self-efficacy: Toward a unifying theory of behavioral change. *Psychological Review, 84*, 191–215.

Bandura, A. (1982). Self-efficacy mechanism in human agency. *American Psychologist, 37*, 122–147.

Bardwick, J. (1979). *Psychology of women: A study of biocultural conflicts.* New York: Harper & Row.

Barnett, R. C., & Baruch, G. K. (1985). Women's involvement in multiple roles and psychological distress. *Journal of Personality and Social Psychology, 49*, 135–145.

Betz, N. E., & Fitzgerald, L. F. (1987). *The career psychology of women. Orlando*, FL: Academic Press.

Betz, N. E., & Hackett, G. (1983). The relationship of mathematics self-efficacy expectations to the selection of science-based college majors. *Journal of Vocational Behavior, 23*, 329–345.

Bird, G. W., Bird, G. A., & Scruggs, M. (1984). Determinants of family task sharing: A study of husbands and wives. *Journal of Marriage and Family, 46*, 345–356.

Boardman, S., Harrington, C., & Horowitz, S. (1989). Successful women: A psychological investigation of family, class and educational origins. In B. Gutek & L. Larwood (Eds.), *Women's career development* (pp. 60–85). Newbury Park, NJ: Sage.

Bram, S. (1984). Voluntarily childless women: Traditional or nontraditional. *Sex Roles, 10*, 195–206.

Brooks, L. (1984). Counseling special groups. In D. Brown, L. Brooks, & Associates, *Career choice and development: Applying contemporary theories to practice*. San Francisco: Jossey-Bass.

Brooks, L. (1990). Recent developments in theory building. In D. Brown, L. Brooks, & Associates, *Career choice and development: Applying contemporary theories to practice* (2nd ed.). San Francisco: Jossey-Bass.

Brown, G. W., Bhrolchain, M. N. & Harris, T. (1975). Social class and psychiatric disturbance among women in an urban population. *Sociology, 9*, 225–254.

Busch, J. W. (1985). Mentoring in graduate schools of education: Mentors' perceptions. *American Educational Research Journal, 22*, 257–265.

Campbell, K. E. (1988). Gender differences on job-related networks. *Work and Occupation, 15*, 179–200.

Campbell, N. K., & Hackett, G. (1986). The effects of mathematics task performance on math self-efficacy and task interest. *Journal of Vocational Behavior, 28*, 149–162.

Castro, J. (1990). Rolling along the mommy track. *Time, 133*, 72.

Cleary, P. D., & Mechanic, D. (1983). Sex differences in psychological distress among married people. *Journal of Health and Social Behavior, 24*, 111-121.

Coverman, S. (1985). Explaining husband's participation in domestic labor. *Sociological Quarterly, 26*, 81–97.

Coverman, S., & Sheley, J. (1986). Change in men's housework and child care time. *Journal of Marriage and the Family, 48*, 413–422.

Dabrowski, I. (1984). The social integration of working class women: A review of employment, voluntary organization and related sex role literature. *The Social Science Journal, 21*, 59–63.

Diamond, E. (1989). Theories of career development and the reality of women at work. In B. Gutek & L. Larwood (Eds.), *Women's career development* (pp. 15–27). Newbury Park, NJ: Sage.

Ehrhart, J., & Sandler, B. (1990). Rx for success: Improving the climate for women in medical schools and teaching hospitals. *Project on the Status and Education of Women* (pp. 1–23).

Farmer, H. S. (1985). Model of career and achievement motivation for men and women. *Journal of Counseling Psychology, 32*, 363–390.

Feuer, D. (1988). How women manage. *Training, 25*, 23–31.

Fischer, C. (1987, March). Toward a more complete understanding of occupational sex discrimination. *Journal of Economic Issues, 21*, 113–135.

Forrest, L., & Mikolaitis, N. (1986). The relational component of identity: An expansion of career development theory. *Career Development Quarterly, 35*, 76–88.

Freeman, S. (1990). *Managing lives*. Amherst: University of Massachusetts Press.

Gaddy, C., Glass, C., & Arnkoff, D. (1983). Career involvement of women in dual-career families: The influence of sex role identity. *Journal of Counseling Psychology, 30*, 388–394.

Gerson, M. J., Alpert, J. L., & Richardson, M. S. (1984). Mothering: The view from psychological research. *Journal of Women in Culture and Society, 9*, 434–453.

Gibson, A., & Fast, T. (1986). *The women's atlas of the United States*. New York: Facts on File Publications.

Gilligan, C. (1982). *In a different voice: Psychological theory and women's development*. Cambridge: Harvard University Press.

Gottfredson, L. S. (1981). Circumscription and compromise: A developmental theory of occupational aspirations. *Journal of Counseling Psychology, 28*, 545–579.

Guinn, S. (1989). The changing work force. *Training and Development Journal, 43*, 38–39.

Gutek, B., & Larwood. L. (1989). *Women's career development*. Newbury Park, NJ: Sage.

Hackett, G., & Betz, N. (1981). A self-efficacy approach to the career development of women. *Journal of Vocational Behavior, 18*, 326–339.

Hansen, L. S. (1987). Career socialization, social change, prevention: Critical issues for dual-career counseling. *The Counseling Psychologist, 15*, 122–130.

Holland, J. L. (1985). *Making vocational choices: A theory of vocational personalities and work environments* (2nd ed.). Englewood Cliffs, NJ: Prentice-Hall.

Hopkins, E. (1990, October). Who is Felice Schwartz and why is she saying those terrible things about us? *Working Woman*, 117–120.

House, E. A. (1986). Sex-role orientation and marital satisfaction in dual and one-provider couples. *Sex Roles, 14*, 245–259.

Information please almanac: Atlas & yearbook. (1990). Boston: Houghton Mifflin.

Juster, F. T. (1985). Investments of time by men and women. In F. T. Juster & F. P. Stafford (Eds.), *Time, goods and well-being* (pp.177–204). Ann Arbor, MI: Survey Research Center/Institute for Social Research.

Kandel, D. B., Davis, M., & Raveis, V. H. (1985). The stressfulness of daily social roles for women: Marital, occupational and household roles. *Journal of Health and Social Behavior, 26*, 64–78.

Kiger, G. (1984). Working women and their children. *The Social Sciences Journal, 21*, 49–57.

King, S. (1989). Sex differences in a casual model of career maturity. *Journal of Counseling and Development, 68*, 208–215.

Kinner, R., Brigman, S., & Hoble, F. (1990). Career indecision and family enmeshment. *Journal of Counseling and Development, 68*, 309–312.

Larwood, L., & Gattiker, U. (1989). A comparison of the career paths used by successful women and men. In B. Gutek & L. Larwood (Eds.), *Women's career development* (pp. 129–156). Newbury Park, NJ: Sage.

Lent, R. W., & Hackett, G. (1987). Career self-efficacy: Empirical status and future directions. *Journal of Vocational Behavior, 30*, 347–382.

Loden, M. (1985). *Feminine leadership, or, how to succeed in business without being one of the boys.* New York: Times Books.

Lott, B. (1973). Who wants the children? Some relationships among attitudes toward children, parents and the liberation of children. *American Psychologist, 28*, 573–582.

Lyons, N. P. (1983). Two perspectives: On self, relationships and morality. *Harvard Educational Review, 53*, 125–145.

Marini, M., & Brinton, M. (1984). Sex typing in occupational socialization. In B. Reskin, *Sex segregation in the work place* (pp. 192–232). Washington, DC: National Academy Press.

Miller, J., & Garrison, H. (1982). Sex roles: The division of labor at home and in the work place. *Annual Review of Sociology, 8*, 237–262.

Morrison, A., & Glinow, M. (1990, February). Women and minorities in management. *American Psychologist, 45*, 200–208.

Morrison, A., White, R., & Velsor, E. (1987). *Breaking the glass ceiling: Can women reach the top of America's largest corporations?* Reading: Addison-Wesley.

Newman, J. L. (1990). A review of issues in the career development of women. *Counseling and Human Development, 23*, 1–12.

O'Hare, M., & Beutell, N. (1987). Sex differences in coping with career decision making. *Journal of Vocational Behavior, 31*, 174–181.

Papalia, D., & Olds, S. (1989). *Human development* (4th ed.). New York: McGraw-Hill.

Perosa, S., & Perosa, L. (1987). Strategies for counseling midcareer changers: A conceptual framework. *Journal of Counseling and Development, 65*, 558–561.

Piotrkowski, C. S., & Katz, M. H. (1982). Women's work and personal relations with the family. In P. W. Berman & E. R. Ramey (Eds.), *Women: A developmental perspective* (Publication No. 82–2298; pp. 221–235). Bethesda, MD: National Institutes of Health.

Powell, G. (1988). *Women and men in management.* Newbury Park, NJ: Sage.

Price-Bonham, S., & Murphy, D. C. (1980). Dual-career marriages: Implications for the clinician. *Journal of Marital and Family Therapy, 6*, 181–188.

Psathas, G. (1968). Toward a theory of occupational choice for women. *Sociology and Social Research, 52*, 253–268.

Ragan, J. (1984). Gender displays in photographs. *Sex Roles*, 33–34.

Ragins, B., & Sundstrom, E. (1989). Gender and power in organizations: A longitudinal perspective. *Psychological Bulletin, 105,* 51–88.

Rapoport, R., & Rapoport, R. N. (1973). Family enabling processes: The facilitating husband in dual-career families. In R. Gasling (Ed.), *Support, innovation, and autonomy* (pp. 245–263). London, England: Tavistock.

Rice, D. G. (1979). *Dual-career marriage: Conflict and treatment.* New York: Free Press.

Richardson, M. (1974). Vocational maturity in counseling girls and women. In D. Super (Ed.), *Measuring vocational maturity and evaluation* (pp. 135–145). Washington, D.C.: National Vocational Guidance Association.

Richman, D. R. (1988). Cognitive career counseling for women. *Journal of Rational-Emotive and Cognitive-Behavior Therapy, 6,* 50–65.

Riverin-Simard, D. (1988). Phases of working life and adult education, *Lifelong Learning, 12,* 24–26.

Rix, S. (1988). *The American woman 1988-89: A status report.* New York: W. W. Norton.

Rix, S., & Stone, A. (1984). Work. In S. Pruitard (Ed.), *The women's annual,* (No. 4). Boston: G. K. Hall.

Robinson, J. P. (1988). Who's doing the housework? *American Demographics, 10,* 24–63.

Sanik, M. M. (1981). Division of housework: A decade comparison—1967–1977. *Home Economics Research Journal, 10,* 175–180.

Schwartz, F. N. (1989a, January/February). Management women and the new facts of life. *Harvard Business Review,67,* 65–76.

Schwartz, F. (1989b, September). Mommy track, daddy track. *Training and Development Journal, 43,* 12–14.

Shelton, B. A. (1990). The distribution of household tasks: Does wife's employment make a difference? *Journal of Family Issues, 11,* 115–135.

Smith, R. (1988, January). Comparable worth: Limited coverage and the exacerbation of inequality. *Industrial and Labor Relations Review, 41,* 2.

Sorensen, E. (1987, Fall). Effect of comparable worth policies on earning. *Industrial Relations, 26,* 227–239.

Stautberg, S. (1987, Summer). Status report: The corporation and trends in family issues. *Human Resource Management, 26,* 277–290.

Stokes, J. P., & Peyton, J. S. (1986). Attitudinal differences between full-time homemakers and women who work outside the home. *Sex Roles, 15,* 299–310.

Super, D. E. (1953). A theory of vocational development. *American Psychologist, 8,* 185–190.

Super, D. E. (1984). Self-concepts in vocational development. In D.E. Super, D. Starishevsky, N. Martin, & J. P. Jordan (Eds.), *Career development: Self-concept theory* (pp. 161–169). New York: CEEP Research Monograph.

Super, D. E. (1990). A life span, life space approach to career development. In D. Brown, L. Brooks, & Associates (Eds.), *Career choice and development: Applying contemporary theory to practice* (2nd ed.). San Francisco: Jossey-Bass.

Taylor, K. M., & Betz, N. E. (1983). Applications of self-efficacy theory to understanding and treatment of career indecision. *Journal of Vocational Behavior, 22,* 63–81.

Wilkie, J. (1981). The trend toward delayed parenthood. *Journal of Marriage and the Family, 43,* 583–593.

Zytowski, D. G. (1969). Toward a theory of career development for women. *Personnel and Guidance Journal, 47,* 660–664.

6

Empowering Women: Gender Issues in Adulthood

Ellen P. Cook
University of Cincinnati

W e live in a society differentiated on the basis of sex. On a daily basis, people confront different messages, opportunities, expectations, and resources because of their biological sex. Individuals' biological sex prompts others to perceive and behave toward them in gender-differentiated ways, and to some extent how we see ourselves as individuals has been conditioned by gender as well.

Gender is a multidimensional construct, referring to the many ways that society is sex-differentiated. The biological differentiation of the sexes is an inheritance from nature, but gender is not. Instead, gender is created by humans. It serves as a central organizing principle in society and in everyday interactions between individuals, prescribing which personal characteristics, life roles, responsibilities, and prerogatives are the province of each sex, and how members of each sex should be treated by others. These contrasting sets of prescriptions constitute the gendered context of women's and men's lives. In many societies, autonomy / dominance / goal-directed activity centered in paid work is "men's world", where emotionalism / nurturing / care of home and family describe "women's world." People tend to assume that this dichotomous social–psychological differentiation of the sexes is as clear-cut and preordained as reproductive differences, when in fact similarities between the sexes and variability within each sex are the rule rather than the exception.

Development throughout adulthood is shaped by gender as individuals attempt to deal with the changing nature of their self-perceptions and the demands placed upon them by their life circumstances. Recent views of gender portray individuals as actively attempting to select and influence their own environments (e.g., Unger, 1989). Men and women alike attempt to negotiate a personally unique blending of individual achievement through a variety of pursuits in work, the home, and in the community, and meaningful personal relationships. Ideally, these attempts lead to a sense of personal empowerment: a conviction and ability to successfully pursue personally meaningful individual achievement and relationships in one's life, with dignity and respect for self and others. Yet gender differentiation makes this process difficult. An individual or others may summarily dismiss certain life options because of gender (e.g., a corporate presidency for a woman). Other possibilities are tolerated but ostracized by others, or promote strong feelings of shame or guilt (e.g., a woman surrendering custody of her children). Depending upon perceptions of the "gender correctness" of a life possibility, a life option can be idealized, barely accepted, punished, or simply invisible to the individual and others in her or his life.

Gender-related behavior is the end-product of a complex reciprocal interaction among the predispositions, expectations, attitudes, and behaviors brought by individuals to situations in their lives; those brought by others to the interaction; and both transient and enduring features of the environment, ranging from characteristics of the immediate setting (e.g., a particular classroom) to those of society at large (cf. Deaux & Major, 1987). To put it simply, we have our own ways of being a man or woman that interact with many potentially concordant or discrepant factors on a daily basis. Counselors need to appreciate the multidimensionality of gender to be able to help clients work through gender-related issues in counseling (Cook, 1985).

Using this reciprocal view of gender as a backdrop, a basic premise of this chapter is that women today are disempowered by several related processes linked to the gender differentiation of our society. First, women learn to view themselves and develop life preferences in ways that restrict the opportunities and rewards open to them. Through the lifelong gender socialization process, women internalize the sex-appropriate prescriptions and associated sanctions explicitly or implicitly taught to them. The nature and the consequences of this socialization are likely to be quite familiar to most counselors by now.

Second, disempowerment of women occurs also because of externally generated factors they face on a daily basis simply because they are women. In our society, women are widely considered to be separate and unequal to men in power, privilege, and status. Their gender-typical characteristics, choices, and contributions at home and in the work force are treated as secondary to those of men. Such obviously "sexist" dynamics have also received considerable attention in the counseling literature most frequently in discussions of women's career issues. In this chapter, I will focus instead upon certain social and relationship issues that illustrate the gender-related disempowerment of women and suggest some ways that counselors can help women cope with the personally and externally generated restrictions and devaluations endemic in women's lives today. Specifically, I will discuss (a) negative consequences of women's relationship orientation in adulthood, (b) the feminization of poverty, and (c) violence by men against women.

CONSEQUENCES OF WOMEN'S RELATIONSHIP ORIENTATION

A central component of women's lives is caring for and about others. Participants in research widely agree that characteristics associated with satisfying relationships such as emotional sensitivity are the essence of psychological femininity, defined as characteristics considered typical and desirable for women (Cook, 1985). Gallos (1989) described how this relationship orientation is a central theme in women's lifelong development and life/career choices. Empathizing with others may be essential to psychological development from early infancy throughout life (Surrey, 1985). Many women may see their life's work, whether paid or unpaid, as defined or qualified in terms of the interpersonal relationships involved (Grossman & Chester, 1990). Whereas men have traditionally been encouraged to view their individual achievement and intimate relationship efforts as belonging to two distinct spheres of life, women are prone to define their accomplishments in terms of the relationships involved or to view work and relationship responsibilities and decisions by necessity as intertwined with each other.

This relationship orientation represents both a source of strength and a liability for women. Counselors are well aware of the importance of satisfying, intimate relationships for the mental health of both women and men. Considerable evidence suggests that relationships with and among women tend to be more intimate and supportive than those of men (Cook, 1990). Women serve as major providers of emotional support at home and in their broader social networks and are likely to respond to others in need (Belle, 1987; Wethington, McLeod, & Kessler, 1987). In turn, they are more likely than men to mobilize a wide range of social support for themselves when in distress (Belle, 1987). This social support may well serve as an important buffer of stress for women.

On the other hand, this relationship orientation may pose real liabilities for women as well. The role of provider of support for others may also mean that women can experience personal stress themselves when involved in the distress of others and experience a support gap if they do not receive sufficient support from others in return for their efforts (Belle, 1987; Wethington et al., 1987). Helping professionals of both sexes frequently experience these stressors as contributing to burnout.

Other liabilities stem from society's definition of relationship building and maintenance as central to women's gender identity and roles. Individual women and others around them are prone to view caring for and about others as *necessary* components in women's life choices, determining a primary commitment to duties of wife/mother/homemaker, career choices in helping and service occupations dominated by women, and a resolve to maintain troubled interpersonal relationships at all costs. Gallos (1989) has stated that "Growing up female has often meant relinquishing freedom of expression and choice in order to sustain relationships" (p. 119). Although traditional life choices are satisfying for many women, many other women have paid a steep price for following life paths socially prescribed as right for women in general rather than developing choices right for them as individuals. Women, in particular mothers of young children working outside of the home, may experience role overload when they maintain the bulk of housekeeping and parenting responsibilities in addition to their paid work (McBride, 1987). Women are also more likely than men to assume complete care of chronically ill and aged individuals. It is assumed that women can and will do the caretaking on their own (Eichler & Parron, 1987).

Women's relationship orientation has been implicated in common mental health problems seen in women. Thoits (1987) labeled women's support-giving obligations as a unique source of stress for them, placing them at a disadvantage in terms of their mental health. Experts have noted that women, because of their gender socialization, may deny their own needs in favor of meeting the needs and wishes of others and work to maintain even those relationships destructive to themselves because they perceive that it is their responsibility to do so. This tendency, when coupled with disappointments in relationships and society's devaluation of women's relationship capacities, may predispose women to depression (Kaplan, 1986). Other women have been labeled "codependent" for this reason, denying themselves while enabling others to continue their own destructive behaviors.

Thus, women may encounter a variety of problems because of their gender-socialized relationship orientation. Some of these problems may be an inevitable consequence of a notable strength that women enjoy; others, an example of a "deficiency" or personal identity issue on the part of an individual woman; still others attributable to the expectations and reactions of others. How counselors address these problems in counseling can have a significant impact upon women's ability to explore new possibilities for themselves with dignity and self-respect.

THE FEMINIZATION OF POVERTY

Our individualistic society today promotes the myth that anyone can "make it in the world" with sufficient motivation and effort (Spence, 1985). To a large extent, wealth is thus seen as a matter of individual merit. The issues contributing to the origins and maintenance of poverty are too complex to unravel here. Yet, without debating the validity of the sociopolitical ideology underlying this myth about success, it can be argued that the sexes in our society today face somewhat different sets of gender-related factors influencing their economic standing. The intersection of the personal and the social recognized in the reciprocal perspective on gender is endemic in many women's economic plight today.

The widely repeated phrase "the feminization of poverty" succinctly portrays the relationship between economic status and being female in today's society. Factors contributing to the feminization of poverty are diverse, related to women's career development, women's traditional parenting and homemaking responsibilities, society's devaluing of their paid work and domestic contributions, and recently, women's increasing assumption of major or sole economic support for their children and themselves as well.

In particular, divorce means poverty for many women. Numerous experts have pointed out that a woman's income after divorce drops precipitously compared to the income of her husband (e.g., Bianchi & Spain, 1986; Weitzman, 1985; Zopf, 1989), with women less likely to remarry as well. Weitzman (1985) extensively documented the consequences of typical financial and custody settlements for women and children today, arguing the existence of a direct link between divorce, its economic consequences, and the rise in poverty for women. Current divorce laws attempt to be gender neutral, treating the partners as equally able to support themselves at the time of divorce, rather than presuming a right for a woman's continued financial support by her husband after divorce. Weitzman has argued that this assumption of equality does not consider very real differences in opportunities and earning capacity between the sexes as a result of typical role allocation in marriages and sex differentiation of the work force. Consequently, women at every income level predivorce are at risk for a markedly reduced standard of living after divorce. For some women, poverty is the result of a change in role from full-time homemaker to a prospective member of the paid work force with little previous experience and few easily transferable job skills. A 55-year-old counseling client exemplified well the poignant situation of such women. Laura's husband left her for a younger woman after more than 30 years of marriage, during which Laura served as full-time mother and homemaker. Bewildered and trusting, Laura agreed to a divorce settlement leaving her with little more than a small stipend for several years, only until she completed community college. Laura eked out a living with an educational grant, contributions from her church community, and food stamps. She found her classes difficult to master, and with some regret returned to her hometown to care for an aging parent.

Women like Laura are economically vulnerable in part because of choices made early in life to devote themselves exclusively to women's traditional homemaking / nurturing roles. Laura's bewilderment at her predicament reflected her surprise at being punished for making life decisions expected for women of her generation. In Weitzman's (1985) words, Laura and women like her fulfilled their end of the marital bargain, only to discover that society has changed the rules for them.

Female heads of households with young children are particularly prone to experience poverty. An increasing number of women today must depend upon their own earnings or public assistance to support themselves and their families rather than upon a man's financial support (Smith, 1986). A substantial proportion (65% in the years 1969–1978) of persistently poor individuals were members of female-headed households; the proportion for black family members was even higher (Corcoran, Duncan, & Hill, 1986). Such women face a daunting array of factors: the need to provide both primary income and caretaking for their children; decreased ability to work because of their caretaking responsibilities; and the most plentiful employment opportunities in the more transient, poorly paying service sector.

Zopf (1989) starkly analyzed the relationship between numbers of dependent children and poverty for women. Each additional child represents a greater likelihood for poverty than for other types of families. Women can expect little help from public resources: contrary to popular opinion in some sectors, AFDC payments provide poor compensation for the additional financial burdens faced by such mothers. On the other hand, Zopf noted that mothers working outside the home face child care expenses that consume a substantial portion of their income, and there are not enough satisfactory child care facilities to meet the need for them. It may simply not pay some women to work outside of the home.

Female heads of households who are divorced rarely have significant financial help from their ex-husbands, either. Alimony payments are increasingly rare, child support generally does not match the financial burden of raising children, particularly child care expenses, and it is difficult to enforce fathers' compliance with child support arrangements. Current estimates suggest that the noncompliance rate ranges from 60% to 80% (Eichler & Parron, 1987; Weitzman, 1985). Weitzman tartly concluded that "In the end the current legal system places the economic responsibility for children on their mothers and allows fathers the freedom to choose not to support their children" (p. 321).

Women who decide to work outside of the home often face opportunities limited not only by their own career preparation and child care responsibilities, but assumptions about women's work embedded within the job market. Statistics on women and work regularly demonstrate continued sex differentiation of the labor force and that "women's jobs" are paid more poorly than are the jobs men typically occupy (Bianchi & Spain, 1986), observations which Feldberg (1986) attributed to systematic devaluation of women's contributions and skills. Stereotypes that women do not really need to work and do not have a real commitment to their paid work persist. Smith (1986) argued that the very nature of the jobs most readily available to women in need of paid employment—low paying and unstable jobs in the service sector—is a major factor contributing to the feminization of poverty. In Smith's words: "Because of the social relationships and expectations that stereotyped them as nonwage workers in the past, women are expected to accept less than standard employment—employment that is frequently less than full time, considerably less stable, and substantially lower paid" (p. 138). Russo and Denmark (1984) have also pointed out that benefits typically offered in paid work tend to be linked to degree of participation and level of earnings, so that women are further disadvantaged. Covert and overt sex discrimination on the job further disadvantages women singly and as a group, but is beyond the scope of this discussion.

Also, as briefly noted above, poor women can expect little real help from public assistance programs in the United States to cope with their multifaceted problems (Bianchi & Spain, 1986). Kamerman (1986) has provided an enlightening analysis of public assistance programs in the United States and elsewhere that highlights the shortcomings in current policies.

Finally, poverty places women at increased risk for mental health problems as well. Poor women face chronic stress, poor nutrition, and lack of support and social services, all of which can promote or exacerbate psychological problems (Shore, 1987). Minority women are likely to be at particular risk.

Thus, the increasing problem of the feminization of poverty can be attributed to a combination of gender-related factors more or less applicable to an individual woman's situation: life choices not emphasizing or precluding preparation for a stable, economically sound career; women's major responsibility for child care, including financial support (and men's relative lack of involvement as a group); the structure of the present job market, traditional assumptions about women and work, and employment practices discriminatory against women; divorce settlements, public policy, and resources not recognizing the dilemmas characterizing women's lives today. The combination of all of these factors can leave women feeling trapped, with few resources to draw upon and few viable options to choose from. Solutions to the problems need to be multifaceted as well.

MALE VIOLENCE AGAINST WOMEN

The gender socialization of women that predisposes them toward a strong relationship orientation has provided many women with a profoundly satisfying orientation to life (though one not without its stresses and strains). Another aspect of the gendered context of women's lives is a clearly tragic one: the prevalence of male aggression against them. A high percentage of women are likely to become targets of childhood sexual abuse, rape, or battering perpetrated by men at some point in their lives. Accurate statistics on incidence are impossible to obtain, in part because of women's tendency to under-report or to relabel violence against them. Koss's (1987) extensive review suggests that sexually abusive contacts in childhood may have been experienced by 15% to 65% of women, and completed or attempted rape by 15% to 44%. McCann, Sakheim, and Abrahamson (1988) concluded that one third of all women may experience childhood sexual abuse; up to half are victimized by attempted or completed rape; and up to 1.8 million wives are the target of domestic violence each year.

Such violence against women is a gender-related issue because it occurs much more frequently to women than to men and because of the nature of traditionally defined male/female relationships within our society. Hilberman (1984) succinctly summarized the commonalties among varieties of sexual violence against women:

> The large majority of victims of spouse abuse, incest, and rape are female, and their assailants are most often men who (with the possible exception of rapists) are trusted relatives and intimates. In all of these acts of violence, women and girls are perceived by their assailants as legitimate targets for male aggression. (p. 216)

Walker (1989) described "the problem of violence against women as one of misuse of power by men who have been socialized into believing they have the right to control the women in their lives, even through violent means" (p. 695).

The psychological dynamics accompanying forms of sexual violence are complex and differ somewhat according to the form that the violence takes (e.g., father-daughter incest versus physical battering between spouses). However, a common denominator across forms of violence appears to be men's efforts to control or dominate women, attitudes linked to broader social devaluation of women (Herman, 1988; Walker, 1989). This conclusion will be examined more closely by a brief look at rape and battering.

Rape

Hilberman's conclusion that women are much more likely to suffer violence at the hands of men that they know rather than strangers applies to rape as well as forms of violence by definition occurring within a relationship (e.g., battering) (see also Koss, 1987). In a recent survey of college students, acquaintance rape was nearly eight times as common as rape by strangers (Koss, Dinero, Seibel, & Cox, 1988). Why do men sexually attack women, including women that they may know well?

Rape has been stereotypically and incorrectly seen as a crime motivated by sexual desire. Instead, the issue is power rather than sexual gratification (Walker, 1989). Recent studies on sexually aggressive men suggest that the act is typically motivated by anger at women and a need to dominate and control them (Lisak & Roth, 1988). These dynamics may apply to men identified as having the potential to engage in sexually coercive activities falling short of rape as well as convicted rapists. These men are likely to perceive themselves as having been hurt by women and tend to be attuned to power dynamics between the sexes.

Rape continues to be a crime that is difficult to prove. With the exception of attacks committed in public or by groups, there are generally no witnesses. Victims' efforts to gain justice are compromised by negative social attitudes blaming them for being sexually provocative or for not taking enough precautions to prevent it. Contacts with authorities may hurt rather than help their post-rape recovery (e.g., Wyatt, Notgrass, & Newcomb, 1990). The message that women are responsible for preventing men from hurting them is a sad commentary on traditional gender roles that has tragic consequences for women already traumatized by assault.

Battering

Battering is profoundly disempowering to women because the violence is from the hands of a person to whom they are deeply committed, is chronic and often life threatening, and is designed to maintain the man's absolute control over her. Battering men tend to see women as legitimate targets for men's aggression, who in this view are permitted such lengths to control "their" women and sustain their sense of personal adequacy. Although battering men may insist that they cannot control their own battering behavior, paradoxically that behavior is intended precisely to help them regain control in the relationship (Long, 1987; Ptacek, 1988). Romero (1985) likened strategies used by battering men to those commonly suffered by prisoners of war: psychological abuse intended to terrorize the woman, efforts to strengthen her emotional dependency upon him and isolation from others, to strengthen the power of the batterer's beliefs and behavior over her. Coercion and manipulation are the keys.

Women battering victims are stereotypically blamed for provoking the violence, especially by the batterers themselves (e.g., Ptacek, 1988), or for not leaving because of feminine passivity, masochism, or true love. A more accurate composite picture of these women is being anxious, depressed, paralyzed, isolated, afraid for their own and their children's safety, with few personal economic resources or alternatives to insure their safety (Hilberman, 1984; Rosewater, 1985; Walker, 1989). Battered women often work hard to actualize their belief that they can somehow find a way to increase the periods of love that occasionally occur in such relationships and to eliminate the ever-increasing violence. Rather than being "passive," battered women often have strong coping skills developed to increase the probability of their own and their children's safety. Their perceptions that life and death issues are at stake are quite accurate (Walker, 1989).

Traditional gender socialization increases the likelihood that women can be trapped within a battering relationship. Women taught that they will derive their primary sense of identity from "their" man, that they must honor and obey him, or that they must rely upon a man for economic sustenance are less likely to leave a destructive relationship. Generally speaking, women have traditionally had the responsibility to care for others, and men have been seen as entitled to women's care of them (Westkott, 1986). Women may feel that they must protect men and their own identity as men's partners by giving up or hiding their own strengths (Gilbert, 1987). Conversely, Gilbert argued that, because men are dependent upon women (e.g., to validate their masculinity), men are motivated to exert power over them, including through jealousy and violence.

Traditional socialization thus makes individual women more vulnerable to the dynamics inherent in battering relationships (Romero, 1985). However, such individual socialization does not cause battering to occur. The roots of battering are broader gender-related attitudes encouraging men to use physical aggression to maintain a sense of control over others.

The Psychological Consequences of Violence

Sexual violence is profoundly disempowering to women for a variety of reasons. Women frequently suffer serious and chronic psychological symptoms as a consequence of the act(s). Across types of sexual violence, certain sequelae are common: anxiety, fear, and avoidance; depression and affective constriction; poor self-esteem; suicidal behaviors; substance abuse; disturbed social functioning and intimate relationships; and often sexual dysfunction as well (Koss, 1987; McCann et al., 1988). A diagnosis of post-traumatic stress disorder is often appropriate. The long-term effects of incest can persist into adulthood, years after the offense occurred (Browne & Finkelhor, 1986). The symptoms manifested by battered women can be severe enough to be confused with indicators of schizophrenia or severe personality disorder (Rosewater, 1985). For survivors of rape, there may be little difference in psychological consequences whether the rapist was known to the survivor or was a stranger (Koss et al., 1988).

Coping after sexual violence requires the survivor to challenge basic assumptions about herself and the world (cf. Janoff-Bulman & Frieze, 1987; Koss & Burkhart, 1989; McCann et al., 1988). How an individual woman copes with victimization may depend upon her preexisting cognitive schema related to herself and others in the areas of safety, trust, power, esteem, and intimacy. Violence can profoundly wound a woman's sense of self and others (McCann et al., 1988). She may no longer view herself as relatively invulnerable and others as good or trustworthy. She can doubt her own sense of worth and competence and her ability to judge situations and to protect and nurture herself. Her sense of comfort in the world is especially shaken because the violence occurred within an interpersonal context rather than the impersonal violence of a natural disaster. When the violence is personally directed at her by someone she knows, she cannot comfort herself with the reassurance that it was a random event that coincidentally occurred to her.

Paradoxically, the coping strategies survivors typically employ after an assault to help them reestablish a sense of coherence to the world can be further disempowering. Some women may attempt to deny, avoid, minimize, or reinterpret the nature of the event (e.g., "It wasn't really rape"; " It was just the liquor that made my husband beat me and it won't happen again"). Self-blame can help to reestablish some sense of personal control at the same time that it damages the survivor's already shaken sense of self. Negative responses from others can reinforce her self-blame: acquaintance rapists who "remember" her willing participation, memories of incest perpetrators who told her that she was "bad," battering partners who blame her for provoking them. Perpetrators of violence are likely to minimize their responsibility for the act and the damage done to the victim (Ptacek, 1988; Scully & Marolla, 1984). Others not directly involved in the incident itself are frequently prone to blame her at least in part, whether from damaging gender stereotypes (e.g., "Men can't control themselves sexually when a woman acts or dresses like a slut") (Koss & Burkhart, 1989; Walker, 1989) or from a desire to reassure themselves that, because they are somehow different from the victim, such violence cannot happen to them (Janoff-Bulman & Frieze, 1987).

Invalidating responses from others compound the trauma of rape. One former client was repeatedly raped by several men who broke into her apartment at night and broke in again later that week to rob her. In her interactions with the police, she had difficulties convincing them that, contrary to her assailants' story, she did not willingly let them in for a wild party! Friends and members of a rape survivors' group told her that she was "too" upset and angered by the experience. What they meant was that they found her reactions overwhelming to cope with themselves.

Koss and Burkhart (1989) suggest that a central task in recovering from sexual violence is for a survivor to realize that she was not to blame for her victimization. The difficulty of this recovery task is compounded by the nature of her efforts to cope and by broader gender-relevant ideologies that blame women for their victimization and condone male violence to solve problems or dominate others. Counselors can help women work through their trauma once they understand the nature of sexual violence in general and detect it in an individual client. Unfortunately, cases of sexual victimization often go undetected because many victims will not or cannot offer that information, and counselors may not explore or deal with the possibility of victimization with their clients because of ignorance or their own negative attitudes about victims (Downing, 1988; Dye & Roth, 1990).

Sexual violence can also be disempowering to women who have never personally experienced it. Because of its ubiquitousness, the very possibility of sexual violence shapes the choices of women who fear it. To prevent it, women may make relatively minor and common compromises such as choosing parking spaces for safety rather than for convenience, up to drastic measures to control their own behavior and their environments in the hopes of discouraging men from committing such violence. It may, in fact, be accurate to argue that coping with the possibility of sexual violence is part of every adult woman's life experience.

Women do have some control over whether they choose to tolerate some abusive situations, how they cope with violence when its occurs to them, and choices they might make to minimize or maximize chances of its occurrence. These options are all shaped to some extent by an individual woman's sense of herself as a woman, linked to her experiences in a society organized according to gender. Yet counselors must remember that women are not the frequent targets of sexual violence *because* of their socialization. Sexual violence happens to so many women because the gendered context of the world around them permits and even sanctions it. Empowerment of women against sexual violence requires coping and confrontation with it as a reality in women's lives, rather than simply asking why an individual woman may have suffered from violence on a given occasion.

COUNSELING WOMEN

Counseling women toward empowerment involves helping them explore the issues that facilitate or interfere with their efforts to realize a personally satisfying blending of individual achievement and relationship issues in their lives. In this process, because of the gendered context of their lives, women must directly or indirectly grapple with what it means to them to be a woman in today's society. Before discussing some specific implications for counseling of insights into gender and women's lives, it is worthwhile to consider more carefully the implications of the conceptual perspective proposed earlier. How counselors understand the nature of the problems that clients present in counseling plays a major role in deciding what goals and counseling strategies seem most appropriate in helping them work through their issues.

Implications of Counselors' Conceptual Perspective

The most familiar explanations for gender differences focus upon gender as a property of the individual. This individualistic perspective stresses that the sexes behave the way that they do because they were born or taught to be that way from early life on. Consequently, men and women bring two different sets of personality traits, attitudes, behaviors, and so on to various situations. To explain psychological problems faced by the sexes, proponents of the individualistic perspective assume that each sex is predisposed to experience certain problems because of their gender socialization (Cook, 1990). O'Neil (1981) stated this perspective concisely: "Men and women have each learned only about one-half of the attitudes, skills, and behaviors necessary to cope with life" (p. 64).

Counselors adopting this perspective would be likely to ask: "What gender-socialized characteristics of this client are contributing to his or her problems?" The next step in counseling would be to design remedial strategies to overcome these deficiencies, such as teaching new behaviors (e.g., assertion skills) or working to expand a client's gender-restricted notions of appropriate life roles.

The reciprocal perspective briefly described earlier extends the individual perspective to recognize the influence of gender in the very context of our lives. Individuals act the way they do not only because of their own gender-socialized personal characteristics, but because of how gender shapes essential features of the environment in which they live. Counselors implementing the reciprocal perspective would need to ask a broader range of questions than those proposed by the individual perspective in order to determine the most appropriate way to work with the client's problem. In addition to looking at the client's gender-socialized personal characteristics, the counselor might ask, for example, "How are others responding to the client's behavior? Is the client struggling with contradictory or extremely demanding messages from others about what she as a woman should be doing? Is she expected to behave as a woman very differently in different situations? Is she being devalued or otherwise punished for making choices considered appropriate for a woman (e.g., being a full-time homemaker)?"

To put it briefly, counselors thinking about gender issues today must consider whether they consider gender to be an individual characteristic that they must empower individuals to overcome, or whether it is a feature of daily life that individuals must learn to cope with in other ways as well. Poor women present one such challenge for counselors. Counselors focusing upon individual characteristics may look to a woman's inadequate educational and career development and attempt to empower her by clarifying work options, training opportunities, job search skills, and so on. For some women, such a skills-oriented problem solving approach may be sufficient. For many other women, however, the approach is doomed to failure because it fails to consider the broader context in which she lives: the caretaking responsibilities to which she has committed herself; attitudes about women's roles and responsibilities she confronts from others and how she copes with those environmental prescriptions and constraints; experiences she has had as a woman that shaped her sense of possibilities for herself (e.g., educational and career, previous relationships including violent ones); resources she can draw upon in making life changes, including family and friends' support and community resources including welfare and job training programs.

These questions would automatically occur to many counselors accustomed to thinking in terms of person/environment interactions for issues that are not specifically gender-related. However, the common tendency to view gender primarily as a property of the individual (as is biological sex) can restrict a counselor's ability to think about the complexity of gender issues in a client's life. Our ability to help these women is correspondingly restricted as well.

Counselors interested in helping women work through these gender-related issues in their lives need to develop an approach to counseling that explicitly recognizes the role of gender in women's lives today. Good, Gilbert, and Scher (1990) have proposed an approach to "gender-aware therapy" based upon principles that can be incorporated into a variety of counseling approaches. These principles include viewing gender as a central part of counseling and mental health; considering how clients' problems are affected by their societal context; working actively to change gender injustices; developing collaborative and egalitarian relationships with clients; and respecting clients' freedom to choose what is right for them as individuals, rather than because of preconceived ideas about gender correctness. These ideas are consistent with the reciprocal perspective on gender issues and offer challenges to counselors in the areas of problem identification and goal setting/design of strategies. Some specific counseling applications are briefly described next.

Problem Identification

As noted above, counselors need to be aware of how they conceptualize the gender-relevant nature of the client's problem: Is she having difficulties because of her own gender-socialized personal characteristics (e.g., her self-concept as a woman, traditional attitudes, or restricted life role options), characteristics of the gendered context in which she lives (e.g., expectations and sanctions imposed by others), or a combination? Brown (1986) provided a detailed guide for doing a gender role analysis for an individual that yields a comprehensive picture of what an individual client learned about gender in her life and how she has translated these lessons in her own decisions and reactions. Another guide to gender role analysis is outlined in Cook (1985).

Counselors should be aware that what they define as a psychological problem attributable to gender socialization is influenced by what they look for and how they interpret what they see. Ever since the publication of the highly influential study by Broverman, Broverman, Clarkson, Rosenkrantz, and Vogel (1970) on sex bias in standards for mental health for men and women, the issue of whether practitioners' own gender-related values and beliefs affect their work with clients has attracted considerable attention. There are large sex differences in diagnosis of psychological problems (e.g., Cleary, 1987), so that simply diagnosing a particular disorder more frequently in one sex is not automatically a sign of sex bias.

What is of greater concern is whether counselors' values, and those of the diagnostic tools they use, cause them (however innocently) to apply different standards to identify psychological problems in each sex, often to the detriment of women. Kaplan (1983) argued that simply behaving in a feminine stereotypic manner is enough to earn a woman a "disturbed" diagnostic label (e.g., dependent or histrionic personality disorder) where masculine stereotypic behavior is not similarly diagnosed (e.g., being independent to the point of insensitivity to others). In other words, women may be diagnosed as disturbed for behaving in a way that they are socialized to do, where men are not. This difference reflects the devaluing of women's socialized characteristics relative to men's in our society.

Counselors should also be aware that common and predictable reactions to sexual abuse may appear to take the form of serious psychological disturbance. For example, as noted earlier, childhood sexual abuse has been linked to serious psychological reactions lasting for years. Battered women may exhibit symptoms identified as indicative of schizophrenia or borderline personality disorder, though in their case such symptoms may be quite realistic responses to the terror and the chaos of their lives (Rosewater, 1985).

There is little doubt that interpersonal trauma can contribute to the development of serious psychological problems in women. However, with few exceptions (e.g., adjustment disorders and post-traumatic stress disorder), current diagnostic categories are notably silent about the central role of environmental stress in these disorders. Debate about whether and how counselors should use such diagnostic systems at all is beyond the scope of this chapter. Counselors *should* seriously question whether the use of certain specific diagnoses can suggest a "blaming the victim" mentality, where the helper sees only woman's "deficiencies" rather than appreciating what a woman's behavior communicates about what she has experienced. Problem identification and diagnosis can be disempowering rather than an empathic summary of a client's pain.

Goal Setting

The next major step in counseling practice involves setting goals for the counseling relationship. Goals such as "helping a woman become more androgynous" are too ambiguous and do not represent the complexities of being a woman in a gendered society (Cook, 1985). Specific goals may be consistent with a variety of counseling approaches (e.g., person-centered, behavioral, cognitive). In my own counseling practice, I have found several basic themes related to the topics discussed here to apply to many women's situations.

First, women clients tend to be demoralized, feel powerless in their lives, and have low self-esteem. Experiences commonly associated with being a woman today—for example, sexual and emotional abuse in relationships, societal devaluing of their life role and career choices, multiple role demands and struggles in caring for others— coupled with the particulars of their own experience can leave women emotionally exhausted and blaming themselves for their inadequacies in dealing with the challenges of their lives. Enhancing a woman's sense of control over her life and its personal value is usually an important focus in counseling. Framing her behavior as representing positive (though perhaps ultimately ineffective) efforts to cope with her life situation can be helpful.

Second, I have observed that many women do not think about their lives as separate problems that can be handled sequentially with problem solving techniques. For example, relationship issues frequently appear in different guises across disparate types of problems, and relationship and career/educational/economic issues are often closely intertwined. Certain goals may be prioritized as most important, but many women also seem to appreciate the flexibility to explore interconnections inherent in their lives by exploring different aspects of their problems simultaneously.

Third, counselors should be aware that changes made as a consequence of counseling do not occur within a vacuum. The interactional nature of gender guarantees that changes a woman makes in her self-concept, attitudes, behavior, and so on will lead to corresponding changes in others' treatment of her as a woman. This is particularly true for social/family issues, which by their very nature are rooted in relationships. Because of the importance of relationships in many women's lives, the impact of their behavior upon others is likely to be of special concern. In the case of sexually violent relationships, consequences may well be life threatening. Counselors have a responsibility to discuss explicitly with women the effect personal changes may have in their lives.

Finally, a woman's career development and individual economic resources can have a significant impact upon her current life choices, possibilities, and her sense of herself in other areas of her life as well (e.g., her ability to assert herself in intimate relationships). Counselors can help her to define personal success in her own terms, and to expand her range of future options for herself.

Counseling Applications

A variety of counseling approaches and strategies can be useful in helping women work through gender issues in counseling, ranging from supportive exploration of personal perceptions to skills-oriented behavioral techniques (Cook, 1985). Individual, family/marital, and group counseling modalities have been recommended, with some specific recommendations for their application.

In individual counseling, the establishment of an egalitarian relationship between the counselor and the client appears to be particularly important (Good et al., 1990). Positioning the counselor in the role of expert is avoided. Instead, the client's rights as a consumer are emphasized, and the counselor attempts to validate her experiences as a woman and serves as a role model, including engaging in self-disclosure (Gilbert, 1980). Stiver (1986) has provided one view on how traditional helping approaches have, in contrast, been distancing and disempowering to women.

In family and marital approaches, counselors need to be aware that certain views of family relationships and emphasis upon maintaining relationship unity and stability above all can unwittingly reinforce traditional asymmetry of power among its members. The result can be the counselor serving as yet another social agent enforcing traditional gender roles in the family, rather than working with the family to promote change. For example, some approaches to work with battering couples can avoid confronting the nature of and responsibility for the violence (Adams, 1988). Hare-Mustin's (1984) article is a classic statement of gender issues in family therapy, while Walters, Carter, Papp, and Silverstein (1988) have discussed and provided examples of gender-fair family counseling.

From the beginning of the feminist movement, counselors have also recognized the power of the group in helping women struggle with gender issues, ranging from professionally led counseling/psychotherapy groups to less structured self-help or exploration groups (e.g., Kravetz, 1980). Groups have become a preferred modality for working with survivors of sexual violence (e.g., Courtois, 1988). Counselors can serve such groups as leaders, trainers, consultants, supervisors, and program developers, in the role of advocate for women working through gender-related issues with other women sharing such experiences (e.g., Walker, 1989).

Whatever counseling modalities or strategies are used, counselors need to think carefully about the implications of their approaches for the choices that women eventually make as an outcome of counseling. The case examples that follow illustrate some of these issues.

CASE EXAMPLES

The Case of Lisa

Women frequently feel responsible for caring for others in their lives, even though those responsibilities may seriously limit their lives in a number of ways. Lisa was an unmarried woman in her twenties who had adopted sole responsibility for caring for her invalid father, despite having siblings who could take more responsibility and provide some resources to hire nursing help. She was her father's only "pal," the only caretaker who attempted to amuse him as well as care for his physical needs. Yet she felt guilty and defensive about her failure to establish a career other than the several service-sector jobs she performed. She also complained about the lack of support and understanding about her predicament from others, who criticized her touchiness and moodiness.

From a developmental framework, a counselor might note the importance of Lisa's establishing a stable career path for herself at this time in her life and wonder about the stress related costs to her of dealing with an invalid whose demands were occasionally capricious and over time more onerous with his decline. Also, shouldn't Lisa be striving to be more independent economically and emotionally independent from her family at this time in her life? However, Lisa's counselor recognized the importance of her caretaking to her self-image and to her preparation for his impending death. Empowerment for Lisa meant providing validation for her caretaking efforts while helping her to pursue temporary job possibilities that enhanced her self-esteem and emphasizing the importance of her obtaining nurturing support from others. Lisa became more selective in her social contacts as her self-esteem increased and more patient with her self-labeled "problems" in coping with stress.

The Case of Christine

Christine's caretaking role helped to keep her in poverty and involved with a disturbed man. Her pervasive depression was linked to her self-perceived "abandonment" of her children into a family member's care when she had to do so. When one child died, she blamed herself for not somehow preventing it by being a better mother. She could not leave her partner because he needed her and had been there for her earlier. Yet he refused her permission to leave the house to work, and she resorted to selling her blood plasma for pocket money.

Empowerment for Christine meant coming to view herself as a resourceful person who had indeed been a good caretaker in her own way. Her counselor regularly expressed admiration for her creative efforts to cope with her grief and financial stress. Grieving for her child essentially reestablished the relationship in symbolic ways. She lost patience with her partner's demands, rapidly gained responsibility on her first full-time job in years, and reveled in her new role of grandmother.

The Case of Pat

Pat entered counseling convinced that she was codependent (as labeled by another counselor) because she could not order her intermittently chemically abusing child to leave her house. She also wondered what was wrong with her because she appeared to be more generous with her time and resources than did others. Counseling focused upon helping her to clarify what she wanted and expected from a variety of relationships and how relationship difficulties could be attributed to others' problems as well as shortcomings for which she was always ready to blame herself. She came to view herself as gifted in relationships, as indeed her counselor viewed her, and became more direct about what she desired from others in return. Her child continues to live with her.

The Cases of Amy and Sandra

Two mothers supporting their families on public assistance reached different decisions about their work: Amy decided that job training was not for her, though she did eventually find a part-time job "to get away from the kids for a while." Sandra initially pursued paid employment to provide a better Christmas for her children and was elated to find how much her employers valued her skills and personal style. Counselors accustomed to valuing career planning activities specifically for career enhancement may need to think about their reactions to such clients, whose job related motivations may (at least initially) appear to be quite different or absent. In the case of Amy, she felt that her income pieced together from a variety of public assistance programs was satisfactory, and she did not feel that it was relevant to explore further in counseling. Knowing the importance of financial independence for women and the value many counselors may place upon paid work as a result of their own backgrounds and professional training, how can and should counselors react to Amy's perceptions? What would "empowerment" mean in the lives of women similar to Amy? Such questions can be difficult to answer, but are essential to consider in counseling women today.

In these situations, the counselor may well wonder whether the client should be helped to be less of a caretaker and more autonomous in her life choices. Are women too passive, dependent, or otherwise too feminine when their caretaking causes them problems? Perhaps, but a counselor who automatically concludes this about caretaking and women is communicating more about his or her oversimplification and devaluation of women's choices than concern about the sexism inherent in women's lives. In each of these situations, the counselor helped the client to define caretaking for herself, value her own capacity to care for others, explore the consequences of her choices, and make choices for herself in the context of relationships that she desired to nurture.

The counselor in each situation also recognized the central importance of others' reactions to each woman's behavior. Each client was acutely aware that others expected her to be a good caretaker, yet she felt criticized for how she did it. Counseling for empowerment helps women to see the double binds their caretaking may immerse them in, and to consider life choices that respect the value of connections with others while meeting their own needs as individuals.

As suggested earlier, counselors should consider that, for many women, decisions about career and economic independence also need to be made in the context of the rest of their lives, including important relationships. Some women's decisions may not be consistent with counselors' own values about work.

COUNSELING RESOURCES

Multifaceted issues such as those discussed in this chapter can require resources and skills beyond those available to the individual counselor. Indeed, counselors need to be aware of the community resources available to help women cope with these issues. Victim service programs (cf. Young, 1988), community rape crisis centers and support groups, battered women's shelters, incest and rape survivors' counseling groups, programs providing education and support to female heads of households, and public assistance programs especially designed for women's and children's needs are examples of the types of programs counselors need to be familiar with in their communities. In some cases, referral may be all that is needed to empower women to deal with their life situations. In other cases, counselors may help women integrate the support and changes offered by such community resources into a broader perspective on their lives.

For community resources to be empowering for women, they need to feel that they have the right both to use and to refuse the services. Ideally, the resources should be seen as an extension of rather than a substitute for their own strengths. Finally, gender aware therapy emphasizes that an individual's problems must be understood within his or her societal context—the personal is political (Good et al., 1990). Counselors can help women clients see that their personal problems may be shared by many women, rooted in a societal context that limits their options and does not value the choices that they do subsequently make. Thus, women's efforts to empower themselves through counseling and other resources can be a self-affirming response to an environment that has negated their personal value rather than a final admission of personal inadequacy.

PROBLEM PREVENTION AND SOCIAL INTERVENTIONS

Proponents of gender-fair counseling recognize that counselors must be willing to work actively to change the societal conditions promoting the injustices experienced by women (Good et al., 1990). In the case of the issues discussed in this chapter, the essence of broader social change lies in an understanding of the power and consequences of the gendered context shaping all of our lives.

Part of this necessary understanding can be gained through counseling and education on the individual level. However, there is a danger in individual interventions: failing to appreciate the social context that has inevitably molded our individual experiences (Hare-Mustin & Marecek, 1988; Mednick, 1989). The reciprocal perspective on gender reminds us that, for fundamental change to occur, the interaction between the individual and the environment must receive our attention.

Counselors may work toward such fundamental changes through an expanded range of roles. For example, Downing (1988) proposed a framework for victim services recognizing different possible combinations of counseling target, purpose, and method based upon Morrill, Oetting, and Hurst's (1974) classic cube model for counselor interventions. This model can be adapted to a variety of problems to stimulate thinking about innovative interventions. Among other possibilities, counselors can take a proactive role in working toward legislation and policies designed to improve women's economic situation, such as fair labor practices, parental leave policies of employers, and adequate public support programs for mothers and their families.

In working toward social changes, counselors need to ponder just what would constitute gender-fair practices. Simply failing to engage in sexist practices may inadvertently reinforce the gendered status quo—a sin of omission rather than commission (Good et al., 1990). Policies that openly espouse "equality" between the sexes in the guise of gender neutrality may be unwittingly dangerous in how they overlook very real differences in the sexes' needs, resources, and power. Hare-Mustin and Marecek (1988) have argued that when there are differences between the groups, "neutral" policies can have the result of favoring the group with the advantages. Weitzman's (1985) analysis of gender-neutral divorce proceedings illustrates how this can occur. Nor is it sufficient simply to help women adapt to a "man's world" by aspiring to men's prerogatives and adopting men's strategies in attaining them. This goal of assuming that "men means women too," in Gentry's (1989) words, fails to address the societal values that permit such pervasive gendered problems as the feminization of poverty and violence against women, and also does not work very well for women.

Ideally, social interventions will need to occur on two levels: intermediate interventions designed to help women cope with the consequences of the current gendered context of their lives and more pervasive changes promoting a new, less oppressive world for both sexes. Focused, intermediate interventions such as victim assistance or affirmative action programs not only help the individuals involved, but can communicate a clear message about what individual attitudes and behavior are considered acceptable today. The reciprocal perspective on gender suggests that such interventions can serve an invaluable role in the evolution of gender change in our society.

SUMMARY

Gender is a central organizing principle in society and our everyday life, prescribing personality characteristics and behaviors, attitudes, life roles, responsibilities, and prerogatives for each sex. Gender-related behavior is the end product of a reciprocal interaction among individual characteristics, others, and features of the environment. The gendered context of women's and men's lives affects how individuals negotiate a blending of individual achievement and relationship satisfactions for themselves. Ideally, through this process individuals develop a sense of personal empowerment, though gender differentiation can make this process difficult.

For women, disempowerment can be attributed to individual factors such as problematic self-perceptions and restrictive life preferences, externally generated factors, or a combination. Three categories of social and relationship issues illustrating the gender-related disempowerment of women are the negative consequences of women's relationship orientation, the feminization of poverty, and violence by men against women.

How counselors view the causes of these gender-related problems will have a marked impact upon how they choose to address them in the counseling relationship: as a personal, gender-socialized problem that they must empower women to overcome for themselves, a consequence of everyday coping in a gender-differentiated society, or a combination. Counselors' perspective on gender issues have implications for problem identification, goal setting, and specific counseling strategies used. Case examples illustrated some of these implications for the choices that women make as an outcome of counseling and the importance of helping women to explore personally meaningful possibilities in their lives.

Issues discussed in this chapter are multifaceted, requiring the coordination of community resources available to women. Women need to feel that they have a right to use or refuse such services, that the services are an extension of their own personal strengths, and that their problems are unique to themselves, but shared by many women in a gender-differentiated society. Counselors must be willing to work actively in order to change the social conditions maintaining the injustices experienced by women. An expanded range of roles for counselors can help to work toward fundamental changes in women's lives.

REFERENCES

Adams, D. (1988). Treatment models of men who batter: A profeminist analysis. In K. Yllo & M. Bograd (Eds.), *Feminist perspectives on wife abuse* (pp. 176–199). Newbury Park, NJ: Sage.

Belle, D. (1987). Gender differences in the social moderators of stress. In R. C. Barnett, L. Biener, & G. K. Baruch (Eds.), *Gender and stress* (pp. 257–277). New York: Free Press.

Bianchi, S. M., & Spain, D. (1986). *American women in transition.* New York: Sage.

Broverman, I. K., Broverman, D. M., Clarkson, F. E., Rosenkrantz, P. S., & Vogel, S. R. (1970). Sex-role stereotypes and clinical judgments of mental health. *Journal of Consulting and Clinical Psychology, 34*, 1–7.

Brown, L. S. (1986). Gender role analysis: A neglected component of psychological assessment. *Psychotherapy, 23*, 243–248.

Browne, A., & Finkelhor, D. (1986). Impact of child sexual abuse: A review of the research. *Psychological Bulletin, 99*, 66–77.

Cleary, P. D. (1987). Gender differences in stress related disorders. In R. C. Barnett, L. Biener, & G. K. Baruch (Eds.), *Gender and stress* (pp. 39–72). New York: Free Press.

Cook, E. P. (1985). *Psychological androgyny*. Elmsford, NY: Pergamon.

Cook, E. P. (1990). Gender and psychological distress. *Journal of Counseling and Development, 68*, 371–375.

Corcoran, M., Duncan, G. J., & Hill, M. S. (1986). The economic fortunes of women and children: Lessons from the panel study of income dynamics. In B. C. Gelpi, N. C. M. Hartsock, C. C. Novak, & M. H. Strober (Eds.), *Women and poverty* (pp. 7–24). Chicago: University of Chicago Press.

Courtois, C. A. (1988). *Healing the incest wound: Adult survivors in therapy*. New York: Norton.

Deaux, K., & Major, B. (1987). Putting gender into context: An interactive model of gender-related behavior. *Psychological Review, 94*, 369–389.

Downing, N. E. (1988). A conceptual model for victim services: Challenges and opportunities for counseling psychologists. *The Counseling Psychologist, 16*, 595–629.

Dye, E., & Roth, S. (1990). Psychotherapists' knowledge about and attitudes toward sexual assault victim clients. *Psychology of Women Quarterly, 14*, 191–212.

Eichler, A., & Parron, D. L. (Eds.). (1987). *Women's mental health: Agenda for research*. Rockville, MD: U.S. Department of Health and Human Services, National Institute of Mental Health.

Feldberg, R. L. (1986). Comparable worth: Toward theory and practice in the United States. In B. C. Gelpi, N. C. M. Hartsock, C. C. Novak, & M. H. Strober (Eds.), *Women and poverty* (pp. 163–180). Chicago: University of Chicago Press.

Gallos, J. V. (1989). Exploring women's development: Implications for career theory, practice, and research. In M. B. Arthur, D. T. Hall, & B. S. Lawrence (Eds.), *Handbook of career theory* (pp. 110–132). Cambridge, England: Cambridge University Press.

Gentry, M. (1989). Feminist perspectives on gender and thought: Paradox and potential. In M. Crawford & M. Gentry (Eds.), *Gender and thought: Psychological perspectives* (pp. 1–16). New York: Springer-Verlag.

Gilbert, L. A. (1980). Feminist therapy. In A. M. Brodsky & R. Hare-Mustin (Eds.), *Women and psychotherapy* (pp. 245–266). New York: Guilford.

Gilbert, L. A. (1987). Female and male emotional dependency and its implications for the therapist-client relationship. *Professional Psychology, 18*, 555–561.

Good, G. E., Gilbert, L. A., & Scher, M. (1990). Gender aware therapy: A synthesis of feminist therapy and knowledge about gender. *Journal of Counseling and Development, 88*, 376–380.

Grossman, H. Y., & Chester, N. L. (Eds.) (1990). *The experience and meaning of work in women's lives*. Hillsdale, NJ: Lawrence Erlbaum.

Hare-Mustin, R. T. (1984). A feminist approach to family therapy. In P. P. Rieker & E. Carmen (Eds.), *The gender gap in psychotherapy: Social realities and psychological processes* (pp. 301–308). New York: Plenum. [Originally published in *Family Process*, (1978), *17*, 181–194.]

Hare-Mustin, R. T., & Marecek, J. (1988). The meaning of difference: Gender theory, post-modernism, and psychology. *American Psychologist, 43*, 455–464.

Herman, J. L. (1988). Considering sex offenders: A model of addiction. *Signs, 13*, 695–724.

Hilberman, E. (1984). Overview: The "wife-beater's wife" reconsidered. In P. P. Rieker & E. Carmen (Eds.), *The gender gap in psychotherapy: Social realities and psychological processes* (pp. 213–236). New York: Plenum. [Originally published in American *Journal of Psychiatry*, (1980), *137*, 1336–1347.]

Janoff-Bulman, R., & Frieze, I. H. (1987). The role of gender in reactions to criminal victimization. In R. C. Barnett, L. Biener, & G. K. Baruch (Eds.), *Gender and stress* (pp. 159–184). New York: Free Press.

Kamerman, S. B. (1986). Women, children, and poverty: Public policies and female-headed families in industrialized countries. In B. C. Gelpi, N. C. M. Hartsock, C. C. Novak, & M. H. Strober (Eds.), *Women and poverty* (pp. 41–64). Chicago: University of Chicago Press.

Kaplan, A. (1986). The "self-in-relation": Implications for depression in women. *Psychotherapy, 23*, 234–242.

Kaplan, M. (1983). A woman's view of DSM-III. *American Psychologist, 38*, 786–792.

Koss, M. P. (1987). *The women's mental health research agenda: Violence against women*. Rockville, MD: U.S. Department of Health and Human Services, National Institute of Mental Health.

Koss, M. P., & Burkhart, B. R. (1989). A conceptual analysis of rape victimization: Long-term effects and implications for treatment. *Psychology of Women Quarterly, 13*, 27–40.

Koss, M. P., Dinero, T. E., Seibel, C. A., & Cox, S. L. (1988). Stranger and acquaintance rape: Are there differences in the victim's experience? *Psychology of Women Quarterly, 12,* 1–24.

Kravetz, D. (1980). Consciousness-raising and self-help. In A. M. Brodsky & R. Hare-Mustin (Eds.), *Women and psychotherapy* (pp. 267–283). New York: Guilford.

Lisak, D., & Roth, S. (1988). Motivational factors in nonincarcerated sexually aggressive men. *Journal of Personality and Social Psychology, 55,* 795–802.

Long, D. (1987). Working with men who batter. In M. Scher, M. Stevens, G. Good, & G. A. Eichenfield (Eds.), *Handbook of counseling and psychotherapy with men* (pp. 305–320). Newbury Park, NJ: Sage.

McBride, A. B. (1987). Position paper. In A. Eichler & D. L. Parron (Eds.), *Women's mental health: Agenda for research* (pp. 28–41). Rockville, MD: U.S. Department of Health and Human Services, National Institute of Mental Health.

McCann, I. L., Sakheim, D. K., & Abrahamson, D. J. (1988). Trauma and victimization: A model of psychological adaptation. *The Counseling Psychologist, 16,* 531–594.

Mednick, M. T. (1989). On the politics of psychological constructs: Stop the bandwagon, I want to get off. *American Psychologist, 44,* 1118–1123.

Morrill, E., Oetting, E., & Hurst, J. (1974). Dimensions of counselor functioning. *Personnel and Guidance Journal, 52,* 354–359.

O'Neil, J. M. (1981). Male sex role conflicts, sexism, and masculinity: Psychological implications for men, women, and the counseling psychologist. *The Counseling Psychologist, 9,* 61–80.

Ptacek, J. (1988). Why do men batter their wives? In K. Yllo & M. Bograd (Eds.), *Feminist perspectives on wife abuse* (pp. 133–157). Newbury Park, NJ: Sage.

Romero, M. (1985). A comparison between strategies used on prisoners of war and battered wives. *Sex Roles, 13,* 537–547.

Rosewater, L. B. (1985). Schizophrenic, borderline, or battered? In L. B. Rosewater & L. E. A. Walker (Eds.), *Handbook of feminist therapy* (pp. 203–213). New York: Springer.

Russo, N. F., & Denmark, F. L. (1984). Women, psychology, and public policy: Selected issues. *American Psychologist, 39,* 1161–1165.

Scully, D., & Marolla, J. (1984). Convicted rapists' vocabulary of motive: Excuses and justifications. *Social Problems, 31,* 530–544.

Shore, B. K. (1987). Position paper. In A. Eichler & D. L. Parron (Eds.), *Women's mental health: Agenda for research* (pp. 74–79). Rockville, MD: U.S. Department of Health and Human Services, National Institute of Mental Health.

Smith, J. (1986). The paradox of women's poverty: Wage-earning women and economic transformation. In B. C. Gelpi, N. C. M. Hartsock, C. C. Novak, & M. H. Strober (Eds.), *Women and poverty* (pp. 121–140). Chicago: University of Chicago Press.

Spence, J. T. (1985). Achievement American style: The rewards and costs of individualism. *American Psychologist, 40,* 1285–1295.

Stiver, I. P. (1986). The meaning of care: Reframing treatment models for women. *Psychotherapy, 23,* 221–226.

Surrey, J. L. (1985). *Self-in-relation: A theory of women's development* (Works in progress, no. 13). Wellesley, MA: Wellesley College, Stone Center for Developmental Services and Studies.

Thoits, P. (1987). Position paper. In A. Eichler & D.L. Parron (Eds.), *Women's mental health: Agenda for research* (pp. 80–105). Rockville, MD: U.S. Department of Health and Human Services, National Institute of Mental Health.

Unger, R. (1989). Sex, gender, and epistemology. In M. Crawford & M. Gentry (Eds.), *Gender and thought: Psychological perspectives* (pp. 17–35). New York: Springer-Verlag.

Walker, L. E. A. (1989). Psychology and violence against women. *American Psychologist, 44,* 695–702.

Walters, M., Carter, B., Papp, P., & Silverstein, O. (1988). *The invisible web: Gender patterns in family relationships.* New York: Guilford.

Weitzman, L. J. (1985). *The divorce revolution: The unexpected social and economic consequences for women and children in America.* New York: Free Press.

Westkott, M. (1986). Historical and developmental roots of female dependency. *Psychotherapy, 23,* 213–220.

Wethington, E., McLeod, J. D., & Kessler, R. C. (1987). The importance of life events for explaining sex differences in psychological distress. In R. C. Barnett, L. Biener, & G. K. Baruch (Eds.), *Gender and stress* (pp. 144–156). New York: Free Press.

Wyatt, G. E., Notgrass, C. M., & Newcomb, M. (1990). Internal and external mediators of women's rape experiences. *Psychology of Women Quarterly, 14*, 153–176.

Young, M. (1988). Common bonds of victimization. *The Counseling Psychologist, 16*, 642–646.

Zopf, P. E. (1989). *American women in poverty*. New York: Greenwood Press.

7

The Hardy Woman:
Health Issues in Adulthood

Judith A. Lewis
Governors State University

W omen live longer than men, but have more illnesses along the way. We use health services more frequently than males, but are less likely to be taken seriously by our physicians. We receive more than our share of drug prescriptions, but are left out of the research studies that determine whether these drugs are safe. We seek wellness but may be deprived of the internal control and power that are associated with optimal health.

All health matters should be considered from the perspective of a biopsychosocial approach (Engel, 1977; Schwartz, 1982), which recognizes the interaction of biological, psychological, and social components in each individual's well-being. Any considera-tion of adult women's health must address the interactions among these factors. Women's special health concerns are affected not only by their biological sex but also by gender-based behavior differences, social stressors, and discrimination. In answer to the question, "Why a focus on *women's* health?" Rodin and Ickovics (1990) pointed out that some health concerns are unique to women, that sex differences in mortality and morbidity have been documented, that our knowledge of women's health has been limited because of the male focus of health research, and that health risks differ between women and men. Moreover:

> Psychosocial factors are also likely to differentially affect women's and men's health. Women and men engage in social roles that often differ, if not in quantity, certainly in quality. Sex differences in role expectations, environmental qualities, role burdens related to the domains of work and family, and abilities to adapt and cope with stressful situations may also have a

distinctive impact on health. Imbalances in social roles, and subsequently in power, equality, and control, are likely to affect women's health adversely. Within these roles, women are more likely than men to be subjected to interpersonal violence, sexual discrimination, and harassment. (p. 1018)

WOMEN'S HEALTH CONCERNS

In discussing women's health concerns, we need to examine differences in mortality and morbidity rates between females and males, as well as issues and problems affecting women only.

Sex-Related Differences in Mortality and Morbidity

Although it would be inappropriate to take male health as the norm against which women's concerns are compared, it is appropriate, and in fact necessary, to consider the sex-related differences that characterize health and illness.

Mortality

In terms of mortality rates, females show a distinct advantage over males.

In every moment across the life span, from conception to death, girls and women are, on the average, biologically more advantaged and live longer than boys and men. Approximately 125 male fetuses are conceived for every 100 female fetuses, and 106 live male babies are born for every 100 female babies. Almost 33% more boys than girls die in the first year of life, and an equal sex ratio does not occur until age 18, when 100 young men are alive for every 100 young women. This ratio steadily decreases so that by age 87, only 1 man is alive for every 2 women....Women now comprise 53% of our country's population, a proportion that is steadily increasing. (Strickland, 1988, pp. 381–382)

In each of the leading causes of death among Americans, age-adjusted mortality rates are higher for men than for women (Rodin & Ickovics, 1990). For instance, coronary heart disease is the leading cause of death for both men and women in the United States, but men have three times the risk of developing a major cardiovascular event before the age of 60; women at any age have half the risk of men of the same age (Strickland, 1988). Men are also much more likely to die prematurely as a result of such behaviorally influenced events as homicide, accidents, or suicide, a fact that is not surprising given the greater likelihood that a man will "engage in life threatening, high risk, competitive behaviors" (Strickland, 1988, p. 389).

Because differences between male and female mortality rates begin before birth, the female advantage must be attributed, at least in part, to biological factors. Some scientists have explained differences in mortality in terms of a protective function played by the second X chromosome or by hormonal differences. Clearly, however, lifestyles also have an important role to play. In today's society, the diseases that account for most deaths are preventable, controllable, and affected by such behavioral risk factors as cigarette smoking, drug and alcohol use, diet, and exercise ("Preventable Diseases," 1990). Traditionally, men have been more likely than women to engage in risky behaviors. Now, the gap between male and female mortality rates has begun to close. Men's death rate from heart disease has decreased in recent years, while the mortality rate for women has remained constant. Cancer rates also declined more rapidly for men than for women during the 1980s (Rodin & Ickovics, 1990). Lung cancer has replaced breast cancer as the leading cause of cancer death for women (Strickland, 1988). In fact, between 1979 and 1986, lung cancer deaths rose 7% among men and 44% among women, a statistic that can be attributed to increased smoking by women. Even now, women's smoking rates are declining more slowly than men's. As women intensify their participation in health compromising behaviors, their advantage in terms of mortality rates can be expected to decrease. Smoking and alcohol use increase risks for a number of health problems. In addition, some risk behaviors hold particular dangers for women. For instance, the combination of smoking with use of birth control pills appears to increase the risk of stroke. As dangerous and controllable health compromising behaviors increase among women, the need for counselors to play a role in risk reduction becomes more and more apparent.

Morbidity

Whether morbidity is defined in terms of the presence of specific illnesses or general poor health, women's morbidity rates are higher than men's. In general, females are more likely than males to suffer from both chronic and acute diseases. They are more likely to suffer from illnesses resulting in restricted activity and use of health care facilities. One common explanation for this phenomenon is that women, more than men, report their illnesses and seek help. Women are, in fact, more likely than men to seek health care, but this factor does not fully account for high morbidity rates. Hypertension, rheumatoid arthritis, lupus, diabetes, anemia, and a number of other diseases are more prevalent in women than in men. Women also have more surgeries than men and are more likely to suffer from acute conditions.

A number of ideas have been put forth to explain women's high rates of illness. Wilson (1988) suggested that morbidity is associated with poverty and that a disproportionate number of women live in poverty. Albino and Tedesco (1984) wrote that poverty contributes to the disproportionate deaths of black women from anemias and from complications of pregnancies and abortions and that women in lower socioeconomic groups have an extremely high incidence of obesity, which in turn places them at risk for such problems as hypertension, coronary heart disease, diabetes, gall bladder problems, arthritis, varicosities, and foot problems. Weisensee (1986) pointed out that, though most explanations for gender differences in illness focus either on stress or on the compatibility of the sick role with cultural norms for women, a number of other explanations might also be plausible:

1. Mothers are exposed more frequently to the symptomatically acute illness of their children.
2. Proxy effects in surveys may distort the reporting of illness.
3. Bias on the part of medical practitioners may define women's complaints as hypochondriacal or inconsequential, resulting in palliative treatments, repeat visits for recurring symptoms or both.
4. Normal but exclusively female functions may have been assigned definitions as illnesses requiring medical intervention.

5. Ways women demonstrate distress may be considered "ill behavior," while ways men exhibit distress are defined as something else.
6. Women misunderstand the nature of their ills and overuse doctors.
7. Men are genetically or biologically superior to women and therefore are less susceptible to illness.

Obviously, some of Weisensee's explanations seem more intuitively correct than others, but her general point is an important one. None of the available models fully explains sex differences in morbidity. Any attempt at a more comprehensive answer must take into account biological, social, and economic phenomena.

Mental Health Issues

Differences between females and males in physical health concerns are joined by sex-related differences in mental health. "Frequencies and patterns of mental disorder are vastly different for women and men" (Russo, 1990, p. 368). Women are much more likely than men to receive diagnoses of major depression, agoraphobia, or simple phobia, while antisocial personality disorders and alcohol related problems are much more prevalent among men. In fact, depression among women is so prevalent that it can be seen as a major health crisis. The American Psychological Association's National Task Force on Women and Depression addressed this problem and found victimization, discrimination, poverty, and gender socialization at its core (McGrath, Keita, Strickland, & Russo, 1990). Highlights of their findings on risk factors associated with women's depression included the following:

❏ Women are at higher risk for depression due to a number of social, economic, biological, and emotional factors.
❏ Women's depression is related to certain cognitive and personality styles, that is, avoidant, passive, dependent behavior patterns; pessimistic, negative cognitive styles; and focusing too much on depressed feelings instead of action and mastery strategies.
❏ The rate of sexual and physical abuse of females is much higher than previously suspected and is a major factor in women's depression. Depressive symptoms may be long-standing effects of post-traumatic stress syndrome for many women.
❏ Marriage confers a greater protective advantage on men than on women. In unhappy marriages, women are three times as likely as men to be depressed. Mothers of young children are highly vulnerable to depression; the more children in the house, the more depression is reported.
❏ Poverty is a "pathway to depression."

Clearly, poverty is associated with psychological distress (Belle, 1990), and being a woman or a minority group member increases the likelihood that one is poor. Low-income and ethnic minority women face serious concerns, both in mental and in physical health.

Health Concerns of Low-Income and Ethnic Minority Women

In the United States, ethnic minority women share a number of common health concerns.

> Minority women in the United States suffer a disproportionate share of illness....(They) experience higher infant and maternal mortality rates; greater prevalence of chronic diseases such as diabetes, hypertension, cardiovascular disease, and certain types of cancer; and a lower life expectancy than their White counterparts. (Manley, Lin-Fu, Miranda, Noonan, & Parker, 1984, p. II-37)

Each minority group also faces unique health problems. Among American Indian and Alaska Native women, for instance, health issues include high infant and maternal mortality and morbidity rates; serious problems with alcoholism and alcohol abuse, with associated pregnancy problems and fetal alcohol damage; extremely disadvantaged economic conditions; and high degrees of stress exacerbated by single parenthood and cultural conflicts (Manley et al., 1984). Asian and Pacific Island women face the special challenges of "socioeconomic deprivation, cultural barriers (including severe language problems) and unfamiliarity with the health care system" (Manley et al., 1984, p. II-42). African-American women are more prone than white women to be affected by hypertension, obesity, and high blood cholesterol levels, all of which are associated with heart disease (Cope & Hall, 1987). Black women are almost twice as likely as white women to have strokes, with sickle cell anemia increasing susceptibility for some individuals. Mortality due to diabetes is also disproportionate, with the death rate for African-American women with diabetes being 35% higher than that for white diabetics. Maternal mortality is also a major problem in the African-American community; black women are three times as likely to die while pregnant as white women. Lupus is also three times more common in black women than in their white counterparts. Hispanic women, too, are disproportionately affected by high risk pregnancies, obesity, diabetes, and hypertension (Manley et al., 1984).

Running through all of the special health concerns of minority women are problems related to poverty and lack of access to good health care.

> In studying the physical health of women, it is obvious that the problems of minority and poverty women are overwhelming in their magnitude....For women of poverty and their families, the inability to obtain health care that is responsive to their needs is just one more cycle in an interminable downward spiral that has already included physical and material want, social alienation, powerlessness, and despair. (Albino & Tedesco, 1984, p. 170)

Issues Related to Women Only

Issues Related to Reproduction

Although many health concerns affect women and men differentially, a few are exclusive to women. The fact that women's health issues are unique becomes especially clear when we consider reproduction.

Through the 20th century, pregnancy and childbirth have become increasingly medicalized in the sense that they have come to be seen as medical events to be controlled by physicians (Riessman, 1983). Riessman has suggested that the medicalization of childbirth served first to increase the dominance of professional physicians over midwives and healers and then to differentiate obstetricians from general practitioners. Identification of childbirth as a medical—even pathological—process brought with it a tendency to use more complex technologies, including the Caesarean section. Writing in 1983, Riessman pointed out:

> There is a trend toward more Caesarean births. Although some of these are necessary for maternal health as well as infant survival, evidence suggests that many Caesareans are unnecessary. In view of medicalization, it is important to point out that the potential need for a Caesarean places childbirth squarely and exclusively in the hands of the physician. (pp. 7–8)

This trend continues today. In fact, 23% of births in the United States are by Caesarean section, and it has been predicted that this average could rise to 50% of all births in the United States over the next 20 years (Rodin & Ickovics, 1990). Moreover, new technologies, such as *in vitro* fertilization, embryo transfer, and artificial insemination have created new and unforeseen problems.

Currently, problems related to medicalization are being overpowered by a still more serious issue: politicization of reproduction.

> Less than a decade ago, forums on childbirth and childbirth technology focused on the rights of women to be involved in decisions about their care, and debates raged over rooming in, licensing of midwives, and the superiority of the home or the hospital as a birthplace. The current discourse pits birthing women against their babies and puts obstetricians in the role of adjudicating disputes over whose interests should come first. The steadily increasing focus on the fetus-as-patient has led to demands by some doctors and lawyers that pregnant and laboring women should be subjected to physical regulation, forced surgery, detention, or even criminal or civil punishment for behavior deemed dangerous to the fetus. (Rodin & Ickovics, 1990, p. 1030)

Recent efforts to punish women for exposing fetuses to cocaine point up the problems that are likely to occur when politics enters the arena of pregnancy and childbirth.

> The legal prosecution of pregnant addicts places mother and fetus in the roles of legal adversaries despite the fact that they constitute a biologically interdependent system and not separate individuals. Since the fetus is totally depend upon the mother until birth, virtually everything she does is likely to impact it. Thus, if the mother is to be held accountable for any behavior which may threaten the health of her unborn child, noncompliance with medical advice, failure to exercise, dietary deficiencies, etc., also become grounds for legal prosecution. Such a position would be difficult to justify. (Smith, 1990, p. 23)

In addition to interfering with women's reproductive rights, such punitive approaches have the practical effect of discouraging pregnant women from seeking prenatal care.

Politicization is nowhere more apparent than in the ongoing controversy over abortion. A woman's right to make the decision whether or not to bear a child would seem to be basic. Yet attempts to limit freedom of choice continue to be a part of the political scene in the United States despite the fact that those limitations may endanger a woman's physical and mental health.

> There is substantial literature that documents the serious health, social, psychological, and economic consequences of unintended and unwanted childbearing. These consequences include increased maternal and infant death and illness, unstable marriages, and the restriction of educational and occupational opportunities leading to poverty and limited roles for women. These adverse effects are not shared equally by all segments of our society, but fall more heavily on those who are poor, black, or young. (Russo & David, n.d.)

Issues Related to Work and Family Stress

Baruch, Biener, and Barnett (1987) have pointed out that research on the relative stressfulness of work and home settings has been based on men's lives.

> Because stress research has tended to focus on men, the work place has both implicitly and explicitly been identified as the primary stressor....The home, in contrast, has been viewed as a sanctuary, as a benign environment in which one recuperates from problems at work. This picture reflects not only a male-based view but also the assumption that for women the roles associated with home—wife, mother, homemaker—are somehow "natural" and free from undue stress....The work role has thus been viewed as the most likely catalyst for psychological distress and impaired health in women. (p. 130)

In fact, the role of paid worker has *not* been found to increase women's risks for mental or physical health problems. For example, some studies have found that homemakers were more vulnerable to depression than employed women, others that family role stressors have a more deleterious effect on psychological states than work-related stressors. In general, differences between employed and unemployed women in mental and physical health outcomes clearly favor the employed woman. "Despite the current media fascination with women who flee the work place, subtracting the role of paid worker is unlikely to reduce a woman's stress level overall, except perhaps on a short-term basis for the mother of very young children" (Baruch et al., 1987, p. 132). The work place can be a source of support, social ties, challenge, and self-esteem enhancement, all of which are correlated with good health.

Of course, carrying out multiple roles is not an unalloyed pleasure. Balancing several roles can be seen either as a source of increased rewards or as a source of role strain. Individual differences depend on the quality of the roles involved. High paid, high status jobs are a source of well-being for women (Baruch, Barnett, & Rivers, 1983); low level, low paid jobs, in contrast, are a source of stress. The effects of multiple roles are also mediated by other characteristics of the roles. Overload is greatest for mothers of very young children and for married women whose husbands contribute little to household labor and child care (Repetti, Matthews, & Waldron, 1989).

> Qualitative aspects of paid work, and of marriage, motherhood, and homemaking, clearly affect interrelationships among social roles, psychological distress, and health....Not all jobs are good for women— neither are all marriages or all parenting experiences. (Baruch et al., 1987, p. 134)

Thus, the unique characteristics of the person and her environment determine both the degree of stress in the individual's life and the health outcomes associated with it.

PERSONAL CHARACTERISTICS ASSOCIATED WITH HEALTH AND ILLNESS

A number of personal characteristics appear to be associated with the individual's vulnerability to health problems. Among the personal factors affecting positive or negative health events are hardiness, a sense of coherence, a disposition toward optimism, and a number of factors related to cognition and coping mechanisms (Lewis, Sperry, & Carlson, in press).

Hardiness

Kobasa (1979) studied business executives who had experienced stressful life events and found that some individuals were able to maintain their health more effectively than others. The "hardy personality style" that differentiated these healthy people from their less healthy peers included three components: commitment, as opposed to alienation; control, as opposed to powerlessness; and challenge, as opposed to threat (Kobasa, Maddi, & Courington, 1981). Hardy individuals show a high degree of commitment, involving themselves fully in life and work and believing that their lives are meaningful. Their belief in the possibility of control is closely related to this sense of commitment. They tend to take responsibility for their own lives and to believe that they can influence events. This perception helps the individual to see change as a challenge and a source of stimulation, rather than as a threat. "Thus a hardy person's attempt to influence the course of some event (control) includes curiosity about how it happened and interest in what it is (commitment), plus an attempt to learn from it whatever will enhance personal growth (challenge)" (Kobasa et al., 1981, p. 369).

Because the subjects of Kobasa's original study included 900 male executives and only 20 females, she has stated that "Hardiness studies are essentially studies of personality and stress resistance in men" (Kobasa, 1987, p. 322). Subsequent studies, however, have included women and addressed gender differences. Hardiness *has* been found to mediate the effects of stress on the well-educated, middle-class women who made up the samples in some studies, though a study of female secretaries showed no such effect.

> The early hardiness work involved executives and professionals....One might speculate that occupational settings serve to enhance or stifle the stress resistance effect of personality. Business executives may find themselves in jobs that allow them to exercise, and perhaps even to grow in, commitment, control, and challenge. Secretaries, on the other hand, may confront jobs which limit their expression of hardiness. It may indeed be the case, for example, that some bosses enjoy expressions of control at the expense of their secretaries' sense of control. (Kobasa, 1987, pp. 324–325)

Sense of Coherence

The concept of the "sense of coherence" (Antonovsky, 1979, 1984, 1987) also includes several components: comprehensibility, manageability, and meaningfulness. A person with a sense of comprehensibility believes that events are ordered and ex-plainable, rather than chaotic and random. An individual with a high sense of manageability believes that events are controllable. Meaningfulness is the emotional counterpart to comprehensibility.

> People who are high on meaningfulness feel that life makes sense emotionally, that at least some of the problems and demands posed by living are worth investing energy in, are worthy of commitment and engagement and are challenges that are welcome rather than burdens. (Antonovsky, 1984, p. 129)

Together, these components make up the "sense of coherence" that Antonovsky saw as health-enhancing.

Dispositional Optimism

Scheier and Carver (1987) identified a disposition toward optimism, or "generalized expectations that good things will happen" (p. 171), as the characteristic explaining positive and negative health outcomes. Several studies seemed to support this idea. In one study (Scheier & Carver, 1985), optimistic college students reported fewer stress-related symptoms than pessimists during the last 4 weeks of an academic semester. Another study (Scheier & Carver, 1987) showed that optimists showed better recovery rates than pessimists after bypass surgery. A later study by Carver and Pozo (Adler, 1991) traced the progress of 60 women with breast cancer, with preliminary results indicating that optimists reported less distress than pessimists throughout their medical ordeals.

The impact of optimism may be due to its effect on behavior, with optimists and pessimists using different types of coping strategies.

> When confronting adversity optimists keep trying, whereas pessimists are more likely to get upset and give up. These coping-strategy differences may provide an explanation (at least in part) for the link that has been established between optimism and physical well-being. (Scheier & Carver, 1987, p. 191)

Sense of Control

The individual's belief in his or her ability to exert control over events seems to be important in maintaining health and minimizing disease. "Study after study (has) reported the commanding role of self-definition, self-perception, and sense of control in the maintenance and enhancement of health" (Seeman, 1989, p. 1108). For instance, Seeman and Seeman (1983) found in interviews with more than a thousand individuals that sense of control was associated with health maintenance activities and health status. Rodin and Langer (Rodin, 1986; Rodin & Langer, 1977; Buie, 1988) found in multiple studies that experiences and perceptions of control affected the health status of older people. Taylor, Lichtman, and Wood (1984) found that cancer patients who believed that they had personal control over the progression of the disease made better adjustments and had better outcomes than those who expressed helplessness and denial. In fact, both Kobasa's hardiness construct and Antonovsky's sense of coherence highlight the importance of the healthy person's sense of control.

In general, control seems to be an important factor for both men and women, but there may be some gender-related differences in the kind and degree of control exerted.

> One can argue for a difference between control conceived of as (1) a sense of personal competence or mastery, and that defined as (2) generalized expectancies regarding control within oneself (rather than in others or fate) over a variety of personal, interpersonal, and broad sociopolitical domains. It may be that the former—that is, feeling effective in what it is that one has to do in life—is more important for women's stress resistance than it is for men's. The latter, more important for men, appears dependent on believing that one holds securely within oneself general influence over all of life's arenas. (Kobasa, 1987, pp. 317–318)

The concept of perceived self-efficacy (Bandura, 1982) is closely related to questions of individual control. The person who judges himself or herself as able to mobilize the skills for dealing with challenging situations is more likely to experience success in these situations than is the person who lacks a sense of self-efficacy and therefore gives up or avoids the challenge.

> In any given activity, skills and self-beliefs that ensure optimal use of capabilities are required for successful functioning. If self-efficacy is lacking, people tend to behave ineffectually even though they know what to do....The higher the level of perceived self-efficacy, the greater the performance accomplishments. Strength of efficacy also predicts behavior change. The stronger the perceived efficacy, the more likely are people to persist in their efforts until they succeed. (Bandura, 1982, pp. 127–128)

Self-efficacy appears to be an important component in health maintenance, affecting such behaviors as the ability to quit smoking (Curry, 1989; DiClemente, 1981), the ability to avoid relapse in addictive behaviors (Marlatt & Gordon, 1985), and the ability to maintain generally healthy lifestyles (Schunk & Carbonari, 1984, p. 244). "When knowledge of health risks is combined with a strong sense of efficacy for avoiding them, long-term maintenance of healthy lifestyles results" (Schunk & Carbonari, 1984, p. 244).

Coping Mechanisms

Although stress plays an important role in health, its effects are mediated by the coping mechanisms people use. If we think of coping as "the process of managing demands (external or internal) that are appraised as taxing or exceeding the resources of the person" (Lazarus & Folkman, 1984, p. 283), we can see that the individual's interpretation of events is an important variable. Stress-related health problems result from a combination of three variables: external demands, individual perceptions, and physiological responses. People can cope with stressors by making changes at any of these three points. They can use problem-solving strategies to exert control over the environment and thereby lessen the stressors; they can alter their mental processes so that they are more likely to view situations as challenging, rather than threatening, or they can alter their physiological responses through relaxation techniques. In general, coping can be categorized as either problem-focused or emotion-focused (Lazarus & Folkman, 1984), with problem-focused coping involving constructive action and emotion-focused coping attempting to regulate the individual's own responses. Coping responses can also be categorized in terms of a distinction between active and avoidance strategies (Cohen, 1988).

Stress seems to affect people's health differently, depending on the effectiveness of the coping strategies selected. No one coping mechanism is always preferred. For instance, Suls and Fletcher (1985) found that avoidance strategies were associated with poor outcomes over the long term but that, in the short term, denial played a helpful role. In general, problem-focused coping strategies are adaptive when situations are amenable to change and emotion-focused coping is more effective when stressors are uncontrollable. Because the most effective coping mechanisms are the ones that are appropriate to the specific situation, the most effective adapters may be people with several types of coping skills in their repertoires.

Social Support

The variable of social support affects both the onset of health problems (Cohen, 1988; Gentry & Kobasa, 1984) and recovery from serious illnesses (DiMatteo & Hays, 1981). Gentry and Kobasa (1984) emphasized the role of social support as a buffer that may protect people from the harmful effects of chronic high stress levels. Cohen (1988) made a distinction between stress-buffering models and main-effect models, which see access to social support as being an important predictor of health regardless of stress levels. Either conceptualization recognizes that the links between social resources and health can result from the interplay of a number of factors, including the availability of information and advice; the role of social support in enhancing self-esteem, identity, and motivation; the presence of social controls and encouragement of health-enhancing behaviors; and the presence of tangible problem-solving assistance.

The preponderance of evidence indicates that social support, along with personality variables, cognition, and coping mechanisms, can have a major effect on health outcomes. Strickland (1988), citing the relevance of hardiness, sense of coherence, control, and active coping to health outcomes, pointed out that women, who have been socialized toward passivity and dependency, may not be able to adapt in the healthiest possible ways to life events.

> Appropriate power, predictability, and perceived control all appear to influence health in positive ways....Yet, in contrast to men, women have less power in this society, less control over their lives, and are less likely to live in a predictable and coherent world. (p. 396)

Strategies aimed toward the health enhancement of women must encourage a sense of control, provide training in the skills that make self-management possible, and use interventions that add to the individual's repertoire of coping mechanisms.

COUNSELING STRATEGIES

Lewis et al. (in press) have suggested a set of guidelines for counselors to follow in dealing with health concerns. These guidelines included the following:

1. Because health problems are complex and multivariate, we should think of health and illness in terms of a continuum, rather than a dichotomy.
2. Because the development of health-enhancing behaviors and the avoidance of health compromising behaviors require personal skills, we need to use psychoeducational methods aimed at skill building.
3. Because a sense of personal control is basic to health enhancement, we need to use interventions designed to increase individual perceptions of control and self-efficacy.
4. Because health is at least partly a function of the interaction between the individual and the social environment, we need to use interventions designed to build social support and lessen environmental stressors.

A positive, nonmedical approach of this kind is especially relevant for women, many of whom experience low self-esteem and feel a lack of control over their lives.

The Health–Illness Continuum

Traditional medical models, which tend to emphasize symptomatology and to make sharp distinctions between health and disease, may fail to help women recognize their competencies and strengths. As Young-Eisendrath and Wiedeman (1987) pointed out,

> Deficit thinking directs our attention toward what is absent, deficient, or wrong in a person or situation.…This kind of framework emphasizes weakness or problematic elements and de-emphasizes—or even ignores—strengths, and leads finally to the medical model of illness or distress.…The illness model often reinforces the sense of defeat a woman experiences in trying to master the circumstances of her life. (p. 4)

Young-Eisendrath and Wiedemann (1987) suggested that deficit thinking is as problematic for assessing mental health concerns as it is for diagnosing physical ailments.

> Unfortunately, when a psychiatric label such as "borderline personality disorder" is affixed to a person, one tends to feel that something "scientific" has been done. We can easily believe that we have objectively isolated an ailment we can treat, when in fact we have done nothing more than reinforce a questionable system of nomenclature. (p. 5)

The assessment process should focus on the client's resources and competence, rather than solely on her deficiencies, and lead in the direction of planning for positive life changes. Thinking of health and illness in terms of a continuum helps in this process by diverting attention away from diagnostic labels and toward health enhancement. This way of conceptualizing health is also more accurate than dichotomous thinking. Consider the chronic illnesses experienced by many women. We cannot, for example, divide the population into the categories of those who have heart disease versus those who are disease-free. Instead, we need to think of a continuum from low risk through higher risk to acute distress. Each individual falls somewhere between the two poles; it is impossible to identify a clear dividing line. The same thing holds true for general assessments of health. At any point in time, an individual can be placed somewhere on the continuum between the poles of serious illness and optimal health. The goal of counseling is to meet the needs of the individual where she is and to help her move in the direction of improved health (see Figure 7.1). Thus, a woman affected by a serious illness or injury may need help coping with her health problems and attaining stabilization or recovery. Another woman may be at a point where, though she is not suffering from serious illness, she is at risk. For her, a goal of risk reduction might involve behavioral interventions to help her lessen or eliminate health jeopardizing behaviors. A woman who has not been identified as being at risk might work toward a goal of health maintenance, possibly participating in a wellness oriented program designed to help her gain increased control over her health. The key factor in this conceptualization is that each client is encouraged to identify the strengths and resources she brings to the process of moving toward optimal health. She is identified in terms of her positive goals, not in terms of her diagnosis.

Self-Management Strategies

Female clients frequently bring to the counseling process a sense of powerlessness and a feeling that they lack the ability to make changes in their lives. A focus on building

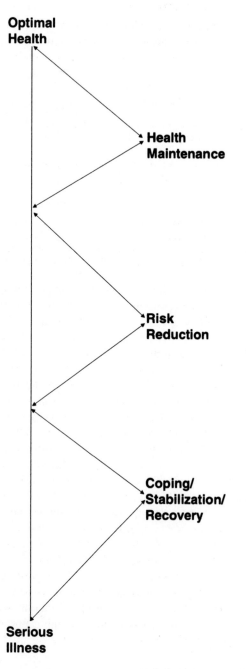

Figure 7.1
The Health–Illness Continuum

the skills and efficacy beliefs that are basic to self-management can prove to be empowering for women.

McGrath et al. (1990) found that therapies emphasizing action, mastery, and competence building were helpful for depressed women, with cognitive and behavioral therapies being particularly important because "they teach women to confront and overcome the passive, dependent role they may have been taught since childhood and that may be feeding their depressions" (p. 59). These approaches are also crucial for women dealing with physical health issues. As Thoresen (1984) pointed out, caring for one's health requires concrete skills, not just information.

> Behaving in personally responsible ways—that is, exercising effective self-management—requires a number of skills that are not necessarily inherent in everyone's repertoire....People need to be taught how to be more caring and more responsible for their own health and well-being, especially when the social environment commonly promotes irresponsible or unhealthy behavior. (p. 300)

Emphasis on skill building and focus on control and self-efficacy are complementary aspects of self-management. As the client begins to achieve success in implementing health enhancement skills, she gains self-efficacy. The sense of self-efficacy, in turn, makes the development and practice of new competencies possible.

Consider, for example, a woman dealing with problems related to alcohol or drug abuse. Skill development can be an important component of her recovery. Relaxation and stress management skills might replace alcohol or drugs as methods for dealing with anxiety, problem solving and decision making skills might help her act less impulsively, interpersonal skills might encourage participation in non-drug related recreational activities, and assertiveness skills might help her avoid the pressure to drink or use drugs in social settings. Skill training focused specifically on substance use would help her single out situations that place her at risk and develop methods for coping with these challenges. If she learns to cope with situations previously associated with drinking or drug use, she will become more aware of her efficacy and more optimistic about the possibilities of control with each success. If she is treated as a responsible person and assumed by the counselor to be capable of making positive decisions, she is likely to be motivated to perform the hard work involved in embarking on new behaviors. Her sense of self-efficacy—and her self-management ability—will give her a sense of positive options that may be missing in medically based treatments that emphasize her powerlessness.

The usefulness of self-management strategies cuts across a variety of health related issues (see Figure 7.2). One client may be learning to manage a chronic disease such as diabetes; another may be attempting weight control or smoking cessation; still another may be addressing behavioral variables putting her at risk for heart disease or stroke. Each of these clients, like the substance abusing client, needs to gain a belief in the possibility that she can control her own life.

Women's Groups

Both powerlessness and isolation are themes that appear again and again as we work with women clients. Because social support is an important component of both physical

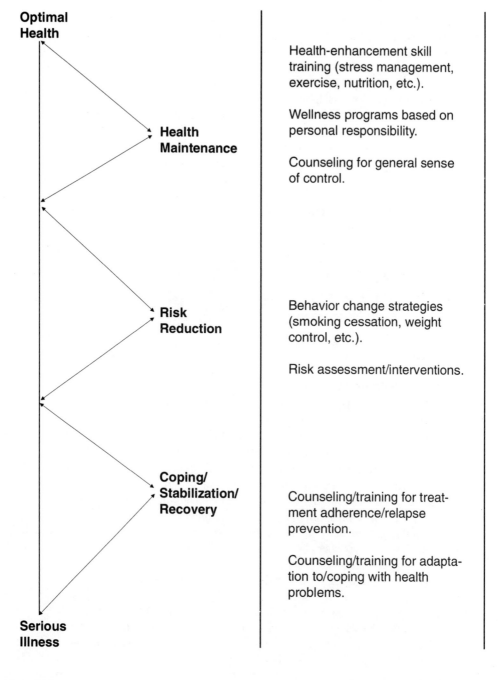

Figure 7.2
Self-Management Strategies

and mental health, strategies designed to break through isolation are needed. Group work, especially through the mechanism of all-women's groups, can engender mutual empowerment and support. Burden and Gottlieb (1987) have suggested that women's therapy groups provide a number of benefits that may be missing in either mixed groups or individual therapy. In mixed groups, men tend to dominate the discussion; in contrast, women's groups provide the opportunity for new behaviors and experiences, especially in the realm of leadership. All-women groups also help to counteract gender role socialization patterns, with women being resocialized to value support from other women. Isolation is decreased. In fact, for many women, the group may provide their first experience in interacting with other women who have similar problems. Women learn to value and trust other women and, concurrently, to trust and value themselves. They receive nurturing from others—possibly also for the first time—and engage in mutual problem solving efforts.

Women who come to groups have frequently been emotionally starved by inadequate nurturing. They have been socialized to be the caretakers of their husbands, their children, their churches, the PTA, their bosses, and their own aging parents. They receive little nurturing in return. The result may be depression, dependence on children or ex-spouses, inappropriate anger, overeating, or reliance on alcohol, drugs, or prescription medication. A major function feminist groups fulfill is to provide women with the opportunity to be nurtured themselves. Women learn that they can gain tremendous support, understanding, and caring from other women in their situation. That discovery provides a major impetus to a woman gaining her own sense of internal locus of control.

Focus on Empowerment

McWhirter (1991), in a discussion of "empowerment counseling," identified several criteria for evaluating the degree to which counseling is empowering. These criteria included (a) a belief in clients' potential for coping with their life problems; (b) a conceptualization of problems based on a recognition of the political, social, and economic context within which the client operates; (c) an understanding of the need to help clients themselves recognize the impact of socialization, discrimination, and economic stratification; (d) a client–counselor balance of power based on collaboration; (e) an emphasis on helping clients gain awareness of power dynamics; and (f) use of skill building strategies to help clients gain control over their environments. Similarly, Good, Gilbert, and Scher (1990) conceptualized gender aware therapy as an approach that could help clients consider problems in a societal context. Feminist counseling, of course, is also based on the notion that "the personal is political."

The empowerment-focused counseling approaches all recognize that, though self-management and personal feelings of control are important goals, these outcomes are most likely to be achieved *after* individuals have come to recognize the political, social, and economic sources of many life problems. Women often make internal attributions for problems that actually have social and political origins. Sometimes they are ready to resolve these difficulties only after they have made more appropriate attributions and recognized that the problems are not within them.

Women have traditionally been socialized to internalize the blame for their problems and to assume that their difficulties stem from personal inadequacies. Their isolation leads them to believe that everyone else is functioning well and that they are alone in their inability to cope....[A feminist approach] offers an alternative explanation for much of the difficulty that women experience....The acknowledgment and ventilation of women's anger at the unfairness of their condition is an important step in reduction of self-blame and in the mobilization of energy toward developing strategies to solve problems. (Burden & Gottlieb, 1987, p. 33)

Even very specifically defined personal health problems may have social components that need to be addressed. For example, a woman dealing with weight control does have to plan and carry out strategies to change her eating habits and embark on an exercise program. She does have to learn how to use self-monitoring and stimulus control methods. At the same time, however, she also needs to recognize the unreasonableness of society's standards concerning women's appearance and the inappropriateness of blaming herself for her inability to conform to them. A woman noticing physical symptoms resulting from the combination of a low pay, high stress job with overwhelming and unshared domestic responsibilities may need to develop stress management skills, but she may also need to recognize that society has placed untenable demands on her.

Good et al. (1990) suggested that therapists "actively seek to address gender injustices" (p. 377). Solutions to gender-based problems, and in fact to all of the health problems faced by women, depend on more than our ability to make individual changes. The reality of oppression makes it necessary that we combine empowering, self-efficacy–enhancing counseling with strong advocacy to make the environment more responsive to the needs of our clients.

CASE EXAMPLES

The Case of Marilyn

Marilyn, a 35-year-old single woman, presented herself as a client because of concern about her stress level. She said that her corporate job was highly demanding and that the only way she was able to relax was by consuming alcohol. She had been drinking rather heavily and had become worried because of some recent events. A friend had refused to accompany her to a corporate function because she knew that Marilyn was likely to drink to intoxication. Then, on an out-of-town business trip, Marilyn had consumed a number of drinks one evening and, by the next morning, was unable to remember what had taken place.

Marilyn works very hard and is trying to get ahead in her corporation. She feels that she must keep striving or others will pass her by. There is pressure to drink with corporate clients and to join the group of employees that goes out on Fridays after work. Yet she also feels pressure to stay in control of herself in front of her male colleagues. She works 60-hour weeks and her social life is limited to work related activities. She says she feels exhausted most of the time.

Marilyn's situation helps to point up the differences between a medical model and a self-management approach. A treatment provider adhering to a dichotomous model of health and illness might identify Marilyn as an alcoholic and urge her to accept this label.

This strategy has several shortcomings: the deficit-oriented thinking that forms the assessment process, the possibility that the very real social pressures affecting the client might be dismissed as rationalization or denial, and an overly narrow focus on one aspect of the Marilyn's health behavior.

Of course, Marilyn does have to make immediate changes in her drinking behavior. She needs to learn to monitor her own behavior, to identify the situations in which she feels the urge to drink, and to use more effective coping mechanisms for dealing with these situations.

Although Marilyn's alcohol use is a pressing issue for her, however, it is not the only important concern in her life. The counseling process also needs to address a number of other issues, including the following:

1. How can she achieve a better balance in her life between work and leisure, shoulds and wants, achievement and human connectedness?
2. How can she respond to the pressures of the work place and still maintain a sense of herself?
3. How can she deal more effectively with the mixed messages that she, as a woman, receives from the corporate setting that is, in fact, her home?
4. How can she deal with work related stress? Do her values suggest that she should make changes in her work setting or that the positive aspects of her work mitigate against a change and make emotion-focused coping more appropriate?
5. How can she enhance her own health by thinking about it in terms of wellness, rather than just as the absence of a specific problem?

The Case of Andrea

Andrea is a 22-year-old mother of two young children. She and the children's father, Charles, live apart, but Andrea and Charles have continued their relationship. Charles has been unable to contribute financially to the children's support, though he does visit them.

Andrea did well in high school, but her early pregnancies kept her from taking seriously any of the career goals she might have pursued. She has always wanted to work, but has had problems with child care and transportation. She and the children have been surviving through public aid. Recently, she entered a special program funded by the city to provide training and job placement for long-term-unemployed women. She moved in with her mother, who has been willing to care for the children while Andrea is in the training program with the understanding that, once Andrea has a job, she will be able to afford a better long-term option. Andrea has been doing well in the program, and the trainers believe that she should be easy to place in a secure job. Now, however, Andrea has been forced to confront still another problem. Finding out that she was pregnant with her third child, Andrea sought an abortion, feeling that this was the best option for her at this time. Unfortunately, Andrea's Medicaid will not cover an abortion unless her life is in danger. The city hospital, which normally provides most of the medical treatment in Andrea's neighborhood, has stopped providing abortions for political reasons.

Andrea feels disappointed in herself and hopeless about her future. She believes that she should have been able to turn her life around and that she has failed. She also believes that the trainers in her program are exasperated with her; in fact, they have expressed frustration with what they see as Andrea's sabotaging of her own success. She has been referred to counseling by the director of the program because the program's funding does provide for short-term counseling.

It is difficult to perceive any way that Andrea can achieve her goals, at least in the immediate future. Everything in the society, from the lack of child care to the lack of reproductive health services for poor women to the lack of support for single mothers and their children, seems to be working against her. One thing that must happen in the counseling process is reframing the problem so that Andrea can begin to overcome the notion that these failures are all her own. As long as she continues blaming herself, she will find it difficult to move in the direction of any active solution. Andrea also needs assistance in problem solving. Unless she can find ways to maneuver more skillfully through the systems that affect her, she will feel—and will in fact be—powerless.

Andrea's situation points up the need for counselors to be proactive, to work toward changes that will make the environment more responsive to the needs of their clients. Unless Andrea's city hospital provides the reproductive health services that women need, she and many others will continue to be victimized.

RESOURCES

A number of sources of information and support are available to women dealing with health problems. Counselors will find that referrals to organizations can provide valuable assistance to clients. Among the resources available are the following:

❑ Breast Cancer Advisory Center
 P.O. Box 224
 Kensington, MD 20895
❑ National Alliance of Breast Cancer Organizations
 1180 Avenue of the Americas
 2nd Floor
 New York, NY 10036
❑ Y-Me National Organization for Breast Cancer Information and Support
 18220 Harwood Avenue
 Homewood, IL 60430
❑ Association of Maternal and Child Health Programs
 2001 L Street, NW
 Suite 308
 Washington, DC 20036
❑ Healthy Mothers—Healthy Babies
 409 Twelfth Street, SW
 Room 309
 Washington, DC 20024

❏ Endometriosis Association
  8525 N 76th Place
  Milwaukee, WI 53223
❏ Woman Health International
  4659 Massachusetts Avenue, NW
  Washington, DC 20016
❏ National Women's Health Network
  1325 G Street, NW
  Washington, DC 20005
❏ Women and Health Roundtable
  1000 Connecticut Avenue, NW
  Suite 9
  Washington, DC 20036
❏ Women's Drug Research Project
  School of Social Work
  4091 Frieze Building
  University of Michigan
  Ann Arbor, MI 48109-1285
❏ Women for Sobriety
  Jean Kirkpatrick, Executive Director
  P.O. Box 618
  Quakertown, PA 18951
❏ Women's Occupational Health Resource Center
  117 St. Johns Place
  Brooklyn, NY 11217
❏ Women Against Violence Against Women
  543 N Fairfax Avenue
  Los Angeles, CA 90036
❏ National Clearinghouse for the Defense of Battered Women
  125 S 9th Street
  Suite 302
  Philadelphia, PA 19107
❏ National Organization for Women
  1000 Sixteenth Street, NW
  Washington, DC 20036-5705
❏ National Abortion Rights Action League
  1101 Fourteenth Street, NW
  Washington, DC 20005

PROBLEM PREVENTION AND SOCIAL INTERVENTIONS

The health problems experienced by individual women can be prevented most effectively through changes in the systems that affect us all. One pressing problem involves the health care system itself. Women and men tend to be treated differently by medical personnel. Women are more likely to receive prescriptions for psychoactive medications and to undergo possibly unnecessary surgeries. At the same time, they are less likely than men to receive careful diagnostic work-ups when presenting with the same symptoms. Although obstetrical and gynecological surgeries are performed in abundance, women may have inadequate access to technology in areas such as coronary health (Rodin & Ickovics, 1990). As Holt (1990) pointed out, "Men get medical work-ups; women get tranquilizers." Public involvement, education, and political action can play an important role in affecting health care. For instance, a number of women have become involved in the effort to mobilize against breast cancer (Kauffold, 1991), with political activists focusing on such issues as the need for more research and better insurance coverage for mammograms and experimental treatments.

Traditionally, women have been omitted from health related research studies. For example, the major studies on risk factor interventions for cardiovascular disease have been based solely on white males (Rittenhouse, Shumaker, Czajkowski, & Chesney, 1990). Among the reasons usually cited for single-sex studies are cost, the need for homogeneity in the populations being studied, and problems related to drop-out rates. In fact, white males are perceived as the human norm and findings from studies of white males have traditionally been considered to be generalizable, while studies of women would never be considered as a basis for generalization to men (Rittenhouse et al., 1990). Although women have been under-represented in studies of pharmacological, medical, and surgical interventions, they have received these interventions as patients.

This continuing problem has made the recent opening of the National Institutes of Health Office of Research on Women's Health a necessity. Although this move holds promise, vigilance continues to be important. Ideally, this office will support new research on women's health problems and, concurrently, review with a critical eye any requests by researchers to exclude women from their studies.

Many of the health problems affecting women are amenable to prevention and change through legislation. In 1991 alone, the United States Congress considered the Family and Medical Leave Act, the Violence Against Women Bill, the Comprehensive Health Care for All Americans Act, the Freedom of Choice Act, the Reproductive Health Equity Act, and the Women's Health Equity Act. As counselors, we need to recognize that active political advocacy on behalf of such legislation can help to prevent many of the problems we see every day.

SUMMARY

Adult women's health concerns are unique to them. There are a number of sex-related differences in mortality and morbidity, making it necessary that women's health be a focus of attention. Poor and minority women face especially pressing and dangerous health problems. Counseling strategies should be based on an understanding of the personal characteristics associated with health and illness. Internal control and self-efficacy, access to social support, optimism, and a sense of coherence seem to be correlated with positive health outcomes. As Kobasa's research indicated, hardiness includes the components of control, as opposed to powerlessness; commitment, as opposed to alienation; and challenge, as opposed to threat.

How can we work with women in such a way that we increase their hardiness? In this chapter, we suggested a number of strategies, including the following: (a) a focus on positive, rather than deficit-oriented, assessments; (b) encouragement of self-management through emphasis on skill building and self-efficacy enhancement; (c) use of women's groups as a means to lessen isolation; and (d) a general focus on empowerment.

Many of the health problems women experience could be prevented through sociopolitical interventions. Counselors need to be aware of inequities in health care delivery and research. Some health problems can be addressed through legislation, making counselors' participation in political advocacy very appropriate.

REFERENCES

Adler, R. (1991, February). Optimists' coping skills may help beat illnesses. *The APA Monitor, 22*(2), p. 12.

Albino, J. E., & Tedesco, L. A. (1984). Women's health issues. In A. U. Rickel, M. Gerrard, & I. Iscoe (Eds.). *Social and psychological problems of women: Prevention and crisis intervention* (pp. 157–172). Washington, DC: Hemisphere Publishing.

Antonovsky, A. (1979). *Health, stress, and coping.* San Francisco: Jossey-Bass.

Antonovsky, A. (1984). The sense of coherence as a determinant of health. In J. D. Matarazzo, S. M. Weiss, J. A. Herd, N. E. Miller, & S. M. Weiss (Eds.), *Behavioral health: A handbook of health enhancement and disease prevention* (pp. 114–128). New York: John Wiley.

Antonovsky, A. (1987). *Unraveling the mystery of health: How people manage stress and stay well.* San Francisco: Jossey-Bass.

Bandura, A. (1982). Self-efficacy mechanism in human agency. *American Psychologist, 37*, 122–147.

Baruch, G. K., Barnett, R., & Rivers, C. (1983). *Lifeprints: New patterns of love and work for today's women.* New York: McGraw-Hill.

Baruch, G. K., Biener, L., & Barnett, R. C. (1987). Women and gender in research on work and family stress. *American Psychologist, 42*, 130–136.

Belle, D. (1990). Poverty and women's mental health. *American Psychologist, 45*, 385–389.

Buie, J. (1988, July). "Control" studies bode better health in aging. *APA Monitor,* p. 20.

Burden, D. S., & Gottlieb, N. (1987). Women's socialization and feminist groups. In C. M. Brody (Ed.). *Women's therapy groups: Paradigms of feminist treatment* (pp. 24-39). New York: Springer.

Cohen, S. (1988). Psychosocial models of the role of social support in the etiology of physical disease. *Health Psychology, 7*, 269–297.

Cope, N. R., & Hall, H. R. (1987). Risk factors associated with the health status of black women in the United States. In W. Jones & M. F. Rice (Eds.), *Health care issues in black America: Policies, problems, and prospects* (pp. 43–58). New York: Greenwood Press.

Curry, S. (1989, August). *Motivation for behavior change: Testing models with smoking cessation.* Paper presented at the 97th annual convention of the American Psychological Association, New Orleans.

DiClemente, C. C. (1981). Self-efficacy and smoking cessation maintenance: A preliminary report. *Cognitive Therapy and Research, 5*, 175–187.

DiMatteo, M. R., & Hays, R. (1981). Social support and serious illness. In B. H. Gottlieb (Ed.), *Social networks and social support.* Beverly Hills, CA: Sage.

Engel, G. L. (1977). The need for a new medical model: A challenge for biomedicine. *Science, 196*, 129–136.

Gentry, W. D., & Kobasa, S. C. O. (1984). Social and psychological resources mediating stress-illness relationships in humans. In W. D. Gentry (Ed.), *Handbook of behavioral medicine* (pp. 87–116). New York: Guilford Press.

Good, G. E., Gilbert, L. A., & Scher, M. (1990). Gender aware therapy: A synthesis of feminist therapy and knowledge about gender. *Journal of Counseling and Development, 68*, 376–380.

Holt, L. H. (1990, October). *How the medical care system has failed to meet women's needs.* Paper presented at the Rush/North Shore Medical Center Women and Mental Health Conference, Evanston, IL.

Kauffold, M. P. (1991, February 10). A new partnership: War on breast cancer shifts to legal action, education. *Chicago Tribune,* Section 6, p. 3.

Kobasa, S. C. (1979). Stressful life events, personality and health: An inquiry into hardiness. *Journal of Personality and Social Psychology, 37*, 1–11.

Kobasa, S. C. (1987). Stress responses and personality. In R. C. Barnett, L. Biener, & G. K. Baruch (Eds.). *Gender and stress* (pp. 308–329). New York: Free Press.

Kobasa, S. C., Maddi, S. R., & Courington, S. (1981). Personality and constitution as mediators in the stress-illness relationship. *Journal of Health and Social Behavior, 22*, 368–378.

Lazarus, R. S., & Folkman, S. (1984). Coping and adaptation. In W. D. Gentry (Ed.), *Handbook of behavioral medicine* (pp. 282–325). New York: Guilford Press.

Lewis, J. A., Sperry, L., & Carlson, J. (In press). *Health counseling.* Pacific Grove, CA: Brooks/Cole.

Manley, A., Lin-Fu, J. S., Miranda, M., Noonan, A., & Parker, T. (1984). Special health concerns of ethnic minority women. Commissioned paper. *Report of the Public Health Service Task Force on Women's Health Issues Vol. II* (pp. II-37–II-47). Washington, DC: U. S. Government Printing Office.

Marlatt, G. A., & Gordon, J. R. (1985). *Relapse prevention: Maintenance strategies in the treatment of addictive behaviors.* New York: Guilford Press.

McGrath, E., Keita, G. P., Strickland, B. R., & Russo, N. F. (1990). *Women and depression: Risk factors and treatment issues. Final report of the American Psychological Association's National Task Force on Women and Depression.* Washington, DC: American Psychological Association.

McWhirter, E. H. (1991). Empowerment in counseling. *Journal of Counseling and Development, 69*, 222–227.

Preventable diseases take high toll (1990, January 19). *Chicago Tribune,* p. 4.

Repetti, R. L., Matthews, K. A., & Waldron, I. (1989). Employment and women's health: Effects of paid employment on women's mental and physical health. *American Psychologist, 44*, 1394–1401.

Riessman, C. K. (1983). Women and medicalization: A new perspective. *Social Policy, 14*(1), 3–18.

Rittenhouse, J., Shumaker, S.A., Czajkowski, S. M., & Chesney, M. A. (1990, July). *Invited panel discussion: Research on women and health: Current trends and future directions.* Present at 98th annual convention of the American Psychological Association, Boston.

Rodin, J. (1986). Aging and health: Effects of the sense of control. *Science, 223*, 1271–1276.

Rodin, J., & Ickovics, J. R. (1990). Women's health: Review and research agenda as we approach the 21st century. *American Psychologist, 45*, 1018–1034.

Rodin, J., & Langer, E. (1977). Long-term effects of a control-relevant intervention with institutionalized aged. *Journal of Personality and Social Psychology, 35*, 897–902.

Russo, N. F. (1990). Overview: Forging research priorities for women's mental health. *American Psychologist, 45*, 368–373.

Russo, N. F., & David, H. P. (n.d.). *When children are unwanted.* (A social issue release from the Board of Social & Ethical Responsibility for Psychology). Washington, DC: American Psychological Association.

Scheier, M. F., & Carver, C. S. (1985). Optimism, coping, and health: Assessment and implications of generalized outcome expectancies. *Health Psychology, 4*, 219–247.

Scheier, M. F., & Carver, C. S. (1987). Dispositional optimism and physical well-being: The influence of generalized outcome expectancies in health. *Journal of Personality, 55*, 169–210.

Schunk, D. H., & Carbonari, J. P. (1984). Self-efficacy models. In J. D. Matarazzo, S. M. Weiss, J. A. Herd, N. E. Miller, & S. M. Weiss (Eds.), *Behavioral health: A handbook of health enhancement and disease prevention* (pp. 230–247). New York: John Wiley.

Schwartz, G. W. (1982). Testing the biopsychosocial model: The ultimate challenge facing behavioral medicine? *Journal of Consulting and Clinical Psychology, 50*, 1040–1053.

Seeman, J. (1989). Toward a model of positive health. *American Psychologist, 44*, 1099–1109.

Seeman, M., & Seeman, T. E. (1983). Health behavior and personal autonomy: A longitudinal study of the sense of control in illness. *Journal of Health and Social Behavior, 24*, 144–160.

Smith, I. E. (1990). Balancing priorities in the prevention of drug related birth defects. *The Community Psychologist, 23* (3), 23–24.

Strickland, B. R. (1988). Sex-related differences in health and illness. *Psychology of Women Quarterly, 12*, 381–399.

Suls, J., & Fletcher, B. (1985). The relative efficacy of avoidant and nonavoidant coping strategies: A meta-analysis. *Health Psychology, 4*, 249–288.

Taylor, S. E., Lichtman, R. R., & Wood, J. V. (1984). Attributions, beliefs about control, and adjustment to breast cancer. *Journal of Personality and Social Psychology, 46,* 489–502.

Thoresen, C. E. (1984). Overview. In J. D. Matarazzo, S. M. Weiss, J. A. Herd, N. E. Miller, & S. M. Weiss (Eds.), *Behavioral health: A handbook of health enhancement and disease prevention* (pp. 297–307). New York: John Wiley.

Weisensee, M. (1986). Women's health perceptions in a male-dominated medical world. In D. K. Kjervik & I. M. Martinson (Eds.). *Women in health and illness: Life experiences and crises* (pp. 19–33). Philadelphia: W. B. Saunders Company.

Wilson, B. J. (1988). Women and poverty: A demographic overview. *Women and Health, 13,* 21–40.

Young-Eisendrath, P., & Wiedemann, F. L. (1987). *Female authority: Empowering women through psychotherapy.* New York: Guilford Press.

Part Four

MATURE WOMANHOOD

8

Career Development in Maturity: Changing Roles and Challenges

Loretta J. Bradley and L.J. Gould
Texas Tech University

T he United States has become an aging society. The lower birth rate, lower mortality, and the aging of the baby boomer generation has guaranteed that by 2020 one of five people will be 65 or over (Neugarten, 1982a). The number of older people is increasing most rapidly among the very old. There are more older women than men. Most men over 65 are married and live with their wives, but women over 65 are more than twice as likely to be single—by choice, divorce, or by widowhood—and live alone. Most of the elderly whose income is below the poverty level are women. Growing old in the United States is not always a pleasant experience.

There are many stereotypes about the elderly. The elderly are seen as poor, isolated and lonely, sick, dissatisfied with life, dependent on others, and not sexual. Although these stereotypes, like others, are most often inaccurate, they are still widely believed. In reality, most older people are active and involved with their families and friends in good, close relationships. They are satisfied with life and have positive self-images. Most elderly people are healthy and live alone by choice. Fortunately, society's concept of age is changing and becoming more fluid. For many people, it is not age but retirement that marks the difference between middle age, when one is still in the labor force, and young old age, when one retires (Neugarten, 1982a).

An examination of portrayals in the media shows both our preoccupation with youth and our attitudes toward older people, particularly women. On television, older adults, in general, are often shown as both mentally and physically weak, dependent on others for monetary and psychological support, and unconcerned with current affairs. Older women are often portrayed as sweet "little old ladies" who spend most of their time involving themselves in the affairs of others. Television advertisements portray a youth cult, with constant emphasis on looking younger by use of makeup, hair color, food and diet products, and exercise devices. Older women are seldom seen in commercials for products other than over-the-counter drugs, often for osteoporosis or constipation, and products for incontinence. Magazines have few older models and few articles directed to older audiences.

Aging for women can be a most unpleasant experience. Myths such as women age swifter and harder than men or women have not had the time to acquire the same level of competence as men and what competence they have decreases with time are commonly believed (Giesen & Datan, 1980). According to Ward (1977), women tend to postpone thinking of themselves as old and are likely to label themselves as younger than men of the same age. Women tend to have a subjective age, the age they think and feel themselves to be, that is several years less than their actual age (Montepare & Lachman, 1989). As De Beauvoir (1970) has stated:

> When we look at the image of our own future provided by the old we do not believe it, an absurd inner voice whispers that that will never happen to us—when that happens it will no longer be ourselves that it happens to. Until the moment it is upon us, old age is something that only affects other people. (p. 13)

The denial of aging may signal the reluctance to accept the negative values and the stereotypes that are applied to women. Women, even professionals, are reluctant to reveal their ages (Sontag, 1979). If a woman thinks of herself and calls herself old, then she tends to exhibit less life satisfaction, lower morale, decreased psychological health, lower self-esteem, and dependence on others because, in describing herself as old, she in turn causes others to perceive her as old. To call oneself old is to act old because the age label connotes stereotyped expectations about personal capabilities that shape the individual's choice and level of activity (Furstenberg, 1989).

Researchers agree that there is a double standard in aging that affects women. Women are expected to marry older men (Cowan, 1984). Sexuality and attractiveness are thought to diminish with age (Berman, O'Nan, & Floyd, 1981; Deutsch, Zalinski, & Clark, 1986; Kogan, 1979; Lipka, 1987; Matlin, 1987; Porcino, 1985). According to Sontag (1979), physical appearance is more important to women than to men; wrinkles on a man's face are signs of character, but on a woman's face they give quite another message. She further stated:

> This society offers even fewer rewards for aging to women than it does to men. Being physically attractive counts much more in a woman's life than in a man's, but beauty, identified, as it is for women, with youthfulness, does not stand up well to age. Exceptional mental powers can increase with age, but women are rarely encouraged to develop their minds above dilettante standards. (1979, p. 464)

CAREER DEVELOPMENT ISSUES FACING OLDER WOMEN

During the last 100 years there has been a major increase in labor force participation of women, especially following World War II. In the 1950s, if they entered the labor force, most women did so after their childbearing years when they were between the ages of 45 and 64. The 1960s saw the beginning of a trend in which women entered the job market between 20 and 34 and either delayed marriage or family or combined them with work (Lyon, 1986). In general, women are now over-represented in the so-called "secondary sector" that is characterized by relatively low earnings, few fringe benefits, poor working conditions, and little job security. Minkler and Stone (1985) noted that in 1985, 80% of women were employed in only 20 of the 420 job categories listed by the Department of Labor.

To demonstrate the differences between the career patterns of men and women, Karp (1985) studied academics in a university setting. The women who were in their 50s held special interest because they were pioneers in the academic world. Most of the women in this survey reported a career path that was almost universal within the sample. Women reported that their careers were interrupted or delayed because of family responsibilities that included child rearing and frequent moves caused by their husbands' careers. Most of the women said that their career aspirations took second place to their marriages for years, but in their mid-to-late 30s dissatisfaction and the women's movement combined to push them toward a career. For some of the women, their marriages suffered in direct proportion to their seriousness and the intensity with which they pursued their work. A critical difference between the men and women in this study was their places on the career path. By the time the men were in their 50s, they knew where they stood in the career world; and they were, at most, questioning if they could do one more significant piece of research in their careers. The men also reported changes in their feelings toward others, stating that they were more interested in their students as people. Many women who were in their 50s felt that they had really just begun their work; they were making their marks and did not take their careers for granted. So, although the men in their 50s were demonstrating Erikson's (1980) generativity (that is, concern with productive work and family involvement as opposed to self-absorption and failure to incorporate the needs of others into one's personal life), the women were "not burdened with the prospect of stagnation. The women are still generating their careers in middle adulthood and are consequently not concerned with generativity" (Karp, 1985, p. 21).

Another reported difference between the men and women in this study is that women distinguished between their chronological ages and their professional ages, which were typically 10 to 15 years lower. Thus, the women tended to identify more with younger colleagues. Karp stated several implications of this study:

❏ Aging is a socially constructed phenomenon.
❏ Women in this age group display more intensity toward work than men.
❏ Men and women in their 50s face different developmental tasks: men are occupied with generativity while women are still occupied with generating their career development.

❏ For women, career position leads to a sense of age that is measured in terms of the beginning of one's professional career.

Karp stressed that this study was not statistically representative, but it was important in understanding women and their careers.

Several issues have significant effects on women and work. These include sexism, ageism, midlife career change, midlife reentry, life satisfaction, and retirement. These issues will be discussed in the following sections.

Sexism

Matlin (1987) has distinguished two types of discrimination against women: access discrimination and treatment discrimination. Access discrimination prevents women from being hired, particularly when the employer holds strong stereotyped beliefs, when a woman is applying for a job that is considered to be inappropriate for her gender or when a woman's qualifications are ambiguous. Treatment discrimination involves actions occurring after a woman is on the job and includes salary inequity, being passed over for promotions or special assignments, and exclusion from social relationships. Sex discrimination guidelines are issued by the Equal Employment Opportunity Commission (EEOC); however, in the past few years it has become increasingly uncommon for the commission to accept sex discrimination complaints unless they deal with sexual harassment.

Women in the labor force are the subject of many stereotypes designed to keep them in secondary-sector jobs. Some of these stereotypes are:

❏ Women work only until they get married or pregnant.
❏ Women work for extra money to buy things they want and not to support a family; therefore, they need less money than a man.
❏ Women are not committed to a career.
❏ A woman cannot do a job as well as a man.
❏ Women are too emotional for certain types of work.
❏ Women take more time off from work because of illness.
❏ Women are more likely to suffer from stress because of conflict between their jobs and their proper career as homemaker/mother.
❏ Women are too young/too old/too pretty to be taken seriously.

It cannot be denied that women do not show the same work patterns as men. Women's careers are often interrupted by child rearing or moving when a husband changes jobs. The burden of child rearing is still the primary responsibility of the woman, even in a stable marriage, which means that she will not be able to devote as much of her life to her job. A woman may not have completed her education before having her family; after she does so, her time in the labor force is often limited. Minkler and Stone (1985) estimated that women start their careers an average of 5 years later than men, with 15% assuming their first major job after age 35. Women, because they are most often in lower paying, lower status jobs may not be eligible for pension-vesting rights. Women have not been socialized to think of work as the center of their lives (Baruch, Biener, &

Barnett, 1987). However, research evidence does not indicate that women are not committed to their work. Keith (1985) noted that women, both married and single, are highly committed to their work, though single women have a stronger orientation and derive more social validity from work than married women.

In fact, most married and formerly married women are working for financial reasons (Collier, 1982; Crosby, 1982; Lyon, 1986; Matlin, 1987; Szinovacz, 1983), with salary being one of the most common areas of sex discrimination. However, women do not always recognize discrimination (Crosby, 1982). For women, job satisfaction is often based on a combination of factors considered desirable and deserved, and salary may or may not be one of those factors (Crosby, 1982). If the reality of the job closely matches the desires of the employee, then the job is satisfactory. If there is a gap between reality and desire, then the job is unsatisfactory. Crosby further noted that, because women are often quite concerned with the social relationships within the work environment, they refuse to recognize discrimination against themselves. Thus, if a woman admits to discrimination, she is aligning herself with a disadvantaged group of workers. Further, if she is truly underpaid, then someone must be responsible for the injustice, and it would be painful to identify a villain in the work environment. Finally, seeing herself as a member of a disadvantaged and underprivileged class would be to invite pity and scorn from others.

An area in which women are often excluded is the social relationship that has come to be called the "good old boy" network. It is in this informal arena—often over lunch, at after work get-togethers, or at the health club—that men exchange information and conduct business. Being excluded from this informal network can be very damaging to a woman's career (Dunnette & Motowidlo, 1982; Lipman-Blumen, 1976; Sexton, 1977).

Rosen and Jerdee (1974) researched the personnel decisions of bank managers and discovered three areas in which women suffered from discrimination: men were more likely to be promoted to bank branch managers; men were more likely to be chosen to attend personnel conferences; the recommendations made by male supervisors on firing employees were upheld more often than those made by women. In a similar study of school superintendents, Frasher, Frasher, and Wims (1982) reported that males were more often selected for work that involved travel; when an employee's spouse was required to move for professional reasons, women were encouraged to move while men were more often encouraged to remain; males who expressed family priorities over job responsibilities were more likely to be promoted than females who did the same; and requests for leaves of absence for child care were considered to be more appropriate for males than the same requests by females.

Ageism

According to Troll (1976), there are three types of age bias. The first type of age bias is age restrictiveness, which affects everyone within a certain group by advocating that certain behaviors are suitable only or primarily for a specific age. The second type is age distortion, in which the behaviors or characteristics of a specific cohort are seen and perceived inaccurately. Finally, there is ageism, which presents an entire age group negatively. Ageism implies segregation, prejudice, discrimination, and inferior social status. Cultural ageism refers to basic values, traditions, and assumptions about the nature of older people; institutional ageism refers to the conceptualization of these beliefs at the institutional level with discriminatory behavior in the form of policies (Williamson, Shindul, & Evans, 1985).

Ageism in the work force most often affects those who are older, but the combination of ageism and sexism is restricted to women (Meade & Walker, 1989). As Collier (1982) stated:

> All of us suffer the pangs of growing older, but women more than men suffer from pain and discrimination on account of age since our society prefers youth and beauty and tends to identify the two. This is not a meaningless generalization; men hire women because they are young and pretty—for jobs which have nothing to do with youth or beauty. They marry them for the same reasons. Women have to fight against being thrown on the scrap heap for reasons which do not apply to men or in circumstances in which men have more options and defenses. Our discrimination against older women is so pervasive that a woman's anxiety about aging has become a matter for joking, while a man's preference for young women is a matter of pride....Women discriminate against themselves in regard to aging, either by fighting it and denying it or by converting the healthy acceptance of the aging process into the internal message that nothing can be done about it—consignment to that dreaded scrap heap is inevitable. (pp. 233-234)

The Age Discrimination in Employment Act of 1967 (ADEA) made discrimination by age illegal. ADEA was amended in 1978 when the retirement age for the private sector was raised from 65 to 70, and again in 1986 when it was amended to eliminate an age ceiling in all but a few special circumstances. Most states have age discrimination laws. The statute is administered by the EEOC. Unlike sexism, ageism is not considered to be an expression of personal animus, dislike, or intolerance by the employer; it is considered to be less malevolent than other types of discrimination (Eglit, 1989). According to ADEA regulations, employers cannot fire older employees because they are seeking younger, more dynamic staffs, nor can they demote older employees in order to promote younger employees; lastly, employers may not refuse a job to older job applicants on the basis of age. However, incompetent workers may not claim immunity simply because they are old, and an age requirement is lawful if the employer can prove that age is a bona fide occupational qualification of the job. In 1987, there were 245 published cases that addressed claims of ADEA plaintiffs.

Midlife Career Change

As the name implies, the midlife career changer is a person in the middle years of life making a career change. The typical age is 35 to 55 years. In 1987, 74.5% of women between 35 and 44 years and 67.1% of women between 45 and 54 years were in the labor force; corresponding figures for men at these age ranges were 94.6% and 90.7% respectively. By the year 2000, it is predicted that 84.2% of women 35 to 44 years and 75.4% of women 44 to 54 years will be in the paid labor force. The corresponding percentages for men are 93.9% and 90.1% (U.S. Department of Commerce, Statistical Abstract, 1989).

Research on the general topic of women's career change at midlife is limited. Jung (1933) was the first to identify the midlife transition. He concluded that upheaval occurs at this time because of the loss of control over life. Erikson (1963) and Havighurst (1953) presented more widely publicized theories related to adult development. According to Erikson, the basic issue facing the individual at midlife is generativity versus self-absorption. For Erikson, the tasks at midlife are to achieve integration of work and family, create for the next generation, and increase social and civic responsibility. Havighurst viewed adulthood as a series of stages in which one must face specific developmental tasks including assisting children to become responsible, happy adults, adjusting to aging parents, adjusting to physiological changes of middle life, and achieving an economic standard of living.

Super (1953, 1957) probably has had the most influence on our ideas of life span career development. His theory of career development includes five stages. His "establishment" and "maintenance" stages cover the period from 25 to 44 and 45 to 65 years, respectively. Thus, the later part of the establishment and early part of the maintenance stage encompass the midlife years. The major task in the establishment stage is settling down in a permanent position, while that of maintenance includes maintaining a career against competition. Super (1990) wrote that "implicit in my formulation of the life-stage model and explicit in the variations in the age limits of the stages are the terms trial and transition to denote recycling" (p. 215). Super made it clear that not only are the ages of the transitions flexible but the transition itself involves a minicycle. Other career development research includes work by Gould (1978), Griffin (1981), Hall (1976), Isaacson (1985), Levinson, Darrow, Klein, Levinson, and McKee (1978), Neugarten (1976), Schein (1978), Sheehy (1976) and Valliant (1977). Despite the growing body of information about midlife and career change at midlife, women remain a neglected group.

Midlife Reentry

After several years of interruption, a growing number of women are entering the paid labor force at midlife. Many of these women are married; some are divorced, widowed, or single. They may be single parents or come from dual-career families. Some have young children while others have children ready to leave home permanently. Many have been homemakers and have been frustrated with that role; others have experienced much satisfaction as homemakers. For some, the reentry into the work force was anticipated, while for others it was not. Despite their classification into a group as "reentry," these women are characterized by their within-group diversity.

Women return to the paid work force for many reasons. One of the most frequent is economic necessity (Healy, 1982; Kiger, 1984). About two-thirds of working women need to work because they are single, divorced, widowed, separated, or married to men earning less than $10,000 per year (Papalia & Olds, 1989). Some women enter the paid labor force to achieve recognition and increase their feelings of self-worth. An increasing number of reentry women indicate that career pursuits have become an important part of their life's plan (Betz & Fitzgerald, 1987).

During midlife, many reentry women return to college. In a national study on reentry women, Astin (1976) found that most reentry women enrolled in college courses to prepare for employment or to upgrade their skills. She described the group of reentry women as more self-confident and happier after they returned to college than they were when they stayed home. Farmer and Fyans (1983) studied achievement and career motivation among first- and second-year married reentry women college students by gender types (androgynous and feminine). Among the first-year college women, the researchers found that, when career motivation is high, fear of success is also high. Although the authors are tentative about the implications of their research for practice, they suggested that feminine women may be highly achieving, given adequate support for achieving behaviors at home and at school or work. The authors concluded that "The fact that fear of success was found to be highest in highly motivated women suggests that much remains to be done before women's full potential is unleashed both for their personal benefit and that of society" (p. 371). MacKinnon-Slaney, Barber, and Slaney (1988) studied the influence of marital status on the career aspirations of single, married, and divorced reentry students. All three groups of women selected increased knowledge as their major career-related goal. The authors stated that "The item rating the emotional support was statistically significant—divorced women believed they received less support than did married women" (p. 330).

Overall, researchers indicated that reentry into the paid work force usually has more positive than negative psychological consequences for women at midlife. The role of paid worker enhances the woman's self-esteem, and provides more social contacts and greater feelings of control, all variables related to the development and maintenance of well-being among reentry women.

In contrast, many women who are reentering the labor force because of job displacement have experienced numerous problems. Foreign competition, often using a less expensive, more productive labor force and technology, has created fewer human resource needs and many plant and business closures. For many women this has meant dislocation from their jobs, often jobs that employed them for many years. For other women displacement means they must be retrained before they can reenter the paid work force. With increased demands placed on the work force, retraining for many women involves beginning again. During the transition period, it is important that the displaced worker receive emotional support in addition to career retraining. Upon completion of training, assistance is often needed with job search methods as the displaced worker prepares to reenter the work force.

Life Satisfaction

Life satisfaction is a complex issue involving many factors. Multiple roles, usually marriage combined with paid employment, have often been considered more stressful than a single role. According to Rosenfield (1989), women benefit from the greater power and resources that are available with employment. However, if a woman is in a situation, at work or at home, where she has high demands combined with low power, she is likely to suffer from more stress, anxiety, and depression. Research has shown that multiple roles in themselves are not inherently stressful (Baruch & Barnett, 1986; Baruch et al., 1987). It is the qualitative rather than quantitative aspects of experience in various social roles that are the best key to understanding psychological well-being, and being a paid worker is associated with higher self-esteem. Life satisfaction is not dependent on gender (Liang, 1982) or on age (Palmore & Kivett, 1977). Bird (1979) compared surveys of women taken in the 1960s to surveys taken in the late 1970s and concluded that women were more satisfied with their lives in the late 1970s. Middle-aged women emphasize self-acceptance and self-knowledge, while older women emphasize positive changes in self-confidence and assertiveness; both middle aged and older women are generally satisfied and happy with their lives (Ryff, 1989).

The "empty nest syndrome" is a depression that supposedly affects adult women when their children go out into the world. Some researchers (Craig, 1990; Herr & Cramer, 1984; Neugarten, 1972) have reported that this period can present a crisis for women. However, most have found that the empty nest is not as stressful and depressing as once thought. Barnett and Baruch (1978) noted that research and theory have overemphasized the importance of women's reproductive role. As Rubin (1979) stated:

> Appearances notwithstanding, for women, at least, midlife is not a stage tied to chronological age. Rather, it belongs to that point in the life cycle of the family when the children are grown and gone, or nearly so—when, perhaps for the first time in her adult life, a woman can attend to her own needs, her own desires, her own development as a separate and autonomous being. (p. 7)

Rubin further stated that the term "empty nest" suggests a picture of a lonely, depressed woman who is clinging pathetically to a lost past when she lived for and through her children. Adelmann, Antonucci, Crohan, and Coleman (1989) suggested that cohort membership and employment status are important main effects of well-being, but empty nest status is not a main effect though it does interact with other factors in life satisfaction. It is a mistake to assume that women automatically become depressed when their children leave home because research shows otherwise (Glenn, 1975; Matlin, 1987; Radloff, 1980).

Oliver (1988) has distinguished between mothering, a role beginning with the birth of the first child and ending with the independence of the last, and motherhood, a relationship that continues throughout life that ends with death. The mothering role is culturally determined, with method, style, and objectives varying from culture to culture, according to need. The transition between active mothering and the relationship of motherhood has the potential for maladaptive behavior largely because society has ignored, distorted, or trivialized its problems. Regarding the empty nest, Oliver (1988) stated:

> The term derogates women who may have difficulty in disengaging from the mothering role. The metaphor implies that women, like birds, passively sit on the eggs until they hatch and fly away, but unlike birds, don't have the good sense to accept the end of their "useful" function. Women have, indeed, been socialized to behave passively with respect to many important areas of their lives. But, in our society, women have not been passive with respect to their mothering role. Mothering and passivity are mutually exclusive. This is a distinction not usually made when arguments are made whether passivity in women is innate, or the result of the socialization process. Mothering is active and goal directed. (p. 104)

Although some women experience distress with the role loss, most women accept (and many welcome) the change in role. For many women, this can be a time to engage in activities which they desired earlier but were unable to find or take the time for.

Retirement

In the past, researchers have tended to think that retirement should not be as important to a woman as it is to a man. Women were perceived to be less involved in their work, which was seen as secondary to their proper role as homemaker and mother. According to Fox (1977), less attention is paid to issues in women's retirement because for most women social status and identity are tied to a man and therefore do not change with employment status. There is little support for this attitude. The issue of retirement is one that affects working women only because homemakers do not have the luxury of retirement (Giesen & Datan, 1980).

Kalish (1982) stated that retirement means different things to different people, and one's lifestyle in retirement tends to reflect one's previous lifestyle. The negative aspects of retirement include reduced income, loss of social contacts, loss of the basis of personal identification, and a sense of meaninglessness. Positive aspects include increased freedom and the chance to take advantage of new options in the pursuit of education, travel, and leisure activities. However, leisure activities depend on income, health, mobility, and personal preference. Women are especially vulnerable to problems caused by low income.

A recent trend in employment is offering early retirement to older employees. Companies usually offer early retirement to older employees because they wish to reduce labor force size or because they are merging with another company. For employees, taking early retirement depends on whether or not they are bored with working and are ready for a change either to pursue leisure activities or to work somewhere else and whether or not the employees see the offer as a one-time-only chance (Seltzer, 1989). Women who take early retirement usually do so for one of four reasons: poor health, their own or that of a husband or parent; job dissatisfaction; financial security; or their husbands' retirement (Kalish, 1982; Minkler & Stone, 1985; Neugarten, 1982b; Szinovacz, 1983, 1987). Single, never-married women, who are more likely to have work histories comparable to those of men, tend to respond to health issues and retirement incentives by considering the relative merits of early retirement as compared to continuing employment and choosing what is best for their situation (Belgrave, 1989; Keith, 1985). Shaw (1984) studied the retirement plans of married women and determined that slightly more than half planned to retire before the age of 65, before, or at the same time, as their husbands. In research on predictors of retirement for women, it has been shown that age is the only independent variable that is significant in the decision to retire; other factors (work history, pension availability, health, etc.) show only interactional effects (George, Fillenbaum, & Palmore, 1984; 1984; Palmore, Burchett, Fillenbaum, George, & Wallman, 1985).

How well do women adapt to and show satisfaction in retirement? Women are not homogeneous in their attitudes toward retirement, and there appear to be several factors that play a part in determining satisfaction and adaptation. Campione (1987) listed finances, age, and husband's retirement as significant issues for women. Anderson, Higgins, Newman, and Sherman (1978) have stated that women do not anticipate retirement as favorably as men. Szinovacz (1983) has said that women who have chosen careers in an attempt to avoid the household routine are likely to suffer when forced to return to it. Atchley (1976) observed that women are more likely than men to express apprehension and anxiety about retirement, especially if there are other issues (widowhood, empty nest, chronic illness of a family member, etc.) with which they have not dealt. Neugarten (1979) stated that transitions are only stressful if they are unanticipated, and research on satisfaction and adjustment in retirement tends to support her statement by stressing the importance of willingness to retire in successful adjustment and satisfaction (Cherry, Zarit, & Krauss, 1984; Holahan, 1981; Kalish, 1982; Levy, 1980-1981). Also important in determining life satisfaction in retirement are social involvement (Dorfman & Moffett, 1987; Johnson & Price-Bonham, 1980; Kaye & Monk, 1984; Steinkamp & Kelly, 1985), family relationships (Johnson, 1983), and the ability to cope with unfamiliar situations (Capsi & Elder, 1986; Porcino, 1985).

Issues in Retirement

One of the issues that is most troubling to retirees is finances. There are three areas from which most retirees derive their income—Social Security, an employer or union pension plan, and private savings (Liebig, 1984). For many, Social Security is the major source of income. If inflation continues to increase, however, it may become impossible for a retiree to exist without additional income. Women who have followed the typical work pattern, which includes gaps caused by marriage, child rearing, and moving with their families, are often disadvantaged when it comes time to retire because they have not worked enough to be eligible for Social Security or pension benefits and because they have been in lower paying jobs. Widows, in the past, have been victimized by a lack of pension benefits; before a recent revision in the Social Security law that allows a divorced woman to retain benefits if married for 10 or more years, women lost all rights to benefits from their husbands' accounts when they divorced (Bernstein, 1980; Redmond, 1980).

In 1962, 30% of total income of elderly people came from Social Security benefits (Holden, 1989). In 1986, that percentage had risen to 45%. Old Age and Survivors Insurance (OASI) paid $164.5 billion to more than 90% of eligible older people in 1985. Again, it is important to recognize that Social Security benefits depend on the wages earned. Therefore, with each successive cohort that becomes eligible for benefits, the amount of benefits rises. Another potential source of retirement income is pensions. The Employee Retirement Income Security Act of 1974 (ERISA) increased the probability of pension coverage by establishing minimum standards for funding, administration, participation, and vesting in pension funds. ERISA also states that pension funds should be structured so that employees are paid in joint and survivor benefits, thus eliminating a problem faced by many widows who found that their husband's pensions ended when he died. The Retirement Equity Act of 1984 (REA) requires spouse approval if the employee decides to take any option other than joint and survivor benefits.

Tager (1984) has noted that health is another problem for the older adult. Not only is it a common reason for retirement, but it is a concern of healthy retirees as well. Although people over 65 are automatically covered by Medicare Part A (which covers inpatient hospital care, skilled nursing facilities, some home health care, and hospice care), Medicare Part B is a health insurance plan that requires premiums, deductibles, and coinsurance amounts that must be paid by the insuree or another insurance plan (U.S. Department of Health and Human Services, 1990). Health care in the United States currently consumes 12% of the Gross National Product; and by 2010 that figure is likely to rise to 28.5% (Matthiessen, 1990). This forces older adults to rely on personal savings, expensive and often uncertain insurance policies, or state Medicaid programs that require different, and often onerous, levels of spending down or lowering the amount of money available, either by the retiree or by the health care provider, for health care services. Beyond the cost of health care, older adults often have problems with access to care facilities, chronic illness not covered by insurance or Medicare, transportation to medical facilities, and income that limits receiving benefits (Henry, 1990).

Another issue in retirement is family relationships. In a survey on wives' attitudes toward their husbands' retirement, Fengler (1975) found that women's attitudes were evenly divided into three groups: optimistic—women looked forward to having time for companionship and living an exciting life together; neutral—women expected no change in the relationship; and pessimistic—women expected the stereotypical bored, retired husband with too much time on his hands intruding into his wife's activities. For many women, whether they are retired or not, problems arise when their husbands retire and are suddenly home all day (Atchley, 1976; Vinick & Ekerdt, 1989). Wives may feel that they have lost their personal freedom and their privacy, that there is too much together-ness, and that their established routine has been disrupted. More problems are likely to occur if employed wives feel that their husbands, who are home all day, are taking either too much or not enough responsibility for the household (Plowman, 1984). Because of increases in longevity, many retired adults have parents still living; if the parent is ill or in need of other assistance, they feel responsible, which may lead to resentment (Vinick & Ekerdt, 1989). Retirees may also find that their adult children need their help (Plowman, 1984). Thus, retirees often find themselves sandwiched between the demands of older parents and of adult children. Women, who have been the primary caregivers in the past, may no longer be as inclined to give up their careers and take the responsibility for others. Plowman (1984) stated:

> It is quite possible that many women will not be willing to withdraw from the labor force in order to minister to elderly family members or to provide child care to grandchildren. Also, many women may choose to postpone retirement even if their husbands have already retired. (p. 154)

A final issue of retirement is post-retirement work. There is some disagreement over the importance of work to older adults. Parnes (1989) has stated that the desire to work is a misconception about retirement; people retire because of poor health, work dissatis-faction, or because they have the money to do so. Having retired they have no desire to go back to work. Other researchers have pointed out that many retirees would like to work if they could do so without jeopardizing their Social Security and other financial benefits (Lazarus & Laver, 1985; Moon & Hushbeck, 1989). Eisler (1984) stated that independence is important to the elderly, and the continuation of a career is one way in which an older person may maintain independence, pride, and a sense of autonomy. Further, he says, with longer life spans and earlier retirement, more middle aged retirees will be reentering the work force and will often be making changes in career because they can afford to risk the time and effort involved in experimentation. Fleisher (1984) noted that more people would delay retirement or return to work if corporations were more flexible in work hours.

COUNSELING STRATEGIES

Two types of counseling will be considered in this section: midlife career counseling and preretirement counseling. Both types are especially important to women because of their pattern of labor force involvement.

Career development theories have overlooked half of the population. Like other developmental theories, career theories are based on the developmental processes of men. There are three basic types of career theories: the developmental approach (Ginzberg, 1972; Super, 1953; Tideman & O'Hara, 1963); the psychological need approach (Holland, 1966; Roe, 1957); and the social learning approach (Krumboltz, Mitchell, & Jones, 1976). Women are expected to fit the model, but they do not fit the model. According to Brooks (1984), some theorists—Super, Krumboltz, Hotchkiss and Borow, and Roe—have attempted to address issues of gender but no one has yet developed a theory geared to the uniquely female experience. Women are socialized to think of work as something that they do until they marry and have children, not as a career that requires extensive training and commitment. Therefore, women have jobs, not careers. Women are further socialized to place more emphasis on their husbands' careers than on their own and so often do not take advantage of career advances. Gilligan (1982) believes that it is this process of socialization that causes women to face developmental tasks that are different from those faced by men.

Midlife Career Change

Heald (cited in Eisler, 1984) has suggested that middle age is a time of reevaluation of one's life when priorities change and time and options are seen as limited. This can be very stressful and precipitate a midlife crisis, or it can cause a woman who is locked into a dissatisfying and unfulfilling career to make changes in her life. Other issues that cause midlife career changes are reentry into the labor force, change in marital status, and economic need (Bradley, 1990).

The Counseling Process

When a client comes to a counselor, the first step is always an initial interview during which the counselor is able to begin the process of gathering information. Information gathering may take several sessions, and during this time the counselor may discover that the client has problems that go far beyond her career. In this situation, the counselor must determine what is best for the client: refer her to another counselor more qualified to help with her problems, keep her as a client and work on both her personal and career problems, or refer her for personal problems and keep working with her on career problems.

Early in the counseling process it may be helpful to determine why the client has decided to change careers. Entine (1977) developed a classification system of midlife career change based on motivations that are anticipated or unanticipated and internal or external. He has stated that, by knowing the motivation behind the change, a counselor

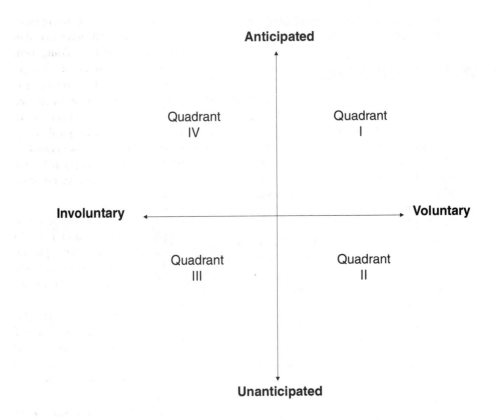

Figure 8.1
Patterns: Midlife Career Change

is better prepared to deal with the client because each type of motivation indicates a different type of intervention. Unanticipated/internal motivations include serious illness, death, or divorce; anticipated/internal motivations include reentry into the labor force after children are grown, or adult education and retraining. Unanticipated/external motivations include layoffs, plant closings, or worker dissatisfaction; anticipated/external motivations include planned retirement or promotion/advancement requiring moving or a change in lifestyle.

Although there is no traditional mold for the woman who is changing careers at midlife, she usually fits into one of the four broad categories depicted in Figure 8.1. As Figure 8.1 illustrates, a career change at midlife is either anticipated (A) or unanticipated (U) and is either voluntary (V) or involuntary (I). The combinations of these patterns are represented in four quadrants. Quadrant I represents a career change that is anticipated and voluntary. For example, Ms. Andrews is 50 years old and has worked as an accountant for 30 years. For the past 5 years she has really disliked her job. She decides to leave her job and start her own company, a yogurt business. Thus, Ms. Andrews anticipated the change and voluntarily decided to change careers at midlife. In contrast, Quadrant III represents a different type of change. In this case, Ms. Belle has worked in an automobile plant for 25 years. Although she thought her department was doing well, she was told that the department would be closed in 2 months. Ms. Belle, at 45 years old, was displaced and therefore forced to make a career change. Her change was unanticipated (did not expect to lose her job) and involuntary (did not want to change careers). Similarly, Quadrant II represents an opposite contrast to Quadrant IV. In Quadrant II, the midlife career change, while initially unanticipated, becomes voluntary. In Quadrant IV, the change is anticipated but involuntary. It is important to conceptualize the career change of the woman at midlife, for her coping skills, stress level, and behavior will be affected by the circumstances surrounding the career change. To consider midlife career change a one-dimensional event is an oversimplification.

Assessment Inventories   Early in the counseling process the client may be given assessment inventories to aid her in the decision making process. The counselor should be familiar with career assessment tools including career interest inventories, aptitude inventories, achievement inventories, personality inventories, retirement inventories, and leisure inventories. This is a brief overview of assessment inventories; for a more detailed listing, see Bradley (1988).

Career interest inventories are based on the assumption that persons in a particular occupation will have interests in common with others in that same occupation, but will not share common interests with those in other occupations. Typically, the client is asked whether she likes, dislikes, or is neutral to various careers. Some of the inventories available include: Strong-Campbell Interest Inventory, Kuder Occupational Interest Survey, Self-Directed Search, and the Career Assessment Inventory.

Aptitude inventories are designed to predict a person's aptitude for a particular career area. The counselor should be careful to note that aptitude and interest are two very different traits; it is possible to be interested in a specific career but lack aptitude for it. Aptitude tests are divided into two broad categories—multiple aptitude test batteries (differential or multifactor) and component ability tests (specific aptitudes, such as music or math). Available multiple aptitude batteries include Differential Aptitude Test, General Aptitude Test Battery, and Flanagan Aptitude Classification Tests. Component tests are available for almost any area.

Achievement inventories measure what a person has learned rather than predicting future performance in a specific area. Some of the more common are California Achievement Tests, Iowa Tests of Basic Skills, and Wide Range Achievement Test.

Personality inventories are often used in career counseling. Some theorists have suggested that personality profiles can be used in much the same way as interest inventories to find a personality type that fits an occupation. Some personality inventories are California Psychological Inventory, Myers-Briggs Type Indicator, and Sixteen Personality-Factor Questionnaire.

Because midlife career changers will be facing retirement in the relatively near future, it is often helpful to give a client both retirement inventories and leisure inventories. Both types of tests are helpful in retirement planning.

Diagnosis Diagnosis is the process by which the counselor determines where, within a categorical system, the client manifests difficulty (Moursund, 1985). Bordin (1968) listed five categories of client career-change difficulty: dependence, lack of information, self-conflict, choice anxiety, and no problem. Healy (1982) listed nine problem areas: unrealistic or unclear goals; insufficient knowledge, ability, interest, training, or resources; does not try hard enough; misconceptions about how the system operates; system itself has defects or is obstructive; cannot decide or commit to one alternative; incomplete or inaccurate problem formulation; interpersonal conflict; and inappropriate affect (anxiety). Certainly diagnosis is most effective when involving both the client and counselor. As Healy stated:

> Many persons have not learned to appraise their attributes and goals and to relate them to working. They have not acquired the habit of gathering information about career opportunities and changes occurring in themselves; nor have they learned to resolve problems, profit from mistakes, and improve their own confidence. These people feel the frustration of such deficits, but often they do not relate it to their own ignorance or their erroneous information and beliefs. (1982, p. 166)

Counseling Techniques The client should be encouraged to set goals for herself that are attainable and realistic. Moursund (1985) noted that "Much of the career counseling task involves teaching the client something, information about jobs and job requirements or skills needed in order to succeed in the world of work" (p. 139). Role playing can be very effective in teaching the client new skills and new social behaviors. Journals may be used to aid in problem solving or meeting career goals; a decision diary where options, advantages and disadvantages, and final decisions are recorded may be especially helpful. Homework assignments that include finding and reading information about careers are helpful in correcting mistaken beliefs about the job market and specific careers. Stress management and relaxation exercises help reduce the anxiety that often accompanies career change. Self-empowerment skills and cognitive restructuring may be used to help the client see herself as a causal agent in the process of problem solution (Kopp, 1989).

Group Work Group therapy has proven especially effective in career counseling (Brown, 1984; Moursund, 1985; Kahn & Ward, 1983). In the group setting, the client will find others who are in the same situation and thus, lessen her feelings of isolation. She will have others with whom to exchange ideas and information. She will be in a supportive environment in which to take chances with change and in which to practice new skills and social behaviors.

Ending Counseling The final phase of counseling should be some type of planning for the future. The counselor and client should anticipate problems that might occur in the future and plan a strategy for problem solving so that the client will not be overwhelmed if something goes wrong. It is usually a good idea to have a follow-up arrangement that allows the client to contact the counselor if something goes drastically wrong or just to let the counselor know that everything has worked out well.

Preretirement Counseling

Unlike counseling midlife career changers, there are few how-to-manuals or standards for preretirement counseling. Therefore, this section will be an overview of what is currently available in the field and suggestions for what might be made available in the future.

Preretirement counseling is geared to preparing employees for retirement. Approximately one-third of the major corporations in the United States offer some sort of retirement planning programs for their employees. The importance of preretirement counseling becomes clear when one realizes that the average person will spend approximately 20% (10 to 30 years) of his or her life in retirement (Dennis, 1989).

Comprehensive preretirement programs include information on financial and estate planning, health, leisure, housing, interpersonal relations, use of time, role adjustment, second careers, and issues affecting women. Very few programs are comprehensive; most cover financial planning only (Dennis, 1989; Ramsey, 1984). When programs are offered, they are usually directed at men who are in the upper echelons of the company and are within 5 years of retirement (Block, 1984).

According to Block (1984), women are most often excluded from preretirement programs for four reasons. First is occupational status and education; women are usually in nonprofessional jobs and have less education than men. Second is readiness to retire; women are more likely to retire suddenly because of family responsibilities. Third is existence of social networks; people feel women will be able to rely on their husbands during retirement, which is a mistake because the likelihood of being widowed and left in poverty is quite high. The final reason is access to programs; women most often work for companies that have no retirement programs or inadequate ones that place little importance on female concerns.

Another area that is often neglected in preretirement counseling is leisure. Many older adults have no idea what to do with themselves after they retire (Edwards, 1984). Liptak (1990) has stressed the importance of goal setting to provide motivation. Long-term goals are the final result that the person wishes to achieve. Medium-term goals are to be achieved in the near future; they are more specific and lead to the accomplishment of the long-range goals. Short-term goals are objectives to be achieved in the immediate future and are very specific. Both medium- and short-term goals can be modified as necessary to lead to the achievement of the long-term goals. For example, a woman wishes to start her own antique store (long-term goal); she plans to learn about running a business and take some courses on antiques (medium-term goals); she registers at the local community college for a course in bookkeeping and a course in Early American furniture (short-term goals).

A model for preretirement counseling programs should include approximately five modules. Module one would be devoted to financial planning and include information on Social Security, pensions, estate planning, taxes, and retirement expenses. Module two would focus on health issues, including information on Medicare, chronic and acute illness, health-care costs, mental health, and community resources. Module three would be devoted to interpersonal relations, including marital problems that may occur after retirement, parent-child issues, elderly parent issues, and support networks. Module four would focus on the use of time, including information on opportunities for part-time work, education, volunteerism, and leisure activities. Module five would focus on women's issues and include information on widowhood and growing old alone. To insure female participation, all employers need to offer preretirement programs that are accessible to all occupational levels and are offered at times that are convenient to all employees. Materials should be current and relevant to the subject. Because of the tendency of women to retire earlier than men, programs should begin earlier in women's careers (Block, 1984; Dennis, 1989).

CASE EXAMPLES

The Case of JoAnn

JoAnn has been married to John for 25 years. They have four children ranging in age from 10 to 20 years. When they were married, JoAnn quit college and obtained a job as a secretary to support her husband's medical school expenses. Their life seemed perfect. Upon completion of medical school, John quickly became a successful surgeon. JoAnn was a great wife, and the children were ideal. After John's career was established, JoAnn quit her job and devoted full time to her family and community.

Following their silver anniversary, John heard of a position in Chicago. After much discussion, John and JoAnn decided that John should apply. John obtained the job, and the family planned for their move to Chicago. While driving to Chicago, John told JoAnn that he was in love with another woman, who had worked for him for 2 years. At first, JoAnn could not believe what she had heard. There she was 50 years old, the moving van was en route to Chicago with the furniture, and her husband was asking for a divorce.

After JoAnn realized and admitted John was serious, she found herself confronted with the following: Can I raise these children alone? How can I support myself? Why did this happen to me? What can I do? The questions were numerous and mainly served to frustrate JoAnn even more.

As she experienced the loss of her marriage, JoAnn experienced the stages of grief much like those described by Kubler-Ross (1975). During Stage 1, the denial stage, she met the moving van and began unpacking her furnishings as if nothing were wrong. She told herself, "This is just a stage that John's experiencing. After all, we're both in our 50s, and John's going through a midlife crisis. This will pass and our marriage will be fine."

Within a few weeks, JoAnn admitted John was serious. While she did not want to lose her marriage, she knew it was happening. At this stage (Stage 2), she was hostile and angry. Sometimes her anger was displaced at her children, though most of the anger was directed to John and the girlfriend, a younger woman.

In Stage 3, the bargaining stage, JoAnn tried to reason with John. She told him that if he would give her another chance, she would try to be a better wife. She stated, "I know if we both try, we can make our marriage work as before." John responded by telling her that she just did not seem to understand that he was in love with another woman.

At Stage 4, the depression stage, JoAnn had realized her marriage was lost and admitted "This is really happening to me." Further, JoAnn said, "My marriage is over and there's really nothing that I can do to save it." As she reviewed her 25 years of marriage, she remembered the good times with their friends and children. Soon the

Table 8.1
The Bottom Line

1. At this time in your life, summarize where you see yourself in regard to:
    A. <u>Resources</u>
       Personal
       Financial
       Family
       Other

    B. <u>Goals</u>
       Personal
       Financial
       Educational
       Vocational
       Family
       Other

2. What area the practical obstacles, problems, and constraints with which you must cope to reach your current goals?
    A. In self
    B. In others
    C. In the world

Source: From *Career Actualization and Life Planning* (pp. 16–17) by Donald H. Blocher, 1988, Denver, CO: Love Publishing Company. Reprinted with permission.

memories were replaced by depression. With time, she became more and more depressed, even to the point that she did not want to see family or friends. She constantly had to fight off tears. Finally the despair was so great that she no longer bothered to get dressed and remained in bed all day. A friend visited her and insisted that she seek counseling. After several months of counseling, the depression was reduced.

In Stage 5, the acceptance stage, JoAnn was facing the pain and realization that her marriage was over. She stated, "While divorce isn't what I would have chosen, I realize John isn't coming back." In a similar vein she concluded, "While I dislike being replaced by another woman, I realize it has happened so I just have to accept what is and do the best that I can."

After the divorce, JoAnn continued in counseling for 3 years. During this period the counselor encouraged JoAnn to get together with her old friends and try to make new ones. At first JoAnn resisted any social activities. Because John had left her for another woman, JoAnn was afraid people would pity and feel sorry for her. Further, she said that she did not think she would be good company for others. With time and encouragement, JoAnn met some friends for lunch. As counseling progressed, the counselor helped JoAnn to feel better about herself. As her self-concept improved, JoAnn ventured into new activities. With time, she began to believe that she could succeed in life.

During one of the sessions, the counselor used a technique called The Bottom Line (Table 8.1). As Table 8.1 illustrates, the bottom line asked JoAnn to summarize where

Table 8.2

Issues for the Midcareer Mother

I. Survival Issues
   A. Do I have the ability to learn a new career?
   B. Do I have or can I acquire the skills necessary to survive in the job market?
   C. Who would even want to hire me?
   D. Can I survive financially?
   E. Can I support myself? My child?
   F. Will I be able to get along with my supervisor? Others at the job?

II. Personal Issues
   A. Am I bright enough to make it on a job?
   B. What will my family think when I go to work?
   C. What will my friends think when I go to work?
   D. Can I be both a good mother and successful careerist?
   E. Can I adapt to working outside the home?
   F. Will I be able to organize my time?
   G. Will I have time left to spend with my child? Children?
   H. Will my child still love me even though I am not with him/her as much?
   I. Can I share my child's love with others (babysitters)?
   J. Can I develop my career and be successful?

III. Work/Family Issues
   A. Will I be able to find and afford adequate babysitting?
   B. What will happen if my child becomes ill when I am scheduled to work?
   C. Will my working hours be rigid or flexible?
   D. When my child has events at school, will my job be flexible enough to allow me to attend?

Source: From *Counseling Midlife Career Changers* (p. 49) by L. J. Bradley, 1990, Garrett Park, MD: Garrett Park Press. Reprinted with permission.

she sees herself—her resources, goals, and obstacles. Following this exercise, JoAnn expressed some interest in making future plans.

After the divorce, she had been living on the money John was providing for her and the children. While her settlement was good, JoAnn realized she could not depend on John's support forever. During counseling, she mentioned that, though she had little experience, she had always wanted to own her own business. The counselor administered some aptitude, interest, and work values tests similar to those described by Bradley (1990). The results seemed to be congruent with JoAnn's expressed interest in owning her own business.

In discussing JoAnn's career plans, she was initially plagued by a number of questions that seemed to center on survival, personal, and work/family issues. Some of the questions are presented in Table 8.2. The counselor was supportive and helped JoAnn deal with the issues. As Table 8.2 illustrates, the issues are typical concerns that women face when they are planning to return to the world of work. A more comprehensive list of issues that women face can be found in an article by Lee (1984).

Once JoAnn decided to establish a catering business, she spent a lot of time planning for her business. She read books and talked with individuals who had successful businesses. She planned trips and met with three successful owners of catering businesses in another state. As per their suggestions, she began her catering business on a small scale. During the first 6 months, her business did not go well. JoAnn realized she needed help in organizing and advertising her business. She employed a consultant part-time. Slowly her business began to prosper. Within a year, she was making a profit and was able to employ an assistant. At the time of this writing, her business is going well. JoAnn continues to attend counseling sessions, though she has transferred from individual to group counseling.

The Case of Mildred

Mildred is a 67-year-old woman who has been retired for almost 2 years. She has been married for almost 45 years to Gilbert, who is 70 years old. They have two children who live across the country. Both Mildred and Gilbert, who retired about 6 months ago, are in excellent health. Barring a catastrophic illness, their finances are in excellent shape.

Mildred has come to counseling because she has been feeling resentful of Gilbert since his retirement. "I expected him to get involved with things, go fishing with his friends, something. But all he does is sit around the house and watch soap operas. Or he follows me around the house trying to help. Help! He has no idea how to do anything. We have a dishwasher, but he insists on washing the dishes and he does a really bad job." She paused and then continued, "I'd expected to enjoy time with my husband when he retired, but he doesn't want to go out or travel. He says he wants to enjoy his retirement by doing nothing, and, believe me that is exactly what he is doing. I'm so tired of him."

Mildred is involved in activities at her church and volunteers 3 days a week at one of the local hospitals. She says, "I use every excuse possible to get out of the house. I may even volunteer to teach adult reading classes 2 days a week. At least, that would get me away from Gilbert."

During a counseling session, the counselor asked Mildred to make a list of the things that bothered her the most about Gilbert being at home all of the time. Mildred thought for a moment and then took a pen and a piece of paper and began to write. When she finished her list it contained the following: "I have no privacy in my own home"; "I can no longer take my time and enjoy my household work"; "We no longer talk to each other about anything interesting, like politics or current events, only about what is on TV"; "I feel like I am suffocating."

Looking over the list, Mildred said, "I hadn't realized that I was so bothered by my lack of privacy. If I tell him what is bothering me, he will be crushed." The counselor suggested that Mildred spend the time between sessions thinking about various ways of confronting the issue.

At the next session, Mildred reported that she had been thinking of ways to tell Gilbert that she needed more privacy but "I just can't think of any way to tell him that I need more time to myself without sounding like I want to spend no time with him at all." The counselor used the empty chair technique and role playing to give Mildred practice in talking to Gilbert.

When Mildred came in the next week, she was beaming. "I talked to Gilbert and you can't imagine what he said. He told me that he was unhappy with all of the time we were spending together as well. He thought that, after all of those years he worked, he owed me all of his time. We've been a couple of old fools who didn't know enough to talk to each other." Mildred and Gilbert learned to communicate with each other and learned that it is best to ask what another person wants rather than to assume that one knows automatically.

The Case of Jessica

Jessica is a 55-year-old single woman who holds an executive position in sales at a small drug manufacturing company. She has recently learned that her company is merging with a larger company within a year. The president of her company has offered Jessica early retirement because the merger will cause her position to be discontinued, and, because she has been with the company for 29 years, she is eligible for full pension. Jessica has come to counseling to discuss her options.

"I really hadn't considered retiring this early. Truthfully, I have never considered retirement at all. I guess that I thought I would work forever. I really have no idea what to do." Jessica admitted that she has lived for her work and has few contacts outside of the company. Her parents are dead, and her sister lives in Europe.

Jessica is not worried about finances because she has invested in an IRA and her pension pays at two-thirds of current salary. She is more concerned by the sense of loss that she feels when she thinks of her career. Mancini (1979) defined role loss as a critical factor in stress because it "excludes and devalues people, sorely undermining their social identity" (p. 292).

An unanticipated/external change is extremely stressful and caused Jessica to ask questions such as "What do I do now?" "Can I get another job?" and "Why did this happen to me?" Jessica suffered from depression for several weeks while she struggled to make up her mind about what she would do when her job ended.

Her interest inventories had shown that she had a high interest in the arts combined with an interest in business. The counselor suggested that she begin researching a way to combine her interests into one occupation. Having something for which to work gave Jessica motivation to move forward. She spent several weeks researching businesses that involved art and decided that she would like to work in a gallery or museum.

Finally, Jessica came to a counseling session with the news that she had found a small art gallery that needed a manager. She went to talk with the owner and was hired on the spot. She says, "The money isn't that great, but I have my pension so I need very little. I love being surrounded by art and helping people to choose something beautiful, and I've been able to use my business experience to reverse some of the expenses that have plagued the owner for years." After Jessica had been with the gallery for 3 years, the owner offered to sell her half of the business.

RESOURCES AVAILABLE

It is important for counselors to know what services and resources are available to adults. A counselor should become familiar with local networks and support groups, programs available in the area, and the people to call when help is needed (Humple, 1984; Neugarten, 1982b).

A number of organizations serve as advocates for older people. National organizations include the American Association of Retired Persons (AARP), Action for Independent Maturity (AIM), the Gray Panthers, the Older Women's League, and the National Organization on the Aging, Inc. Government agencies concerned with aging include the Administration on Aging (AoA), ACTION, the National Institute on Aging (NIA), the Social Security Administration, the United States House of Representatives Select Committee on Aging, and the United States Senate Special Committee on Aging.

Information on state organizations and committees are available from state departments of human services. Most large cities have an age-advocate office. In addition, states have ombudspeople to advocate and assist older adults. Community networks are often formed around senior citizen centers, the YMCA/YWCA, and local hospitals. The local library may have books and periodicals that are helpful.

PROBLEM PREVENTION AND SOCIAL INTERVENTIONS

Cultural change is a slow process, and it is the only way to change stereotypes. One need only examine the history of civil rights legislation in this country to discover that "laws do not change attitudes." Although the Equal Employment Opportunity Commission is mandated to deal with issues of sexism and ageism in the labor force, it has often failed to do an adequate job. Cases of sexism, with the exception of sexual harassment, are usually refused (Matlin, 1987). Unions and labor organizations often do not support their women members as well as they support men. In listening to and reading the national news, one hears of more and more incidents about employers who refuse to hire women for certain jobs because the jobs may be dangerous to women in their childbearing years. This is access discrimination hidden behind paternalism: "This is too dangerous for you, little woman. If you took this job, you might not be able to fulfill your proper role and have children. Listen to us; we know what's best for you."

Older adults suffer from discrimination as well. Unlike sexism, ageism is covered by a specific law, but the question arises of how stringently it is enforced. Considering the number of older Americans, 245 cases of age discrimination seems very low. Ageism in employment, especially in hiring, seems to be a case very difficult to prove. If companies and union officials would commit themselves to equal treatment for adult women and make equal treatment standard operating procedure with sanctions against those in the company who failed to follow the guidelines, then progress in eliminating sexism and ageism would be made.

Budget cuts in social programs—food stamps, legal aid, subsidized housing, Medicare, and so on—have affected the older adult more than any other single group. It has been suggested that part of the problem with social programs for older adults results from using age as a criterion. As Kutza and Zwiebel (1982) stated:

> The weakness of using chronological age as a criterion by which to focus public benefits is straightforward: changes within persons are related to more factors than their age. The individual's development is unique. It is shaped not only by number of years lived, but by the particular life events the person has experienced....Because of their diversity, older people are a difficult group for whom to plan. This conclusion contradicts the presumption on which current aging policy rests, that the group as a whole is characterized by a specific, identifiable, and consistent set of attributes and, hence, needs. (pp. 61-63)

Faulkner and Micchelli (1988) have noted that public policy often requires the older adult to liquidate all assets before providing aid. This is especially true of the health system, which fails to consider that by forcing a couple to spend all of their joint assets on one member's illness, the surviving member may be forced into destitution. An alternative is legal separation. In addition, the health care system has failed to make a distinction between caregiver and spouse that would allow children to receive aid for caring for parents. The system also emphasizes institutional rather than home care, when home care might be less expensive and more beneficial to the mental and emotional health of the patient.

For public policy change, people must be involved. Each person must be responsive to the plight of women and especially the elderly, and each person must take the responsibility for either acting or not acting as an agent for change. Policy makers are influenced by the electorate. If they are told by a significant number of voters that a certain piece of legislation is needed, they will respond. However, if the voters do not inform the policy makers, the status quo will be maintained. All social change begins with the individual.

SUMMARY

We live in an aging society; by the year 2020 one person in five will be 65 or older. The media is preoccupied with youth, which leads to special problems for women, including double standards toward aging and denial. Our preoccupation with youth has led to stereotypes about the elderly that are pervasive in our society.

Career development theory, like other developmental theories, is based on the male experience. The increase in the number of women in the labor force has underscored the need for a career theory for women that takes into account the patterns and developmental tasks unique to women.

Women in the labor force are victims of gender role stereotyping. Sexism, both in access and treatment, results in lower status jobs and lower pay. Women are seldom invited to join the informal social network in which information is exchanged away from the office. Married women, in particular, suffer from interrupted career patterns because of child rearing and other family obligations. Despite the problems that women face at work, employed adult women are satisfied with their lives. The empty nest syndrome that has portrayed the adult woman as a depressed, over-involved mother unable to relinquish that role and allow her children autonomy has been proven a fallacy.

In general, women in retirement adapt well and are satisfied. They are involved with friends, family, and social roles. The two issues that cause the most stress in retirement are finances and health. Women retire earlier than men, often to care for an ailing husband or parent.

Counseling women who are older adult career changers requires a knowledge of what developmental tasks they are facing. The counselor should be acquainted with assessment tools to aid the woman in choosing new options. The process of counseling includes assessment, diagnosis of problems, and the use of techniques—role playing, journals, homework, and so on—to learn new skills and behaviors. Group therapy can be very effective in career counseling because it allows the practice of new skills and behaviors with others, and it fosters the exchange of information and support.

Preretirement counseling is an area in which there is much room for growth. Approximately one-third of the corporations in the United States provide some form of retirement counseling, although it is often limited both in scope and applicability. Retirement counseling should include information on financial planning, health issues, interpersonal relationships, use of time, and issues that face women.

Resources from the federal and state governments, national advocacy groups, and the community are available to assist older women. State ombudspeople and city age advocates are often able to aid in problem solving. Community groups provide older adults with support and offer activities in which they may become involved. Counselors are urged to acquaint themselves with information on the resources available in their areas.

Women and older people are victims of stereotypes. Our culture's emphasis on youth and beauty undermines self-confidence and identity. The laws that have been made to protect women and older people are often ineffective and sporadically enforced. Health care and other social programs have suffered from budget cuts that have limited or eliminated aid to affected groups.

Change is needed. Commitment is required at both the individual and institutional levels. Each of us is responsible for being sure that change happens.

REFERENCES

Adelmann, P. K., Antonucci, T. C., Crohan, S. E., & Coleman, L. M. (1989). Empty nest, cohort, and employment in the well-being of midlife women. *Sex Roles, 20*, 173–189.

Anderson, K., Higgins, C., Newman, E. S., & Sherman, S. R. (1978). Differences in attitudes toward retirement among male and female faculty members and other university professionals. *Journal of Minority Aging, 3*, 5–13.

Astin, H. S. (1976). Continuing education and the development of adult women. *Counseling Psychologist, 6*, 55–60.

Atchley, R. C. (1976). Selected social and psychological differences between men and women in later life. *Journal of Gerontology, 31*, 204–211.

Barnett, R. C., & Baruch, G. K. (1978). Women in the middle years: A critique of research and theory. *Psychology of Women Quarterly, 3*, 187–197.

Baruch, G. K., & Barnett, R. C. (1986). Role quality, multiple role involvement, and psychological well-being in midlife women. *Journal of Personality and Social Psychology, 51*, 578–585.

Baruch, G. K., Biener, L., & Barnett, R. C. (1987). Women and gender in research on work and family stress. *American Psychologist, 42*, 130–136.

Belgrave, L. L. (1989). Understanding women's retirement. *Generations, 13*, 49–52.

Berman, P. W., O'Nan, B. A., & Floyd, W. (1981). The double standard of aging and the social situation: Judgments of attractiveness of the middle-aged woman. *Sex Roles, 7*, 87–96.

Bernstein, M. C. (1980). Forecast of women's retirement income: Cloudy and colder; 25 percent chance of poverty. In M. M. Fuller & C. A. Martin (Eds.), *The older woman: Lavender rose or gray panther* (pp. 234–246). Springfield, IL: Charles C Thomas.

Betz, N. E., & Fitzgerald, L. F. (1987). *The career psychology of women*. Orlando, FL: Academic Press.

Bird, C. (1979). The best years of a woman's life. *Psychology Today, 12*, 20–26.

Blocher, D. H. (1988). *Career actualization and life planning*. Denver: Love Publishing.

Block, M. R. (1984). Retirement preparation needs of women. In H. Dennis (Ed.), *Retirement preparation: What retirement specialists need to know* (pp. 129–140). Lexington, MA: Lexington Books.

Bordin, E. S. (1968). *Psychological counseling* (2nd ed.). New York: Appleton-Century-Crofts.

Bradley, L. J. (1988). Career assessment across the life span. In R. Hayes & R. Aubrey (Eds.), *New direction for counseling and human development*. Denver: Love Publishing.

Bradley, L. J. (1990). *Counseling midlife career changers*. Garrett Park, MD: Garrett Park Press.

Brooks, L. (1984). Counseling special groups: Women and ethnic minorities. In D. Brown & L. Brooks (Eds.), *Career choice and development* (pp. 255–368). San Francisco: Jossey-Bass.

Brown, D. (1984). Midlife career change. In D. Brown & L. Brooks (Eds.), *Career choice and development* (pp. 369–387). San Francisco: Jossey-Bass.

Campione, W. A. (1987). The married woman's retirement decision: A methodological comparison. *Journal of Gerontology, 42*, 381–386.

Capsi, A., & Elder, G. H., Jr. (1986). Life satisfaction in old age: Linking social psychology and history. *Journal of Psychology and Aging, 1*, 18–26.

Cherry, D. L., Zarit, S. H., & Krauss, I. K. (1984). The structure of post-retirement adaptation for recent and longer-term women retirees. *Experimental Aging Research, 10*, 231–236.

Collier, H. V. (1982). *Counseling women: A guide for therapists*. New York: Free Press.

Cowan, G. (1984). The double standard in age discrepant relationships. *Sex Roles, 11*, 17–24.

Craig, G. (1990). *Human development*. Englewood Cliffs, NJ: Prentice-Hall.

Crosby, F. J. (1982). *Relative deprivation and working women*. New York: Oxford University Press.

DeBeauvoir, S. (1970). *The coming of age*. New York: Warner Books.

Dennis, H. (1989). The current state of retirement planning. *Generations, 13*, 38–41.

Deutsch, F. M., Zalinski, C. M., & Clark, M. E. (1986). Is there a double standard of aging? *Journal of Applied Social Psychology, 16*, 771–785.

Dorfman, L. T., & Moffett, M. M. (1987). Retirement satisfaction in married and widowed rural women. *The Gerontologist, 27*, 215–221.

Dunnette, M. D., & Motowidlo, S. J. (1982). Estimating benefits and costs of antisexist training programs in organizations. In H. J. Bernardin (Ed.), *Women in the work force* (pp. 156–182). New York: Praeger.

Edwards, P. B. (1984). Leisure counseling. In H. Dennis (Ed.), *Retirement preparation: What retirement specialists need to know* (pp. 97–107). Lexington, MA: Lexington Books.

Eglit, H. (1989). Ageism in the work place: An elusive quarry. *Generations, 13*, 31–35.

Eisler, T. A. (1984). Career impact on independence of the elderly. In W. H. Quinn & G. A. Hughston (Eds.), *Independent aging: Family and social system perspectives* (pp. 256–264). Rockville, MD: Aspen Publications.

Entine, A. D. (1977). Counseling for midlife and beyond. *Vocational Guidance Quarterly, 25*, 332–336.

Erikson, E. H. (1963). *Childhood and society*. New York: W. W. Norton.

Erikson, E. H. (1980). *Identity and the life cycle*. New York: W. W. Norton.

Farmer, H. S., & Fyans, L. J. (1983). Married women's achievement and career motivation: The influence of some environmental and psychological variables. *Psychology of Women Quarterly, 7*, 358–372.

Faulkner, A. O., & Micchelli, M. (1988). The aging, the aged, and the very old: Women the policy makers forgot. *Women and Health, 14*, 5–19.

Fengler, A. P. (1975). Attitudinal orientations of wives toward their husbands' retirement. *International Journal of Aging and Human Development, 6*, 139–152.

Fleisher, D. (1984). Alternative work options. In H. Dennis (Ed.), *Retirement preparation: What retirement specialists need to know* (pp. 53–60). Lexington, MA: Lexington Books.

Fox, J. H. (1977). Effects of retirement and former work life on women's adaptation in old age. *Journal of Gerontology, 32*, 196–202.

Frasher, J. M., Frasher, R. S., & Wims, F. B. (1982). Sex role stereotyping in school superintendents' personnel decisions. *Sex Roles, 8*, 261–268.

Furstenberg, A. (1989). Older people's age self-concept. *Social Casework: The Journal of Contemporary Social Work, 70*, 268–275.

George, L. K., Fillenbaum, G. G., & Palmore, E. (1984). Sex differences in the antecedents and consequences of retirement. *Journal of Gerontology, 39*, 364–371.

Giesen, C. B., & Datan, N. (1980). The competent older woman. In N. Datan & N. Lohmann (Eds.), *Transitions of aging* (pp. 57–72). New York: Academic Press.

Gilligan, C. (1982). *In a different voice*. Cambridge: Harvard University Press.

Ginzberg, E. (1972). Toward a theory of occupational choice: A restatement. *Vocational Guidance Quarterly, 20*, 169–176.

Glenn, N. D. (1975). Psychological well being in the post-parental stage. *Journal of Marriage and the Family, 37*, 105–110.

Gould, R. L. (1978). *Transformations: Growth and change in adult life*. New York: Simon & Schuster.

Griffin, J. (1981). Midlife career change. *Occupational Outlook Quarterly, 25*, 2–5.

Hall, D. T. (1976). *Careers in organizations*. Santa Monica, CA: Goodyear.

Havighurst, R. J. (1953). *Human development and education*. New York: Longman.

Healy, C. C. (1982). *Career development: Counseling through life stages*. Boston: Allyn & Bacon.

Henry, S. (1990). Barriers to access. *Modern Maturity, 33*, 33–36.

Herr, E. L., & Cramer, S. H. (1984). *Career guidance and counseling through the life span*. Boston: Little Brown & Co.

Holahan, C. K. (1981). Lifetime achievement patterns, retirement, and life satisfaction. *Journal of Gerontology, 36*, 741–749.

Holden, K. C. (1989). Do retirement resources hold up? *Generations, 13*, 42–46.

Holland, J. L. (1966). *The psychology of vocational choice*. Waltham, MA: Blaisdell.

Humple, C. S. (1984). Resources and networks for the retirement planner. In H. Dennis (Ed.), *Retirement preparation: What retirement specialists need to know* (pp. 167–187). Lexington, MA: Lexington Books.

Isaacson, L. (1985). *Basics of career counseling*. Boston: Allyn & Bacon.

Johnson, C. K., & Price-Bonham, S. (1980). Women and retirement: A study and implications. *Family Relations, 29*, 380–385.

Johnson, E. S. (1983). Suburban older women. In E. W. Markson (Ed.), *Older women: Issues and prospects* (pp. 179–193). Lexington, MA: Lexington Books.

Jung, C. (1933). The stages of life. In *Modern man in search of soul (W. S. Dell & C. F. Baynes, Trans.)*. New York: Harcourt Brace, Jovanovich.

Kahn, S. E., & Ward, V. G. (1983). Evaluation of group vocational counseling for women. *Journal of Employment Counseling, 20*, 34–41.

Kalish, R. A. (1982). *Late adulthood: Perspectives on human development*. Monterey, CA: Brooks/Cole Publishing.

Karp, D. A. (1985). Gender, academic careers, and the social psychology of aging. *Qualitative Sociology, 8*, 9–29.

Kaye, L. W., & Monk, A. (1984). Sex role traditions and retirement from academe. *The Gerontologist, 24*, 420–426.

Keith, P. M. (1985). Work, retirement, and well-being among unmarried men and women. *The Gerontologist, 25*, 410–416.

Kiger, G. (1984). Working women and their children. *The Social Sciences Journal, 21*, 49–57.

Kogan, N. (1979). A study of age categorization. *Journal of Gerontology, 34*, 358–367.

Kopp, J. (1989). Self-observation: An empowerment strategy in assessment. *Social Casework: The Journal of Contemporary Social Work, 70*, 276–284.

Krumboltz, J. D., Mitchell, A. M., & Jones, G. B. (1976). A social learning theory of career selection. *The Counseling Psychologist, 6*, 71–81.

Kubler-Ross, E. (1975). *Death, the final stage of growth*. Englewood Cliffs, NJ: Prentice-Hall.

Kutza, E. A., & Zwiebel, N. R. (1982). Age as a criterion for focusing public programs. In B. L. Neugarten (Ed.), *Age or need? Public policies for older people* (pp. 55–99). Beverly Hills, CA: Sage Publications.

Lazarus, M., & Laver, H. (1985). Working past retirement: Practical and motivational issues. In R. N. Butler & H. P. Gleason (Eds.), *Productive aging: Enhancing vitality in later life* (pp. 47–75). New York: Springer Publishing.

Lee, R. (1984). When midcareer mothers first return to work: Counseling concerns. *Journal of Counseling and Development, 63*, 35–39.

Levinson, D. C., Darrow, C., Klein, E., Levinson, M., & McKee, B. (1978). *The seasons of a man's life.* New York: Knopf.

Levy, S. M. (1980–1981). The adjustment of the older woman: Effects of chronic ill health and attitudes toward retirement. *International Journal of Aging and Human Development, 12*, 93–110.

Liang, J. (1982). Sex differences in life satisfaction among the elderly. *Journal of Gerontology, 37*, 100–108.

Liebig, P. S. (1984). The three-legged stool of retirement income. In H. Dennis (Ed.), *Retirement preparation: What retirement specialists need to know* (pp. 43–51). Lexington, MA: Lexington Books.

Lipka, R. P. (1987). Women: Why does society age them sooner? *Contemporary Educational Psychology, 12*, 110–118.

Lipman-Blumen, J. (1976). Toward a homosocial theory of sex roles: An explanation of the sex segregation of social institutions. *Signs: Journal of Women in Culture and Society, 1*, 15–31.

Liptak, J. J. (1990). Preretirement counseling: Integrating the leisure planning component. *The Career Development Quarterly, 38*, 360–367.

Lyon, E. (1986). The economics of gender. In F. A. Boudreau, R. S. Sinnott, & M. Wilson (Eds.), *Sex roles and social patterns* (pp. 149–189). New York: Praeger.

MacKinnon-Slaney, F., Barber, S., & Slaney, R. (1988). Marital status as a mediating factor on career aspirations of reentry female students. *Journal of College Student Development, 29*, 327–334.

Mancini, J. (1979). Family relationships and morale among people 65 years of age and older. *American Journal of Orthopsychiatry, 49*, 292–300.

Matlin, M. W. (1987). *The psychology of women.* New York: Holt, Rinehart & Winston.

Matthiessen, C. (1990). Bordering on collapse. *Modern Maturity, 33*, 30–32, 38–40, 82–85.

Meade, K., & Walker, J. (1989). Gender equality: Issues and challenges for retirement education. *Educational Gerontologist, 15*, 171–185.

Minkler, M., & Stone, R. (1985). The feminization of poverty and older women. *The Gerontologist, 25*, 351–357.

Montepare, J. M., & Lachman, M. E. (1989). "You're only as old as you feel": Self-perceptions of age, fears of aging, and life satisfaction from adolescence to old age. *Psychology and Aging, 4*, 73–78.

Moon, M., & Hushbeck, J. (1989). Options for extending work life. *Generations, 13*, 27–30.

Moursund, J. (1985). *The process of counseling and therapy.* Englewood Cliffs, NJ: Prentice-Hall.

Neugarten, B. L. (1972). Education and the life cycle. *School Review, 80*, 209–216.

Neugarten, B. L. (1976). Adaptation and the life cycle. *The Counseling Psychologist, 6*, 16–20.

Neugarten, B. L. (1979). Time, age and the life cycle. *American Journal of Psychiatry, 136*, 887–894.

Neugarten, B. L. (1982a). Older people: A profile. In B. L. Neugarten (Ed.), *Age or need? Public policies for older people* (pp. 33–54). Beverly Hills, CA: Sage Publications.

Neugarten, B. L. (1982b). Policy for the 1980s: Age or need entitlement? In B. L. Neugarten (Ed.), *Age or need? Public policies for older people* (pp. 19–32). Beverly Hills, CA: Sage Publications.

Oliver, R. (1988). "Empty nest" or relationship restructuring? A rational-emotive approach to a midlife transition. *Journal of Rational-Emotive and Cognitive-Behavior Therapy, 6*, 102–117.

Palmore, E. B., Burchett, B. M., Fillenbaum, G. G., George, L. K., & Wallman, L. M. (1985). *Retirement: Causes and consequences.* New York: Springer Publishing.

Palmore, E. B., & Kivett, V. (1977). Changes in life satisfaction: A longitudinal study of persons aged 46–70. *Journal of Gerontology, 32*, 311–316.

Papalia, D., & Olds, S. (1989). *Human development* (4th ed.). New York: McGraw-Hill.

Parnes, H. S. (1989). Post-retirement employment: How much is there? How much is wanted? *Generations, 13*, 23–26.

Plowman, V. (1984). Retirement and the family. In H. Dennis (Ed.), *Retirement preparation: What retirement specialists need to know* (pp. 141–157). Lexington, MA: Lexington Books.

Porcino, J. (1985). Psychological aspects of aging in women. *Women and Health, 10*, 115–122.

Radloff, L. S. (1980). Depression and the empty nest. *Sex Roles, 6*, 775–781.

Ramsey, G. P. (1984). Financial planning. In H. Dennis (Ed.), *Retirement preparation: What retirement specialists need to know* (pp. 35–41). Lexington, MA: Lexington Books.

Redmond, R. (1980). Legal issues involving the older woman. In M. M. Fuller & C. A. Martin (Eds.), *The older woman: Lavender rose or gray panther* (pp. 228–233). Springfield, IL: Charles C Thomas.

Roe, A. (1957). Early determinants of vocational choice. *Journal of Counseling Psychology, 4*, 212–217.

Rosen, B., & Jerdee, T. N. (1974). Influence of sex role stereotypes on personnel decisions. *Journal of Applied Psychology, 59*, 9–14.

Rosenfield, S. (1989). The effects of women's employment: Personal control and sex differences in mental health. *Journal of Health and Social Behavior, 30*, 77–91.

Rubin, L. B. (1979). *Women of a certain age: The midlife search for self.* New York: Harper & Row.

Ryff, C. D. (1989). In the eye of the beholder: Views of psychological well-being among middle-aged and older adults. *Psychology and Aging, 4*, 195–210.

Schein, E. H. (1978). *Career dynamics: Matching individual and organizational needs.* Reading, MA: Addison-Wesley.

Seltzer, M. (1989). Early retirement programs. *Generations, 13*, 36–37.

Sexton, P. C. (1977). Women and work. *R&D Monograph, 46.* Washington, DC: U.S. Government Printing Office.

Shaw, L. B. (1984). Retirement plans of middle-aged married women. *The Gerontologist, 24*, 154–159.

Sheehy, G. (1976). *Passages: Predictable crisis of adult life.* New York: E. P. Dutton.

Sontag, S. (1979). The double standard of aging. In H. Williams (Ed.), *Psychology of women: Selected readings* (pp. 462–478). New York: W.W. Norton.

Steinkamp, M. W., & Kelly, J. R. (1985). Relationships among motivational orientation, level of leisure activity, and life satisfaction in older men and women. *Journal of Psychology, 119*, 509–520.

Super, D. E. (1953). A theory of vocational development. *American Psychologist, 8*, 185–190.

Super, D. E. (1957). *The psychology of careers.* New York: Harper & Row.

Super, D. E. (1990). A life span, life space approach to career development. In D. Brown, L. Brooks, & Associates (Eds.), *Career choice and development: Applying contemporary theory to practice* (2nd ed.). San Francisco: Jossey-Bass.

Szinovacz, M. E. (1983). Beyond the hearth: Older women and retirement. In E. W. Markson (Ed.), *Older women: Issues and prospects* (pp. 93–120). Lexington, MA: Lexington Books.

Szinovacz, M. E. (1987). Preferred retirement timing and retirement satisfaction in women. *International Journal of Aging and Human Development, 24*, 301–317.

Tager, R. M. (1984). Health promotion. In H. Dennis (Ed.), *Retirement preparation: What retirement specialists need to know* (pp. 29–34). Lexington, MA: Lexington Books.

Tideman, D. V., & O'Hara, R. P. (1963). *Career development: Choice and adjustment.* New York: College Entrance Examination Board.

Troll, L. E. (1976). The nature of the adult client: Developmental needs and behavior. In N. C. Seltz & H. V. Collier (Eds.), *Meeting the educational and occupational planning needs of adults.* Bloomington: Indiana University (ERIC Document Reproduction Service No. 143 885).

U.S. Department of Commerce. (1989). *Statistical abstract of the United States.* Washington, DC: U.S. Government Printing Office.

U.S. Department of Health & Human Services. (1990). *The Medicare Handbook* (No. HCFA 10050). Baltimore: Author.

Valliant, G. E. (1977). *Adaptations to life.* Boston: Little Brown.

Vinick, B. H., & Ekerdt, D. J. (1989). Retirement and the family. *Generations, 13*, 53–56.

Ward, R. A. (1977). The impact of subjective age and stigma on older persons. *Journal of Gerontology, 32*, 227–232.

Williamson, J. B., Shindul, J. A., & Evans, L. (1985). *Aging and public policy: Special control or social justice?* Springfield, IL: Charles C Thomas.

9

Mature Women: Confronting the Social Stereotypes

Jane E. Myers
University of North Carolina at Greensboro

The graying of America and indeed the world is an accepted fact of the 20th century. People are living longer—into their 80s today compared to the late 40s in 1900. A less well-known but equally significant demographic trend with important implications for the future is the "feminization of aging" (Wisniewski & Cohen, 1984). Women are living longer than men and are thus at risk for extended years of widowhood, living alone, institutionalization, poverty, and mental health problems. A recent national ecumenical conference that sought to raise awareness of the issues facing older women underscored the following facts:

❑ Women make up almost 60% of the over-65 population and nearly 75% of the over-75 population.
❑ Women make up 72% of the aged poor.
❑ Almost 75% of nursing home patients are women.
❑ 70% of women over age 75 are widowed, while 70% of men in this age group are married.
❑ Single older women are most likely to have no significant source of income other than Social Security.
❑ More than 2 million women over age 65 live in poverty compared to fewer than 1 million older men. (American Association of Retired Persons [AARP], 1986)

Gender differences in the experience of aging have led many researchers to define the problems of aging as the problems of women. Many of these problems are based in pervasive social stereotypes that limit the lifestyle choices available to women in their later years. It is the purpose of this chapter to confront those stereotypes and suggest strategies and resources for intervening to enhance the lives of today's mature women, while working to prevent similar difficulties for later generations of women. Case examples are used to clarify the issues presented.

SOCIAL AND FAMILY ISSUES AFFECTING MATURE WOMEN

Aging occurs in a social as well as family context, and factors affecting the adjustment of mature women can be best understood from these perspectives. Social stereotypes of later life and the resultant devaluation of older persons in general are considered first, with an emphasis on those concerns specific to older women. Issues related to poverty and loneliness are reviewed in detail, as these are among the most significant problems facing mature women today. This section ends with an exploration of relationships between adult children and aging parents and how these relationships can enhance or detract from life satisfaction in the later years.

Social Stereotypes and Devaluation of Older Women

Older women are affected by numerous social stereotypes, including those that relate to older persons in general, those that relate to various minority groups or subgroups, and those that relate specifically to being female and being older simultaneously. Each of these sets of stereotypes is examined in this section, which concludes with a discussion of how these stereotypes contribute to the devaluation of older women in our society.

Stereotypes of Aging and Older Persons

"Ageism," a term first used by Butler (1975) in his Pulitzer Prize–winning book, *Why Survive? Growing Old in America*, refers to the negative stereotypes of and discrimination toward older persons prevalent in our society. Similar to racism and sexism, ageism is a perspective that views all older people as similar. Many people view all older persons as senile, unattractive, and in poor health. The National Council on the Aging defined the most persistent and widespread—and also untrue—stereotypes of older persons as follows (Kermis, 1984):

❏ Old people are all alike.
❏ Old people are all poor.
❏ Old people are all sick.
❏ Old people are all depressed.
❏ Old people are all a drag on everyone else.
❏ Old people cannot function in society.
❏ Old people all live alone.
❏ Old people all die in institutions.
❏ If we live long enough, we will all be senile.

As is true with young children, adolescents, and college students, much of the research that has given us what we "know" about older persons we have learned from captive populations. Young children and adolescents are most easily accessible through schools and college students through university classes. Older persons are most easily found in long-term care institutions. In spite of popular misconceptions to the contrary, only 5% of older people reside in such settings. Another 10% to 15% are largely homebound due to physical or emotional illnesses, and at least 80% are functioning independently in the community. Much of our "common knowledge" of older people has been gained from a small minority of the older population, most notably those who are ill.

While stereotypes tend to be generalizations, there remains at least a kernel of truth in each one. For example, older persons are alike in many ways, many of them are poor, at one time or another most of them are sick, and often many are depressed. The fact that these characteristics are shared at one time or another by many older people has contributed to our myths about later life. However, one of the most salient characteristics of the 26 million Americans over age 65 is that they are a very heterogeneous group. Any single older person may be wealthy and/or healthy and/or happy, and show evidence of any of the other characteristics found in younger people.

Harris and Associates (1975), under contract to the National Council on the Aging, conducted an extensive national survey of public perceptions of older people. They divided their respondents into two groups, those under 65 and those 65 and over. They found that younger people described older people as senile, inactive, unfriendly, and uncooperative. While individual older people described themselves as intelligent, active, and friendly, they maintained negative perceptions of their age peers ("those old people"), which matched the views of the younger respondents in the sample.

Younger people thought that older people spend a lot of time watching television, sitting and thinking, and socializing with friends (in that order), and little time participating in sports, full- or part-time work, and political activities. Older persons reported their top three activities as socializing with friends, gardening or raising plants, and reading. Sleeping ranked 10th out of 15 activities, and their three lowest ranked were participating in sports, political activities, and volunteer work. There were even more enlightening data (Harris & Associates, 1975) on public expectations of very serious problems of the over age 65 group. Table 9.1 gives a sample of the results.

Although the Harris study (1975) is now more than 15 years old, numerous studies of age discrimination within the last decade suggest that attitudes toward older persons are universally negative. Negative attitudes have been found among children (Nishi-Strattner & Myers, 1983), adolescents (Doka, 1986), psychiatrists (Ray, Raciti & Ford, 1985), rehabilitation practitioners (Bearden & Head, 1985), and gerontologists (Hickey, Bragg, Rakowski, & Hultsch, 1979), among others. A few researchers have reported a shift in public attitudes in a slightly less negative (not be confused with positive) direction (Austin, 1985; Chandler, Rachal, & Kazelskis, 1986), however, negative myths, "myth-conceptions," and negative attitudes toward older persons prevail.

Table 9.1
Personal Experience vs. Public Perception of Very Serious Problems for People Over Age 65

Problem Area	Very Serious for Older People Personally	Public Perception of Very Serious Problem	Difference
Fear of crime	23%	50%	+27
Poor health	21%	51%	+30
Not enough money to live	15%	62%	+47
Loneliness	12%	60%	+48
Not enough medical care	10%	· 44%	+34

Source: Data drawn from *The Myth and Reality of Aging in America* by L. Harris and Associates, 1975, Washington, DC: The National Council on the Aging, Inc., 409 Third Street SW, Washington, DC 20024.

Multiple Jeopardy: The "isms" and More

Being old in America places one at risk, "in jeopardy." Ageism, described above, is a danger caused by negative societal perceptions of people who are old. Other "isms" are prevalent in our society. These include racism (prejudice against people of a particular ethnic background), handicapism (stereotypical views of those with disabilities), and sexism (bias against people based on their gender). A person who happens to be old *and* a minority is placed in a situation of *double jeopardy.* One who is old, a member of a minority group, *and* disabled is in a situation of *triple jeopardy.* Clearly, women in their later years experience at least double jeopardy and frequently are best described as being in *multiple jeopardy.*

The isms are not the only source of negative bias or stereotypical views of older women. For example, people who are poor in our society experience decreased social status. Those who are homeless are significantly devalued compared to those who are self-supporting. Those for whom English is not the native language, or who are not fluent, are often viewed as less intelligent than others.

People whose sexual preference is for a partner of the same gender face discrimination and frequently homophobic reactions from the majority of society. Kimmel (1979) estimated that 10% of the general population is gay. By inference, therefore, as many as 10% of older people, some 2.5 million individuals, may be gay. Many fail to declare their lifestyle openly due to the social stigma, and in later life may have few social supports. Among the more negative concomitants of a homosexual lifestyle for older people are the inability to visit a terminally ill partner in the hospital, inability to maintain community property or grieve openly upon the death of a partner, or ostracism by family members in times of bereavement (Martin & Lyon, 1979).

Marital status can be a significant source of bias against older women. Recent studies reviewed by Keith (1986) substantiate the existence of negative stereotypes against unmarried persons. Among this group, widowed people have the highest status, followed by those who never married, with divorced people being seen as undependable, troubled, and unstable. Even widows may be viewed negatively by married couples, especially wives, who view them as threats to marital stability. The rapid exclusion of new widows from social groups in which they participated as couples is widespread. Several years ago a letter in Ann Landers' column urged couples to read the fine print when signing contracts to live in retirement communities. One older woman who did not do so was forced to move out when her husband died. Older single women most likely have experienced a lifetime of stigma and social pressure, since marriage has been the predominant role for women during most of their lifetimes. Because most psychosocial theories of development favor marriage and parenting as "normal" adult roles, older women who are childless as well as single are placed in "a socially deviant role" (Myers & Navin, 1984, p. 93).

Divorce among older people today is not common however, the proportion of adults who have been divorced before reaching old age will increase rapidly in the near future. Today's older people were raised in an environment where divorce was considered unacceptable. The social stigma attached to "divorced" status probably contributes to an under reporting of being divorced and resultant inaccurate data for the current older population. Using the census and vital statistics, Uhlenberg and Myers (1981) estimated that 10% to 13% of older people have been divorced. This represents between 2.6 and 3.4 million individuals.

Being Female and Being Old

Women experience aging differently than men; as a consequence their lives become more difficult as they get older (Porter, 1984). Older women in contemporary society are viewed as "poor, dumb, and ugly" (Troll, 1984, p. 1) and are stereotyped as unattractive, passive, complaining, asexual, and useless (Livson, 1977). Media portrayals of women as invisible, irrelevant, or victimized add to the negative picture (Steenland & Schmidt, 1985). The image of youthful bodies, active lifestyles, and romantic involvements urged by the media as the American ideal places aging women who do not fit the desired stereotype into one of two primary modes: (1) denial of aging, often requiring purchases of expensive treatments and cosmetics and (2) acceptance of aging and devalued status. This is a double bind; aging *will* occur as a natural process, even if one tries to delay or cover the physical effects.

Wolleat (1980) noted that "the psychological costs of being an elderly female in the latter half of the twentieth century are as devastating as economic impoverishment" (p. 110). These costs are related to (1) a double standard of aging for men and women that makes men become "distinguished" while women become "hags," (2) loss of the roles of wife and mother through which women have become socialized and through which their lives have had meaning, and (3) inadequate coping mechanisms women have learned to use.

The internalization by an individual of negative societal perceptions and stereotypes leads to a loss of self-esteem. Looking at older people, Barbado and Feezel (1987) found that language can affect attitudes. Older people who refuse to label themselves as "old" maintain more positive self-concepts and a higher sense of self-esteem than those who use this label to describe themselves. Another negative consequence of internalization of the bias against older people is a tendency to dislike other older people and a consequent failure to develop satisfying peer relationships. Older women are likely to internalize negative societal stereotypes of aging people as well as females. As a result of the many stereotypes that affect their lives, older women are "likely to receive little affirmation of [their] worth in our society" (Wolleat, 1980, p. 110). Jacobs (1976) suggested that many older women are "underemployed, underpaid, underfinanced, underhoused, undervalued, and underloved, sometimes even by themselves" (p. 34).

Wolleat (1980) noted that stereotypes of older people resemble feminine more than masculine stereotypes and suggested that the close association between concepts of older people and females have negatively influenced our treatment of older people. She further suggested that the deleterious effects of inferior status that accompany being born female and socialized in a feminine gender role "are dramatically exacerbated as a woman advances in age" (p. 109). Women are socialized to depend on males for economic and social support, and thus learn to undervalue other women. The high rate of isolation among older women, discussed below, reflects a failure to develop supportive relationships with the people who are most likely to be a source of companionship in later life. Many older women view not only older people but specifically older women as undesirable or inferior companions. Thus, they may choose to be alone rather than in the company of other older women. The effects of inferior status are clearly psychological in nature, and often also economic.

Poverty in the Later Years

Although public media promote a view of older people as financially better off today than 10 or 20 years ago, studies of older women support the fact that older people are not relatively better off in 1980 than they were in 1960 (Uhlenberg & Salmon, 1986). The media image is derived from aggregate data, which obscure the fact that a substantial portion of older women are now living in poverty (McKenna & Nickols, 1986). This section includes demographic information concerning the financial status of older women, followed by a discussion of factors that contribute to poverty in this population and the effects of being poor late in life.

Financial Status of Older Women

According to the American Association of Retired Persons (1986), the poverty rate for all older persons was 12.4% (3.5 million people) compared to 10.8% for people aged 18–64. These figures were determined using the official 1986 definition of the poverty level as $6,630 for an older couple household or $5,255 for an older individual living alone. An additional 8% (2.3 million people) were classified "near-poor," reflecting an income between the poverty level and 125% of poverty level. Overall, more than one fifth (21%) of the older population were classified as poor or near-poor in 1986. One in nine (11%) older Caucasians were poor in 1986, compared to one in three (31%) older blacks and one in four (23%) older Hispanics. The nine states with the highest poverty rates for older persons were all in the South.

The poverty rate for older women in 1986 was almost twice that for older men (15% compared to 8%). In fact, older women continue to be the single poorest subgroup in this country (Wolleat, 1980). Almost one half (44.9%) of all single women over age 65 fall below the poverty level. In the early 1980s, older women received an average of $363 per month from Social Security. Nonmarried older women had little or no income from assets. Overall, 36% had no asset income, 43% earned between $1 and $999 annually from assets, and the median annual asset income was $320 (McKenna & Nickols, 1986).

A report prepared for the Select Committee on Aging in 1979 revealed that the poverty rate for older women was 60% higher than it was for older men. The average amount of retirement benefits received by older men was substantially greater, with the women's average monthly Social Security benefit being only about two thirds that of men (Select Committee on Aging, 1979). The Senate report did note that changes were expected to occur in the poverty rate for women in the future, based primarily on civil rights legislation of the 1960s and 1970s. The report also noted that the changes would be indirect, based on laws designed to end discriminatory hiring practices that restrict opportunities for women and other minorities. To the extent that the laws result in women being employed for longer periods at higher pay, their benefits would be expected to increase. If the change from 1979 to 1986 is used as a guideline, it will still be several decades before women's retirement benefits equal those of men.

Income inequality differs within the older population as well as between older and younger persons. Not surprisingly, old–old people (older than 75) have lower incomes than young–old people (ages 65-75) (AARP, 1987). Income inequality between people recently turning 65 and younger people has been steadily decreasing over the past 10 years, for both married and unmarried older women. In addition, the marked disadvantage of old–old compared to young–old women has decreased in recent years, as women over age 75 now have incomes closer to those of women under age 75. At the same time, though, "the drop in income associated with entering old age has increased for women more recently making the transition" (Uhlenberg & Salmon, 1986, p. 170). The median income for older people in 1986 was $11,544 for males and $6,425 for females (AARP, 1986). In 1989, the median income of white families of all ages was $35,980.

Older people living alone or with nonrelatives were most likely to have low incomes in 1986, with almost half (44%) reporting incomes of under $7,000. One fifth (22%) had incomes under $5,000; one fifth (21%) had incomes over $15,000 (AARP, 1986). The 43% of older women who live alone (compared to 17% of older men who do so) are the poorest of the poor in the United States, with an annual income of just over $3,000 for Caucasian women and $2,000 for black women (Uhlenberg & Salmon, 1986).

Factors That Contribute to Poverty in Later Life

Poverty may begin or continue in old age. People who have lived independently and with some degree of financial comfort may find themselves living at the poverty level for the first time in old age. Savings that seemed adequate prior to retirement may be rapidly depleted due to illness, the effects of inflation when living on a fixed income, fraud, elder abuse, or other factors. Within the older population, women are more likely to be poor, widowed, and living alone than are men (Special Committee on Aging, 1985). A complex array of factors contribute to the risks older women face for living in poverty.

McKenna and Nickols (1986) discussed two sets of factors that contribute to poverty for older women. The first are economic and demographic factors. These include low pay, child rearing preferences, and women's longevity. Women who leave the labor force permanently after the birth of their first child experience a 50% (college graduates) to

57% (high school graduates) reduction in lifetime earnings, which is reflected in retirement benefits. Dropping out of the labor market only temporarily results in a drop in lifetime earnings of 21% to 18%, respectively. The second set of factors are personal, social-psychological ones. These include women's financial decision-making strategies and willingness to plan and prepare for retirement. Math anxiety, fear of taking risks, and an external locus of control or passive view of control combine to make women unwilling to plan for their financial needs in retirement.

The poverty experienced by older women reflects a lifetime of gender discrimination in employment. Many did not work outside the home and thus did not receive monetary compensation or retirement benefits. Even if they did work outside the home, salaries were likely to be one half those of their male counterparts (Wolleat, 1980). Today's older women were relegated to low-paying jobs in teaching and service industries, with lower retirement benefits as a result. Because retirement benefits are based on earnings, a vicious cycle of low incomes is perpetuated.

Labor force participation rates for both men and women decline with age. Even those older people who would like to continue working are often kept from doing so by mandatory retirement age requirements and widespread age discrimination in employment (National Coalition on Older Women's Issues, undated).

Marital status has a significant effect on poverty rates for older women, with married women faring best. Older unmarried women are most disadvantaged, with never-married women having slightly higher incomes than divorced or widowed women (Keith, 1986). Divorce is associated with a decrease in the standard of living for women (Uhlenberg & Myers, 1981), with older women facing greater barriers to employment than younger women and thus relatively unable to supplement their incomes.

The Effects of Poverty on Older Women

Poverty in later life can lead to inability to purchase needed health care services, followed by increasing rates of disability and eventual institutionalization and death. Quality of life is significantly reduced and can be especially traumatic for those who were not poor until old age. Older men who need assistance typically receive it from family members. Older women needing help are far more likely to be institutionalized. Older women who are poor are more likely to experience stress, depression, and mental illness. In addition, lack of adequate nutrition and medical care can lead to irreversible mental and physical deterioration. The effects of poverty are pervasive and cumulative. Public policy needed to affect poverty among older women is discussed in a later section of this chapter.

Loneliness and Isolation

As seen in the results of the Harris (1975) survey, some 12% of older people report that loneliness is a "very serious problem." An even larger proportion report that loneliness is a "somewhat serious problem." This section discusses factors contributing to isolation and loneliness among older women, as well as the effects of loneliness on psychological adjustment in later life.

Factors Contributing to Isolation and Loneliness among Older Women

A number of factors have been identified that correlate with isolation and loneliness among older women. These may be discussed under the broad categories of marital status and socialization patterns.

Marital Status   Older women who are not married are at increased risk for loneliness, whether or not they have ever been married. However, it is important to distinguish between older women who were never married and those who go through divorce or widowhood. In all instances, roles that are chosen, or over which one has control, result in more life satisfaction and better adjustment.

Ward (1979) noted that there is little literature concerning never-married people in later life, and what is available is inconclusive. Some evidence suggests that the well-being of single persons is equivalent to that of those who are married. Single older persons may be more isolated, but not necessarily more lonely. They presumably have developed strategies for coping with being single over the course of their lifetime, in addition to which they do not experience the "desolation" of widowhood or divorce (Ward, 1979, p. 861). On the other hand, being single may be less satisfying than marriage in a couple-oriented society such as ours. The lack of institutional support for single lifestyles among today's older women can contribute to feelings of guilt, embarrassment, loneliness, and isolation.

The overall conclusion of Ward's (1979) study was that never-married people are a vulnerable segment of the older population. They belong to fewer clubs than married persons, see friends and neighbors less frequently, express less satisfaction from friendships (presumably because they expect more from them), and require more access to institutional care as a result of receiving less family assistance. Divorced and separated older people are even more vulnerable than those who are single, having to cope with sometimes undesired role changes as well as single status.

Children are a major source of support and assistance for older people. Thus, childless older women have fewer resources to help them cope with life changes and are more likely to become isolated and lonely (Myers & Navin, 1984). Further, "to be old, alone, and without children or husband, and physically incapacitated is (almost by definition) to have a poor quality of life" (Beckman & Houser, 1982, p. 250).

Half of all older women are widows, and most of them live alone. Because women tend to marry older men and also to outlive them, women can expect to be widows in later life. The median length of widowhood for a woman today is 25 years (Special Committee on Aging, 1983). Older men tend to remarry after the loss of a spouse, but older women do not. Currently, more than 80% of older men live in family environments, while almost 60% of older women do not.

Socialization Patterns   Traditional gender-role socialization patterns that devalue women result in fewer same-sex friendships in later life. Women are still being raised with the "American dream," believing that they will grow up, marry, have children, and live happily ever after. Many of today's older women lived with family until they married, lived with children and spouse until their children left home, lived with their spouse until the day he died...then, for the first time in their life, began to live alone.

Lacking role models, adequate warning, a network of female friends, and unprepared to spend up to one third of their lives alone, these women are significantly at risk for depression.

Many older persons do lead active social lives, and many date, though little is known about those who do so. Pressure from adult children, perceptions of older women as asexual, and simply lack of access to male partners prevent many older women from seeking male companionship through dating. This is unfortunate, as dating can be a hedge against loneliness in later life (Bulcroft & O'Conner, 1986).

Effects of Loneliness on Psychological Adjustment in Later Life

Schlossberg (1984) discussed transitions in life and the greater effort required to adjust to those that occur off-time. She further noted that the lack of expected events, such as marriage and birth of children, requires an adjustment as well. Role changes that are involuntary are most difficult to accept. Involuntarily occupying a role or status that is perceived as unchanging (e.g., single, widowed, divorced) tends to be highly stressful for most people. Older people who are involuntarily single and moving from a superimposed temporary status to a permanent single status may feel frustration, disappointment, resentment, anger, and depression (Keith, 1986). These feelings in turn lead to isolation, then loneliness.

Women commonly experience an identity crisis in reaction to the loss of a spouse (Atchley, 1983). Being identified as the wife of someone throughout most of their adult lives contributes to the onset of this crisis. Gilligan (1982) found that, for women, the issues of identity and intimacy are fused. Thus, particularly for older women today, successful socialization was equated with marriage and the roles of spouse and mother. For many older widows, the identity crisis is never resolved. These women remain isolated and lonely.

Loneliness is known to have a major negative effect on morale. Lee and Ishii-Kuntz (1987) found that feelings of loneliness are reduced and morale improved through interactions with friends and to a smaller extent with neighbors. Interestingly, they found that interaction with children and grandchildren had no such effects.

Lonely people tend to exhibit poor social skills and are less assertive, often experiencing such disabling emotions as depression, hostility, and anxiety. Lonely people tend to be dissatisfied with a broad range of interpersonal relationships and allow their predominant negative feelings to inhibit the development or restoration of satisfying interactions with others. Lonely older persons experience low self-esteem, a sense of hopelessness about the future, and a variety of maladaptive behavior patterns, such as inability to plan for life changes (Hansson, Jones, Carpenter, & Remondet, 1986).

Lowenthal and Haven (1968) found that the presence of a confidant is the single most important factor that correlates with emotional well-being in later life. Having a confidant also helps to moderate the effects of role losses and changes in old age. Simply stated, many older women lack a confidant, a single person to whom they feel close, with whom they feel safe, and whose company they both enjoy and seek. The inability to access a support network has a negative effect on older women's physical health and overall ability to live independently.

Relationships with Adult Children

Contrary to popular misconceptions, aging occurs in a family context. Older people, including older women, are not forgotten or ignored by their adult children and in fact have frequent interactions with them. The nature of these interactions, which is not universally positive, is discussed below in the context of developmental issues for adult children and aging parents. Filial maturity, related to needs for caregiving, is discussed in terms of the needs of both adult children and their aging mothers. Other outcomes of caregiving needs, including elder abuse and institutionalization, are briefly considered. This section concludes with a review of family relationships and patterns in later life.

Developmental Issues for Adult Children and Aging Mothers

Adult children of aging parents typically are in midlife, a period known as "middlescence" for its similarity to adolescence; however, adolescents move toward increased status and midlife adults move toward decreased status (Dobson & Dobson, 1985). Midlife adults are referred to as the "command generation," because they occupy more positions of power and authority than persons of any other age group. Increasingly, midlife adults, especially women, are referred to as the "sandwich generation," having their own needs sandwiched between those of their teen-age children seeking increasing independence and their aging parents, who may be becoming increasingly less independent.

Midlife is viewed in varying ways by developmental theorists. For Erikson (1963), the central psychosocial crisis is one of generativity, or leaving something of value to the next generation. Midlife adults thus are greatly concerned with helping their teen-age children reach adulthood. Havighurst (1972) adds to this the tasks of adjusting to the physical changes of midlife; developing work, civic, and leisure pursuits; and adjusting to aging parents. Buehler (1967) suggested that midlife is a time of personal assessment, for reviewing one's life, accomplishments, and goals. Neugarten (1968) identified a shift in time perspective as the onset of the transition to midlife. That is, people cease to see their lives in terms of time since birth (e.g., immortality) and begin to see life as time remaining until death (e.g., mortality). The awareness that life is finite contributes to the self-assessment process and setting of goals for the future or second half of life.

Many adults in midlife look forward to the empty nest and new freedom from child rearing responsibilities. Hobbies, leisure, educational, and work pursuits that were postponed during the years of active parenting may now become possible. These freedoms may be abruptly curtailed when the needs of aging parents increase.

Aging parents, on the other hand, experience what Erikson (1963) refers to as the search for ego integrity. Through a process of life review, older people come to accept their lives as being the best they could have lived. Having little time left to make changes, the feeling of contentment accompanying a sense of integrity prepares older people to live the remainder of their lives and face death without serious regrets. Older people who review their lives and conclude that they made too many mistakes, are unhappy with their decisions, and hold on to multiple regrets and self-recriminations experience despair, the opposite of integrity. Wishing they could change and facing limited time and resources to do so, many become overwhelmed and immobilized by depression.

There is some evidence that the crisis of ego integrity is typically resolved in the 60s and 70s, leaving 20 or more years of useful life—or depressed life—for older individuals (see Riker & Myers, 1990). The major developmental tasks older persons face include adjusting to retirement and reduced incomes, adjusting to the death of spouse and friends, establishing peer relationships, and establishing satisfactory physical living arrangements (Havighurst, 1972). Peck (1968) suggested three additional conflicts for older adults: body transcendence versus body preoccupation, ego differentiation versus work-role preoccupation, and ego transcendence versus ego preoccupation. The latter conflict refers to one's view of the meaning of life and of the world after death, which could include leaving a legacy or a belief in life after death.

The retirement years include greater amounts of free or discretionary time. Older people freed from work tasks are free to create new lifestyles. In some instances, relationships with adult children and grandchildren take on primary importance. Investment in relationships with family members can be especially important for older people who are attempting to achieve ego integrity through righting past wrongs in child rearing and relationships with their children. Adult children may not welcome the time and responsibility of the close relationships desired by their aging parents. Alternately, as older persons age and experience an increased sense of physical and emotional vulnerability, their relationships with their adult children may become increasingly important and desirable.

Aging is often referred to as a time of loss—loss of the work role through retirement, loss of income, loss of health, loss of spouse, loss of friends, and so on. The experience of multiple losses without a sense of control or choice can and often does lead to a sense of learned helplessness in older persons (Troll, 1982). Older women may generalize the experience of lack of control to increasing numbers of life circumstances, becoming immobilized in decision making and increasingly dependent on adult children and others for support and assistance.

Filial Maturity and Caregiving

The "crisis of filial maturity" begins for adult children when they first recognize the onset of vulnerability and fallibility of their aging parents. The feeling that they should help their aging parents is referred to as a sense of filial responsibility (Brubaker, 1985). Unfortunately, it is now possible to spend more years caring for aging parents than raising one's children to adulthood. Because more than 80% of the care needed by aging parents is provided by family members, and because more than 80% of kin care is provided by women, adult women in midlife face significant pressures from parent-care. Further, while the raising of children has a logical end in sight, the deterioration and needs of aging parents may seem without end, contributing to feelings of depression for caregivers.

One third of caregivers are themselves over age 65. Caregivers face competing demands for their time such as child care responsibilities and work conflicts, and almost one in ten must quit their own jobs in order to care for aging relatives (Stone, Cafferata, & Sangl, 1987). In 1988, 63% of caregivers had been providing care for 5 years or less, 66% received no outside or family help with caregiving, and 86% used no paid assistance

(Caregivers in the Work place, 1988). The typical recipient of their care was female, over age 70, physically or mentally disabled, and alone.

Caregiving creates conflicts over use of time, role strains, a sense of burden and stress, frustration, and resentment. Guilt is commonly experienced, along with a sense that nothing one does will ever "be enough." Anger and depression are common reactions. All these negative reactions may be expected to increase when the older person's health declines. Alternately, caregivers may feel a sense of pride in their ability to provide parent care and a sense of accomplishment in attempting to repay parents for a lifetime of support and love.

Aging parents who become dependent experience a sense of low self-esteem, accompanied by fears of future decline and disability, fear of possible institutionalization, grief, anger, resentment, and depression. Each loss one experiences must be grieved if it is to be resolved, but older people experience multiple losses and may be unable to resolve one before another occurs. A condition of "bereavement overload" can occur (Kastenbaum, 1969), leading to a pervasive sense of despair, immobilization, and hopelessness. Experiencing a loss of control in so many areas of life, older people may react by becoming demanding and self-centered. This provides at least some control, though negative, over the reactions of their caregivers.

Coping with the role reversal that occurs when adult children become caretakers for their aging parents is a painful process. Interpersonal conflict and unresolved family issues may exacerbate the difficulties. When the parent suffers from organic brain impairments, caregiver reactions are intensified. In general, family caregivers tend to be highly committed, to enter caregiving gradually, and to become overcommitted and fail to relinquish caregiving responsibilities when it might be prudent for all concerned to do so.

Crisis Situations: Elder Abuse and Institutionalization

The stress of providing care for aging parents is constant and tends to increase over time. Few sources of respite are available to caregivers. When caregivers' attempts to cope with the stress are unsuccessful, abuse may result. Alternately, a decision may be made that institutionalization is the only viable option. Each of these situations creates unique sources of stress for older women and their adult children.

Elder Abuse   Elder abuse takes many forms. It can be physical, as in passively withholding food or medicine, or active, as in hitting or sexually mistreating an older person. Abuse can be psychological, including isolation, neglect, ignoring the older person's requests for assistance, humiliation, insulting and otherwise demeaning the older person's sense of self-worth. Material abuse, theft or misuse of money or materials, is another form of elder abuse. Violation of rights can include inappropriate adjudication of incompetence or eviction from one's housing. Reports indicate that 4% of older Americans (over a million individuals) are abused annually. Because families fail to report elder abuse, it has been estimated that the actual incidence is closer to one in ten older persons in caretaking situations (Giordano & Giordano, 1984).

Victims of elder abuse are those older persons typically needing assistance: older than 75, white, female, middle class, and dependent on an adult child for care. The profile of the typical abuser is middle age, white, female, middle class, caregiver, adult child. Frail older persons, those with physical and emotional disabilities, are most likely to experience abuse. The incidence of abuse increases when the older person has an organic brain disorder.

Past unresolved conflicts between adult children and their aging parents can contribute to abuse (Pillemer, Wolf & Gwynther, 1987). Adult children may feel that their parents do not appreciate the care they are providing (Giordano & Giordano, 1984). Situational factors contributing to abuse include role conflicts and strains, disappointment over not being able to pursue personal interests and goals, decreased income or purchasing power, unemployment, substance abuse, marital instability, and conflicts with adolescent children, to name a few. Negative attitudes toward older people place them in a devalued and hence vulnerable position, complicated by low self-esteem, learned helplessness, and an acceptance of victimization as a consequence of low status. It is extremely difficult for older people to report abuse by family members, not just because of shame, but also because the alternative to family care is often an institution. Family members who abuse their parents do not do so consistently, so the parent always hopes that change will occur for the better.

Institutionalization Butler (1975) described nursing homes as halfway houses— halfway between society and the cemetery. The perception of long-term care settings as places where people go to die, rather than rehabilitative settings from which people may be discharged, contributes to negative perceptions. The fear of institutional placement is very prevalent among older people, especially older women, and the fear of guilt over having to make a decision to institutionalize is prevalent among adult children. In both instances, these fears are realistic responses to the risk factors.

More than 80% of residents of nursing homes are women, 90% of whom are over the age of 65, with 20% aged 85 and older. Approximately 85% have no living spouse; many have no relatives at all. More than half have a psychiatric diagnosis in addition to physical diseases. Most are isolated, even within the long-term care setting, and have few interactions with peers. Most have no confidant available.

Although families consider an average of at least six options before deciding to institutionalize (Zweibel, 1984), adult children universally report that this decision was among the, if not *the* most difficult in their lives. Options other than long-term care include in-home companion and chore services, supportive congregate housing, counseling, foster care, and independent housing. The decision for long-term care usually is based on the best interest of both the older person and the family, with the family unable to continue providing the level and quality of care required. Still, taking the responsibility for choosing a nonindependent living situation for an older relative can never be made easily, and usually is made with apprehension, doubt, and guilt. These fears cause families to postpone the decision until a crisis occurs, potentially leading to poor decision making.

Taking the time to explore options in advance, particularly with the older person when she is able to participate and express opinions, is better for all concerned. Unfortunately, older people frequently refuse to participate in such planning, leaving their children to do so but without the permission to do so without guilt. The extent to which families can discuss such decisions openly depends both on the unique characteristics of older mothers and their daughters and on typical family relationship patterns in later life.

Family Relationships and Patterns in Later Life

Family relations differ in later life for men and women, as is true earlier in life. Men's relationships are couple-based, while those for most older women are cross-generational. For women, relationships with adult children take on increasing importance with advancing age (Troll, 1982).

Within the family development literature, families with aging members are least well researched. A number of authors have noted that family roles and ties become increasingly important sources of affirmation and meaning as people grow older (e.g., Cherlin, 1983; Morgan, 1981). Aging parents, particularly mothers, most often turn to adult children when they need assistance. Sometimes they turn *only* to their adult children not just for help but for companionship as well. This is understandable, considering that most of us want to be with those we love and who presumably love us when we are feeling vulnerable. What is difficult for adult children to grasp is the pervasive nature of the feelings of vulnerability that can become a part of the experience of later life. Adult children want some "time out" from the relationship, while frail, aging parents may fail to consider any need for separation, taking an increasingly egocentric perspective.

Treas (1983) suggested that the multigenerational family living together in harmony is a myth. In the past, people did not live long enough to live in multigenerational households; when they did, it was for economic reasons. Anyone who has lived independently for any length of time may be expected to have difficulty accommodating to the lifestyles of others in close quarters. That leaves today's multigenerational families living with Mom as the pioneers who will teach later generations how to do it—if they succeed.

Another common myth is that older people want to live with their adult children. Most would like to live near them, but maintain their independent households (Harris & Associates, 1975). Almost 90% of older people report seeing family members within the last month, and 75% live within a 35-minute drive of one adult child (Treas, 1983). Older people are not abandoned by their families, in spite of popular misconceptions to the contrary.

The geographic mobility of our society has resulted in many adult children living far from their aging parents. This creates problems when crisis situations arise, though often one sibling lives near enough to provide the assistance needed. It is when decisions such as institutionalization must be made that the whole family needs to be involved. Families with healthy patterns of relating are most apt to cope successfully with difficult situations in the lives of older relatives. Those with a history of dysfunction may be expected to cope in less than satisfactory ways with the same situations.

An extended discussion of relationships with adult children and aging parents is beyond the scope of this chapter. The interested reader is referred to Myers, *Adult Children and Aging Parents* (1989). At this point it may be more useful to consider strategies for counseling with older women in relation to the issues already discussed.

COUNSELING STRATEGIES

The situations discussed in the first part of this chapter—social stereotypes, poverty, loneliness, and relationships with adult children—create needs for adjustment on the part of older women. In many instances, counseling interventions may be helpful or even necessary to facilitate successful adjustment to aging and changing life circumstances. Counseling interventions in this section are divided into three parts: group and individual counseling focused on empowerment and maintenance of self-esteem, supportive interventions to address isolation, and multigenerational family interventions.

Individual and Group Counseling for Older Women

Older women are a heterogeneous group with diverse needs. Counselors must consider such factors as marital status, ethnicity, disability, role losses, and mental status in determining appropriate interventions. It is important to assess the nature of current life transitions, history of coping mechanisms for dealing with transitions, and developmental task accomplishment as part of the initial assessment of functioning with older female clients. Several strategies may be more effective in working with subgroups of the older female population. These include social reconstruction, empowerment, and group counseling interventions.

Social Reconstruction

Kuypers and Bengtson (1973) developed the Social Breakdown Theory as an explanation of negative adjustment in later life. This theory is useful for counselors as it incorporates a systems perspective that includes individual, familial, and societal contexts. Further, the theory suggests possible intervention strategies through a social reconstruction approach.

The Social Breakdown Syndrome explains the process of interaction between social inputs and self-concept in later life. Social inputs that devalue older women contribute to a self-perpetuating negative cycle of depression, learned helplessness, and decreased psychological functioning. The four-stage cycle proceeds as follows:

❏ **Stage 1.** There is an existing condition of psychological susceptibility. For older women, this could be due to identity problems or low self-esteem. Contributing factors could be age, gender, ethnicity, poverty status, marital status, declining health, loss of social roles—in short, any of the risk factors identified earlier in this chapter.
❏ **Stage 2.** The older woman is labeled as incompetent or deficient in some aspect of behavior. The labeling may be a result of negative social perceptions of people who are old, or it may come from family, friends, neighbors, or service providers. These labels may be communicated in both overt (e.g., forced retirement) and covert (e.g., ignoring) ways. Common injunctions include admonitions to "not act" in a certain way because of one's age.
❏ **Stage 3.** The older woman moves into a sick role, a dependent position with some temporary secondary gains. These gains include freedom from responsibilities, caregiving from others, and time-out from dysfunctional relationships until the person is better. For younger persons, this role is temporary. Because it tends to become

permanent for older persons, the secondary gains are eventually eliminated. The older woman learns and maintains the sick role, and her independent living skills accordingly atrophy through disuse.

❑ **Stage 4**. The older woman in this stage will identify even more with the sick role and perceive herself as increasingly less capable and inadequate. Self-esteem and self-efficacy are extremely impaired at this stage.

The cycle begins again after stage four is reached, with the older woman being even more susceptible to negative, demeaning inputs from others. A negative, downward spiral is perpetuated. Left unchecked, the eventual result can be a vegetative state and even death. The psychological reactions that contribute to the syndrome include depression, discouragement, learned helplessness, and a change from an internal to an external locus of control.

The Social Reconstruction Model is designed to counteract the negative effects of social breakdown. Its purpose is to increase competence and self-esteem through social inputs. An important assumption of this model is that inputs may be made at any point in the breakdown process with positive results. Successful interventions will result in a reversal of the four stages, so that positive inputs will lead to an enhanced sense of self-worth and increased ability to live independently. Individual inputs alone will not suffice. For example, the predominant work ethic in our society results in older people who are retired taking on the same devalued status as younger persons who are unemployed. Developing a social definition of retirement that is positive and desirable can free older people from the stress of being in a devalued role. The availability of better housing, transportation, and in-home assistance could enable more older people to live independently in their own homes for longer periods. One of the most important components of the Social Reconstruction Model is an empowerment perspective that helps older women develop a view of themselves as capable, self-determined, self-confident, and in control of their lives.

Empowerment

Empowerment of older women will require major social changes, but also changes within individuals. A first step will be awareness of their lack of power, followed by education and training to help them realize their own ability to influence the events in their lives. Patience will be required, because people with a low sense of self-esteem will function in a way that reinforces their self-perceptions. On the other hand, people with a strong sense of self-efficacy will tend to persevere in the face of challenges, seeing difficulties and failures as due to something external to themselves rather than the result of internal qualities. Over the course of a lifetime, women are much more likely to attribute failures to themselves and successes to external forces or others. This is exactly opposite to men's perceptions of success and failure. It is easy to understand, then, how it is that older women become so very immobilized when faced with the challenges of later life. After all, if failures are due to their own inabilities or lacks, and there are so many "failures," must they not be very *non*–worthwhile?

The strong interaction between mental and physical health is well-documented in the literature on aging (Myers, 1989). It is essential in working with older women that counselors use holistic approaches, because a focus on only one life arena may miss both important areas of concern and important strengths for building a sense of self-esteem. One philosophy that offers promise for helping in the empowerment process is currently termed "wellness." Wellness refers to an active process of living in which people are encouraged to achieve a sense of optimum functioning and balance in body, mind, and spirit (Leafgren & Elsenrath, 1986). Wellness approaches have the advantage of increasing an individual's ability for self-care, making them more self-sufficient and empowered to make healthy choices in their own best interests (Hetherington & Loganbill, 1985).

Hettler's (1980) six-dimension model is one that can be useful in counseling with older women. The six dimensions are emotional, intellectual, physical, social, occupational, and spiritual development. Counselors can help older women define strengths and limitations in each area (using a life span approach), and set and work toward goals to optimize their functioning in all six dimensions. Fortunately, the effect of change in any one area is change in the others. So, it is possible to choose one area, set goals, work toward the achievement of those goals, and provide the type of encouragement that enables women to accept their successes and develop an enhanced sense of self-efficacy and empowerment. With severely impaired older women, such interventions are best accomplished through individual counseling interactions. For a large majority of older women, group counseling interventions may be even more effective.

Group Counseling Interventions

Numerous advantages of using group counseling approaches with older people have been identified. Groups may enhance self-esteem, encourage socialization, provide suggestions and role models for problem solving, increase motivation to renew former interests, encourage reality orientation and reality testing, clarify and resolve intrapsychic conflicts, and clarify the diagnosis or prognosis for impaired older persons (Blazer, 1982). Groups can also help improve social status, enhance family relationships, and provide outlets for emotional expression (Kalson, 1982).

The Social Breakdown Syndrome described how the losses of aging contribute to low self-esteem among older women. Groups focused on reminiscence can provide ego support by emphasizing past accomplishments and coping skills developed over a lifetime. Further, sharing memories of common life experiences can build a sense of rapport, camaraderie, and friendship among the older women participants. Once a sense of self-worth has been established, it can become the foundation for developing strategies to cope with the current challenges and realities of later life.

Groups offer an opportunity for social contact to combat loneliness as well as the chance to develop friendships, which can help overcome feelings of rejection. The development of peer relationships and support can contribute to successful accomplishment of developmental tasks. Groups also can provide a supportive environment for coping with age-related changes and the many losses associated with aging. They can provide an opportunity to learn and model new social and interpersonal skills (Burnside, 1984; Zimpfer, 1987).

Counselors working in groups with older people will find the entire repertoire of group counseling skills to be useful. In addition, there are certain special considerations in conducting groups with older people that will contribute to successful outcomes. First, greater time may be required for building trust and rapport. Thus, the earlier stages of the group may need to be more structured and may last longer than with groups of younger persons. Older people typically are reluctant to seek counseling in part due to predominant values of independence in problem solving. To expect them to "air their dirty laundry in public" before a high level of trust has been established would be unrealistic. The activities selected should be meaningful to older women and should assist them in developing a feeling-focused vocabulary. That kind of vocabulary is usually not common in their experience, as evidenced by the tendency to discuss physical ailments rather than emotional reactions.

Sites selected for groups with older women should be comfortable, quiet, well lit but without the glare of windows or mirrors, and close to their homes. Times should be planned that do not interfere with normal routines. It is important to have a site close to a bathroom and to plan sessions that are relatively short (45 to 90 minutes) to accommodate physical limitations and a tendency to tire more rapidly. Sensory deficits, session length, and the tendency of some older persons to "tell their story" reflect a need to limit group sizes to no more than six persons to assure adequate time for participation of each individual (Waters, McCarroll, & Penman, 1987).

While the setting may be the primary determinant of group composition, screening is still important. Heterogeneous groups comprising people of differing social, ethnic, and educational backgrounds, and health status, are recommended. Alternately, persons considered inappropriate for groups include those who are disturbed, wandering, psychotic, severely depressed, hypochondriacal, and severely hearing impaired (Burnside, 1984). Older women who talk excessively can benefit from the group experience as a way to learn appropriate skills for listening and social interaction. Group leaders need to be willing to interrupt and refocus the discussion when story-telling is detrimental to the other members of the group. Those who talk too much tend to do so in reaction to isolation and fear of loneliness.

Supportive Interventions to Address Isolation

Counselors working with older women need to devote a significant amount of time to interventions designed to remediate or prevent isolation and loneliness. Even those older women who seem to have few needs in this area may find their circumstances changing rapidly upon the death of a spouse or confidant. Awareness of the importance of support networks and strategies for building and using support networks should be a routine part of the counseling process with older women. Strategies for empowerment should focus on the need to maintain control over one's life and decisions throughout the totality of the life span.

Ashinger (1985) described the use of social networks and social network inventories in problem resolution and also as a follow-up means of support after the termination of formal counseling interventions. She defined social networks as "interrelated groups of people organized along the pattern of their own culture" (p. 519), structures commonly taken for granted that represent the total social field of an individual. The network approach requires an analysis of existing supports, identification of needed supports, and the development of strategies for gaining and maintaining supports needed to function independently and happily.

A typical network inventory will take 30 to 60 minutes to develop and explain. The older woman should be asked to list all network members with whom she has had contact in the last year. Typically resulting in a listing of 40 or so names, these contacts should be grouped according to immediate and extended family, neighbors and friends, work associates, educational associates, recreational associates and formal helpers (e.g., doctors, senior center staff). Time should be allowed for the older woman to discuss each component of the network and the functions served by various individuals. The network can be used to foster self-esteem, identify sources of support, and help target areas where support is needed or could be generated.

Another type of network inventory might ask older women to draw a circle with themselves in the middle, then draw lines similar to the spokes in a wheel for each source of support. Thin lines can depict distant support, strong lines strong support, and broken lines conflicted but important relationships. Women should be encouraged to list supports relative to each of the six aspects of wellness; for example, physical exercise could be a strong source of personal support as it contributes to a sense of well-being. Spiritual beliefs and practices may be a strong source of support, as may the existence of pets. A comprehensive analysis with older women will allow enumeration of hobbies and activities. This is especially important with isolated older women, for whom major sources of support may not be individuals. Counselors should be prepared to assess the risk of loss of any of these supports. For example, the age of pets can be a clue as to their longevity. Primarily visual activities such as watching television and reading can be jeopardized as a result of degenerative, progressive visual disorders. Travel may be sharply curtailed if one can no longer drive. Again, this technique can be an important means of identifying risks of major losses as well as sources of strength.

Multigenerational Family Interventions

Because aging occurs in a family context, an understanding of developmental family history can be helpful in working with older female clients. Further, an examination of family members as individuals and in interaction with older female members can be an important means of identifying potentially conflicting developmental stages and tasks as well as sources of support in later life. A family systems approach can identify dysfunctional communication patterns that limit the life satisfaction of older as well as younger family members. Communication patterns take on increased significance when decisions concerning an older person's lifestyle and needs are considered. One of the most critical decisions would be moving in with adult children. This would result in a special type of blended family system and requires flexible family rules if cohabitation is to be successful.

Counselors working with families need to understand the family system and mobilize the family to be effective problem solvers (Herr & Weakland, 1979). It is essential to determine the extent of the family system, then involve all members who have an investment in or influence on decision making. At times, neighbors, friends, or service providers may need to be involved. In fact, one of the most important steps in intergenerational counseling is the determination of who the participants will be (Baruth & Huber, 1984).

Initial steps in family counseling will be to assess the family power base, decision making strategies, and communication patterns. Taking time to review the solutions that have been tried can help family members understand how some solutions may contribute to a perpetuation of problems. Each family member's perceptions, needs, feelings, and goals in relation to the problem areas should be assessed.

Family assessment is an ongoing process that needs to be undertaken on a continuing basis to determine appropriate interventions. Some key questions to consider are how the family member who initiated contact with the counselor represents the family system, how the presenting problem (or individual) is connected to the family system, what recent events prompted the request for counseling, what types of dysfunctional communication patterns exist and which are acute or chronic, how effective therapy will be based on the family members' willingness to invest in the process, whether the system is an engaging or enmeshing one, and whether there are significant intergenerational influences on family functioning (Nicholls & Everett, 1986).

Genograms, a graphic form of family assessment (McGoldrick & Gerson, 1985), offer a means of family assessment that can contribute to older women's need for life review and reminiscence. This technique allows one to display family information in a way that allows ready analysis of complex family relationships and patterns of interaction. Because they are subjective self-report measures, they offer clinicians a rich source of information for the development of hypotheses and interpretations. An advantage of genograms is that they can be used in family assessment even if the older woman is the only client. By describing their family and relationships with various family members, older women can provide much information about their needs, values, support system, and developmental history. For older women whose sole focus is family members, this technique may be less useful in some ways than support network analysis. The latter technique could help reduce family strain by focusing the older woman's attention on other resources and supports. Perhaps the best approach would use both strategies for assessment, combining family systems with a holistic view of the older woman's social environment.

CASE EXAMPLES

A few case examples are presented here to stimulate the reader's thinking about the reality and applications of the concepts presented here for counseling with older women. These examples are meant to be illustrative of some of the common problems faced by older women.

The Case of Harriet—A Reluctant Widow

Harriet, a 72-year-old Caucasian woman, was the quietest member of a group of four widows who participated in a four-session group experience explained by the leader as an opportunity to discuss "the experience of aging." She appeared neatly dressed but with a wig that sat somewhat askew on her head and was pulled forward to the point that her eyes were not visible behind her glasses. She talked in a monotone and only when prompted. About a year ago, her husband had retired and they had moved to our town to be near her adult daughter, her only child. The first night in their new apartment, before the telephone was installed, her husband suffered a heart attack in the middle of the night. She ran from door to door in the retirement complex trying to get someone to let her use a telephone. By the time help arrived, he was dead.

Harriet reported that she had lived with her parents until the day she married, and with her husband until the day he died. She had not worked outside the home during her adult life. When he died she found herself alone, in a strange town with no friends, and had only the hope of a relationship with her adult daughter and grandchildren to look forward to each day.

Several months ago she began receiving treatment for polymyalgia, which is non-specific pain in multiple joints with no clear antecedent cause. The medication for this condition resulted in "heart trouble" for which she is now taking additional medication. Her medical costs continue to escalate, but her income remains stable and low. She has developed friendships with several other women in a low-income senior housing apartment complex, and participates in some activities, such as the painting class, at their urging.

By outward appearances, Harriet has developed a support system and some activities that keep her busy and in contact with other older people. However, she remains severely depressed over the loss of her husband and the role of wife, which gave meaning to her life. She was totally unprepared for widowhood and feels as if she is just waiting around to die. She has a very poor sense of self-esteem, and no desire to change her lifestyle.

The Case of Eileen—Active and Involved

Eileen never married and was a teacher in a small rural town most of her life. After several years of retirement, she decided she needed to keep busy so she sought assistance in opening a senior center. She was successful in obtaining an old home on a main street in town (next door to her home) for the center. She had it painted mustard yellow and called it "The Golden Age Center." She was also successful in obtaining state and federal funds under the Older Americans Act for the operation of the center. Ten years later, Eileen's center was recognized as among the best in the state. Her administrative skills were not the best, but with the assistance of competent staff she was able to maintain a smooth operation.

One of Eileen's less desirable characteristics was an inability to listen coupled with a tendency toward excessive talking. As she began to experience physical disabilities that kept her from working full time, younger staff members began to exclude her from decision making and took over many of her functions in operating the center. A nutrition program she had worked to have funded was operated in a separate location under the leadership of a new director. Eileen felt she was being pushed out, and rightly so. Eventually she was unable to continue working and became a recipient of services from the center.

Eileen was difficult to work with in counseling. Her excessive talking set up a smoke screen that effectively prevented her from talking about or dealing with her feelings. Because the feelings were primarily negative and related to a perceived loss of control, interventions instead were focused on her successes in life and the contributions she had made to an improved quality of life for so many older people in her home town. Although she had never had children, Eileen was able to feel a sense of accomplishment, perhaps a feeling of generativity, for what she had given to others through her years of teaching and senior center administration.

The Case of Geraldine—Isolated from All but Family, by Choice

Geraldine was 75, still working part-time as an adult education instructor after a career teaching special education students, and lived alone in her five bedroom house. She had lived in the house for 30 years, during which time the neighborhood had changed. It was now considered almost inner city. The crime rate was high: She was robbed several times over a 4-year period. Her house smelled of dog excrement, a fact she explained with the statement "my dogs are more important to me than my rugs." Her hobbies included television game shows, reading a wide array of material, playing scrabble and card games, and working in her yard. She had virtually no friends and interacted only with her adult daughters, only one of whom lived in the area.

Attempts to get her to participate in senior center activities generated statements such as "those old people are boring"; "I'm not old!"; "Those places are filled with older women!" When confronted about her dislike of women, she admitted that "I find the company of my own gender particularly boring." This statement helped explain some of the difficulties she experienced in relating to her four daughters.

Her oldest daughter bought the house next door to be available to her mother as she grew older. The move was a disaster. When daughter's kitchen light went on in the morning, mother arrived at the front door for coffee. She expected that all meals would be taken together, including the times when daughter's boyfriend (later husband) was present. To save her marriage, the daughter finally moved from the state, aided by harsh words from Geraldine on moving day that included a desire to "never see you again."

All attempts to get Geraldine in for counseling failed. She had completed a master's degree in guidance in the 1950s and believed firmly in Freudian analysis and not at all in counseling. She did go to see a psychiatrist, who affirmed that she had "enough problems for three people" and did not suggest she come back. Her daughter later moved home when her marriage failed. Their inability to get along with one another resulted in abusive behavior by the daughter.

The Case of Susan—Learned Helplessness

Susan, a 77-year-old female, had raised two children and worked her entire life as a homemaker and mother. Her husband retired and they continued to live in the same house for 10 active years. One day, driving home from church, he pulled the car to the side of the road, said goodbye, and died of a heart attack. Like Harriet, she found herself alone for the first time in her life. Her immediate response was to sell the house and move into a one bedroom apartment in a senior citizen's apartment building. She lived there for 10 years, establishing friendships with several women. They attended church together, went to dinner regularly, and spent a lot of time visiting one another. She enjoyed periodic visits from her only son, who lived a 4-hour drive away. She could not understand why she had lived so long, as no one before in her family lived that long. She had no real goals for the future or purpose in living other than being with her son whenever possible.

Susan also had macular degeneration and was slowly becoming blind. She refused to watch much television (though she had it turned on for "the company") or read (even her mail), as she said she was "saving my eyes in case I need them."

As Susan passed the age of 75, her health became what is termed "frail." Living alone, she often chose not to eat and sometimes could not recall if she took her medications. On several occasions when she did not eat, her potassium and other electrolytes became imbalanced. She began to experience paranoid hallucinations and delusions, especially at night, which were hidden from most except an occasional neighbor. One bad episode occurred when her son visited, resulting in a hospital stay and return to normal functioning. The scenario was repeated on more than one occasion, until her physician and son realized that she could no longer live alone. A difficult decision was made to place her in foster home care.

Two years later, she is experiencing extreme forgetfulness as a result of organic brain deterioration, perhaps Alzheimer's disease. Her son tries to call daily, though each time she talks about wanting to move into her own apartment. She wants his total attention and would like to live with him. When they are together, she requires total and constant attention and assistance.

The Case of Tillie—Living Vicariously

Tillie is in her late fifties and lives with her husband. She has a recliner in her living room where she spends most of her time. Beside the chair is a police band radio that is always on. Anytime there are voices on the radio, all conversation in the room ends and Tillie becomes excited, wondering aloud which officer is responding, pulling out her map to determine the exact location of a call. She knows each officer in her precinct by name. Tillie has no other desire in life than to live vicariously the life of a Miami police officer. She reads little, has few friends, and reports being very happy with her life.

Does Tillie need counseling? Would she accept it? What would be a counselor's goals? These and other obvious and not so obvious questions are left to the reader to decide.

RESOURCES AVAILABLE

Resources available to assist counselors in addressing the concerns of older women include organizations and publications. Within local areas, many community colleges have over-60 programs and displaced homemaker programs to help meet the needs of older women. The Older Americans Act mandates that information and referral services for older persons be available in every community. A call to the local information operator can quickly lead to the source of information on services for older people in a particular community. The major national organizations which counselors should be aware of are as follows:

❏ American Association of Retired Persons (AARP)
  601 E Street, NW
  Washington, DC 20049

❑ National Coalition of Older Women's Issues (over 40 constituent organizations)
2401 Virginia Avenue, NW
Washington, DC 20037
❑ National Policy Center on Women and Aging
University of Maryland, Center on Aging
College Park, MD 20742
❑ Older Women's League (OWL)
1325 G Street, NW, Lower Level B
Washington, DC 20005

AARP publishes a wide array of self-help books as well as materials for service providers to older persons. Three useful books for older women are:

❑ *AARP Guide for Widowed Persons*, 1987, Washington, DC.
❑ *Survival Handbook for Widows (and for Relatives and Friends Who Want to Understand)* by R. J. Loewinsohn, 1984, Washington, DC.
❑ *Alone—Not Lonely: Independent Living Guide for Women over Fifty* by J. Seskin, 1985, Washington, DC.

PROBLEM PREVENTION AND SOCIAL INTERVENTION

Counselors need to look beyond the immediate therapeutic setting and consider ways to function as change agents on behalf of older women. Three areas which can be explored include community education efforts, consultation with decision makers, and strategies for influencing public policies.

Community Education

Prevention of the problems described in this chapter is the ideal solution, but it simply will not work for women in their later years today. If prevention is to be effective, it must start early, perhaps as early as infancy, with the socialization of women to be independent, to value the friendships and support of other women, and to prepare for changing lifestyles that could incorporate radically different alternatives at different ages and life stages. The "American dream" of marriage, two children, and a two car garage should not be fostered on women at a time when soon 20% of older women will be single and childless over the course of their lifetime, compared to only 5% today. A major key is to teach women to be flexible, and to develop an internal locus of control and sense of esteem and value for who they are.

Older women today can benefit from educational efforts to assist them in becoming and remaining independent. For example, women need to learn more about financial tools and information, how to use comprehensive retirement planning materials, how to develop a balanced investment portfolio, and how to use a strategy of total resource management in planning for later life (McKenna & Nickols, 1986). Local schools and colleges can be encouraged to develop programs to meet these and other needs of older women. Community education programs can teach courses on topics such as strategies for building social networks, developing habits of life-long learning, and how to use basic communications skills to enhance the quality of family interactions. Women need to be encouraged to take advantage of educational opportunities, to view themselves as empowered rather than helpless in responding to the changing circumstances of later life.

Consultation with Decision Makers

An effective way to achieve changes in a system is to advocate with decision makers. The problem in trying to change the life circumstances of older women is that many of the systems that need to be changed are complex and diverse, and access to decision makers is difficult. Within a local community, volunteering to serve on the board of agencies that provide services to older persons is a good first step. At the national level, becoming a member of AARP, OWL, or another active advocacy group is a way to support needed change on behalf of older women. It is important to understand that change is a very slow process. An example may clarify this point.

Within the counseling profession, the concerns of older persons first began to be addressed in 1975. Through a series of national projects on aging funded by the U.S. Administration on Aging (AoA) in cooperation with the American Association for Counseling and Development (AACD), interest in gerontological counseling was stimulated. The number of counselor education programs offering course work to train counselors to work with older persons increased from 6% to 33% in fewer than 10 years (Myers, 1983). In 1990, standards for training counselors to work with older persons were submitted to the AACD Council on Accreditation, and a statement of competencies for gerontological counselors was prepared (Myers & Sweeney, 1990). Also in 1990, the National Board for Certified Counselors approved a specialty certification in gerontological counseling to help assure the public of a minimum level of preparation on the part of National Certified Gerontological Counselors (NCGCs). Fifteen years, relatively speaking, is not a long time, at least when viewed retrospectively. At no time during those 15 years could anyone have predicted or guaranteed what would become of the growing minority of counselors with an interest in serving older persons.

The same may be said of any efforts to obtain needed change. What is important is to identify the issues that can be changed, the individuals and groups that can help to bring about change, and strategies for working with those groups. This chapter has provided a very sketchy overview of some of the issues facing older women; the list of organizations above can be a good starting point for finding out what efforts to effect change are planned and in progress.

Strategies for Influencing Public Policy

Legislative advocacy is the primary strategy used today for influencing economic and social policies, and there is strength in numbers. Continuing policy changes are needed to assure equal employment opportunities for women across the life span and equal pension benefits regardless of time spent out of the labor market in child rearing activities. Although stereotypes and biases cannot be legislated, policies that allow women to live meaningful lives with adequate incomes and access to health care will result in a picture of older women much different than that of today. Many older women do not now fit the stereotypes, yet they are viewed as unique among their peers. We need to set and maintain a national policy agenda that assures that women are able to choose and maintain healthy lifestyles across their life span, in all areas of their functioning. National organizations working with and on behalf of older women have that as their goal. Counselors can and should support these initiatives. For those of us who are female, it is an investment in our own future.

REFERENCES

American Association of Retired Persons. (1986, Fall). Conference on women's issues: A joining of minds. *AARP Program Update, 5(4)*, 1ff.

American Association of Retired Persons. (1987). *A profile of older Americans.* Washington, DC: Author.

Ashinger, P. (1985). Using social networks in counseling. *Journal of Counseling and Development, 63*, 519–521.

Atchley, R. (1983). *The social forces in later life* (3rd ed.). Belmont, CA: Wadsworth.

Austin, D. (1985). Attitudes toward old age: A hierarchical study. *The Gerontologist, 25*, 431–434.

Barbado, C. A., & Feezel, J. D. (1987). The language of aging in different groups. *The Gerontologist, 27*, 527–531.

Baruth, L. G., & Huber, C. H. (1984). *An introduction to marital theory and therapy.* Monterey, CA: Brooks/Cole.

Bearden, L. J., & Head, D. W. (1985). Attitudes of rehabilitation professionals toward aging and older persons. *Journal of Applied Rehabilitation Counseling, 17*, 17–19.

Beckman, L. J., & Houser, B. B. (1982). The consequences of childlessness on the social-psychological well-being of older women. *Journal of Gerontology, 37*, 243–250.

Blazer, D. (1982). *Depression in later life.* St. Louis: C. V. Mosby.

Brubaker, T. H. (1985). *Later life families.* Beverly Hills, CA: Sage Publications.

Buehler, C. (1967). Human life as a central subject of humanistic psychology. In J. Bugental (Ed.), *Challenges in humanistic psychology* (pp. 83–91). New York: McGraw-Hill.

Bulcroft, K., & O'Conner, M. (1986). The importance of dating relationships on quality of life for older persons. *Family Relations, 35*, 397–401.

Burnside, I. (1984). *Working with the elderly: Group processes and techniques.* Monterey, CA: Wadsworth.

Butler, R. N. (1975). *Why survive; Being old in America.* St. Louis: C. V. Mosby.

Caregivers in the work place. (1988). *Working Age, 3(5)*, 4–5.

Chandler, J. T., Rachal, J. R., & Kazelskis, R. (1986). Attitudes of long-term care personnel toward the elderly. *The Gerontologist, 26*, 551–555.

Cherlin, A. (1983). A sense of history: Recent research on aging and the family. In M. Riley, B. Hess, & K. Bond (Eds), *Aging in society: Selected reviews of recent research* (pp. 57-84). Hillsdale, NJ: Lawrence Erlbaum.

Dobson, J. E., & Dobson, R. L. (1985). The sandwich generation: Dealing with aging parents. *Journal of Counseling and Development, 63*, 572–574.

Doka, K. J. (1986). Adolescent attitudes and beliefs toward aging and the elderly. *International Journal of Aging and Human Development, 22*, 173–178.

Erikson, E. (1963). *Childhood and society.* New York: Norton.

Gilligan, C. (1982). *In a different voice.* Cambridge: Harvard University Press.

Giordano, N. H., & Giordano, J. A. (1984). Elder abuse: A review of the literature. *Social Work, 29*, 232–236.

Hansson, R. O., Jones, W. H., Carpenter, B. N., & Remondet, J. H. (1986). Loneliness and adjustment to old age. *International Journal of Aging and Human Development, 24*, 41–53.

Harris, L., & Associates. (1975). *The myth and reality of aging in America.* Washington, DC: National Council on the Aging.

Havighurst, R. J. (1972). *Developmental tasks and education.* New York: McKay.

Herr, J. J., & Weakland, J. W. (1979). *Counseling elders and their families.* New York: Springer.

Hetherington, C., & Loganbill, C. R. (1985). Wellness promotion: A new strategy for counselors. *Journal of NAWDAC, 48,* 32–37.

Hettler, B. (1980). Wellness: Encouraging a lifetime pursuit of excellence. *Health Values, 8,* 13–17.

Hickey, T., Bragg, S., Rakowski, W., & Hultsch, D. (1979). Attitude instrument analysis: An examination of factor consistency across two samples. *International Journal of Aging and Human Development, 9,* 359–375.

Jacobs, R. H. (1976). A typology of older American women. *Social Policy, 7,* 34–39.

Kalson, L. (1982). Group therapy with the aged. In M. Seligman (Ed.), *Group psychotherapy and counseling with special populations* (pp. 187–198). Baltimore: University Park Press.

Kastenbaum, R. (1969). Death and bereavement in later life. In A. H. Kutscher (Ed.), *Death and bereavement.* Springfield, IL: Charles C Thomas.

Keith, P. M. (1986). The social context and resources of the unmarried in old age. *International Journal of Aging and Human Development, 23,* 81–96.

Kermis, M. D. (1984). *The psychology of human aging: Theory, research, and practice.* Boston: Allyn & Bacon.

Kimmel, D. C. (1979). Adjustments to aging among gay males. In B. Berezon (Ed.), *Positively gay* (pp. 146–158). Los Angeles: Mediamix.

Kuypers, J. A., & Bengtson, V. L. (1973). Competence and social breakdown: A social-psychological view. *Human Development, 16,* 37–49.

Leafgren, F., & Elsenrath, D. (1986). The role of campus recreation programs in institutions of higher education. In M. J. Barr & M. L. Upcraft (Eds.), *Developing campus recreation programs in institutions of higher education* (pp. 3–18). San Francisco: Jossey-Bass.

Lee, G. R., & Ishii-Kuntz, M. (1987). Social interaction, loneliness, and emotional well-being among the elderly. *Research on Aging, 9,* 459–482.

Livson, F. B. (1977, August). *Cultural faces of Eve: Images of women.* Paper presented at the annual meeting of the American Psychological Association, San Francisco.

Lowenthal, M. F., & Haven, C. (1968). Isolation and interaction: Intimacy as a critical variable. *America Sociological Review, 33,* 20–30.

Martin, D., & Lyon, P. (1979). The older lesbian. In B. Berezon (Ed.), *Positively gay* (pp. 134–145). Los Angeles: Mediamix.

McGoldrick, M., & Gerson, R. (1985). *Genograms in family assessment.* New York: Norton.

McKenna, J., & Nickols, S.Y. (1986). Retirement planning strategies for midlife women. *Journal of Home Economics, 78,* 34–37 ff.

Morgan, L. A. (1981). Aging in a family context. In R. H. Davis (Ed.), *Aging: Issues and prospects* (pp. 98–112). Los Angeles: University of Southern California.

Myers, J. E. (1983). Gerontological counseling training: The state of the art. *Journal of Counseling and Development, 61,* 398–401.

Myers, J. E. (1989). *Adult children and aging parents.* Alexandria, VA: American Association for Counseling and Development.

Myers, J. E., & Navin, S. (1984). To have not: The childless older woman. *Humanistic Education and Development, 22,* 91–100.

Myers, J. E., & Sweeney, T. J. (1990). *Gerontological competencies for counselors and human development specialists.* Alexandria, VA: American Association for Counseling and Development.

National Coalition on Older Women's Issues. (undated). *It's about time...* Washington, DC: Author.

Neugarten, B. (1968). *Middle age and aging.* Chicago: University of Chicago Press.

Nicholls, W., & Everett, C. A. (1986). *Systemic family therapy: An integrative approach.* New York: Guilford Press.

Nishi-Strattner, M., & Myers, J. E. (1983). Attitudes toward the elderly: An intergenerational examination. *Educational Gerontology, 9,* 389–397.

Peck, R. C. (1968). Psychology developments in the second half of life. In B.L. Neugarten (Ed.), *Middle age and aging* (pp. 88–92). Chicago: University of Chicago Press.

Pillemer, K., Wolf, R. S., & Gwynther, L. P. (1987). Elder abuse: Conflict in the family. *Journal of Gerontology, 42,* 234–235.

Porter, S. V. (1984). *Age discrimination: The invisible barriers. Proceedings of the conference Women, Work, and Age: Policy Challenges.* Lansing, MI: Institute of Gerontology.

Ray, D. C., Raciti, M. A., & Ford, C. V. (1985). Ageism in psychiatrists: Associations with gender, certification, and theoretical orientation. *The Gerontologist, 25,* 496–500.

Riker, H., & Myers, J. E. (1990). *Retirement counseling: A practical approach for a new decade.* New York: Hemisphere.

Schlossberg, N. (1984). *Counseling adults in transition.* New York: Springer.

Select Committee on Aging. (1979). *Women and retirement income programs: Current issues of equity and adequacy.* (Comm. Pub. No. 96–190). Washington, DC: U.S. Government Printing Office.

Special Committee on Aging. (1983). *Developments in aging, Volume I.* Washington, DC: U.S. Government Printing Office.

Special Committee on Aging. (1985). *How older Americans live: An analysis of census data.* (Comm Pub No. 99–D). Washington, DC: U.S. Government Printing Office.

Steenland, S., & Schmidt, L. (1985). *Trouble on the set: An analysis of female characters on 1985 television programs.* Washington, DC: National Commission on Working Women.

Stone, R., Cafferata, G. L., & Sangle, J. (1987). Caregivers of the frail elderly: A national profile. *The Gerontologist, 27,* 616–626.

Treas, J. (1983). Aging and the family. In D. S. Woodruff & J. E. Birren (Eds.), *Aging: Scientific perspectives and social issues* (pp. 92–108). Los Angeles: University of California.

Troll, L. (1982). Family life in middle and old age: The generation gap. *Annals of the American Academy of Political and Social Science, 464,* 38–46.

Troll, L. (1984, August). *Poor, dumb, and ugly: The older woman in contemporary society.* Paper presented at the annual convention of the American Psychological Association, Toronto, Ontario, Canada.

Uhlenberg, P., & Myers, A. P. (1981). Divorce and the elderly. *The Gerontologist, 21,* 276–282.

Uhlenberg, P., & Salmon, M. A. P. (1986). Change in relative income of older women, 1960-1980. *The Gerontologist, 26,* 164-170.

Ward, R. A. (1979). The never-married in later life. *Journal of Gerontology, 34,* 861–869.

Waters, E., McCarroll, J., & Penman, N. (1987). *Training mental health workers for the elderly: An instructor's guide.* Rochester, MI: Continuum Center.

Wisniewski, W., & Cohen, D. (1984, November). *Older women: A population at risk for mental health problems.* Paper presented at the Annual Scientific Meeting of the Gerontological Society of America, San Antonio, TX.

Wolleat, P. L. (1980). Counseling the elderly woman: A sex-role perspective. *Counseling and Values, 24,* 108–117.

Zimpfer, D. (1987). Groups for the aging: Do they work? *Journal for Specialists in Group Work, 12,* 85–92.

Zweibel, N. R. (1984, November). *Analysis of family decision making in selection of alternatives to institutionalization.* Paper presented at the annual scientific meeting of the Gerontological Society of America, San Antonio, TX.

10

Midlife and Beyond: Health Counseling Issues Affecting Older Women

Ann Q. Lynch
Florida Atlantic University

Marilyn M. Patterson and Martin Uher
California University of Pennsylvania

Discussions of health issues concerning midlife and aging women, and the aging process in general, often fail to distinguish normal aging from pathological aging. However, it is important for counselors to understand this distinction if they are to provide comprehensive interventions and appropriate referrals when necessary. The first section of this chapter identifies major health issues related to women, with distinctions made between physical changes that occur with the normal aging process and disease processes of particular concern to midlife and older women. Specific counseling strategies, case examples, and relevant resources are presented. The remainder of the chapter addresses the role of problem prevention and social interventions including consultation with family caregivers and medical personnel and community education programs, as well as the impact of health policies on older women.

HEALTH ISSUES IN THE LATER YEARS

Due to advances in medical sciences and public health, longevity for women has increased tremendously during the 20th century. In 1900 the life expectancy for females was 48; it is 78 today (Older Women's League, 1988). The primary factor in this increase has been the drastic reduction in the infant mortality rate. Reduction in maternal death during childbirth and the control of infectious diseases are also complementary factors (Ferrini & Ferrini, 1989).

Life Expectancy

Because longer life expectancy results in greater incidence and prevalence of chronic diseases, factors influencing life expectancy should be examined. Many theories have been advanced to explain why women have a longer life expectancy than men. These can be separated into genetic-biological factors and sociological-lifestyle factors.

Genetic-Biological Factors

It has been suggested that females have a genetic advantage in life expectancy because this advantage extends to almost all animal species. According to Waldron (1976), females are more resistant to infectious diseases and cell damage because all females have two X chromosomes and men have only one. The X chromosome is believed to carry genes for immune system functioning and for the repair of free radical damage. In addition, the estrogen produced by women prior to menopause, protects against atherosclerosis build up, and consequent heart disease. However, women become more susceptible to circulatory disease after menopause. On the other side, the output of the male hormone testosterone, which promotes blood clotting and subsequent greater susceptibility to circulatory problems, is at its peak in men between ages 20 and 40. This results in greater vulnerability to circulatory diseases earlier in life for males (Ferrini & Ferrini, 1989).

Sociological-Lifestyle Factors

Another reason that men have a higher mortality rate earlier in life is their higher incidence of violent deaths (wars, auto accidents, killings), as well as job-related deaths stemming from greater occupational dangers in the male's work place. Other gender-linked lifestyle behaviors such as the male's greater tendency to smoke and drink more than females have been cited. These factors suggest that the difference between male and female longevity will decrease as women gain more equality in the work force and in social behaviors. According to the latest census figures, death rates for men declined more rapidly than those of women between 1940 and 1989 (National Center for Health Statistics, 1990). The reason seems to be changing patterns of disease as more women began smoking and moving into traditionally male-dominated jobs and lifestyles. Moreover, another reason for women's longevity is that women tend to use health services to a greater extent than do men, and generally take more and better health precautionary measures than do men (Grambs, 1989).

Normal Age-Related Physiological Changes

In midlife women begin to face health related issues that accompany the normal aging process. Although every woman goes through the aging process in her own unique way, certain normal age-related physiological changes will occur. The rate of these changes varies depending on a woman's biological system and individual lifestyle. The counselor needs to understand normal age-related changes in order to communicate about them from a wellness rather than a disease oriented perspective. Menopause has been the focus of much attention for midlife women and is an example of a normal age-related process that should not be confused with a disease process.

Menopause

The terms *menopause* and *climacteric* are used interchangeably in the literature to refer to a single event or changes occurring over 20 years or more. Dyer (1979) has clarified the terms: Menopause refers to the "actual cessation of menstruation and can be said to have occurred after a woman has not had menstrual bleeding for at least one year"; the female climacteric refers to the period of life characterized by changes in the body that accompany the decreasing function of the ovaries, encompassing "the time period and those events leading up to and following the actual cessation of menstruation" (p. 305). Menopause then is one physical event in the entire climacteric experience.

Physiological Process of Menopause Prior to the termination of menstruation, a woman may experience irregular menstrual periods, hot flushes, and atrophic vaginitis. These changes result from decreased sensitivity of the hypothalamus and pituitary glands (Tyler & Woodal, 1982). These symptoms may persist over a 5 to 10 year period as a woman goes through the gradual transition from reproductive to nonreproductive status. Menopause usually occurs at about age 50, though it can occur as early as age 45. Ninety percent of women between the ages of 45 and 55 will have experienced menopause (Treloar, 1974).

Hot flashes or flushes are a common occurrence for women during the climacteric, though not all women experience them. Vasomotor dilatation causes an intense sensation of body heat and excess perspiration. Sometimes a reddening of the skin is apparent. Even though hot flashes may be uncomfortable, only 10% of women report them to be a severe problem (Pearson & Beck, 1989).

Atrophic vaginitis results in vaginal dryness, a thinning of the vaginal walls, and a decrease in elasticity of the vagina due to reduced secretion of vaginal mucosa. As a result women may report uncomfortable irritation during sexual intercourse and a susceptibility to vaginal and urethral infections.

With the cessation of menses, vaginal discomforts and hot flushes are the only physiological symptoms proven to be the result of menopause. Women sometimes report headaches, dizzy spells, palpitations, fatigue, backache, nausea, weight increase, and various other physical maladies during the climacteric. However, there is little evidence that these symptoms are a direct result of menopause.

Psychosocial Aspects of Menopause Psychological symptoms of depression, impaired memory, nervousness, and mood swings have not been shown to be psychologically linked to menopause (Rosenthal, 1979). Recent research efforts have attempted to dispel the notion that emotional difficulties associated with midlife women can be directly attributed to menopause. Instead, factors affecting a woman's physical and emotional state may be linked to general health, medication, physical activity level, life events, heredity, and attitude (National Institute of Health, 1983). In addition, natural transitions involving gender roles, family interactions, self-concept, and various external events affect a woman's behavior in midlife (Parlee, 1984).

The way in which women are socialized in our society contributes to the belief that menopause is a time of instability and depression. The view of femininity as directly related to women's reproductive capabilities was promoted in the literature until recently. Counselors need to understand this heritage of women's psychological history because many of the women in the older age cohort have this view as a legacy. Deutsch (1944), a Freudian, defined menopause as a loss of all that was feminine, and believed that a major psychological adjustment was needed to cope with this loss and to preserve one's womanhood. Without the capacity to reproduce, it was thought that women merely coped with the inevitable feelings of uselessness, hopelessness, and lack of sexual identity associated with the onset of old age. Themes that pervaded medical definitions of menopause were summarized by McCrea (1983) as: (a) a woman's potential and function are biologically destined, (b) a woman's worth is determined by fertility and attractiveness, (c) rejection of the feminine role will bring physical and emotional havoc, and (d) aging women are useless and unattractive. Survey data collected by Cowen, Warren, and Young (1985) suggest that physicians and nurses view menopausal symptoms as more pathological than do the women themselves. With stereotypical views of menopausal women promoted in the psychological, medical, and popular literature, it seems inevitable that some women would accept these stereotypes themselves.

An important question to be asked is: Do the ways that American women are socialized contribute to the continuation of the belief that menopause is a period of emotional instability? Following an examination of data on 30 societies worldwide, Bart (1971) concluded that, in cultures in which women reported the greatest amount of distress during the climacteric, social power was patriarchal, with few social roles for older women. By contrast, in cultures in which older women were valued and grandmother and mother-in-law roles carry responsibilities and privileges within the extended family, menopause was viewed as a less traumatic event. Many Western women have been socialized to view their self-worth and femininity as directly related to sexual attractiveness, youth, fertility, and motherhood (Baruch, Barnett, & Rivers, 1983). Moreover, in our society there have been few positive roles associated with aging women.

Life events and various changes including children leaving home, obtaining a job, furthering an education, divorce, remarriage, caring for aging parents, widowhood, and declining income can be stressful for midlife women. Cooke and Green (1981) examined the relationship between life stressors and the psychological symptomatology associated with menopause. They found that the loss of significant others was the primary stressful life event experienced by women at the climacteric. Symptoms were attributed to loss and the capacity for coping rather than the event of menopause. Moreover, the timing of menopause may determine the amount of psychological distress experienced by a woman. In earlier research, Neugarten, Wood, Kraines, and Loomis (1968) found that when menopause was viewed as a normal life event, occurring within an expected time frame, any deviation from the time frame may become overly stressful. After examining data from the Health and Nutrition Examination Survey on a nationally representative sample of more than 3,000 women, Lennon (1982) concurred that when menopause occurred on time, in midlife, it was not associated with psychological distress. When it occurred earlier or later in the life course, however, the event itself was the source of psychological stress.

In studying attitudes toward menopause across age groups, Neugarten et al. (1968) concluded that middle-aged women do not necessarily view menopause negatively or even as a significant event in their lives. When asked to respond to statements related to how women feel following menopause, only 20% of the respondents in the 31–44 age group stated they would feel better, whereas 68% in the 45–55 age group responded favorably. Most of the middle-aged respondents viewed the post-menopausal woman as freer, feeling better, more confident, and calmer than before menopause. Experiencing menopause may relieve some of the fears and misconceptions women hold prior to that event.

Health Problems Associated with Aging

Besides the normal aging process, there are a number of health problems associated with aging. These affect women in different ways. The diversity among women in terms of heredity, biological makeup, ethnicity, and lifestyles adds to the complexity of making generalizations. The following section presents some of the more common health problems of aging women, including cardiovascular disease, cancer, osteoporosis, incontinence, chronic conditions, depression, and dementia.

Cardiovascular Disease

The leading cause of death for both women and men in the United States is cardiovascular disease. As mentioned above, it is believed that the female's estrogen production protects her from cardiovascular disease. Estrogen is associated with high density lipoproteins (HDL), which aid in decreasing blood cholesterol and thus reducing the incidence of circulatory disorders. As stated by the National Institute on Aging (1987), women develop cardiovascular disease on the average about 10 to 20 years later than do men. This delay holds true even when women have the same risk factors as men, which include smoking, high blood cholesterol levels, and family history of heart disease. Following menopause, females' incidence of cardiovascular mortality increases, until by age 65, the incidence (1,958 per 100,000) is about the same as for males. However, women tend to develop less severe heart problems. Apparently the symptoms of angina pectoris, which indicate cardiac oxygen insufficiency, are more prevalent in aging females. Thus, signs of impending cardiac complications are more apparent in aging females than in males.

However, when an elderly female does develop severe cardiovascular problems, her prognosis is not as encouraging as the male's. A woman is two to three times more apt to have a second heart attack, and less likely to benefit from aspirin therapy or from bypass surgery than a man (National Institute on Aging, 1987). Several studies summarized by Eastman and Glasheen (1990) indicated that many more elderly women died during or after bypass surgery than did men. At one time it was assumed that the higher death rates resulted from technical difficulties of performing delicate surgery on women's smaller hearts and coronary arteries. Yet indications were that the women were older and much sicker than the men by the time they received bypass surgery. The implications of this finding were that the delay in getting the women into surgery could be tied to physicians' tendencies to ignore the same early warning symptoms in women that were treated as serious in men.

Being overweight or obese seems to present a formidable heart disease risk factor for aging women. Approximately 40% of women's heart attacks could be attributed to being overweight; almost three fourths of obese women's heart attacks were caused by weight (Wolfe, 1991). Smoking has definitely been shown to have a deleterious effect also on women's cardiovascular systems.

Several important facts relative to women and heart disease should be noted.

❑ Diagnosing heart disease in women is more difficult than diagnosing it in men because women's symptoms are less obvious. (In 65% of women, the first indication is chest pain, frequently mistaken for some other symptom.)
❑ Treadmill exercise tests are not as reliable for women as they are for men.
❑ Women have a higher initial death rate with angioplasty than do men.
❑ Women who do have successful angioplasty and bypass surgery have survival rates comparable to those of men. (Eastman & Glasheen, 1990)

High blood pressure is also more prevalent in elderly women than elderly men, particularly in black females. This blood vessel–damaging condition can lead to renal failure, blindness, and strokes as well as to heart attacks. Menopause also seems to lead to higher cholesterol levels which are closely linked to cardiovascular disease and probably caused by an inherited tendency to accumulate blood fats or a diet high in saturated fats and cholesterol.

Cancer

Cancer is the second highest ranked cause of death in the United States. The primary types of cancers affecting elderly women are breast, lung, colorectal, uterine, and skin cancers.

The most common form of cancer in women, breast cancer, will strike 1 in 11 women during their lifetimes. That rate has not changed for many years (Wolfe, 1991). Breast cancer is most common in post-menopausal women. The good news is that more women than ever are surviving breast cancer because of early diagnosis and better treatment. Moreover, Gee and Kimball (1987) have reported the survival rate of older women with breast cancer seems to be even better than for younger women. Because breast cancer is so common, all women are considered to be at risk and should be examined by a physician annually, especially after the age of 50 (Moe, 1985). Continuing monthly breast self-examinations (BSE) are also strongly recommended by the National Cancer Institute. Despite the success rates, mammography, as well as BSE, is now recommended by the American Cancer Society, starting with baseline mammography at age 35 and yearly for women age 50 and older, in order to detect cancers too small to be palpated. After menstrual periods stop, women should continue to perform BSE once a month at a regular time.

The leading cause of all cancer deaths is lung cancer because it is difficult to detect in the early stage, making treatment generally ineffective. Deaths from lung cancer are presently four times more common in men than in women. However, the increase in women smokers has dramatically increased the incidence of lung cancer in women until now it surpasses breast cancer as the leading cancer killer in women (U.S. Surgeon General, 1986). The average age of women with newly diagnosed lung cancer is 60 years.

According to the National Cancer Institute (1990), people age 65 and older account for three-fourths of the cases of colorectal cancer, and the rate increases beyond that age. There does not appear to be a gender difference in the prevalence of colorectal cancer, but more a lifestyle basis for its occurrence. This type of cancer is almost nonexistent in developing nations, but is peculiar to industrialized nations, pointing to our diet, lifestyle, and environment.

Elderly women are particularly at risk for cancer of the reproductive organs. The highest incidence of cervical cancer occurs in women ages 50–59. Most cases of endometrial cancer (cancer of the lining of the uterus) occur in women between the ages of 55 and 64; and it rarely occurs in women under age 40 (National Cancer Institute, 1990). Factors that increase the risk of developing cervical cancer are early age of first intercourse and multiple sex partners, while high risk factors for endometrial cancers are a history of infertility, failure to ovulate regularly, obesity, abnormal bleeding, late menopause, and prolonged estrogen therapy. Although the Pap test is considered to be highly accurate in detecting cervical cancer, it is not nearly as effective in detecting cancer in the body of the uterus. More extensive diagnostic techniques (dilation and curettage, and aspiration curettage) are used to obtain tissue samples of the lining of the uterus for microscopic examination. These latter procedures can detect precursors of cancer as well as established cancer growth.

Osteoporosis

Demineralization and loss of supporting bone matrix is characteristic of aging bones. This process, part of natural aging, results in bones becoming more porous and subsequently more susceptible to fractures. Bone loss is greater in older women than older men. Women lose 20 to 30% of their bone mass over their life span (Aviola, 1982), while men lose only about 10 to 15% (Mazess, 1982). Essentially, this is considered normal.

Osteoporosis, on the other hand, is greater-than-normal bone loss. This greater-than-normal loss results in reduced bone strength, which makes fractures, particularly in the back and hip, more common. It can also cause deterioration of the vertebrae leading to spinal deformities, reduced height, and back pain. Women are four times more likely to have osteoporosis than men, and women begin bone loss earlier and their rate of loss is faster. White women are more prone to this accelerated bone loss than nonwhite, and women whose ethnic origins are closer to the equator fare better than women from higher latitudes (Ferrini & Ferrini, 1989).

There are many theories about the cause of this accelerated bone loss, particularly in aging women. Because the condition of accelerated bone loss occurs after menopause, estrogen deprivation must certainly be considered a major factor. What estrogen does to aid in the reduction of osteoporosis is not fully understood, but that a relationship exists can hardly be disputed. According to Aviola (1982), a woman's bone mass may drop as much as 5% a year in the first few years after menopause. Estrogen Replacement Therapy (ERT) treatment has been effective in preventing excessive bone loss if treatment is initiated soon after menopause. However, many doctors have been reluctant to prescribe ERT since earlier studies linked estrogen with uterine and breast cancer.

Other factors that seem to be regarded as causes or contributors to osteoporosis are insufficient consumption of calcium, lack of exercise, particularly weight-bearing exercise, cigarette smoking, excessive alcohol consumption, and high intake of protein. The typical picture of an osteoporotic candidate is a small-framed, thin, fair-skinned woman who smokes, is inactive, and does not get enough calcium. "There is little evidence that any therapy can reverse the bone loss associated with osteoporosis, but its progression can be retarded. Prevention and treatment measures include increased calcium intake (1200–1400 mg), Vitamin D, exercise, smoking cessation and, in some cases, estrogen therapy" (Ferrini & Ferrini, 1989). Again, Wolfe (1991) has cautioned against the use of ERT for the prevention of osteoporosis because of the implications for breast and uterine cancer.

Incontinence

Incontinence is the inability to control bladder function. This condition ranges from mild to severe and from temporary to chronic. Temporary incontinence is usually associated with acute illness, drugs, or some circumstance that reduces the urge or ability to get to the toilet on time. One form of persistent chronic incontinence more closely associated with women than men is stress incontinence. This type of incontinence is more common in older women because the pelvic floor muscles have been weakened by the rigors of childbirth. Overweight women are also more susceptible. In stress incontinence, small amounts of urine are expelled involuntarily when pressure is increased in the abdominal muscles by sneezing, coughing, laughing, jumping, and so on. Stress incontinence may be alleviated in many cases by strengthening the muscles in question through exercise. When warranted, surgical procedures may also be used to correct the problem.

Chronic Conditions

According to Atchley (1991), chronic conditions are "long term, leave residual disability, require special training for rehabilitation, or may be expected to require a long period of supervision, observation, or care" (p. 78). The nature of chronic illnesses is such that: they cannot be cured; they have uncertain prognoses; they often have many physical, social, and psychological problems; they require a wide variety of services; and they are costly. The U.S. Senate Special Committee on Aging reported on chronic conditions in order of prevalence in all persons age 45 and over. Rates quoted here are for those age 65 and older: arthritis (47%), hypertension (39%), hearing impairment (33%), heart condition (30%), sinusitis (15%), orthopedic impairment (18%), arteriosclerosis (10%), diabetes (9%), and visual impairment (11%) (U.S. Department of Health and Human Services, 1990).

Fortunately, chronic conditions do not automatically result in severe limitation of activities, especially for women ages 65 to 74. Only about 2% of women in this age group must considerably limit their daily activities due to chronic conditions; though limitations increase with age for those age 85 and older, the percentage of older adults who must severely limit their activities due to chronic conditions has only increased to

12% of that population (Atchley, 1991).

One chronic condition associated with the sensory processes is hearing loss. Approximately 80% of hearing impaired individuals are over the age of 45. An estimated 6.5 million persons over the age of 65 have total or partial hearing loss (U.S. Department of Health and Human Services, 1990). Different degrees and types of hearing loss impede communication differently. Presbycusis is the term used to define age-related changes in hearing ability that include a decline in the ability to hear high frequency tones, impaired frequency discrimination, and impaired ability to tell the direction from which the sound is coming (Olsho, Harkins, & Lenhardt, 1985).

Degrees of hearing loss influence the ability of an individual to interact in the social environment and can be mistaken for symptoms associated with depression or mental confusion. However, just as with changes in vision, older adults are rarely severely hearing impaired due to normal age-related changes, as their ability to adapt and compensate is generally sufficient to prevent overwhelming dependency.

Depression

Counselors and other health care professionals need to understand the difference between normal reactions to loss and crises and dysfunctional reactions. Symptoms of depression are often confused with symptoms associated with organic brain disorders (Public Health Service Task Force on Women's Health Issues, 1985). According to the DSM-IIIR (American Psychiatric Association, 1987), the symptoms of depression include feeling sad and blue, fatigue, concern, or difficulty with doing everyday tasks, constipation, sleeping difficulties, poor appetite, weight-loss, persistent feelings of loneliness, inability to enjoy activities, and suicidal thoughts.

When symptoms of depression are noted or reported, the counselor must be aware of the multitude of factors that complicate the picture. First, medication side effects, misuse, and abuse must be considered. Second, severity and duration of the depressed mood/symptoms should be evaluated. Older adults experience multiple losses and stressors. Consideration should be given to what social and environmental factors could be associated with the behavior. Personality and lifelong coping mechanisms should be assessed, as well as lifestyle and health factors. Chronic conditions, diet, and social isolation are all associated with affective changes in older adults.

Symptoms of depression are more common in women than in men and are associated in older women with age and gender roles (Rodeheaver & Datan, 1988). Women with a traditional gender-role orientation are more likely to suffer from depression in late life (Markides & Vernon, 1984). Counselors need to be sure that they do not see problems associated with aging as irreversible, negative "disease-oriented" consequences of aging, because women are more likely to report somatic complaints.

Dementia Including Alzheimer's Disease

Dementia and depression are the most prevalent mental disorders among older adults and can present the counselor with a complex web of degrees of symptomatology to evaluate. Both disorders are easily subject to misdiagnosis and therefore incorrect treatment, if the counselor is not informed about the many factors relevant to their assessment and treatment. In addition to medical personnel, it is also crucial for counselors to realize that mental disorders are not a part of the normal aging process.

Alzheimer's disease is now the most common form of dementia. It accounts for approximately 55% of all dementia among the elderly (Atchley, 1991). Because its incidence increases with age and women live longer, the disease is more prevalent in older women than in older men (National Institute on Aging, 1987).

Clinical diagnosis of Alzheimer's disease involves a complete evaluation that includes family/client history, physical assessment, neurological and psychiatric evaluation, mental status exams, psychometric tests, laboratory studies, and computerized axial tomography (Older Women's League, 1988). The symptoms of progressive decline in mental and physical functioning are not easily distinguishable from symptoms associated with other dementias, depressive reactions, clinical depression, drug interactions, or even physical and mental problems associated with poor diet and living conditions. Gurland, Dean, Cross, and Golden (1980) have estimated that between 10% and 20% of clients diagnosed as having dementia have reversible conditions.

COUNSELING STRATEGIES

Aging women are at risk. With women living longer, the goal is not just longevity, but as high a quality of life as possible for as long as possible. Because women in our society have been socialized to defer to authority figures, counselors must become aware of health issues affecting all women. With their different life experiences and variety of circumstances, it should be remembered that older women represent greater diversity and are a more heterogeneous group than younger women (Waters, 1984). Counselors must be proactive and become advocates for improving health conditions for women of all ages, especially older women. Through greater awareness of issues and strategies to impact them, mental health professionals can empower women to take control of their lives for their own fulfillment as well as that of their families and society in general.

Counselors need to be aware of the following dimensions of client-centered services as defined by the U. S. Department of Health and Human Services (1990):

❑ Maximize individual independence.
❑ Provide the least restrictive setting for care.
❑ Encourage client input to decision making.
❑ Respect individual differences.
❑ Serve the chronically ill, as well as provide proactive treatment for those with chronic disabilities.
❑ Promote wellness.

Awareness of these dimensions can help counselors provide the best quality of care for midlife and older women clients. Each of these stances can empower women.

Attitudes toward aging are changing, and the aging process no longer is primarily associated with disease and dependency. Lifestyle factors, most notably diet, exercise, and stress management, and early intervention are now considered to be directly associated with the prevention of debilitating conditions, including strokes and hip fractures (U.S. Department of Health and Human Services, 1990).

Prevention is the key to a healthy and satisfying life. Given that older women may not have had the advantage of educational interventions at a time in their lives to make a significant difference in terms of total prevention of chronic health problems, it is never too late to begin to change patterns of poor health maintenance to those promoting a healthy lifestyle. Traditionally, physicians and nurses have been the health professionals who have offered health counseling to older women, while social workers visited them in their homes and in nursing homes. Now is the time for all mental health professionals to recognize their role in helping midlife and older women to prevent chronic illness, to ameliorate serious health problems, and to promote wellness.

To identify strengths and help women build on them, counselors need knowledge about organic factors, whether controllable or not, and about ways to reduce stress, whether it is environmental, interpersonal, or intrapersonal. They also need strategies for increasing competence, self-esteem, coping skills, and support systems. This paradigm is based on a formula proposed by George Albee, the grandfather of preventive mental health. Albee (1982) proposed this formula for the prediction of the incidence of emotional disturbance:

$$\text{Incidence of Emotional Disorders} = \frac{\text{Organic Factors} + \text{Stress}}{\text{Competence} + \text{Self-Esteem} + \text{Coping Skills} + \text{Support}}$$

Thus, if organic factors can be controlled or at least brought into awareness, if stress can be reduced, and if competence, self-esteem, coping skills, and support can be increased, the incidence of emotional disturbance will be decreased. This formula is also quite applicable to improving the health of older women.

Several years ago Blocher (1966) suggested that "human behavior is too complex and the interaction effects among the various behavioral determinants too intricate for a simple set of diagnostic constructs tied to causal factors to be adequate" (p. 128). Blocher defined five levels of human effectiveness in terms of the degree of control that individuals can exert over their environment and their affective responses. *Mastery* is the highest level of human effectiveness; the individual enters into active, planful interaction with the environment rather than merely reacting to it and has feelings of adequacy, mastery, and security in most roles. At the *coping* level, behavior is planful and largely goal-oriented, with the individual reacting to life as a challenge rather than with defeatist attitudes. Anxiety does not extinguish appropriate risk taking behavior. Individuals at the *striving* level have some degree of control over their affective responses but often alternate between feelings of hope and confidence and feelings of resignation and despair. The person's life is likely to consist of a series of crises and emergencies that would be preventable if planning and organization were more effective. At the *inertia* level, the person is unlikely to be economically or socially self-sufficient or independent and reacts to environmental demands in ways to avoid immediate punishments or failures or to secure very immediate gratifications. Such individuals have difficulty accepting responsibility for their behavior or its consequences and tend to project responsibility for difficulties upon others, often feel at the mercy of fate, and tend to show indifference and distrust. The *panic* level is characterized by actual loss of control over affective responses and over the immediate and short-term environment.

The person may have intense feelings of being out of control and of being at the mercy of hostile and uncontrollable forces. She or he may make active attempts at suicide, become violently aggressive, or show extreme withdrawal behavior, and require short- or long-term hospitalization.

Five treatment modalities for working with older adults and their families that interact with Blocher's levels of human effectiveness were proposed by Sterns, Weis, and Perkins (1984). Their treatment modalities range from more cognitively oriented and less intense to more affectively oriented and more intense. They suggested the modalities of educational intervention, peer support, group counseling, family therapy, and individual counseling. Their modalities parallel Blocher's levels of human functioning from mastery to panic, depending upon the individual's needs and the family's effectiveness in dealing with the issues facing it in providing support and care for the older adult.

Women who are currently functioning at a mastery or coping level can be reached more efficiently through educational interventions. All women need to be encouraged to take more responsibility for their own health and can benefit from increased, up-to-date knowledge about health issues. Some women who may currently be functioning at the striving level may also benefit from peer support. Those women who are at the inertia or panic levels may need group, family, or individual counseling. These different educational and counseling interventions will now be addressed. Later, broader-based interventions involving consultation, community programs, and health care policies will be presented.

Educational Interventions

Women can be empowered by greater awareness and encouragement to be more active in their own health care. Aging women are a highly diverse group. It is important to understand differences stemming from ethnic and cultural diversity and cohort groups. Taking cohort perspective means understanding social and historical circumstances that characterize different developmental experiences of various age groups (Riley, 1985). For example, members of younger cohorts may be more receptive to educational, prevention oriented approaches to counseling because they are more likely to have more education, hold higher level jobs, and have been less socialized to accept subservient roles than members of older cohorts.

Because illness robs many women of their sense of mastery and sometimes throws them into a panic state, it is important for all women to have regular medical examinations to prevent and monitor health problems. These examinations should include the usual blood tests, heart exam, PAP smear, breast exam, and for women over 50, a yearly mammogram. Doctors should be alert to early signs of heart disease, cancer, osteoporosis, arthritis, incontinence, hearing impairment, alcoholism, depression, and dementia. Women need to be encouraged to be more active in their relationships with their physicians. Asking for their blood pressure, cholesterol level, weight, PAP smear and mammogram results and recording those readings would give women a greater sense of control over their own bodies. When they have their next check-up, they can compare their results and know how changes in their diet and exercise patterns have affected the test results.

Beyond the regular medical exam, women who are susceptible to osteoporosis should be tested for bone loss regularly. Of course, physicians should encourage their women patients to do breast self-examination (BSE), to stop smoking, and to control their weight, cholesterol, and blood pressure through nutrition and exercise. Because over-medication is a major problem (Wolfe, 1991), women must become more proactive in asking the reason for different medications, if they are absolutely necessary, what the side effects are, and the dosage and duration of treatment. They must also be encouraged to remind physicians of any other medication they are taking, especially if they are seeing more than one doctor, and to ask if there is any interaction among the different medications. Women need to monitor their response to new medications carefully and call the physician immediately if they have undesirable side effects. They should maintain their own records of the different medications they have taken over the years and their responses to them, especially if they move or change physicians.

Specific recommendations regarding various health problems can be encouraged by the counselor who is working in concert with the physician and client to promote a healthy lifestyle. Masling (1988) has pointed out that menopausal symptoms can be easily relieved, but women often do not know where to seek help or information. In working with midlife women, counselors can be supportive of their concerns regarding the climacteric, such as hot flushes and vaginal dryness. Knowing that women who have gone through menopause often need to use a topical jelly for lubrication can be valuable to a post-menopausal woman who becomes concerned about painful intercourse. Relieving a menopausal woman's fears about the strangeness of her symptoms of hot flashes and early morning wakefulness can help her feel more comfortable and accept the universality of her symptoms. This approach often helps to put other major life events into their proper perspective because most of the research indicates that menopause is not a significant problem for women unless it is accompanied by another major life event, such as a divorce or the loss of a sex partner.

The use of Estrogen Replacement Therapy (ERT) should be understood by those counseling midlife women. ERT has advantages in terms of prevention of osteoporosis and the relief of menopausal symptoms, but raises concerns regarding the research findings on uterine cancer. Many midlife women need support when they are faced with the recommendation to have a hysterectomy, because as Wolfe (1991) has indicated, approximately 25% of such operations are unnecessary. Since many women are isolated from other women because of their primary responsibility to their families, putting a woman who is considering such an operation in touch with other women who have had a hysterectomy or who have chosen not to have one can be helpful, especially if varied viewpoints are presented. The final decision must be a medical one, and should be made with the wisdom of a second or third unbiased medical opinion. All risk factors need to be explained clearly by the physician; including the possibility of cancer; the continuation of menstrual bleeding, the likelihood that fibroid tumors, if present will shrink after the cessation of menses; and the necessity of ERT, if the ovaries are removed. Women need to be reassured that menopause or a hysterectomy will not interfere with their capacity for sexual enjoyment.

Women who are prone to have osteoporosis need to do whatever they can to prevent the onset of significant bone loss. It is difficult to predict which women might be susceptible, so all women should be aware of the need to fortify their diets with calcium.

Because many women do not drink milk or their bodies become intolerant of milk in later years, dietary supplements are often necessary. The role of exercise in strengthening supportive muscles can not be overstated. Perhaps, in the future, all women's groups will start or end with brisk walking to encourage women to become more physically active. Women who already have osteoporosis need to be encouraged to be as active as they can and to be tolerant of their need to rest when they are in pain. Counselors should remember that each person has a different pain tolerance level, so that listening to the client about how she feels may help relieve some of the pain. Just as with other serious health problems, osteoporotic women need support and encouragement to find other outlets in their lives that give them satisfaction, whether that is continuing to work, talking on the phone with friends, watching TV, or pursuing a hobby. Having something to look forward to can help sustain life and make pain tolerable.

Exercise seems to be the treatment of choice among health conscious counselors for alleviating menopausal symptoms (Gannon, 1988) and among prevention oriented physicians for weight loss and preventing hypertension leading to possible stroke (Wolfe, 1991). After high blood pressure has been detected, if diet and exercise do not reduce it, medication may be indicated. Women who are on medication need to be encouraged to continue taking it with physician monitoring until their condition has sufficiently improved, which may take months or years. Salt intake needs to be eliminated or severely restricted for controlling blood pressure, with salt substitutes proving quite satisfactory.

Because incontinence is a problem that keeps many women at home, they need to learn that there are many solutions to this condition. Preventing and relieving the problem can take the form of learning and practicing exercises to strengthen the muscles of the bladder. These exercises consist of constricting the muscles around the vagina, holding for 10 to 20 seconds, and releasing. Women can work up to 10 contractions done 20 times per day in a month's time. When these exercises are done several times a day over a few weeks, the muscles become tighter and better able to restrict the flow of urine. The recent introduction of a new product on the market, unobtrusive absorbent pads, allows many women who are afraid of having "an accident" to participate fully in activities outside the home. Restricting the intake of fluids may also help. Some women may need minor surgery to tighten the muscles that became displaced in childbirth and that lost their elasticity over the years. The procedure that is least invasive, exercise, should be the first to be tried. Some women will be delighted to learn that the bladder-strengthening exercises are also those recommended to increase sexual pleasure.

The prevention of many forms of cancer is still basically a mystery. Cigarette smoking certainly has the clearest link to lung cancer. The prevention of lung cancer should begin as early as possible by encouraging girls and women to never start smoking or (for those who do) to stop smoking as soon as possible. The belief that smoking will keep one's weight down should be balanced with an understanding of the facts about the devastation of lung cancer. With so many more women dying of lung cancer now than ever before, counselors need to be very proactive in encouraging women to stop smoking and to stay abreast of the research on the effects of passive smoking on lung cancer and other health problems.

For many forms of cancer, such as breast, uterine, and colorectal, early detection is the best that can be done. BSE, yearly check-ups, and mammograms are essential in the early signal network for breast cancer. All women's support groups should address the procedure of BSE's and how to get women to have mammograms. PAP smears provide a reading of precancerous uterine and cervical cells. Stool tests can indicate the need for further exams to detect colorectal cancer. Using sunscreen to avoid the sun's harmful ultraviolet rays can help prevent skin cancers. A family history of cancer is important information to forewarn the woman and her physician. It goes without saying that hazardous environmental conditions need to be avoided, but what all these conditions are has not been clearly delineated by research.

Women who must have a mastectomy or lumpectomy and chemotherapy need all the support that they can get from family, friends, physicians, and counselors. Exploring how she will feel about her body after surgery can often help a woman deal with her concerns and those of her husband or partner. Facing the encouraging statistics about survival with early detection can help many women in the decision making process.

Peer Support Groups

Many midlife and older women can benefit from peer support groups which are becoming much more readily accessible today for all types of physical and mental health concerns (Waters & Goodman, 1991). Many support groups can be found in vocational-technical and adult community schools; in community colleges through displaced homemaker programs; in college and university programs for returning women (Schlossberg, Lynch, & Chickering, 1989); in community agencies for stroke victims, cancer patients, or alcoholics; in hospitals for menopausal concerns, hysterectomy, breast surgery, or depression; and through churches and synagogues for bereavement and spiritual guidance. Senior centers offer mutual support groups for elders coping with limited vision or blindness, Alzheimer's disease (Mace & Rabins, 1981), or loss.

Conyne (1991) summarized the common denominators in successful primary prevention programs, in which they

—targeted a population or setting based on a data base.
—changed life trajectories of participants.
—developed new skills.
—strengthened natural support systems.
—emphasized cultural and ethnic diversity.
—evaluated their effectiveness appropriately.

Described in *14 Ounces of Prevention: A Casebook for Practitioners* (Price, Cowen, Lorion, & Ramos-McKay, 1988), Widow-to-Widow, a mutual help program for the widowed, is an exemplary program by these standards.

These mutual support groups help their members gain knowledge about their physical or mental problem, but more importantly, they share their experiences and coping strategies. By sharing in groups, individuals come to realize that they are not alone in facing their illness and they gain strength through feeling understood and accepted.

Family Therapy

The family context is very important in considering counseling interventions with middle-aged and elderly women. Most midlife women are a vital part of their family. They often do have problems that involve other family members, whether it is a concern about "What am I going to do with the rest of my life now that I am no longer needed as a mother?" or a worry about how to deal with boomerang kids and aging parents, how to fulfill their own needs by returning to school and having a career, or how to reassess the marriage relationship. Marriage counseling can be very helpful for motivating the midlife couple to achieve new intimacy and goals. Family therapy can help family systems achieve higher levels of functioning both in communicating and problem solving.

When families are called upon to deal with an elderly family member, they can bring issues out into the open and involve the older person with the help of the family therapist. Mother-daughter relationships can be strengthened through family counseling. The genogram developed by Bowen (1978) is an excellent tool for looking at families over three generations and can be helpful in exploring family patterns of disease, such as cancer and alcoholism, and emotional problems, such as schizophrenia and dementia.

Although there is a perception that most older women live in nursing homes, actually only 5% of the elderly population (adults 65 and older) are institutionalized (Hooyman & Kiyak, 1991). The vast majority of elderly women live in their own homes with support from family, friends, and agencies, or live with relatives. When and if the time comes that a family must make a decision that they must move an older person into their own homes or that they can no longer care for the older relative in their homes due to illness or other circumstances, the family can benefit from the help of a counselor with a family systems perspective in considering different options ranging from assisted care to a nursing home.

Group and Individual Counseling

Many women can improve their lives with group or individual counseling by learning to manage their physical or mental problems more effectively. Group counseling can motivate clients at the inertia level of functioning through recognition that others in similar circumstances have learned coping skills and strategies. Individual counseling can empower women who are at a panic level of functioning by helping them to gain control of their lives and to cope with the problems that life has presented to them in the best way possible for themselves. Basic counseling skills of listening, attending, and reflecting can be unobtrusive in helping women reclaim their identities or reinvent themselves. Knight (1986) has cautioned psychotherapists to be aware of countertransference issues when working with older clients. Chiriboga (1989) suggested that some midlife and older women may want to see a therapist with a Jungian approach because reflecting on the "second half of life" (Jung, 1960) can be very enriching.

Physical and psychological problems are so often intertwined that it is difficult for the woman to separate them by herself. Menopausal women who are experiencing the loss of children or a marriage partner and who are confused about future career options may focus on their hot flashes and feel overburdened with the stress with which they are confronted. Patterson and Lynch (1988) have recommended that individual counseling from a supportive counselor well-educated about midlife issues can help women make significant changes. Counselors trained in Schlossberg's (1990) transition theory can help their clients cope with life events and nonevents more effectively. Elderly widows may focus on their pain and physical symptoms, especially if they are isolated at home or been recently moved to a son or daughter's home or into an unfamiliar nursing home. Rather than write off the older woman as unable to cope, or worse, support over-medicating her, a counselor trained in gerontological issues (Ganikos, 1979; Myers, 1989b) can provide a listening ear through the transition.

With the leadership of a skilled and knowledgeable therapist, group counseling can give women the opportunity to share their concerns about their symptoms with other menopausal women, relieve them of feelings of isolation, and normalize their worries. Relaxation techniques taught by experienced counselors and practiced in groups can help hypertensive patients to relax and not allow stress to take its toll. Biofeedback methods also are helpful to people recovering from a heart attack and to those with high blood pressure. Kegel exercises can be taught in a woman's group or individually to women who are becoming incontinent. Behavioral techniques and support systems to maintain motivation have been shown to be very effective in helping people stop smoking and lose weight.

In dealing with late-onset hearing impairment, counselors can recognize that two or more of every eight clients will have hearing problems severe enough to cause significant communication problems (Hittner & Bornstein, 1990). Specific strategies that can be employed to improve the physical environment for group counseling are a quiet room, improved acoustics, hearing rehabilitation referrals, group hearing aids, specific placement of group members, and use of visual aids. Hittner and Bornstein also suggested behavioral techniques such as repetition, increased loudness, clearer enunciation, special seating, and use of nonverbal cues.

Although alcoholism is a greater problem for older men than for older women, there are many elderly women who are alcoholics, especially silent alcoholics. Dealing with the specific drinking of the individual older client requires a greater range of counseling goals and a broader range of treatment strategies than is needed for alcoholism treatment programs for younger clients (Blake, 1990). Looking at the increasing numbers of older persons, the increased consumption of alcohol by women, and the decline of values that mediated against women drinking, we can expect that the number of older women problem drinkers will increase in the future (Finney & Moos, 1984). In conjunction with Alcoholics Anonymous and other 12-step treatment programs, family, group, and individual counseling may also prove effective with midlife and older women who are alcoholics.

Many adjunct therapies help women cope with the aftermath of the mastectomy. Positive thinking, meditation, and guided imagery have been shown to provide support and strength to many women who are exploring ways to control the spread of cancer throughout their bodies. Women clients coping with the nausea, vomiting, and hair loss of chemotherapy need extra support from their counselors and families through these extremely trying times. Helping a woman through the cycle of loss, whether for a breast, her uterus, or facing death as cancer metastasizes, can be one of the most difficult and important roles that a counselor fulfills. Helping women find the inner strength to face disfigurement or death takes maturity and a special compassion on the part of the counselor.

For women who are in institutions such as nursing homes, the staff and mental health counselors can lead groups with different approaches for different problems. Life review (Waters, 1990) and the use of early recollections (Sweeney, 1990) can be helpful to elderly women to give them a sense of accomplishment and to recognize that their lives have been fulfilling.

For mildly agitated and mildly confused patients, Reality Orientation has traditionally been the treatment of choice used by staff and counselors to remind patients of who they are and what day it is and to calm their concerns (Hogstel, 1979). However, a review of the literature yielded insufficient evidence to support the routine use of Reality Orientation when compared to less behavioral therapies (Miller, 1987). Research indicates that Validation therapy (Feil, 1982) could be more effective with more severely disoriented and agitated nursing home patients. Music therapy has also been found to calm agitated patients. Bright (1986) found that music therapy was helpful in reducing wandering, aggression, agitation, and apathy among institutionalized older persons. Poetry therapy and various media of expressive art have been shown to be helpful adjuncts to counseling for older clients (Silvermarie, 1988).

Because the causes of dementia, particularly Alzheimer's disease, are not known, we cannot yet prevent or treat it. Physicians must be alert to not misdiagnosing depression, delirium, over-medication, malnutrition, or dehydration as early signs of Alzheimer's disease. As the population ages, counselors who become trained in gerontological counseling will be working more and more with women and men Alzheimer's patients and with their family caregivers. Sensitivity to the confusion and sense of loss that women experience as they come to understand that they are no longer functioning as they once did is essential for the counselor.

Finally, when women do make choices about their right to die, counselors can fulfill an important function in helping them to prepare. Understanding the developmental phases and emotional states that accompany loss and death is essential for counselors working with the terminally ill (Kubler-Ross, 1969). Knowing the procedure for having a valid living will and knowing state laws regarding such issues as the right to die, forced feeding, and family responsibility are important for the counselor.

CASE EXAMPLES

The following are case examples of a midlife and an older woman with health concerns who were helped through counseling interventions.

The Case of Mercedes—A Midlife Woman

Mercedes is a 49-year-old married Hispanic woman who has been working as a secretary for an office supply company for the past 10 years. She has had irregular periods for about a year and has had trouble sleeping recently. She wakes several times during the night drenched in perspiration and then is wide awake at 4 a.m. She told her friend, Carmen, that she has been having "strange feelings" in her head, but when

Carmen suggested that Mercedes see a doctor, she refused. Mercedes' son, 26, an auto parts salesman, married a year ago and was transferred out of state. Last summer, her daughter, 21, returned to Venezuela to help her aunt open a school for children. After their daughter left, Mercedes's husband Manuel lost his job, and started drinking more heavily, and they argued constantly. Then Mercedes had a call from her sister that their mother, 69, a widow, had fallen and broken her hip. Mercedes rushed to the hospital and learned that, after surgery, her mother would need a long period of recuperation with physical therapy. Mercedes's world began falling apart, and she became depressed.

At more urging by Carmen, Mercedes reluctantly agreed to see her physician. After a careful examination, the doctor prescribed estrogen and explained the advantages and risks involved. He also suggested that Mercedes could benefit by talking with a counselor. Carmen, who when her father died, had talked with Mrs. Diaz, the counselor, went with Mercedes for her first appointment. Mrs. Diaz helped Mercedes sort through her problems and together they developed the following plan. Mercedes' immediate concern about her mother could be handled through the hospital's physical therapy and rehabilitation program. Mercedes and her sister visited their mother every day while she was in the hospital. When returned to her own home, Mercedes' mother was to be followed by a home health care nurse and a social worker.

Manuel found another job and agreed to go with Mercedes to talk with the parish priest about their marital disputes. At the urging of the counselor, Mercedes joined a women's support group in the community center addressing issues of midlife women, such as menopausal symptoms and health care. Meanwhile, Mercedes and Carmen started an exercise program that involved brisk walking. Through individual counseling, Mercedes decided to enter the community college to explore a new career. Later she joined a Women in Transition group at the local community college. When she completed her program, she moved into an advertising job with her company and felt more satisfied with her life.

The Case of Mrs. M.—An Older Woman

Mrs. M. is a 76-year-old woman who has been living alone in a rural area since the death of her husband a year ago. She has several chronic conditions, specifically arthritis, hypertension, poor hearing, and poor vision (she is legally blind and is unable to drive). She relies on her daughter for weekly visits to the grocery store and other errands. Recently her memory seems to be deteriorating, she is losing weight, and she has been sleeping most of the day. She is also having difficulty managing her personal affairs.

Mrs. M.'s daughter feels that her mother is no longer able to live alone and is considering a nursing home placement. She is afraid that her mother will leave the stove burner on or will fall. Mrs. M. refuses to accept help from "strangers" and insists that she is capable of managing her own affairs. When her daughter mentioned the possibility of moving, Mrs. M. was highly distressed and refused to discuss the matter further.

Mrs. M.'s daughter finds it increasingly stressful to manage her own life as she works full time and has two teen-age children at home. Her husband owns a small business and often works 50 to 60 hours a week to cut back on the expense of hiring extra help. Finally, Mrs. M.'s daughter telephoned the community mental health center's geriatric assessment program for assistance. She was introduced to a counselor and encouraged to bring her mother for an assessment.

The assessment information is crucial to determining intervention. The geriatric assessment included a complete medical evaluation as well as an assessment of cognitive and emotional factors. Social, environmental, and dietary factors are also evaluated. Following the evaluation process, it was determined that Mrs. M. was confused because she was not following her medication regime correctly. In addition, she appeared to be reacting to the loss of her husband with depression. She missed his constant companionship and had not cultivated many friends or social activities over the years because she devoted herself to meeting his needs, especially over the few years before his death as he had lung cancer and needed quite a bit of care.

The counselor conferred with Mrs. M. on three areas: (1) allowing some outside assistance which would let her remain independently in her own home, (2) ventilating feelings related to her husband's illness and death, and (3) taking risks to meet new people and attempts to socialize weekly outside her home. Mrs. M. received calls from the peer telephone assistance program set up by the local senior center. The peer helpers made contact with Mrs. M. and helped her arrange transportation to the center for weekly meetings. Mrs. M. agreed to meet with the counselor in her home to talk about her feelings and gave her daughter permission to hire a college student to stay with her at nights and to run errands for her. A visiting nurse helped to regulate and monitor Mrs. M.'s medication; thus she was no longer confused and her nightly insomnia and daytime sleeping went away. She found that she could continue to manage her affairs effectively.

RESOURCES FOR MIDLIFE AND OLDER WOMEN

The following is a list of some of the resources that counselors will find helpful in working with midlife and older women.

Wellness and Health Promotion

❏ National Women's Health Network
224 7th Street, SE
Washington, DC 20003
(202) 543-9222

❏ National Institute on Aging
Information Office
Bldg. 31, Room 5C35
Bethesda, MD 20205

❏ National Council on Aging
Publications
600 Maryland Avenue, SW
Washington, DC 20024

❏ American Association of Retired Persons Health Advocacy Services
1909 Kent Street, NW
Washington, DC 20049

❏ Healthwise, Inc.
P. O. Box 1989
Boise, ID 83701

❏ Healthy Older People's Hotline
1-800-336-4797

Midlife Women

❏ Midlife Counseling Associates
1361 South Eliseo Drive
Kentfield, CA 94904
(415) 461-0900

❏ Women in Transition
112 South 16th Street
Philadelphia, PA 19102
(215) 563-9556

❑ Hot Flash (A Newsletter for Midlife and Older Women) Center for Continuing Education, S.B.S. State University of New York Stony Brook, NY 11794-4310

Major Health Problems

❑ American Heart Association
7320 Greenville Avenue
Dallas, TX 75231
(214) 750-5300
❑ National Cancer Institute
Cancer Information Service (CIS)
Bldg. 31, Room 10A18
Bethesda, MD 20205
(800) 638-6694

❑ Breast Care Advisory Center
P.O.Box 224
Kensington, MD 20795
❑ Alzheimer's Disease and Related Disorders Association
70 East Lake Street
Chicago, IL 60601

Support Services

❑ Displaced Homemaker Network
1411 K. Street, NW
Washington, DC 20005
❑ The American Bar Association
Commission on Legal Problems of the Elderly
1800 M Street, NW
Washington, DC 20038

❑ Children of Aging Parents
2761 Trenton Road
Levittown, PA 19056
❑ National Association for Home Care
519 C Street, NE
Washington, DC 20002

Policy Information

❑ National Health Policy Forum
2011 I Street, NW Suite 200
Washington, DC 20006
❑ National Conference of State Legislatures
Health Policy Publication Series
1050 Seventeenth Street Suite 2100
Denver, CO 80265

❑ Health Policy Advisory Center
17 Murray Street
New York, NY 10007
(212) 267-8890

PREVENTION, SOCIAL INTERVENTIONS, AND HEALTH-CARE POLICIES

Prevention

Prevention in a restricted sense means inhibiting the development of disease before it occurs. However, the definition of prevention (Albee, 1982) has been expanded to include three levels: *Primary prevention* is the prevention of disease by altering susceptibility or reducing exposure for susceptible individuals; *secondary prevention* refers to early detection and treatment of disease; and *tertiary prevention* is the alleviation of disability resulting from disease and attempts to restore effective functioning. Counselors are in an excellent position to promote all levels of prevention for women.

The President's Commission on Mental Health, Task Panel on Prevention (1978) defined the essential characteristics of primary prevention as a network of strategies qualitatively different from the field's dominant approach.

1. Prevention is proactive, building adaptive strengths, coping resources, and health.
2. Prevention is concerned with total populations, especially groups at risk.
3. Prevention assumes that equipping people with personal and environmental resources for coping is the best way to ward off maladaptive behavior.
4. Prevention's main tools and models are those of education and social engineering.

Nowhere are these principles more applicable than in the field of health counseling for women.

Health Service Utilization Models

There are several possible reasons why many older people fail to seek medical help for chronic conditions. One is the belief that these conditions are natural concomitants of aging and that a physician can do little to relieve or cure them. Many older people do not report symptoms or seek help because they fear they have a serious illness and are concerned about the expense of physician visits, diagnostic tests, and hospitalizations. They also do not want to be a burden or dependent. Another problem is the negative attitudes of health professionals, some of whom believe that older patients are more difficult to manage and that the diseases associated with aging cannot be reversed. Such perceptions by health professionals interact with older patients' attitudes to decrease the likelihood that the elderly will receive adequate care.

Three models of utilization of health services are relevant to understanding the differential use of services by midlife and older women. The first model is behavioral (Aday & Andersen, 1974). It has three important variables: (1) Predisposing, such as sex, ethnicity, and education; (2) Enabling, such as income level, perception of ability to pay, insurance including Medicare and Medicaid, transportation, and information about availability, costs, and criteria for receiving services; and (3) Need, such as symptoms of health or illness, perceived need for health care, and functional health problems. This model gives counselors some tangible factors to consider in helping women clients to use the health services they need.

The second model of health services use is called a health belief model (Maiman & Becker, 1974). This model proposes that people will not seek health services unless (1) they view themselves as vulnerable or susceptible to a disease that (2) they perceive as having severe consequences. Further, (3) they must see an association between performing particular health practices and outcomes, and (4) they must be convinced that the benefits outweigh the barriers. All four conditions must operate simultaneously. This model focuses on the individual's perceptions, motives, and self-reported likelihood of taking action rather than on demographic and social conditions, as the behavioral model does.

Many women do not believe or see the relevance of services for themselves; for example, the need to quit smoking does not apply to them. Often women do not believe that they can change their behavior or believe that if they do, it will not make a difference, for example, watching one's cholesterol level to reduce the likelihood of a heart attack. Further, they must be convinced that the benefits exceed the costs. For example, only if an older woman sees herself as susceptible to breast cancer will she do monthly breast exams. This model is important for counselors to know so that clients can be helped to move toward an internal locus of control and understand the consequences of their health-care behavior. Counselors are in an excellent position to help their women clients expand their belief systems, provided they have access to their clients, which means that counselors may need to be assertive and outreaching.

The third model is called a congruence model or person-environment (P-E) fit model (Kahana, Liang, & Felton, 1980). This model has been applied to the integration of older people with their physical and social environments. Health-care behavior is a fit between a person's perceived and objective needs, cognitive and physical capacities to handle the health-care system, informal support systems, and the health-care delivery system's characteristics, constraints, and opportunities. If there is a fit between the environment and the individual's perceived objective health needs, he or she will utilize the services. If there is not a fit, the person will not use the services.

This congruence model holds promise for planning alternative health-care delivery systems that meet the needs of midlife and older women clients. Its greatest strength is that it does not view the health-care delivery system as static and that it recognizes that the system needs to be modified to meet the needs of older people and members of different ethnic and socioeconomic groups. The emphasis is on developing services that fit the needs of all types of clients. The model predicts use can be most effective if (1) patients' attitudes, values, and knowledge about health care can be enhanced and (2) health-care settings can be designed to be more sensitive to the needs of all types of clients. This model has been most effective in San Francisco in modifying health-care services to be responsive to the particular needs of Chinese, Filipino, and Italian elderly who do not speak English, and whose health beliefs are often not congruent with the prevailing American model (Hooyman & Kiyak, 1991).

Consultation with Family Caregivers and Medical Personnel

Counselors will provide much consultation for family caregivers because, as the population ages, more families will be involved with health-care issues. More consultation with families who are caring for their elderly loved ones with Alzheimer's disease will be a part of the counselor's role. Respite care provided by professionals and volunteers can challenge counselors to provide training to those participating in these helping programs. Security and freedom from harm is most needed by dementia patients because generally many of them have years of reasonably sound physical health. When families need to make decisions about their limits in keeping the person in the home, counselors can be most helpful in considering all the alternatives (Myers, 1989a). Advocacy and consultation with physicians, nurses, and other medical personnel will be essential elements in the counselor's work.

Community Programs

Because mental health professionals are in such short supply, community programs must be developed to help women take their health more seriously. One important role for a counselor is to become a trainer for peer helpers and volunteers in senior centers and in community agencies. The outreach model of community mental health in which health services are taken to the neighborhoods, homes and even the streets is a very important concept in working with midlife and older women. This outreach approach is especially important in dealing with different ethnic groups of women. For example, counselors must be aware of the beliefs about health among Hispanic and African-American women and change the services to meet the cultural needs of those clients. Many elderly women are homebound and need home services rather than having to be transported to the doctor for medication monitoring. In other words—let's change the system, not the person.

Counselors working with midlife and aging women must know their resources and be able to give clients information about community services, support programs, Medicare, Medicaid, insurance, and so forth. This means counselors must network with various agencies to develop positive working relationships, as referrals must often be made to provide comprehensive counseling services.

Health-Care Policies and Aging Women

National policies on aging do not adequately address the needs of the diverse group of aging women in our society. With the majority of elderly women living at or below the poverty level, many lack needed services. Most older adults live in households with a spouse. However, women are far more likely to be living alone, and this likelihood increases dramatically after age 75. For example, approximately 39% of women over the age of 65 live alone, compared to 14% of men. Approximately 50% of women over the age of 75 live alone compared to 20% of men (Brody, Brock, & Williams, 1987).

This information highlights the importance of health services specifically geared to the needs of aging women. Unfortunately, many needed services are not readily available. Aging women experience a distinct disadvantage when it comes to the delivery of health services in our nation because public policies have not adequately addressed the health-care needs of the aging population in general, let alone address the specific health care needs of midlife and older women. This situation is ironic considering that women consistently make greater use of the health-care system than men. Because women have not had economic or political power, they have not had much of a voice in changing the health delivery system. They have had to leave much of the determination of their needs to an unresponsive, bureaucratic system.

Medicare does not cover health-care needs associated with chronic conditions, preventive care, outpatient care, long-term care, or supportive care. Private and public insurance often does not cover routine preventive procedures important to wellness for midlife women, who are increasingly assuming the role of primary caregiver to the older population (Older Women's League, 1988).

Three shortcomings in public health policy that directly affect women as caregivers and care receivers have been listed by Faulkner and Micchelli (1988). First, the current

Medicaid policy requiring couples to spend down resources to cover the cost of nursing home care leaves the remaining spouse impoverished. Because women generally outlive men and men are usually several years older than their wives (at least in the current cohort of elderly), the results have had a devastating effect on elderly women. Second, public policies are designed to provide services that replace rather than support the family unit. Families are most likely to turn to social services when they have exhausted their own resources in order to justify the use of the programs. Female caregivers are expected to "manage without support until their emotional exhaustion or stress-produced physical illness creates a crisis in caregiving, to which the community will finally make a crisis response" (Faulkner & Micchelli, 1988, p. 13). Finally, public policy is oriented toward institutional rather than home care despite the preference for home care by the consumer. In essence, public policy often encourages families to seek institutional care because needed services such as day care and home assistance are inadequately covered by Medicaid. Moreover, for the middle class working family, the expenses may be overwhelming. It should also be emphasized that health policies are not sufficiently "culturally sensitive" and flexible when it comes to meeting the needs of diverse ethnic groups in our society (Padgett, 1988).

Policies and services required to meet the mental health needs of older adults are even more inadequate than those for physical health. This problem is a result of the shortage of mental health professionals trained to provide psychological treatment to older adults and a reimbursement system that limits outpatient treatment and does not adequately cover inpatient expenses. The reluctance of older adults to seek treatment, especially prevention-oriented programs, due to the stigma they and society in general attach to receiving mental health-care compounds the problem (Older Women's League, 1988).

Policy changes are needed to find ways to finance and deliver a continuum of mental and physical health-care services, particularly community based programs to reduce the strain on families (Rodeheaver & Datan, 1988). Because the majority of people over the age of 85 in need of care are women and the majority of caregivers are middle-aged women, health-care policy reform is clearly a women's issue. Counselors aware of these problems are in a better position to promote programs that will influence policy changes. We must assume a proactive role in health-care policy reform as advocates for less empowered women.

CONCLUSION

Women are more interested and involved in their own health-care than ever before. A well-informed counselor is in a unique position to help women manage their lifestyles, get in touch with their beliefs and attitudes concerning health and the aging process, and promote wellness in the later years.

REFERENCES

Aday, L. A., & Andersen, R. (1974). A framework for the study of access to medical care. *Health Services Research, 9,* 208–220.

Albee, G. (1982). Preventing psychopathology and promoting human potential. American *Psychologist, 37,* 1043–1050.

American Psychiatric Association. (1987). *Diagnostic and statistical manual, DSM III-R* (3rd ed. rev.). Washington, DC: Author.

Atchley, R. C. (1991). *Social forces and aging* (6th ed.). Belmont, CA: Wadsworth.

Aviola, L. V. (1982). Aging, bone and osteoporosis. In S. G. Korenman (Ed.), *Endocrine aspects of aging* (pp. 149–230). New York: Elsevier Biomedical.

Bart, P. (1971). Depression in middle-aged women. In V. Gornick & B. K. Moran (Eds.), *Women in sexist society: Studies in power and powerlessness.* (pp. 99–107). New York: Basic Books.

Baruch, G., Barnett, R., & Rivers, C. (1983). *Lifeprints: New patterns of love and work for today's women. New York: New American Library.*

Blake, R. (1990). Mental health counseling and older problem drinkers. *Journal of Mental Health Counseling, 12*, 354–367.

Blocher, D. H. (1966). *Developmental counseling.* New York: Ronald Press.

Bowen, M. (1978). *Family therapy in clinical practice.* New York: Jason Aronson.

Bright, R. (1986). The use of music therapy and activities with demented patients who are deemed "difficult to manage." *Clinical Gerontologist, 6*, 131–-144.

Brody, J., Brock, D., & Williams, T. (1987). Trends in the health of the elderly population. *Annual Review of Public Health, 8*, 211–234.

Chiriboga, D. A. (1989). Mental health at the midpoint: Crisis, challenge, or relief? In S. Hunter & M. Sundel (Eds.), *Midlife myths: Issues, findings, and practical implications.* (pp. 116-144). Newbury Park, CA: Sage Publications.

Conyne, R. K. (1991) Gains in primary prevention: Implications for the counseling profession. *Journal of Counseling and Development, 69*, 277–279.

Cooke, D. J., & Greene, J. D. (1981). Types of life events in relation to symptoms at climacterium. *Journal of Psychosomatic Research, 25*, 5–11.

Cowen, G., Warren, L., & Young, J. (1985). Medical perceptions of menopausal symptoms. *Psychology of Women Quarterly. 9*, 3–14.

Deutsch, H. (1944). *The psychology of women: A psychoanalytic interpretation, (Vol. 2).* New York: Grune & Stratton.

Dyer, R. A. (1979). Menopause: A closer look for nurses. In D. K. Kjervik & I. M. Martinson (Eds.), *Women in stress: A nursing perspective.* (pp. 303-318). New York: Appleton-Century-Crofts.

Eastman, P., & Glasheen, L. K. (1990, July-August). Women's special risks. *AARP Bulletin. 31*, 3.

Faulkner, A. O., & Micchelli, M. (1988). The aging, the aged, and the very old: Women the policy makers forgot. *Women and Health, 14*, 5–19.

Feil, N. (1982). *Validation: The Feil method.* Cleveland: Edward Feil Productions.

Ferrini, A., & Ferrini, R. (1989). *Health in the later years.* Dubuque, IA: William C. Brown.

Finney, J. W., & Moos, R. H. (1984). Life stressors and problem drinking among older adults. In M. Galanter (Ed.), *Recent developments in alcoholism (Vol. 2).* (pp. 267–288). New York: Plenum.

Ganikos, M. L. (Ed.). (1979). *Counseling the aged: A training syllabus for educators.* Falls Church, VA: American Personnel and Guidance Association.

Gannon, L. (1988). The potential role of exercise in alleviation of menstrual disorders and menopausal symptoms: A theoretical synthesis of recent research. *Women and Health, 14*, 105–127.

Gee, E. M., & Kimball, M. M. (1987). *Women and aging.* Toronto, Ontario, Canada: Butterworths.

Grambs, J. D. (1989). *Women over forty: Visions and realities.* New York: Springer.

Gurland, B., Dean, L., Cross, P., & Golden, R. (1980). The epidemiology of depression and dementia in the elderly: The use of multiple indicators of these conditions. In J. O. Cole & J. E. Barrett, (Eds.), *Psychopathology in the aged.* (pp. 37–60). New York: Raven.

Hittner, A., & Bornstein, H. (1990). Group counseling with older adults: Coping with late-onset hearing impairment. *Journal of Mental Health Counseling, 12*, 332–341.

Hogstel, M. (1979). Use of reality orientation with aging confused patients. *Nursing Research, 28*, 161–165.

Hooyman, N. R., & Kiyak, H. A. (1991). *Social gerontology: A multidisciplinary perspective* (2nd ed.). Boston: Allyn & Bacon.

Jung, C. G. (1960). The stages of life. *Collected works. Vol. 8: The structure and dynamics of the psyche.* New York: Bollingen Foundation.

Kahana, E., Liang, J., & Felton, B. (1980). Alternative models of P-E fit: Prediction of morale in three nursing homes for the aged. *Journal of Gerontology, 35,* 584–595.

Knight, B. (1986). *Psychotherapy with older adults.* Newbury Park, CA: Sage Publications.

Kubler-Ross, E. (1969). *On death and dying.* New York: Macmillan.

Lennon, M. C. (1982). The psychological consequences of menopause: The importance of timing of a life state event. *Journal of Health and Social Behavior, 23,* 353–366.

Mace, N. L., & Rabins, P. V. (1981). *The thirty-six hour day: A family guide to caring for persons with memory loss in later life, Alzheimer's disease, and other dementing illnesses.* Baltimore: Johns Hopkins University.

Maiman, L. A., & Becker, M. H. (1974). The health belief model: Origins and correlates in psychological theory. *Health Education Monographs, 2,* 336–-353.

Markides, K. S., & Vernon, S. W. (1984). Aging, sex role orientation, and adjustment: A three-generation study of Mexican Americans. *Journal of Gerontology, 39,* 586–591.

Masling, J. (1988). Menopause: A change for the better? *Nursing Times, 84,* 35–38.

Mazess, R. B. (1982). On aging bone loss. *Clinical Orthopedics and Related Research, 165,* 239–252.

McCrea, F. B. (1983). The politics of menopause: The "discovery" of a deficiency disease. *Social Problems, 31,* 11–123.

Miller, M. H. (1987). The effects of validation therapy and reality orientation with disoriented nursing home residents. *Dissertation Abstracts International.* 2953A.

Moe, R. E. (1985). Breast disease in elderly women. In R. Andres, E. L. Bierman, & W. R. Hazzard (Eds.), *Principles of geriatric medicine.* (pp. 636–646). New York: McGraw-Hill.

Myers, J. E. (1989a). *Adult children and aging parents.* Alexandria, VA: American Association of Counseling and Development.

Myers, J. E. (1989b). *Infusing gerontological counseling into counselor preparation: Curriculum guide.* Alexandria, VA: American Association of Counseling and Development.

National Cancer Institute (1990). *Cancer statistics review, 1973-1987.* Washington, DC: Author.

National Center for Health Statistics. (1990). *Vital Statistics of the United States, 1987, Vol. 2, Mortality, Part A.* Washington, DC: Public Health Service.

National Institute of Health. (1983). *The menopause time of life.* (Publication No. 83-2461). Bethesda, MD: Author.

National Institute on Aging. (1987, July). *Answers about aging: The aging woman* (NIH Publication No. 87-2756). Washington, DC: Author.

Neugarten, B. L., Wood, V., Kraines, R. J., & Loomis, B. (1968). Women's attitudes toward menopause. In B. L. Neugarten (Ed.), *Middle age and aging* (pp. 195–200). Chicago: University of Chicago Press.

Older Women's League. (1988). The picture of health for midlife and older women in America. *Women and Health, 14,* 53–74.

Olsho, L. W., Harkins, S. W., & Lenhardt, M. L. (1985). Aging and the auditory system. In J. Birren & K. Schaie (Eds.), *Handbook of the psychology of aging.* (2nd ed.) (pp. 332–377). New York: Van Nostrand and Reinhold.

Padgett, D. (1988). Aging minority women: Issues in research and health policy. *Women and Health, 14,* 213–225.

Parlee, M. B. (1984). Reproductive issues, including menopause. In G. Baruch & J. Brooks-Gunn (Eds.), *Women in midlife* (pp. 303–313). New York: Plenum.

Patterson, M. M., & Lynch, A. Q. (1988). Menopause: Salient issues for counselors. *Journal of Counseling and Development, 67,* 185–188.

Pearson, B. P., & Beck, C. M. (1989). Physical health of elderly women. In J. D. Garner & S. O. Mercer (Eds.), *Women as they age: Challenge, opportunity, and triumph.* (pp. 149–174). New York: Hawthorne.

President's Commission on Mental Health, Task Panel on Prevention. (1978). *Report to the President.* Washington, DC: U.S. Government Printing Office.

Price, R., Cowen, E., Lorion, R. & Ramos-McKay, J. (Eds.). (1988). *14 ounces of prevention: A casebook for practitioners.* Washington, DC: American Psychological Association.

Public Health Service Task Force on Women's Health Issues. (1985, January-February). Women's health. (Vol. 1). *Public Health Reports, 101,* 73–106.

Riley, M. W. (1985). The changing older woman: A cohort perspective. In M. Haug, A. B. Ford, & M. Shaefor (Eds.), *The physical and mental health of aged women.* (pp. 3–15). New York: Springer.

Rodeheaver, D., & Datan, N. (1988). The challenge of double jeopardy: Toward a mental health agenda for aging women. *American Psychologist, 43*, 648–654.

Rosenthal, M. (1979). Psychological aspects of menopause. *Primary Care, 6*, 359.

Schlossberg, N. K. (1990). Training counselors to work with older adults. *Generations, 14*, 7–10.

Schlossberg, N. K., Lynch, A. Q., & Chickering, A. W. (1989). *Improving higher education environments for adults: Responsive programs and services from entry to departure.* San Francisco: Jossey-Bass.

Silvermarie, S. (1988). Poetry therapy with frail elderly in a nursing home. *Journal of Poetry Therapy, 2*, 72–83.

Sterns, H. L., Weis, D. M., & Perkins, S. E. (1984). A conceptual approach to counseling older adults and their families. *The Counseling Psychologist, 12*, 55–61.

Sweeney, T. J. (1990). Early recollections: A promising technique for use with older people. *Journal of Mental Health Counseling, 12*, 260–269.

Treloar, A. E. (1974). Menarche, menopause, and intervening fecundability. *Human Biology, 46*, 89–107.

Tyler, S., & Woodal, G. (1982). *Female health and gynecology across the life span.* Bowie, MD: Robert Brady.

U. S. Department of Health and Human Services. (1990). *Geriatric training curriculum for public health professionals.* Washington, DC: Public Health Service, Health Resources and Services Administration.

U.S. Surgeon General's Report (1986). *The health consequences of involuntary smoking.* (USDHHS Pub. No. 87-8398). Washington, DC: U.S. Government Printing Office.

Waldron, I. (1976). Why do women live longer than men? *Journal of Human Stress, 2*, 2–13.

Waters, E. B. (1984). Building on what you know: Techniques for individual and group counseling with older people. *The Counseling Psychologist, 12*, 63–73.

Waters, E. B. (1990). The life review: Strategies for working with individuals and groups. *Journal of Mental Health Counseling, 12*, 207–278.

Waters, E. B., & Goodman, J. (1991). *Counseling older adults: Practical strategies for counselors.* San Francisco: Jossey-Bass.

Wolfe, S. M. (1991). *Women's health alert.* Reading, MA: Addison-Wesley.

Part Five
CONCLUSION

11

Gender-Fair Counseling

Jan Van Buren
University of Missouri, Columbia

Counselors are expected to address a multitude of issues. As Scher and Good (1990) indicated, counselors are likely to be knowledgeable about the dynamics of counseling; however, their graduate training programs tend to ignore gender issues and multicultural concerns. They emphasized that for counselors to ignore the impact of gender roles in their work is an invitation to disaster. Because many people believe that gender characteristics are inherent in their nature rather than learned, they have difficulty facing the possibility of changing gender roles (Good, Gilbert, & Scher, 1990).

It is imperative that all counselors provide gender-fair counseling as they address gender issues in their work. Gender-fair counseling has been prescribed by professional counseling organizations such as the American School Counselors Association (ASCA) and the Council for Accreditation of Counseling and Related Educational Programs (CACREP). The federal government has passed legislation stating that sexism in federally supported educational operations is illegal (Title IX of the Education Amendments of 1972, Title II of the Education Amendments of 1976, and the Carl D. Perkins Vocational Education Act of 1984).

A comprehensive definition of gender-fair counseling has been developed by Van Buren et al. (1989). They defined gender-fair counseling as counseling services that facilitate the development of full client potential based upon the individual's unique characteristics (e.g., values, beliefs, interests, abilities, and personality), regardless of gender. There are four steps in gender-fair counseling: (1) examination of values and beliefs (of counselor and client) for the presence of sex bias, discrimination, or stereotyping, (2) confrontation of biased perceptions that limit client options, (3) initiation of action toward gender-fair goals, and (4) evaluation of outcomes.

Gender inequity has led to personal, social, and economic costs for many people in a variety of ways. Awareness of these inequities has prompted counselor certification and accreditation bodies to mandate gender-fair training in preservice counselor education programs. ASCA (1985) has as one of its basic goals delivering counseling to people equitably. One of ASCA's primary efforts involves working with school faculty members and the broader community to develop sensitivity to the concepts of race, sex, and the exceptional student.

CACREP (1988) also recognized the need for access and equity and mandated certain requirements for program objectives and curriculum. These requirements included the study of gender issues, trends, and changes in human roles that encompass traditional and nontraditional female and male roles. They also added the study of the changing roles for women and men as related to career development and counseling.

In this chapter I examined selected gender issues throughout the life span. The life span has been divided into the early, working, and retirement years. That section is followed by a discussion and presentation of a set of gender-fair counseling competencies designed for inclusion in either preservice or inservice programs. The competencies are organized into the following four categories: socialization and developmental issues, helping relationships, professional and ethical issues, and advocacy and change agentry issues. Selected teacher and student competencies for enhancing gender fairness are included. Strategies for making gender-fair counseling a reality are presented in the final section of the chapter. Parental involvement strategies are included.

GENDER ISSUES ACROSS THE LIFE SPAN

As people have recognized the costs of gender inequities, a number of issues have arisen that may require the attention of a counselor. According to Van Buren, Daines, and Burtner (1990), these issues may change as people move through the stages of the life span. The issues they identified include differential parenting received by females and males; different educational opportunities that are gender-based; comparable worth; and gender discrimination in the work place, in retirement benefits, and in health care. Other gender issues include violence against women and increasing levels of depression among women.

Women continue to earn less, in most cases, than men when performing the same type of work. Female workers must address such issues as the "mommy track" and the "glass ceiling." Men, however, are expected to be strong and competitive, and die, on average, 7 years younger than women. Men historically have to plan to work throughout their entire lives to provide financial security for their families. Barring unusual circumstances, divorced males are infrequently granted full custody of their children. Often they are not granted shared custody even in favorable circumstances. Females are increasingly expected to provide both financial and emotional security for their families.

The Early Years

The acquisition of gender-typed behavior begins early in life. The types of toys and games young children receive influence the role they ultimately perceive for themselves. Children's games help reinforce the development of delicate social skills in girls. Toys often reinforce girls' preparation for roles as wives and mothers. Much of their play concerns family roles and relationships. These role perceptions are reinforced by the conversation and behavior of many adults, including parents and teachers. Children's aspirations for and perceptions of adult occupations may become gender-stereotyped by the age of 3 or 4. These children's early experiences create challenges for gender-fair counseling as many personal, social, educational, occupational, and economic decisions are made as the result of subtle gender influences.

Counselors and others have noted that, as children proceed in the educational system, girls frequently receive an entirely different education from boys. These educational consequences are critical for girls; they lose out academically, financially, psychologically, and occupationally because of the educational system's structure. Girls frequently are rewarded for pleasing others and being nice, while boys are rewarded for mastering tasks and acquiring skills (Block, 1982; Brooks-Gunn & Matthews, 1979). These different expectations of parents and teachers continue to be internalized and communicated through traditional patterns of play.

Educational professionals, including teachers and counselors, communicate both negative and positive task feedback differently to female and male students. According to Dweck, Davidson, Nelson, and Enna (1978), there appears to be an inverse relationship between the way educators view and communicate the concepts of success and failure to girls and to boys. Girls are told their successes occur as a result of effort and that their failures are due to lack of innate ability. In contrast, boys are told that their successes stem from their innate ability and that their failures result from lack of effort.

There are a number of other examples of different treatment by gender. Educators tended to instruct male students in performing a task but often do the task for female students. Different expectations for girls and boys in the use of math, science, and computer skills are communicated by teachers. More girls than boys expect to perform poorly in math, especially those girls who think math is inappropriate for girls and women (Fauth & Jacobs, 1980).

Parents' expectations have a powerful impact on children's beliefs about successful academic performance. Parents appeared to expect more academic achievement from their sons than from their daughters. For example, a Girls Club of America, Inc. report (1985) found that middle-class white parents of second graders expected higher grades from their sons than from their daughters.

Children in the early elementary grades increasingly project themselves into adult roles. Sex-typing of occupations is already established and may limit the economic potential of female students by this early age. It has been found that (a) girls' range of career choices is more limited than boys'; (b) more boys than girls see limits on the occupations open to women; (c) teacher and nurse are the occupations girls and boys associate most often with women; and (d) girls report expectations for parenting roles more often than boys (Girls Clubs of America, Inc., 1985). Counselors need to be aware of these beliefs in children and to examine their own beliefs about the appropriateness of certain occupations for women and men.

In a 1988 study by the National Organization for Women's Project on Equal Education Rights (PEER), more than half of the 75 teen-age females interviewed reported that female students were treated differently from male students by teachers, counselors, and principals. In addition, these young women felt they would need greater credentials, that is, at least a high school diploma, to find jobs that less qualified males could obtain.

Different treatment of school age parents is another issue that requires gender-fair counseling. Pregnant and parenting female teens in the PEER study (1988) described the added burdens of shouldering the ultimate responsibility for the emotional and material well-being of their children. These young women frequently had been deserted by the fathers of their children, and they frequently were not provided support services that would enable them to finish their high school education. Consequently, additional personal, economic, and social barriers are created for them.

Even though fewer young women than young men have traditional attitudes toward women's work roles, many more working young women than working young men are expected to make adjustments for family responsibilities. Most young women expected to be personally and privately responsible for resolving child care problems during work (Girls Clubs of America, Inc., 1985). Few of these young women considered that their future husbands might reduce their work hours to care for their children.

For many young people, the pattern of attitudes toward and behaviors regarding gender appropriateness is established during the preschool years. Parental, teacher, counselor, and peer attitudes and behaviors influence school performance, self-concept, occupational selection, and the choice of a post-secondary education. These early factors and choices, often based upon gender perceptions, set the foundation for economic, emotional, and social well-being throughout an individual's entire life span.

The Working Years

A number of the gender issues that affect people in the working years have roots based on the different treatment individuals received in the early years. Van Buren et al. (1990) noted that the phrases "women's work" and "men's work" have usually conjured up images of people doing certain things, "pink collar," "blue collar," and "white collar" jobs in the work place. An examination of these color coding reveals that they are all based in green turf—that of the dollar. When these collars are associated with women's work, they cling to a much smaller piece of turf. That turf was described for a long time as the 59-cent dollar. That is, women earned 59 cents for every dollar earned by men. By 1985, that turf was described as the 70-cent dollar. This income gap increases with age and is affected only slightly by education. For example, in 1984 the ratio of women's earnings to men's in the 16- to 24-year-old cohort was 87.5; at ages 55 to 64, it was 60.8 (Women's Research and Education Institute of the Congressional Caucus for Women's Issues, 1987). Even though limited progress is being made, there is still a noticeable disparity between women's wages and men's wages. Despite increased labor force participation, women continue to be over-represented in poverty statistics. In 1984 women college graduates who worked full-time earned about the same amount as male high school dropouts. Baum (1987) noted that 37% of corporate managers were women but cited a study that showed executive women earned 42% less than their male counterparts.

There are several factors that may contribute to these disparate wages. One factor is the "glass ceiling," described by Morrison, White, and Van Velsor (1987) as the invisible but effective barrier encountered as women seek to advance to higher levels within an organization. Another possible factor is the "mommy track," a metaphor that has been used by Schwartz (1988) to describe a corporate strategy that separates "family-centered" women from "organization-centered" women.

The "organization-centered" women are placed on a track where they would presumably make the organization their top priority. Women are often forced to choose between a family and a career or to balance commitments to work and family in an era when it is increasingly difficult to find jobs that provide adequate incomes. It has, however, historically been expected that men will have a career and provide for their families.

Occupational segregation continues to be a gender issue that often creates economic problems for women. The Women's Research and Education Institute of the Congressional Caucus for Women's Issues (1987) found in 1985 that 70% of all women employed full-time were working in occupations in which over three quarters of the employees were female, with even higher percentages of part-time workers found in female-dominated occupations. Over one-third of all employed women work in clerical occupations. When women have moved into areas that have been predominately male, these women have remained on the bottom rungs of the ladder in low-paying subcategories of jobs.

Discrimination is operating in occupational classifications, and greater status is frequently assigned to jobs held by men. Women doctors tend to be in the lower-paying specialties, women attorneys in family law, and women in computer operations working as operators and word processors rather than as programmers. Counselors and teachers need to examine the implications of these occupational classifications and perceived status assignments and then develop strategies for changing them.

An examination of the academic world revealed there are more women with heavy teaching loads than with heavy research programs (Dwyer, 1985). There is further segregation by subject area, with more women than men in home economics, health related occupations, and teaching. More women than men are in part-time or nontenured academic positions. In 1983 women accounted for 27.3% of faculty members and held only 10.7% of the full professorships.

Attainment of public office is another area in which women are still outnumbered by men. This is slowly changing; however, in 1988 at no level of government did women hold more than 15.5% of the available positions. Perhaps if more women were in the political arena, greater progress would be made in resolving issues such as comparable worth, parental leave, health research and care, and sexual harassment and violence against women.

The Retirement Years

For women poverty continues to be a gender issue in the retirement years. The experiences and quality of life of women and men age 60 and over are the results of decisions made in the earlier years, whether in childhood or early adulthood (Van Buren et al., 1990). One result of these earlier decisions for elderly women is often living in poverty. Older women's poverty is often rooted in the gender-based expectations, roles, and work experiences of women throughout the life cycle. Through a combination of low-paying jobs, episodic work participation, and part-time work, these older women had little opportunity to save, were probably not covered by a private pension plan, and consequently receive low income from Social Security.

The state of a person's health, the cost of health care, and care-giving roles are another gender equity issue during the retirement years. Older women are more prone to long-term chronic diseases that older men (Older Women's League, 1986). This report noted that women age 65 and over have more days of restricted activity and longer average stays in hospitals. These women were more likely to be transferred from a hospital to a nursing home than were men age 65 and over.

Perhaps because young girls are socialized to be caring and nurturing, our society accepts the fact that women will become caregivers to their aging parents or to a spouse who is ill. Because women often outlive men, the family savings is spent down and women who have spent most of their lives as part of the middle class suddenly find themselves among the poor or the near poor.

Women face many problems as they age. The Social Security system, as noted by the Older Women's League (1986) shortchanges women when they retire. The health care reimbursement system ignores chronic health problems and the need for long-term care. Counselors must be aware and knowledgeable about these economic and health issues if they are to be of assistance and present a gender-fair perspective to clients during their retirement years.

Counselors and other educators must remember that early life choices based on gender-role perceptions affect all people through the life span. Gender-role attitudes and behaviors are learned at a very early age. The quality of human life throughout the life span is influenced by the role expectations of counselors, parents, teachers, peers, and others; education and employment decisions; parenting decisions; the lack of equal access to education and employment; occupational segregation; retirement benefits; and provision of health care. In order to develop full client potential gender-fair counselors must examine a myriad of gender issues, including many that have been discussed in this section of the chapter.

GENDER-FAIR COUNSELING COMPETENCIES

There is need for a list of concrete and comprehensive gender-fair counseling competencies if gender inequities are to be eliminated. DeVoe (1990) has stated that the role of counselors is increasing in importance as a potential way to eliminate sexism. He stressed that the literature has often failed to emphasize the critical role counselors can play in making a social change toward egalitarianism.

Van Buren and Miller (1988) discovered that, even though counselors believe gender-fair counseling is important, they did not feel they had the knowledge and skills needed to provide gender-fair counseling. A survey of 279 school, rehabilitation, and employment counselors revealed that a majority (91%) felt that specific training in gender-fair counseling practices should be included in their graduate programs. Only 20% reported that they had received training in gender-fair counseling practices as the result of a graduate counseling program. These data provided some of the impetus for the development of the gender-fair counseling competencies presented later in this chapter.

A review of counseling literature suggested that school counselors tend to adopt and maintain traditional values, attitudes, and beliefs that are reflected in the delivery of career counseling services to their students (Van Buren et al., 1989). Consequently, both female and male students tended to be counseled into occupational slots based upon counselors' preconceived notions of sex-appropriate or socially sanctioned work roles.

Marini and Brinton (1984) found that gender bias in high school career counseling is consistent with sex-typical occupational choices. Several studies indicated that counselors have tended to hold traditional attitudes about the appropriate occupations for female and male students, to discourage nontraditional aspirations, and to lack knowledge of issues related to women's employment (Karpicke, 1980; Medvene & Collins, 1976).

Several studies (Beyard-Tyler & Haring, 1981; Haring & Beyard-Tyler, 1984; Haring, Beyard-Tyler, & Gray, 1983) revealed that counselors' attitudes were a possible barrier when females were considering nontraditional career areas. Haring et al. (1983) noted more negative attitudes were expressed by counselors, regardless of sex, toward men than women who were considering nontraditional careers. In addition, these researchers noted that some counselors, especially males, still needed to have training interventions to help them separate their own gender biases and stereotypes from their school counseling practices.

Based upon these studies and given the various professional and legislative mandates for provision of gender-fair counseling, a set of gender-fair counseling competency statements was developed to focus preservice and inservice instruction. Competencies should focus directly on actual skills, knowledge, attitudes, values, and appreciations that are critical to success in a profession or life (Kaufman & Sample, 1986). Viewed as professional goals and as measures for performance evaluation, competencies provide a learning framework and help to insure consistency in an educational program.

Competency Development

The process used to develop the gender-fair counseling competencies involved four basic steps and more than 60 professionals who were either directly or indirectly involved with the counseling profession. An advisory committee clarified the scope of counseling programs and expectations for counselors upon post-baccalaureate graduation. This committee identified gender-equitable knowledge and skill deficits. The list was revised and sent to a group of 15 highly regarded counselor educators from throughout the United States for their input. During a 2-day meeting, these counselor educators evaluated and restated the deficit list. These deficit statements were rewritten as competency statements.

An attempt to organize the competency statements into the eight topic areas encompassed in the National Board of Certified Counselors, Inc. (1988) certification requirements did not prove workable. After a reexamination of the competencies, four major topic areas emerged. These areas were (1) socialization and developmental issues, (2) helping relationships, (3) professional and ethical issues, and (4) advocacy and change agentry (Van Buren et al., 1989).

A final verification of these competency statements was provided by 20 counselors representing secondary, post-secondary, and adult education and human services agencies. When asked whether each competency was critical to success in their current counseling position, these counselors confirmed the utility of the competency statements that follow with the exception of the fourth area Advocacy and Change Agentry. Several counselors felt discomfort with that role.

The following competencies, if included in preservice and inservice counselor education, will prepare people to practice gender-fair counseling. Applying these competencies will contribute to the elimination of inequitable gender practices.

Gender-Fair Counseling Competencies

Gender-fair counselors are knowledgeable about socialization processes and developmental issues as they relate to gender and are skilled in applying this knowledge. The following competencies address gender fairness in socialization and developmental issues. The gender-fair counselor:

❑ Assumes responsibility for personal gender biases, stereotypes, and discriminatory behaviors and can specify how they influence his or her delivery of counseling services.

❑ Appraises how gender-biased socialization processes influence attitudes, values, and behaviors.

❑ Assesses both her/his own and the client's world views through the use of both standardized and nonstandardized measures. This assessment should include an examination of how sociocultural variables (e.g., socioeconomic status, age, race/ethnicity, sex/gender, philosophy/spirituality/religion, economic system, family norms/dynamics and lifestyle) serve to increase or restrict clients' options.

❑ Integrates multicultural counseling theory and techniques in the delivery of counseling services.

❑ Assesses the different impact of gender inequity on men and women.

❑ Uses counseling techniques that reflect comprehension of the unique developmental needs (e.g., cognitive, emotional, moral, physical, and psychosocial) of females and males across the life span.

❑ Assumes responsibility for informing clients of how curricular and occupational requirements may be applied differently to women and men.

❑ Uses the knowledge of gender-biased differential hiring practices, job duties, and evaluation criteria to enable clients to make informed decisions.

It is important to note that counselors can affect the roles their clients perceive as acceptable. Role perception boundaries can severely limit an individual's self-esteem, self-worth, and self-understanding as well as a job or career choice. Failure to practice gender-fair counseling may limit a client's career options and potential level of living. In addition to counselors' influence on individuals, they can use their advocacy and change agentry competencies to influence community, state, and national legislators on gender-equity issues.

The gender-fair counselor understands the philosophical and theoretical bases that underscore the helping process and skillfully applies this knowledge to facilitate understanding of self and client, client self-development, and client/consultee change. A set of competencies developed to address the helping relationship follows.

The gender-fair counselor:

❏ Assesses her/his own world view as it relates to gender-fairness and recognizes limitations imposed upon the helping process by this idiosyncratic view.
❏ Assumes responsibility for his/her limitations by examining options and taking ethically appropriate action.
❏ Assesses client and counselor/client communications for the presence of gender issues.
❏ Applies relevant and appropriate counseling/consultation theories (e.g., systems, multicultural, and learning).
❏ Comprehends cognitive, affective, and behavioral change processes and uses this knowledge to facilitate client change in regard to gender issues.
❏ Incorporates gender issues in the conceptualization of career development over the life span.
❏ Creates a counseling environment in which the client feels safe to address gender issues.
❏ Nurtures personal characteristics that enable clients to enter and survive in nontraditional careers.
❏ Empowers females and males differently in negotiating gender-inequitable environments.
❏ Integrates technological resources that enhance the delivery of gender-fair counseling services.
❏ Evaluates clients for evidence of cognitive, affective, and behavioral changes related to gender issues.

If counselors are gender-fair in the helping relationships, they can contribute greatly to the elimination of different treatment of female and male clients. This can help parents be more equitable in their child rearing practices and help teachers treat the students more equally when it comes to behavioral expectations and task assignments. People will be encouraged to explore occupational opportunities based on their interests, abilities, and skills and not because they are male or female. Ultimately these decisions will help to decrease discrimination in the work place. Perhaps as women are guided in ways that increase their feelings of empowerment, their levels of depression will decrease.

As counselors strive for gender-fairness in the helping relationship, they are challenged with a variety of professional and ethical issues. Gender-fair counselors are knowledgeable about professional roles and functions as well as ethical standards that undergird the delivery of counseling services. The gender-fair counselor skillfully applies this knowledge to promote equitable treatment of females and males across multiple roles and settings. The following set of competencies addresses professional and ethical issues. The gender-fair counselor:

❏ Is alert to ethical dilemmas related to gender issues (e.g., power differential).
❏ Resolves ethical dilemmas in counseling through the application of ethical guidelines.
❏ Assumes responsibility for confronting colleagues who exhibit gender-biased attitudes and gender-discriminatory behaviors.

❏ Exemplifies gender-fair attitudes and behaviors in personal, professional, and public interactions.

❏ Accesses and evaluates professional literature related to gender issues.

❏ Assesses and adapts print and nonprint materials for gender fairness.

❏ Assesses and selects psychological instruments, including paper-and-pencil and computerized versions, for gender fairness.

❏ Incorporates gender fairness into case management decisions.

❏ Establishes and uses a referral system sensitive to gender issues.

❏ Establishes and uses professional relationships that foster and reinforce gender-fair attitudes and behaviors.

❏ Evaluates current legislation, pending legislation, and public policy related to gender issues.

❏ Assesses the impact of gender bias, stereotyping, and discrimination on local, regional, state, and national problems.

❏ Conducts or participates in research related to gender issues in counseling.

Questions of when to intervene in domestic or other relationships must be considered as counselors strive to be gender fair. Intervention questions are critical in dealing with violence against females of all ages, a problem that appears to be increasing on university campuses and in the home. For counselors who have clearly developed their professional and ethical beliefs regarding gender fairness and who wish to be more proactive, a series of competencies for advocacy and change agentry have been written. The gender-fair counselor is knowledgeable regarding the role and function of the advocate/change agent in a variety of settings and skillfully applies this knowledge to achieve change at personal, institutional, and societal levels. Following are the advocacy/change agentry competencies. The gender-fair counselor:

❏ Comprehends the role, function, and process of advocacy and change agentry in counseling.

❏ Responds to gender inequity through the use of techniques such as confrontation, negotiation, and conflict resolution.

❏ Assesses changing demographic data for their impact on gender issues in counseling.

❏ Assesses changing social, political, economic, and global trends for their impact on gender issues in counseling.

❏ Conducts gender-fair program development, including needs assessment, design, implementation, and evaluation.

❏ Exercises the "politics of power" by demonstrating the ability to influence decision making in both formal and informal hierarchical structures.

❏ Provides programmatic and personal support to clients considering or working in nontraditional careers.

Including these gender-fair counseling competencies in a counselor education curriculum is one approach to prepare professionals to address the gender inequities that operate in our society. These competencies could be included in a specific course or integrated across the curriculum into a variety of counseling courses.

TEACHER COMPETENCIES FOR ENHANCING GENDER-FAIRNESS

In addition to counselors, teachers are of major importance in providing a gender-fair atmosphere in school settings from preschool through post-secondary education. Frequently, as noted in the early part of this chapter, teachers at all educational levels have different expectations for their female and male students. Sadker and Sadker (1986) have demonstrated that teacher behavior can be changed and that these changes benefit students. Shakeshaft (1986) stated that there is a positive relationship between a supportive nonsexist environment and the productivity of students. Unless counselors and teachers provide some consistency in their gender-fair attitudes and behaviors, students may become confused and limit their educational and career options based on gender stereotypes. Therefore, teacher education programs need to provide opportunities for preservice and inservice teachers to develop or enhance their gender-fair teaching competencies.

In the late 1970s the Iowa Department of Public Instruction developed a set of competencies that a gender-fair teacher should possess. Many of these competencies seem to be appropriate for today as well. I will present selected competencies to illustrate common themes between counselor and teacher competencies in the hope that this will encourage cooperation between these two groups. Selected teacher competencies taken from the *Guide to Implementing Multi-Cultural Non-Sexist Curriculum Programs in Iowa* (1976) follow:

1. Recognize the origins of prejudice and discrimination and the factors that cause them to exist.
2. Understand the contributions, values, and lifestyles of women and various racial and cultural groups.
3. Identify administrative and instructional materials that show evidence of bias based on race, sex, socioeconomic status, or physical disability.
4. Design activities for the school and the classroom that promote respect for and awareness of the value of diversity in our society.
5. Deal with racist, sexist, or other discriminatory statements or actions that occur in the school or the classroom.
6. Understand how stereotyping of races, the sexes, and other groups results in injustices to individuals in these groups, and how educational institutions have played a role in sustaining such stereotypes.
7. Comfortably lead classroom and staff discussions dealing with intergroup relations, the roles of the sexes, and the students' attitudes toward their own and other groups.
8. Understand how individual racism and sexism have become incorporated into institutional policies and programs.

STUDENT COMPETENCIES FOR ENHANCING GENDER-FAIRNESS

For students to achieve maximum personal fulfillment and satisfaction, they need to develop an awareness of the various roles and lifestyles open to both women and men. One way to accomplish this is to help students develop gender-fair competencies that are incorporated into their daily lives. The following competencies adapted from the

Iowa materials (*Guide to Implementing...*, 1976) can be introduced to students through both counseling and teaching interactions.

1. Develop a positive, realistic self-concept regardless of sex or race.
2. Identify the ways that human beings are alike and ways in which they differ (e.g., race, sex, culture).
3. Know the history, the contributions, the cultures, and the value of various subgroups in American society (e.g, races, sexes, ethnic groups).
4. Explain the history and the contributions of women as well as men in developing this country.
5. Comprehend that a wide range of careers are open to both men and women in our society.
6. Be familiar with the writings, music, art, and discoveries of both women and men in our society.
7. Understand the concept of stereotyping and the negative effects it has on human beings.
8. Recognize that certain terms, language, and behavior may be offensive to members of the opposite sex.
9. Comprehend the origins, causes, and the effects of gender prejudice and discrimination.

These competencies are not meant to be a comprehensive list. They are included to provide guidelines for integrating gender fairness throughout the school environment. It is important to remember that students will be most influenced to practice gender fairness if those attitudes and behaviors are modeled by both counselors and teachers.

STRATEGIES FOR MAKING GENDER-FAIR COUNSELING A REALITY

There are numerous strategies for making gender fairness and gender-fair counseling a reality in our society. Counselors, teachers, students, parents, employers, and workers can benefit from exposure to gender-fair strategies. In addition to personal and group interactions, both print and nonprint materials can be used to introduce gender-fair concepts. Print materials might include books, pamphlets, newsletters, and newspaper or magazine articles. Nonprint materials could include public service announcements, videos, and films. This final section of the chapter is devoted to the discussion of gender-fair counseling strategies that might be used to help create a gender-equitable society. Many of these strategies can be used in both school and nonschool settings.

Counselors must deal with their own biases before they can address those of other individuals or other systems. After counselors have addressed their own biases through acquisition of gender-fair counseling competencies in either preservice or inservice education, they may wish to use the following strategies for building gender-equity in the counselor and student/client relationship. These strategies are taken from *Gender-Fair Career Counseling Strategies*, prepared by Van Buren and staff (1988).

Only through awareness and tempering their own biases can counselors be fully available to individuals who seek their services. The following strategies relate to addressing one's own biases.

1. Evaluate your own language, behaviors, and counseling practices periodically for gender fairness. Audiotape yourself when possible and ask for feedback from others to assess your performance.
2. Attempt to represent all educational and occupational options without bias. Consider the attractions and liabilities of each option.
3. Resist stereotyping based on a student's physical characteristics but do communicate actual physical requirements for various jobs.
4. Resist the temptation to counsel only students of the same sex.
5. Avoid "leading" students to predetermined responses.
6. Consider the impacts of early tracking on students and their educational and occupational opportunities.

Another area where bias may occur is in counseling adjuncts such as interest inventories and other assessment instruments. Although these materials are known to be more or less biased, counselors must seek to compensate for known biases with thorough knowledge and understanding of the instruments combined with the context and unique qualities of the student. Selected strategies for evaluating these materials follow.

1. Take great care in selecting a battery of assessment instruments in order to provide the broadest and least biased scope of information.
2. Employ a variety of assessment instruments and devices, including personal interviews and experiences.
3. Consider that interest inventories may reflect only the student's perceptions of a career, rather than the reality of the career.
4. Be alert to the wording in the content of assessment instruments.
5. Provide sufficient and gender-fair interpretive feedback after assessment is completed. This may require familiarizing yourself with manuals and norming techniques.
6. Acknowledge that interpretation of assessment is usually performed by a single individual and is, therefore, biased.
7. Search out research data describing the effects of nonbiased counseling. Use these studies to support your bias-free counseling practices when working with parents, administrators, or other colleagues.

Assisting students and clients in individual exploration and permitting freedom of choice is an important counselor role. Counselors need to emphasize confidentiality and active listening in order to create a climate in which individuals feel free enough to begin ongoing self-exploration. Following is a selection of appropriate strategies for that process.

1. Allow students to choose course work from within any subject area offered.
2. Ask students to acknowledge and examine their own gender stereotypes.

3. Stress that exploration of interests is more easily implemented in high school; later on, the time and expense to investigate interests is more costly.

4. Affirm values and validate interests by asserting the likelihood that one may change occupations several times throughout one's life.

5. Support students in discovering and appreciating their unique qualities, to do what feels right for them and not what they feel pressured to do by others.

6. Promote the development of hobbies and interests by encouraging membership in extracurricular organizations, such as 4-H, scouting, newspaper or yearbook staff, science club, math club, and vocational student organizations.

7. Strive to help individuals relate interest, values, and aptitudes directly to occupations and career goals.

8. Discuss the topic of individual work goals versus family or relationship goals; explore conflicts with students considering marriage and children as a goal.

9. Consider each student's level of self-esteem and work toward enhancing each student's self-esteem.

10. Urge all students to plan for economic self-reliance by discussing the realities of financial responsibility and independence.

11. Reinforce the availability and utility of career information materials that are available in the counseling office or a career resource center.

Because women have tended to select traditional occupations that are low paying, it is critical that counselors promote exploration of nontraditional courses, occupations, and even behaviors. Strategies of this type may help to eliminate differential educational opportunities as well as gender discrimination in the work place, two of the issues discussed earlier in the chapter.

The counselor may play an educational role in exposing individuals to the idea of traditional versus nontraditional occupations and life roles. Throughout this process, the counselor has the opportunity to identify both the benefits and limitations of considering nontraditional and traditional occupations. Suggested strategies for accomplishing this educational process follow.

1. Challenge students to think outside of their gender when considering career options.

2. Challenge students' stereotypes regarding course options. Ask them to discuss their reasons for selecting or rejecting particular disciplines.

3. Educate students regarding the salary differences and other associated benefits or drawbacks of nontraditional occupations.

4. Alert individuals to the possibility of receiving negative feedback when choosing nontraditional behaviors, course work, or lifestyles.

5. Use terminology that promotes gender-equitable career choices.

6. Announce special events and career related activities sponsored by universities, vocational colleges, and private proprietary schools. Encourage visits to post-secondary institutions.

7. Seek scholarships to encourage female students to pursue ongoing education. Provide additional assistance to those who have no other support network.

In addition to enlightening and educating individuals, the counselor is in the position to help individuals identify allied life skills required for the successful accomplishment of life tasks. These skills include goal setting, assertiveness, communication, decision making, and values clarification. Following are strategies that may help the counselor assist individuals in assessing personal capabilities and positions on these issues.

1. Strive to enhance self-confidence. Encourage risk taking within a realistic framework for both female and male clients.
2. Discuss short- and long-term goal setting and the associated benefits of each.
3. Offer group workshops or courses, such as the Quest Program funded by the Lion's Club, to explore topics of interest or to enhance personal well-being.
4. Stress the appropriateness of delaying decision making until sufficient vocational information is gathered to make satisfying choices.

Besides providing individuals with academic information and assisting them with academic concerns, counselors may be able to provide information concerning the community, labor market, and local economic indicators. Counselors often need to help individuals address such issues as peer pressures and parental influences. The following strategies can be used to help individuals obtain nonacademic information.

1. Ask individuals to consider the unique components of their own occupational success and happiness. What are their priorities? What trade-offs are they willing to make for success? For happiness?
2. Support occupational flexibility and life skills acquisition. Ask learners to assess the transferable skills needed to facilitate occupational flexibility.
3. Encourage individuals to think beyond their present environments and imagine the future differently. Ask them to visualize a different type of support system or no support system. Explore situations in which the individual feels more or less independent than now. What are the attendant responsibilities in each situation?
4. Discuss the realities of living expenses when individuals are self-supporting or supporting others. Ask students to construct a simple balance sheet of monthly income and expenses. Assess the balance sheet for thoroughness and realism.
5. Discuss routes to financial independence and probe both the dynamics and consequences of financial dependence or financial instability.
6. Discuss the impacts of peer pressure, parental pressure, teacher pressure, and community pressure to conform to particular ideals. Discuss the consequences of conformity versus nonconformity.
7. Enlighten individuals about their legal rights regarding sexual harassment on the job or in school. Be especially alert to raising this issue with individuals seeking to enter nontraditional fields.

If counselors are to make gender-fair counseling a reality, students' parents need to be involved in the process. Parents are frequently an untapped resource when developing and implementing strategies for encouraging individuals to explore nontraditional courses and occupational opportunities and to act without gender bias. Alden and

Seiferth (1979) found that high school students ranked parents as having the most influence on their career choices. Parents were followed by friends, teachers, counselors, and siblings, in order of influence. In a study of adolescents' perceptions, Davies and Kandel (1981) found that parents have more influence on their children's educational aspirations than do the children's best friends. When examining adolescents' career aspirations, maturity, and their parents' career values and aspirations for them, Dillard and Campbell (1981) discovered that parent-child interaction may be crucial to career maturity development.

Birk and Blimline (1984) determined that biases and stereotypes of parents are conveyed to children through encouragement, or lack thereof, toward some fields and through their willingness to give financial support to some interests and not to others. Their findings suggest that those parents who talked to their children about occupational goals and daydreams were influencing their children toward "sex-appropriate" goals. For example, girls whose mothers talked to them about occupations discussed those occupations that are traditionally feminine. The results of the Birk and Blimline (1984) study indicated that, in their role as primary career development facilitators, parents frequently reinforce stereotyped career choices. They further asserted that parents and counselors need assistance on working together to promote students' career development. Many parents are eager to participate in their children's career development but are uncertain of their role in the process. These parents desired help in guiding their daughters and sons in making career decisions. Strategies for parental involvement follow.

1. Educate parents about career development and nontraditional occupational options through seminars, workshops, PTO/PTA programs, and parent-teacher conferences. Provide child care during workshops and offer stipends as an incentive to attend.
2. Involve parents in their children's career awareness from an early age by providing the parents of preschoolers and kindergartners a variety of informational resources.
3. Invite parents to participate in the counseling process as much as ethically appropriate.
4. Discuss a broad range of topics with parents as they relate to gender equity. Possible topics to address are the influence of peer pressure, the influence of parental pressure, implications of labor and wage statistics, support for their child's strengths and interests, and development of less-biased attitudes and realization of the limiting consequences of bias.
5. Encourage parents to reduce gender bias in the home by dividing chores equitably (i.e., girls take out the trash, boys wash dishes); eliminating sexist behaviors and language from the household; encouraging children to develop specific hobbies and interests and comprehend their links to possible occupational options; discussing the importance of higher education, math, science, and computer literacy for both girls and boys; and discussing stereotypical television portrayals and movie selections.
6. Select or elect an advisory board, including parents, to plan and execute career education projects in the school and throughout the community.
7. Mail printed brochures or make them available to parents on a continuing basis to keep them abreast of current topics in career development.

8. Design bulletin boards to address career development and career education. Have displays coincide with parents' meetings, career days, open houses, home sporting events, and vocational student organization activities.
9. Consider either parent as equally responsible for resolving school related problems with her/his child. Don't automatically call the parent whose employment you consider to be economically or socially less valuable.

Counselors, in addition to interacting with teachers, students, students' parents, or other clients, need to network with each other. Counselors are all connected through an ongoing, almost intuitively generated number of networks that evolve as their needs evolve. Other levels of networking, such as those that are more strictly planned, can directly benefit counselors in at least two very important ways. These networks can provide counselors with a shared sense of identity and shared reciprocal support and a coalescence of individuals within the community promoting a common goal (i.e., helping others in the community.)

If counselors are to become truly gender fair, they need to help and support each other in their efforts to provide a gender-fair environment for their clients. As a result individuals could move through the life span and obtain gender-fair counseling regardless of their problems or concerns. The chances of improvement in gender problems such as different parenting and educational opportunities, comparable worth, work place discrimination, retirement benefits, health care, and violence against women would increase.

Incorporation of gender-fair counseling competencies into preservice and inservice counselor education may be one way to help eliminate sexism (DeVoe, 1990). Counselor, teacher, and student competencies for enhancing gender fairness have been provided. Students will be most likely to incorporate gender-fair attitudes and behaviors into their lives, if counselors and teachers provide appropriate modeling.

There are numerous strategies that can be used to help make school and work environments gender fair. Counselors must address their own biases, handle biases in counseling adjuncts, help individuals explore and make free choices in both their personal and professional lives, and provide gender-fair information to students and clients.

It is important to remember that gender equity is an issue for both females and males; for persons of all races and creeds; and for the young, the old, and those in-between. Early life choices based on gender-role perceptions affect all people throughout the life span. Gender-role behaviors are learned at a very early age. The quality of human life is affected by role expectations of parents, counselors, teachers, peers, and others; education and employment decisions; the lack of equal access to education and employment; occupational segregation; retirement benefits; and provision of health care.

Because we live in a society in which the activities and contributions of all people are not valued equally, there are challenges for each of us. These challenges continue to include dealing with gender-biased attitudes, behaviors, stereotypes, and myths. Counselors' knowledge and skills in the areas of socialization and development issues, helping relationships, professional and ethical issues, and advocacy and change agentry will provide them with a unique opportunity to meet these challenges and face these issues through counseling, education, and advocacy.

REFERENCES

Alden, E. F., & Seiferth, B. B. (1979, July). *Factors influencing choice of technical careers by women and minorities.* Paper presented at the meeting of the American Educational Research Association's North Central States, Ann Arbor, MI.

American School Counselor Association (ASCA). (1985). ASCA role statement. The role of the counselor in career guidance: Expectations and responsibilities. *The School Counselor, 32,* 164–168.

Baum, L. (1987, June 22). Corporate women. *Business Week,* pp. 72–78.

Beyard-Tyler, K. C., & Haring, M. J. (1981, October) *Investigating attitudes toward nontraditional careers.* Paper presented at the Seventh Annual Conference of Research on Women and Education, Washington, DC.

Birk, J. M., & Blimline, C. A. (1984). Parents as career development facilitators: An untapped resource for the counselor. *The School Counselor, 31,* 310–317.

Block, J. H. (1982). Psychological Development of Female Children and Adolescents. In P. W. Berman & E. Ramsey (Ed.), *Women: A developmental perspective.* Bethesda, MD: National Institute of Health.

Brooks-Gunn, J., & Matthews, W. S. (1979). *He and she: How children develop their sex-role identity.* Englewood Cliffs, NJ: Prentice-Hall.

Carl D. Perkins Vocational Education Act. (1984). Public Law 98-524. Washington, DC: U.S. Government Printing Office.

Council for Accreditation of Counseling and Related Educational Programs (CACREP). (1988). *Accreditation procedures manual and application.* Alexandria, VA: Author.

Davies, M., & Kandel, D. B. (1981). Parental and peer influence on adolescents' educational plans: Some further evidence. *American Journal of Sociology, 87,* 363–387.

DeVoe, D. (1990). Feminist and nonsexist counseling: Implications for the male counselor. *Journal of Counseling & Development, 69,* 33–36.

Dillard, J. J., & Campbell, N. (1981). Influences of Puerto Rican, black and Anglo parents' career behavior on their adolescent children's career development. *Vocational Guidance Quarterly, 30,* 139–148.

Dweck, C., Davidson, W., Nelson, S., & Enna, B. (1978). Sex differences in learned helplessness, II. The contingencies of evaluative feedback in the classroom, and III, An experimental design analysis. *Developmental Psychology, 14,* 268–276.

Dwyer, C. A. (1985). Sex equity from early through post-secondary education. In S. S. Klein (Ed.). *Handbook for achieving equity through education* (pp. 448–462). Baltimore: The Johns Hopkins University Press.

Fauth, G. D., & Jacobs, J. E. (1980). Equity in math education: The educational leader's role. *Educational Leadership, 37,* 485–490.

Girls Clubs of America, Inc. (1985). *Facts and reflections on careers for today's girls.* New York: Author.

Good, G. E., Gilbert, L. A., & Scher, M. (1990). Gender aware therapy: A synthesis of feminist therapy and knowledge about gender. *Journal of Counseling & Development, 68,* 376–380.

Guide to implementing multicultural nonsexist curriculum programs in Iowa. (1976). Des Moines: Iowa Department of Public Instruction.

Haring, M. J., & Beyard-Tyler, K. C., (1984). Counseling with women: The challenge of nontraditional careers. *The School Counselor, 31,* 301–309.

Haring, M. J., Beyard-Tyler, K. C., & Gray, J. J. (1983). Sex-biased attitudes of counselors: The special case of nontraditional careers. *Counseling and Values, 27,* 242–247.

Karpicke, S. (1980). Perceived and real sex differences in college students' career planning. *Journal of Counseling Psychology, 27,* 240–245.

Kaufman, R., & Sample, J. (1986). Defining competencies for training and performance development. *Educational Technology, 26,* 16–21.

Marini, M. M., & Brinton, M. (1984). Sex typing in occupational socialization. In B. R. Reskin (Ed.), *Sex segregation in the work place: Trends, explanations, remedies* (pp. 192–232). Washington, DC: National Academy Press.

Medvene, A. M., & Collins, A. M. (1976). Occupational prestige and appropriateness: The view of mental health specialists. *Journal of Vocational Behavior, 9,* 63–70.

Morrison, A. M., White, R. P., & Van Velsor, E. (1987). *Breaking the glass slipper.* Reading, MA: Addison-Wesley.

National Board for Certified Counselors, Inc. (1988). *National counselor certification information and application.* Alexandria VA: Author.

Older Women's League. (1986). *Mother's Day report on the status of midlife and older women in America.* Washington, DC: Author.

Project on Equal Education Rights of the NOW Legal Defense and Education Fund (PEER). (1988). *In their own voices: Young women talk about dropping out.* Washington, DC: PEER.

Sadker, M., & Sadker, D. (1986). Sexism in the classroom: From grade school to graduate school. *Phi Delta Kappan, 67,* 512–515.

Scher, M., & Good, G. E. (1990). Gender and counseling in the twenty-first century: What does the future hold? *Journal of Counseling & Development, 68,* 388–391.

Schwartz, F. N. (1988). Corporate women: A critical business recourse. *Vital Speeches, 54,* 173–176.

Shakeshaft, C. (1986). A gender at risk. *Phi Delta Kappan, 67,* 499–503.

Title II of the Education Amendments of 1976. (1976). Public Law 94-482. Washington, DC: U.S. Government Printing Office.

Title IX of the Education Amendments of 1972. (1972). Public Law 92-318. Washington, DC: U.S. Government Printing Office.

Van Buren, J. B., Daines, J. R., & Burtner, J. B. (1990). Gender equity: An issue throughout the life span. *Journal of Home Economics, 82,* 3–10.

Van Buren, J. B., & Miller, K. L. (1988). *Vocational guidance and counseling/sex equity services* (Contract No. 306-87-4500). Indianapolis: Indiana Commission on Vocational and Technical Education.

Van Buren, J. B., Miller, K. L., Bolyard, K. L., Cheung, P. C., Deason, M. G., Gipson, R. A., & Hall, A. S. (1988). *Gender-fair career counseling strategies.* Indianapolis: Indiana Commission on Vocational and Technical Education.

Van Buren, J. B., Miller, K. L., Deason, M. G., Gipson, R. A., Goldstein, A. E., Patton, D. M., & Schrader, M. K. (1989). *A model for gender-fair counseling: Viewer's guide.* Indianapolis: Indiana Commission on Vocational and Technical Education.

Women's Research and Education Institute of the Congressional Caucus for Women's Issues. (1987). *The American woman 1987–1988.* New York: W. W. Norton.

Name Index

Subject Index

female students, 19-21, 59, 273-274
interventions to benefit elderly women,
252-253
research centers for studies in gender in, 68
Education Amendments, 1972, 69
Elder abuse, 223-224
Elderly women. *See also* Retirement
abuse of, 223-224
case examples of counseling for, 231-234
counseling strategies for, 226-231
depression in, 249
gender issues affecting, 275-276
health issues affecting. *See* Health issues
of elderly women
institutionization of, 224-225, 258
loneliness and isolation of, 218-219, 229
marital status of, 214, 219
organizations for, 203, 234-236
overview of, 211-212
post-retirement employment for, 192-193
poverty of, 215-218
preretirement counseling for, 197-198
problem prevention and social intervention for, 235-237
and relationships with adult children, 221-
223, 225
socialization patterns of, 219-220
stereotypes regarding, 181-182, 212-213,
216
Elementary school children, 15-16. *See also*
Children
Emotional abuse, 82
Emotional disorders prediction, 251
Employment. *See also* Careers
discrimination in, 125-128
post-retirement, 192-193
Employment Retirement Income Security Act
of 1974 (ERISA), 191
Empowerment
for African-American females, 22
case examples of counseling women
toward, 147-149
counseling resources and, 149
counseling women toward, 143-147
for elderly women, 227-228
feminization of poverty and, 136-138
male violence against females and, 139-
142

problem prevention and social interventions and, 150
programs to achieve, 34
relationship orientation and, 135-136
Empty nest syndrome, 189
Equal Employment Opportunity Commission
(EEOC)
administration of ADEA by, 186
sex discrimination guidelines issued by,
184
Estrogen replacement therapy, 247-248, 253
Expressive identity, 28

F
Families
characteristics of dysfunctional, 89
Family roles
and career aspiration development, 27
stress associated with, 161
view of adolescents regarding, 18-19
Family therapy, 230-231, 256
Females. *See also* Elderly women; Midlife
women
early sexual and health issues unique to,
7-9
organizational strategies to help, 125-129
rate and type of abuse by, 80-82
relationship orientation of, 135-136
substance abuse among, 86-87
suicide rates for, 83
Feminist Press, 68
Feminist therapy, 7

G
Garrett Park Press, 68
Gender
combined effect on teachers of race and,
21-22
explanation of, 14, 133
self-efficacy and, 29
views of, 133-134, 143-144
Gender-fair counseling
competencies, 276-280
explanation of, 271-272
and gender issue across life span, 272-276
strategies for, 282-288
student competencies for enhancing, 281-
282